Behind the 1953 Coup in Iran
Thugs, Turncoats, Soldiers, and Spooks

Ali Rahnema's newest work is a meticulous historical reconstruction of the events surrounding the Iranian coup d'état of 1953 that led to the overthrow of Mohammed Mosaddeq and his government. Mosaddeq's removal from power has probably attracted more attention than any other event that occurred during his tenure because of the role of foreign involvement; the political, economic and social impact on Iran; and the long-term impact the ousting had on Iran–US relations.

Drawing on a wealth of American, British and Iranian sources, Rahnema closely examines the four-day period between the first failed coup and the second successful attempt, investigating in fine detail how the two coups were conceptualized, rationalized and then executed by players on both the Anglo-American and Iranian sides. Through painstaking research into little-studied sources, Rahnema casts new light on how a small group of highly influential pro-Britain politicians and power brokers with important connections revisited the realities on the ground with the CIA operatives dispatched to Iran and how they recalibrated a new – and ultimately successful – operational plan.

Ali Rahnema is Professor of Economics and director of the master's programme in Middle East and Islamic studies at the American University of Paris. His publications include *Superstition as Ideology in Iranian Politics* (Cambridge, 2011) and *An Islamic Utopian: A Political Biography of Ali Shariati*, second edition (2014).

Behind the 1953 Coup in Iran

Thugs, Turncoats, Soldiers, and Spooks

ALI RAHNEMA

The American University of Paris

CAMBRIDGE
UNIVERSITY PRESS

32 Avenue of the Americas, New York NY 10013-2473, USA

Cambridge University Press is part of the University of Cambridge.

It furthers the University's mission by disseminating knowledge in the pursuit of education, learning and research at the highest international levels of excellence.

www.cambridge.org
Information on this title: www.cambridge.org/9781107076068

© Ali Rahnema 2015

This publication is in copyright. Subject to statutory exception and to the provisions of relevant collective licensing agreements, no reproduction of any part may take place without the written permission of Cambridge University Press.

First published 2015

A catalogue record for this publication is available from the British Library

Library of Congress Cataloguing in Publication data
Rahnama, 'Ali.
Behind the 1953 coup in Iran : thugs, turncoats, soldiers, spooks / Ali Rahnema, The American University of Paris.
   pages cm
Includes bibliographical references.
ISBN 978-1-107-07606-8
1. Iran – History – Coup d'état, 1953.   I. Title.
DS316.6.R35   2014
955.05'3–dc23
2014020025

ISBN 978-1-107-07606-8 Hardback

Cambridge University Press has no responsibility for the persistence or accuracy of URLs for external or third-party internet websites referred to in this publication, and does not guarantee that any content on such websites is, or will remain, accurate or appropriate.

To the memory of Amir Houshang Keshavarz-Sadr
Glowing Ray of Grace and Integrity

Contents

Preface and acknowledgements		page ix
The coup d'état chronology: from idea to implementation		xv
	Introduction	1
1	The British reaction to Mosaddeq in power: "Mossie grabs Britain's oil – but Navy to the rescue" (*Daily Express*)	11
2	Mosaddeq's opposition strikes: testing tactics	34
3	Who beckoned and who executed on 28 February (9 Esfand)?	49
4	TPAJAX: company (CIA) commanders and firm (SIS) functionaries operationalizing the coup idea	60
5	The CIA-affiliated organizations: propaganda and combat	79
6	The precision coup flops: back to the drawing-board	95
7	Second coup capabilities of the military networks	110
8	A viable home-spun coup	124
9	The crucial last-minute preparations	138
10	The second coup begins with the pincer movement of the thugs	155
11	Coup agents occupying the city centre	174
12	Attacking ministries and pro-Mosaddeq buildings	193
13	The enigma of the tanks: betrayal or incompetence?	204
14	Mosaddeq overthrown	221
15	Religious representatives and the coup	235

16 Why did the second coup succeed?	249
17 Mosaddeq's exit: legal transfer of power or coup d'état?	270
Conclusion	289
Biographical notes of key figures	298
Bibliography	311
Index	315

Preface and acknowledgements

The historiography of the Mosaddeq era, let alone the overthrow of Mosaddeq, is in its infancy, as is our knowledge of this period. The growth of the infant has been stunted by the political atmosphere that came to reign after the removal of Mosaddeq. In the period immediately following 19 August 1953 (28 Mordad 1332) the official state position represented Mosaddeq as a power-hungry and demagogic statesman who had abused the well-founded nationalist sentiments of Iranians for his anti-constitutional, anti-monarchic and anti-democratic political ends. The victors of a struggle which had ended in the overthrow of Mosaddeq by violent means needed to explain – if not justify – their actions. At Mosaddeq's trial the military prosecutor, Hoseyn Azmudeh, accused the ousted Prime Minister of treason, dishonour, demagogy, ruining the country, rebelling against the constitution, serving the interests of foreigners, attempting to overthrow the monarchy, founding a republic and, finally, seeking to become its President. The punishment for such crimes, if proven, was execution. Mosaddeq, however, was eventually sentenced to three years in prison.

By 24 September 1953, General Fazlollah Zahedi, the new Prime Minister, had "sent five messages to the Shah requesting that the Shah order the Military Tribunal to expedite the execution of Mossadeq and others".[1] Even though the Shah decided that Mosaddeq should be tried and condemned to death, he vacillated between pardoning him and executing him.[2] It would be fair to assume that once the Shah decided against executing Mosaddeq

---

[1] National Security Archives, C01383765, from Roosevelt, 24 September 1953. http://www2.gwu.edu/~nsarchiv/NSAEBB/NSAEBB435/docs/Doc%2015%20-%201953-09-21%20Intrigues%20-%20Behbehani%20son%20-%20etc.pdf.

[2] National Security Archives, C01383775, from Roosevelt, 2 October 1953. http://www2.gwu.edu/~nsarchiv/NSAEBB/NSAEBB435/docs/Doc%2015%20-%201953-09-21%20Intrigues%20-%20Behbehani%20son%20-%20etc.pdf.

(probably because of the negative popular reaction that this would have provoked), he consciously decided to erase Mosaddeq from the collective memory of Iranians. This was an executive decision, which to the Shah served as an act of grace towards Mosaddeq, while ensuring his own place on the throne. Throwing a veil of ignorance over a key historical personality and period lest it rekindled sympathies for Mosaddeq, his ideas and memories of him required quelling the historiography of that period. While the lid was kept tightly on this sensitive period, suspicion, speculation and emotion ran wild among Iranians on what really had happened during those years and why and how it came to an end. The moratorium enforced by some self-censorship and much government censorship created ignorance, breeding intuitive convictions and certainties among those who had experienced Mosaddeq's period, along with a thirst for the truth among the younger generations.

How, why and by whom Mosaddeq was removed from office probably remained the most emotional, sensitive and elusive piece of the puzzle. The activities, arrangements and manoeuvres behind the overthrow of Mosaddeq remained opaque, controversial and complicated, especially because of the suspected role of foreign involvement. The putative foreign-involvement factor created two fundamental problems at the time, rendering proper research almost impossible. First, foreign archival sources, where traces or indications of such intervention could be found, verified or refuted, were not accessible; and second, research in Iran was inhibited by the fear that a serious study may provide evidence that the last act of the Mosaddeq play was indeed the outcome of direct foreign intervention. The Mosaddeq episode, especially its end-point, remained a major sore point, causing anxiety for Mohammad Reza Shah. The Shah's dilemma after the Mosaddeq episode was that as much as he wished to forget the unpleasant interlude, he was aware – and sometimes in the early post-Mosaddeq days was reminded – of the common urban perception that ousting Mosaddeq had been required to secure the economic and political interest of foreign powers.

On 29 December 1953, in a subtle fashion characteristic of a press under tight scrutiny, *Ferdowsi*, an Iranian weekly, demonstrated this common perception by publishing two pictures of the same size, one next to the other, under the title "News of the Week". On the right was a picture of an indignant Mosaddeq, with the caption beneath it stating that at 3 p.m. on 21 December, Mosaddeq's court, which was examining the events of 25 to 29 August, had entered its final deliberation and found Mosaddeq guilty. On the left was a picture of Denis Wright, with the caption beneath it stating that at 3:00 p.m. on 21 December Mr. Wright, the new British chargé d'affaires, and 14 British employees entered Tehran, and on the same night took charge of the British Embassy and started their business. The message was simply that Mosaddeq needed to be imprisoned in order for the British to return to Iran and pursue their interests.

The fall of Mohammad Reza Shah freed up the study of the Mosaddeq period in Iran. The freedom to reflect, speak out about and write on this epoch in Iran opened the door to the publication of all kinds of works – of differing quality – on Mosaddeq's government and legacy. The second impediment was also partially removed as public access to important archives in the UK and the US, as well as key internal CIA reports, became available. A third factor further facilitated research on the details of the events: interviews with foreign and domestic players, especially Iranian dignitaries, who had left Iran after the 1979 revolution and who felt as though they could speak openly about the period, provided valuable information. A growing body of memoirs by Iranian personalities provided additional information, as did the publication of security files on key Iranian personalities by various Iranian organizations with access to these files. With the greater availability of Iranian newspapers and journals of the period at reference libraries in Iran and overseas, the task of an in-depth study based on corroboration and verification of events was facilitated. Some three and a half decades have elapsed since the Shah's departure, and more than six decades since Mosaddeq's. The historiography of the Mosaddeq era, by both Iranian and foreign scholars, has produced important academic works, mostly at the macro and general levels. Yet detailed micro studies and histories exposing and analysing the salient and central aspects of slices or frames of the period required for explaining the broad surveys are still rare.

The specific topic of Mosaddeq's removal from power has probably attracted more attention than other aspects of his tenure. The unknowns surrounding Mosaddeq's overthrow and its political, economic, as well as social and psychological impacts, must to some extent explain the interest in this period. The topic also provides a case study of a third-world country in the early 1950s challenging the interests of a hegemonic world power. The long-term consequences of Mosaddeq's ousting for Iran–US relations has also stimulated interest in this period. Interest in this particular period of Mosaddeq's government is mostly generated by the thirst to learn about whether the overthrow of Mosaddeq's government was the result of a foreign, a purely domestic or a combined plan. How did it take shape? Who initiated it? Who pursued it? Who implemented it and how? Since there were no foreign soldiers involved in the overthrow, then in all three scenarios explanations need to be given as to who the Iranian organizers were, who the planners and perpetrators were and how the coup was carried out.

The results of such a study may feed into the political divide of pro- and anti-Mosaddeq partisans for whom "the truth" about how Mosaddeq was ousted vindicates their a priori judgement of the political nature of the other side. In the political psychology of Iranians, the overthrow of Mosaddeq created a binary perception of forces of light/good warring against the forces of darkness/evil. Pro-Mosaddeq forces accuse the opposing camp of colluding with foreigners and sacrificing the national interests of Iran and Iranians, thereby betraying the oil nationalization movement. For them, Mosaddeq did not waiver from his dedication to upholding the Iranian Constitution, free elections and Iran's right to self-determination over her resources. They believe that Mosaddeq continued to enjoy the support of the people and could not have been removed from power without foreign intervention. His overthrow, they believe, was the price that Iran was forced to pay for pursuing her own economic and political interests. The supporters of Mosaddeq consider his overthrow to have been an act purposefully carried out at foreign instigation.

The anti-Mosaddeq camp generally views the oil nationalization movement as a positive and collective effort. Even though Mosaddeq's role in this process is not denied, his opponents place considerable emphasis on the contribution of figures such as Kashani, Makki and Baqa'i, as well as others who later turned against Mosaddeq. They maintain that even though Mosaddeq was an important figure in defending and obtaining Iran's right to economic and political self-determination, at some point during his tenure he deviated from the right path. His deviation is said to have started when he became dictatorial, seeking excessive executive powers. Mosaddeq is subsequently accused of treason, as he is said to have plotted to exile the Monarch, rebelled against the constitution by limiting the powers of the Monarch and the Majles, called for a referendum to dissolve the parliament, and caused the Monarch's departure from the country by defying his royal edict to step down and hand power over to General Zahedi. In tandem with the above charges goes the argument that once Mosaddeq disenfranchised his old religious (Kashani) and anti-Communist (Baqa'i) allies, he colluded with the Communists, gave them free rein in the country, paved the ground for a Communist takeover, and infuriated the highest ranking Shi'i dignitaries along with their pious followers. Mosaddeq's anti-Monarchism and his final intention to establish a republic is said to have been the last straw in causing his downfall.

For Mosaddeq's opponents, his overthrow was the punishment that the Iranian people meted out to him for his deviation, his rebellion against the constitution, his disrespect for the position of the Monarch in the constitution, and his intention to overthrow the Shah and trample over religious sensitivities. It was the outcome of a domestic crisis settled by domestic forces. Opponents of Mosaddeq minimize, partially ignore or totally deny the role of direct foreign involvement in his overthrow. Their case against Mosaddeq follows the arguments of Azmudeh, the Military Prosecutor at Mosaddeq's trial. They emphasize that Mosaddeq's overthrow was the logical outcome of the grievances of Shah-loving, religious and nationalist Iranians.

This book attempts to construct a detailed micro-history of the events that culminated in 28 Mordad (19 August). It is neither about Mosaddeq nor is it an inventory of his government's objectives, failures or achievements; rather, it is about his overthrow and the context of this. Mosaddeq and his associates and opponents did trigger events, react to them and interact with them; hence, any study of the overthrow has to engage with Mosaddeq and his supporters as well as with those who overthrew them, reporting, assessing and analysing the positions and acts of both sides. On the basis of the evidence researched and employed, this study will eventually have to demonstrate whether Mosaddeq's removal from power was intended and initiated by foreigners or not, and whether it was a coup, a revolution, a spontaneous national uprising, or something other. In the prevailing polarization of positions, any conclusion is likely to summon a verdict of pro-Mosaddeq or anti-Mosaddeq on the work, as well as on its author. As with any history of social and political conflict, recounting the history of 28 Mordad will ruffle feathers and provoke judgements. The present history of 28 Mordad is intended for those who are curious about what happened during that day and how it came about.

In writing this book I am intellectually indebted to many people. Ahmad Ashraf played an important role in prompting me to write this book. I appreciate his role as a learned and inspiring interlocutor: a mentor. Yahya Dehganpour not only helped me find the books that I needed, but one lazy summer afternoon, having fished in his basement for old newspapers and magazines which he remembered having collected from the 1952–1953 period, presented me with a treasure-trove: three large plastic bags filled with rare dust-covered magazines of the time, full of pertinent and precious information. Researching periodicals and books in the National Library of Iran was greatly facilitated by Pouran Soltani, to whom I am always indebted for my research, and by the library staff, for whose generous help I am grateful.

While working on the events of 19 August (28 Mordad) I became ever more conscious that I needed a plan of Tehran in order to visualize the movement of the various actors, why they went where they went, and the logic behind their choices of points of congregation. Firouz Bagherzadeh, a true gentleman-scholar, helped me out by providing me with three maps of Tehran, which enabled me to visualize the events and the logic behind them more concretely. The clarity which the maps provided convinced me of the necessity of a map-history of 19 August. This was realized by Reneé Caoutte, a student in Art History at the American University of Paris, who patiently and efficiently worked on the maps, designed and re-designed the icons, labelled the streets when they were missing, and finally put life and history into the four maps, which have since found their way into the public domain. I am most grateful to her. I am thankful to Zahra for working over the self-explanatory cover picture and to Reza for helping out with the indexing.

I have benefitted from the scholarly generosity and indulgence of many. Abdollah Anvar, John Gurney and Fereydoun Rashidiyan read the first draft of this book, which greatly benefitted from their sharp eyes for details, errors and omissions and subsequently from their precise suggestions, comments and recommendations. Mark Gasiorowski and Ali Gheissari read the text closely, commented on it, and provided me with references which I had overlooked. I am thankful to them. Also, Daniel Gunn kindly applied his magical editing skills to the text and rendered it much more readable than it was.

In conclusion, may I suggest that readers glance over the chronology before reading the main text.

The coup d'état chronology: from idea to implementation

27 April 1951: Mosaddeq becomes Prime Minister after the parliament's (Majles') vote of confidence.

29 April 1951: The Majles ratifies the implementation of the oil nationalization law.

5 May 1951: Herbert Morrison (the British Foreign Secretary) asserts that "it is open to us to retaliate economically or militarily against Persia".

16 May 1951: The US administration opposes the British use of force in Iran.

21 May 1951: The British idea of an indefinite military occupation of Southern Iran's oil fields is tabled by the British government.

10 June 1951: The Iranian flag is hoisted on top of the Anglo-Iranian Oil Company in Khorramshahr.

June 1951: Mrs Lambton suggests that Robin Zaehner, a covert operation agent in Iran, would be the ideal person to contact Iranians friendly to the British cause and create the atmosphere conducive to a regime change.

25 June 1951: Eric Drake, the Anglo-Iranian Oil Company's manager in Tehran, leaves for Basra.

26 June 1951: Morrison informs the US Ambassador in the UK that the Shah should dismiss Mosaddeq and dissolve the Majles.

28 June 1951: Francis Shepherd, British Ambassador to Iran, writes to the Foreign Office, stating that "we must now do all we can to hasten Mosaddeq's departure".

Late June 1951: Operation Buccaneer, involving the direct intervention of the Royal Navy, the Royal Air Force and the Army, is under consideration by the British Cabinet.

12 July 1951: Hillier-Fry of the British Embassy in Tehran recommends that "the strong-arm or rough neck side of the party [Seyyed Zia's National Will Party] should be organized as soon as possible".

19 July 1951: British deployment of forces to the region. Three brigades of airborne troops are flown to the base at Shaiba in Iraq and the Persian Gulf squadron is strengthened by three frigates and four destroyers from the Mediterranean.

Summer 1951: For the purpose of occupying Abadan, an Armada is assembled at the mouth of Shatt-al-Arab in Iraqi waters, under British control.

23 July 1951: The occupation of Abadan is again considered as an option by the British Cabinet.

27 September 1951: Attlee completely abandons the idea of a military operation, arguing that the US government's attitude prevented the British from using force.

29 September 1951: The Shah informs Henderson, the US Ambassador to Iran, that Ayatollah Borujerdi has aligned himself with Mosaddeq on the oil issue and sent a message that all Iran must stand together in the face of British threats, and if Britain should invade the country Iranians must present a solid front.

1 October 1951: Zaehner of the British Embassy in Tehran informs the Foreign Office that Ayatollah Borujerdi has sent a message to the Shah announcing his complete support for Mosaddeq's government.

6 October 1951: Mosaddeq leaves for New York to attend the UN Security Council meeting.

14 October 1951: Pyman of the British Embassy in Iran says: "We thought that Seyyed Zia was the best person to put the country on its feet, but we were not opposed to other candidates, including Zahedi".

15 October 1951: Mosaddeq presents Iran's case before the Security Council.

4 November 1951: Anthony Eden informs Secretary Acheson that the US proposal on the oil issue, seemingly acceptable to the Iranians, is totally unacceptable to the British Government, and that "if Mossadeq fell, there was a real possibility that a more amenable Government might follow".

10 November 1951: Following the British rejection of the US proposal on the oil issue, Dean Acheson reports that the cardinal purpose of British policy is not to prevent Iran from going Communist, but is to preserve what is believed to be the last remaining bulwark of British solvency – that is, British overseas investments and property position.

26 December 1951: Henderson reports that the Shah has thought about a replacement for Mosaddeq. In the absence of organized effective opposition to Mosaddeq in the country, he did not see how any change could be effected except by a coup. A successful coup must be followed, at least temporarily, by a dictatorial regime, but the Shah did not know who could be trusted to head such a regime.

10 January 1952: Seyyed Ziaeddin Tabataba'i informs Middleton, the British chargé d'affaires in Tehran, that "there might be no solution except a coup d'état".

18 February 1952: Hoseyn Fatemi, the powerful assistant to Mosaddeq, is shot at by Abde-Khoda'i of the Fadaiyan Eslam.

The coup d'état chronology: from idea to implementation   xvii

20 February 1952: Major R. Jackson of the British Embassy reports that: "The industrial guilds which may be said to be anti-government – and which could be used against the government if so desired – are the following: Bakers, Butchers, Confectioners, Loaf Sugar makers".

11 March 1952: Pyman of the British Embassy in Tehran reports that: "Zahedi and Kashani have recently exchanged visits".

27 April 1952: The newly elected 17th Majles begins work.

24 May 1952: 'Ala confers with Henderson on whether the Shah should bring about the fall of Mosaddeq when the latter is still in Hague or whether he should wait until the prime minster returns.

27 May 1952: The Shah tells 'Ala that "steps must be taken in the near future to have Mosaddeq replaced".

28 May 1952: Mosaddeq leaves for the Hague to attend the International Court of Justice.

12 June 1952: In his discussion with Henderson, the Shah discusses the possibility of Saleh, Mansour and Qavam as successors to Mosaddeq.

24 June 1952: Mosaddeq returns to Tehran.

5 July 1952: Mosaddeq presents the Shah with the letter of resignation of his government.

6 July 1952: 52 out of 65 Members of the Parliament (Majles) present a vote that Mosaddeq is their preference to succeed Mosaddeq!

16 July 1952: Mosaddeq hands his resignation to the Shah over the latter's insistence that the Minister of War be appointed by the Shah. Mosaddeq had appointed himself as Minister of War.

17 July 1952: The Majles votes in favour of Ahmad Qavam as the new Prime Minister. Qavam has the full support of Henderson and Middleton.

18 July 1952: Demonstrations in favour of Mosaddeq are held in front of the Majles; Qavam issues his famous stern declaration that the "Captain has decided on a new course".

20 July 1952: Ayatollah Kashani issues a powerful declaration against Qavam and invites the people to return Mosaddeq to power.

21 July 1952: Tehran witnesses huge demonstrations and the army opens fire on the people. 'Ala informs Middleton that the British have underestimated Mosaddeq's popularity and that at this time only the resignation of Qavam and the return of Mosaddeq can calm public opinion.

21 July 1952: At 5:00 p.m. Tehran radio announces Qavam's resignation.

22 July 1952: At 9:00 a.m. 61 out of 63 MPs present at the Majles vote in favour of Mosaddeq as the new Prime Minister.

22 July 1952: The International Court of Justice upholds Iran's claim that the Court does not have jurisdiction in the Iranian oil nationalization case, by nine votes to five.

26 July 1952: Seyyed Zia meets Sam Falle of the British Embassy and, having emphasized that a "satisfactory agreement" with Mosaddeq is impossible, suggests ousting him as soon as possible by using the army.

26 July 1952: John Fearnley, of the British Embassy in Tehran, reports that General Zahedi is "very anxious to co-operate with this Embassy" and "that he hoped that Mr Middleton would appreciate his (Zahedi's) genuine desire to co-operate with us".

27 July 1952: Mosaddeq introduces his new cabinet and Ayatollah Kashani opposes some of his appointees.

27 July 1952: Asadollah Rashidiyan meets Sam Falle and recommends "a coup d'état in support of General Zahedi".

27 July 1952: Middleton sends a telegram to the Foreign Office suggesting an immediate "military coup d'état" to remove Mosaddeq again. In his mind such a coup will "need active encouragement and possibly support from outside".

28 July 1952: Mehdi Mirashrafi meets Sam Falle and recommends a rapid, violent coup d'état against Mosaddeq, while suggesting himself as leader of the coup. Falle reports to his superiors that Mirashrafi should be enlisted and encouraged to cooperate with Zahedi.

28 July 1952: Middleton concludes that: "It now looks as though the only thing to stop Persia falling into communist hands is a coup d'état". Middleton adds that "There is no outstanding candidate though General Zahedi has apparently entered himself in the lists and might well be adequate".

31 July 1952: Henderson writes to the Department of State that he and Middleton believe that "it did not seem likely [that] any alternative to Mosaddeq could be brought into power except by [a] military *coup d'état* ... that army officers who seemed to best fitted for leadership effecting [a] *coup d'état* were General Zahedi and General Hedjazi ... Both Middleton and I agreed that neither British nor American Government should undertake to encourage or support [a] *coup d'état* and that our two Embassies should not become involved in any way".

3 August 1952: The Majles accords Mosaddeq extraordinary legislative powers for the duration of six months.

6 August 1952: Anthony Eden writes to Oliver Franks, the British Ambassador to Washington, stating that the UK and the US need to find "a local Neguib" to resolve the problems in Persia.

6 August 1952: "With respect to current talk of the possibility of a coup d'état, Mr. Bruce (The Acting Secretary of State) feels that [it] was practically impossible, since there was no leadership capable of taking over, especially with the prestige of the army diminished".

7 August 1952: Sam Falle of the British Embassy in Tehran reports that he has met with Zahedi and that the General claims that "he has support in the army".

9 August 1952: Disagreeing with the US government's proposal to offer a grant of between $10 and $30 million to Mosaddeq, Anthony Eden informs Dean Acheson that: "there are signs among the generals of a feeling that the Army, whose morale is reported to be improving and which remains loyal to the Throne may have to intervene".

16 August 1952: Churchill writes to Truman that, in the name of Anglo-American unity, "I hope you will do your best to prevent American help for Mosaddeq either Governmental or commercial".

18 August 1952: Truman responds to Churchill: "I hope you will be willing to accept Iran nationalization law ... If Iran goes down [the] communist drain, it will be little satisfaction to any of us that legal positions were defended to [the] last".

23 August 1952: Mosaddeq forces 136 officers of the Iranian Armed forces into retirement.

25 August 1952: Mosaddeq informs Henderson that the "Britishers" who have underplayed the importance of the government's financial difficulties and suggested delaying help to Iran "really hoped, and were working, for some kind of *coup d'état*", and he adds that if the British do not respond by 27 August to his note of 7 August he will sever diplomatic relations with them.

3 September 1952: Sam Falle of the British Embassy in Tehran reports that "I saw General Zahedi today and found him full of the joys of Spring".

20 September 1952: Henderson informs the State Department that "Hints of *coup d'état* or resort to tactics of violence are becoming more open".

25 September 1952: Middleton reports a three hour meeting between Kashani and Zahedi.

30 September 1952: According to Middleton's assessment, "Kashani would like to see Mosaddeq removed, if he could be quite certain that this would not damage his position".

13 October 1952: Hoseyn Fatemi, the newly appointed Minister of Foreign Affairs, announces the arrest of General Hejazi, Habibollah, Asadollah and Qodratollah Rashidiyan in relation to a coup plot in collusion with a "foreign embassy". He names General Fazlollah Zahedi, Mozaffar Baqa'i, Ebrahim Khajehnouri and Mehdi Farrokh, who have parliamentary immunity, as other members of this conspiracy.

18 October 1952: The daily *Ettela'at* reports on a secret meeting during the previous week at which George Middleton, the British chargé d'affaires, was among those plotting a coup.

18 October 1952: The pro-Tudeh Party dailies call on the government to react harshly to Zahedi and the other plotters, calling for their arrest and execution.

22 October 1952: Iran severs diplomatic relations with the UK.

November 1952: British intelligence agents approach Kermit Roosevelt in London, informing him that they are thinking of "nothing less than the overthrow of Mosaddeq" and that they wished to start immediately.

Mid-November 1952: Montague Woodhouse, the SIS station chief in Tehran before the severance of diplomatic relations, arrives in Washington with the plan for "Operation Boot". Woodhouse tries to convince American officials that Mosaddeq "must be removed" and finds "sympathetic hearing within the CIA, but less so in the State department".

November–December 1952: Representatives of British Intelligence meet Near East and Africa (NEA) Division representatives in Washington. At this meeting, British Intelligence representatives (Montague Woodhouse, Samuel Falle and John Lockhart) "brought up the proposition of a joint action to remove Prime Minister Mosaddeq".

2 December 1952: Three senior American officials and two members of the British Embassy meet at the State Department and the senior American official categorically declares that "the State Department did not rule out the possibility of joint action of the kind we [the British] contemplated".

19 December 1952: Eden urges the Americans "in the strongest manner" to postpone a $25 million loan from the Export-Import Bank to Iran.

22 December 1952: Eden thanks Acheson for deferring the consideration of the Export-Import loan to Iran.

6 January 1953: Mosaddeq receives a strong vote of confidence from the Majles (64 out of 65) after the Kashani-Baqa'i faction in parliament attempts to curb his powers through a bill.

7 January 1953: Mosaddeq requests the prolongation of his extraordinary legislative powers by one year.

18 January 1953: Kashani strongly opposes Mosaddeq's request.

19 January 1953: The Majles votes in favour of prolonging Mosaddeq's extraordinary legislative powers (59 votes from 67 MPs present).

20 January 1953: Colonel Kamal, the Chief of Police and close to Kashani, is replaced by Lieutenant General Mahmud Afshartus.

20 January 1953: General Dwight Eisenhower, the Republican candidate, is inaugurated as President of the US.

14 February 1953: Iranian newspapers report that Abolqasem Khan Bakhtiyari has rebelled against the government, attacking an army column and killing 42 military personnel.

14 February 1953: Mosaddeq informs Henderson that the "British while pretending that they desired settlement were using their numerous Iranian contacts to overthrow him through alliances of forces including Bakhtiyari and other tribal elements, fanatical religious groups led by irresponsible mullahs, disgruntled reactionary elements in the army and bureaucracy, discredited politicians and Communist front organizations".

19 February 1953: Mosaddeq sends word to the Shah through an emissary that "he could no longer tolerate the unfriendly attitude of the Shah and Court and that he would resign on 24 February and make a public announcement to that effect".

19 February 1953: Mosaddeq sends word to the Shah that he believes that the Court and the Shah are intriguing against him through the Bakhtiyaris and the retired army officers.

21 February 1953: 'Ala meets Mosaddeq and informs him that the Shah is prepared to leave the country and stay abroad until Mosaddeq requests his return. Mosaddeq responds that the Shah should not leave the country. 'Ala meets with Kashani and Kashani is pleased with the situation.

21 February 1953: The British decide "to gradually taper off" the monthly sum of £10,000 which the Rashidiyans have received for the past 18 months. They instruct the Rashidiyans to "to give up their operational plans and devote themselves entirely to intelligence". The Rashidiyans refuse to follow their instructions.

22 February 1953: The Shah is thinking of General Zahedi and Allahyar Saleh as possible replacements for Mosaddeq, even though he does not "fully trust Zahedi".

24 February 1953: Mosaddeq promises not to press his grievances against the Shah. Differences between Mosaddeq and the Shah are reconciled. According to 'Ala, Kashani, Baqa'i and Makki are not happy with the reconciliation.

24 February 1953: Ardeshir Zahedi informs a member of the American Embassy that his father (General Zahedi) may become Prime Minister in the next few days and that he has already chosen his ministers.

25 February 1953: The Shah decides to leave the country as soon as possible.

25 February 1953: General Zahedi is arrested. His arrest is said to be in connection with his attempt to overthrow the government.

28 February 1953: From around 10:00 a.m. news of the Shah's imminent departure spreads through the city. The second wave of rumours is that the Shah is resigning.

28 February 1953: There are organized demonstrations by Behbahani, Kashani, and retired as well as active army officers in front of the Shah's palace to prevent him from leaving.

28 February 1953: The demonstrators, including the ruffians of South Tehran and members of the Zahmatkeshan, Ariya, SUMKA and Zolfaqar parties, attack Mosaddeq's house, which is in the vicinity of the Shah's palace, trying to break through the gates of Mosaddeq's house and forcing him to flee.

28 February 1953: Under pressure from the crowd surrounding his house and demanding that he should cancel his trip abroad, at 3:00 p.m. the Shah informs his supporters that he will not leave the country.

29 February 1953: The opponents of Mosaddeq gather at Baharestan and clash with Mosaddeq's supporters, while at around noon approximately 300 anti-Mosaddeq demonstrators (mainly from the Ariya Party) try to launch an attack on Tehran Radio's Broadcasting Station.

30 February 1953: Clashes between pro- and anti-Mosaddeq demonstrators continue in Tehran, but they gradually die out as pro-Mosaddeq forces take the upper hand. A number of demonstrators actively involved in the attack on Mosaddeq's house on 28 February, including army officers and key thug leaders, are arrested.

4 March 1953: At the 135th meeting of the National Security Council in Washington, Eisenhower presses for supporting Mosaddeq's government against the possibility of a Communist takeover by persuading the British to leave the Americans to deal with the Iranians and permit the US to put the Iranian oil industry back in operation. The President and Secretary Dulles view the British as an impediment to resolving the oil issue and saving Iran from falling into Communist hands. Eisenhower says that if he had $500,000,000 of money to spend in secret, he would give $100,000,000 of it to Iran "right now".

6 March 1953: Henderson reports from Tehran that the "possibility and advisability of attempting [a] military *coup d'état* continues [to] be surreptitiously discussed".

10 March 1953: Henderson reports that "Mosaddeq would prefer Iran [to] become some kind [of a] republic under his dictatorial control".

10 March 1953: Baqa'i and Ha'erizadeh insist that 28 February happened as the result of Mosaddeq's plan to change the regime, overthrow the constitutional monarchy and impose a dictatorship.

11 March 1953: At the 136th meeting of the National Security Council, Eisenhower says that "he had very real doubts whether, even if we tried unilaterally, we could make a successful deal with Mosaddeq ... the example might have grave effects on US oil concessions in other parts of the world".

17 March 1953: General Zahedi is released.

Mid to late March 1953: "General Walter Bedell Smith, Undersecretary of State, determined that the US Government could no longer approve of the Mosaddeq government and would prefer a successor ... The change in policy was communicated to [the] CIA and the NEA Division was informed that it was authorized to consider operations which would contribute to the fall of the Mosaddeq government".

18 March 1953: British Intelligence is informed that the CIA is in a position to discuss "detailed tactics".

31 March 1953: 'Ala reports to Henderson that "practically all elements really concerned regarding future stability [in] Iran were now convinced" that "energetic steps" needed to be taken "to overthrow Mosaddeq in the immediate future". "Most [of] these elements believed [that the] only person available to replace Mosaddeq was General Zahedi ... Zahedi would have [the] support [of] such political leaders as Kashani, Ha'erizadeh, Baqa'i, [and the] Zolfaqari brothers as well as more conservative elements and [the] army".

31 March 1953: 'Ala asks Henderson on behalf of the "group interested in [the] overthrow [of the] Mosaddeq government" whether the US government still supports Mosaddeq?" Henderson responds: "U.S. Government could not be associated with [a] *coup d'état*. If patriotic Iranians should consider [a] coup necessary in order [to] save Iran, they should act on their own responsibility and not expect any foreign power to become involved in such venture".

31 March 1953: Henderson reports to the State Department that since Mosaddeq "seems persistently to be leading Iran towards disaster, [the] risks involved in change would not be too great".

4 April 1953: "The [CIA] Director approved a budget of $1,000,000 which could be used by the Tehran Station in any way that would bring about the fall of Mosaddeq".

16 April 1953: "A comprehensive study entitled: 'Factors Involved in the Overthrow of Mosaddeq' is completed. The study indicates that a Shah–General Zahedi combination, supported by the CIA local assets and financial backing, would have a good chance of overthrowing Mosaddeq, particularly if this combination should be able to get the largest mobs in the streets and if a sizable portion of the Tehran garrison refused to carry out Mosaddeq's orders".

20 April 1953: Afshartus, the powerful pro-Mosaddeq Chief of Police, is abducted.

26 April 1953: Afshartus' dead body is discovered; a group of military officers, in addition to Zahedi, Baqa'i and Khatibi, are implicated in the murder.

End of April 1953: Donald Wilber is selected to go to Nicosia, Cyprus, and draw up a plan for the overthrow of Mosaddeq, in close collaboration with SIS.

4 May 1953: Iranian authorities seek to question General Zahedi about the murder of Afshartus. He seeks sanctuary at the parliament and is welcomed by Kashani, the Speaker of the parliament.

13 May 1953: In Nicosia, representatives of the CIA and SIS begin discussions to draft the first TPAJAX operational plan for the overthrow of Mosaddeq. The meeting ends on 30 May.

20 May 1953: The CIA Tehran station is authorized to spend "one million rials (90 rials to the US Dollar) per week" for the purpose of purchasing "the cooperation of members of the Iranian Majles".

25 May 1953: Henderson informs Mosaddeq that Secretary of State Dulles, who is on a Middle East visit, regrets the fact that he will not be able to visit Tehran.

30 May 1953: The Shah informs Henderson that Zahedi is acceptable to him as a replacement for Mosaddeq only if: "a) he would come into office through legal, parliamentary means: b) he would come in with [a] wide measure of public support; c) he would be acceptable to [the] US and UK and either [the] US or US and UK would be prepared to give [the] new government emergency financial as well as massive economic aid".

31 May 1953: Henderson leaves Tehran for Washington.

9–14 June 1953: CIA personnel involved in the overthrow project (Kermit Roosevelt, Carroll, Roger Goiran and Wilber) gather in Beirut to consolidate the operational plan.

15 June 1953: Roosevelt and Wilber arrive in London and meet their British counterparts to produce the "London" Draft of the TPAJAX operational plan.

25 June 1953: At a meeting of 11 high-powered government, diplomatic, military and secret service officials in Washington attended by Allen and John Foster Dulles (Director of the CIA and Secretary of State), General Walter Bedell Smith (Undersecretary of State and Allen Dulles' predecessor at the CIA), Charles Wilson (Secretary of Defense), Loy Henderson (the American Ambassador to Iran) and Kermit Roosevelt, the plan to overthrow Mosaddeq is given official approval.

11 July 1953: The directors of SIS and CIA, along with Prime Minister Winston Churchill and President Eisenhower, approve of Operation TPAJAX.

13 July 1953: Mattison, the US chargé d'affaires in Iran, writes about "reports circulating that the Prime Minister may ask for [a] referendum presumably in the streets, and may attempt [to] dissolve Majles".

14 July 1953: Mosaddeq's cabinet agrees to put the question of continuation or dissolution of the 17th Majles to a national referendum.

15 July 1953: Asadollah Rashidiyan meets Princess Ashraf in France and seeks her help to put the overthrow plan in motion.

16 July 1953: Stephen Meade of the CIA and Norman Darbyshire of the SIS meet with Princess Ashraf and ask her to inform the Shah of the plot and secure his participation.

19 July 1953: Kermit Roosevelt, the CIA-designated chief of the overthrow operation, secretly arrives in Tehran from Iraq.

20 July 1953: Zahedi leaves the Majles for a hideout and is in direct contact with the CIA station in Tehran.

21 July 1953: George Carroll, a CIA paramilitary expert responsible for the military planning of the overthrow operation, arrives in Tehran.

24 July 1953: The Secretary of State asks his brother Allen Dulles (director of the CIA) whether "the other matter is off". Allen Dulles responds that "he doesn't talk about it, it was cleared directly with the President, and is still active". Allen Dulles then adds that the Shah is an "unaccountable character but the sister has agreed to go". The "other matter" is a direct reference to the coup plan.

25 July 1953: Princess Ashraf flies to Tehran to try to meet with her brother.

26 July 1953: General Norman Schwarzkopf arrives in Tehran to obtain two royal edicts from the Shah.

30 July 1953: Asadollah Rashidiyan begins the first of his six meetings with the Shah, briefing him on all aspects of the overthrow plot and assuring him that the US and the UK are collaborating on this plan. These meetings last until 9 August.

5 August 1953: In a speech in Seattle (Washington), President Eisenhower says that Mosaddeq has "moved towards getting rid of his parliament

The coup d'état chronology: from idea to implementation xxv

and of course he was in that move supported by the Communist party of Iran".

8 August 1953: Kermit Roosevelt, the CIA-designated chief of the overthrow operation, meets secretly with the Shah for the second time.

9 August 1953: Hasan Akhavi has the first of his two meetings with the Shah, during which he presents "the name of the army officers who were ready to take action upon the receipt of an order from the Shah".

13 August 1953: The Ministry of Interior announces the final results of the referendum: 2,043,389 votes in favour of dissolving the Majles and 1,207 votes against.

16 August 1953: At 7:00 a.m. Radio Tehran announces that a coup d'état against the Mosaddeq government was attempted the previous night but was successfully foiled.

17 August 1953: At 10:15 a.m. the Shah arrives in Baghdad from his Caspian Palace on board a Beechcraft, accompanied by a pilot, one palace official and Queen Soraya.

17 August 1953: Berry, the US Ambassador to Iraq, informs the State Department that the Shah has told him that: "when a fortnight ago it was suggested that he sponsor a military coup he accepted the idea. However, in giving it more thought he decided that such action as he took must be within the framework of his constitutional power, hence, not a coup. Thus, ... [he] decided to appoint General Zahedi as Prime Minister in place of Mosaddeq ... The Shah said that he is utterly at a loss to understand why the plan failed. Trusted Palace officials were completely sure of its succeeding".

17 August 1953: Ambassador Henderson, who was present at the high-level meeting of 25 June in Washington which gave the green light for the coup in Iran, returns to Tehran after two and a half months of absence.

17 August 1953: Within the US Embassy compound, Roosevelt, Carroll, the Zahedis (father and son), Gilanshah, Farzanegan and the three Rashidiyan brothers meet for four hours. This "council of war" decides that "some action would be taken on Wednesday the 19th".

18 August 1953: Undersecretary of State Smith writes to the President that "The move failed because of three days of delay and vacillation by the Iranian generals concerned, during which time Mosaddeq apparently found out all that was happening. Actually it was a *counter-coup*, as the Shah acted within his constitutional power in signing the *farman* replacing Mosaddeq".

19 August 1953: Henderson reports that "Morning August 19 supporters [of the] Shah had arranged a pro-Shah demonstration for [the] purpose of showing [that] sentiment continued [to] exist in [the] country for him". By evening Zahedi is in power and Mosaddeq has been overthrown.

Introduction

In the collective memory and social psychology of Iranians, where individuals stand on 28 Mordad 1332 (19 August 1953) goes beyond politics. On 28 Mordad Mosaddeq was overthrown and Fazlollah Zahedi, basing his claim on a disputed edict from Mohammad Reza Shah Pahlavi, announced himself the rightful Prime Minister of Iran. For many Iranians, the significance of the day itself has become much more symbolically important than the mere mourning of another lost opportunity in Iran's perilous and painful quest for democracy and self-determination. The events of 28 Mordad have come to stand for a reflective moment of assessing Mosaddeq's 28-month government, his domestic and international policies, his strengths and weaknesses, his friends and enemies. The date and the event invariably conjure up ethical issues of right and wrong, just and unjust, chivalry and treachery, loyalty to and betrayal of Iran and Iranians. The forceful removal of Mosaddeq on 28 Mordad – through what was popularly believed at the time and is today factually known to have been the active participation of foreign powers seeking to further their financial and political interests – has permanently marked the viewing, reading and analysis of this event.

Four months after the overthrow of Mosaddeq, a British diplomatic source in Tehran reported to Anthony Eden, Secretary of State for Foreign Affairs in the UK, that "There is a considerable body of opinion here which holds that Dr. Mussadiq and other extreme nationalists still enjoy a greater measure of popular support than the present regime".[1] Even six months after Mosaddeq's overthrow, the assessment of British sources in Iran on Mosaddeq's popular support did not alter. Eden was again informed that there "seems little doubt" that Mosaddeq continues to enjoy "much latent support" through the country; "the majority of the people still favour Dr. Mussadiq" and the Zahedi government "lacks any popular following".[2]

---

[1] FO 416/106, 31 December 1953.
[2] FO 416/107, 7 January 1954; FO 416/107, 12 February 1954.

However, Eden was reminded that "it is clearly in our interest, as well as in Persia's, that the present regime should continue".³ If, in the assessment of Mosaddeq's chief adversaries, some six months after his overthrow the so-called rebellious Prime Minister continued to be more popular with the people than the government which replaced it, then it would be difficult to argue that those who brought about his downfall constituted the majority.

The events of 28 Mordad interrupted Iran's attempt to assert its right of self-determination over its polity and economy as well as over its future. It split the country into a defeated self-righteous majority and a victorious self-conscious and somewhat guilt-ridden minority. On one side stood a proud majority who believed that Mosaddeq did embody the democratic, nationalist and anti-imperialist aspirations of the Iranians and that he had succumbed with honour and dignity. His overthrow convinced many generations of his supporters of his righteousness, patriotism and valour. On the other side stood a minority, lacking popular following, whose numbers the Shah needed to inflate and whose morale he buttressed by addressing them as "my people". Their self-interest, preservation of status, loyalty, conviction, or ideological devotion to Britain and the US had motivated them to throw in their lot with the Anglo-American plan to remove Mosaddeq. To achieve this end they were obliged to acquiesce in the political and military leadership as well as in the financial largesse of the British and Americans both before and after Mosaddeq's overthrow. However, this group of collaborators – the petty-mercenary thugs, the middle-ranking but politically influential theologians, the suave Saville Row-suited intermediaries, politicians, parliamentarians, courtiers, the ambitious and fiery journalists, soldiers and officers – all wished to wear the mask of the true patriot. They needed to convince themselves – and, more importantly, others – that they had accepted and collaborated with foreign powers at some point in the process of overthrowing Mosaddeq, only to dispel the greater danger of Communism by ridding Iran of its "mentally unstable" Prime Minister and re-instating the Shah, the symbol of "national unity".⁴ The political, clerical and military leaders of the overthrow project and not necessarily the perpetrators knew only too well how the British and American administrations were pulling the main strings that had led to 28 Mordad. A significant majority of them tried to either hide their connections with foreigners or to put a nationalist "spin" on these in order to assuage their feeling of guilt. Reconciling claims to patriotism with acts of servility and subordination to the British and American administrations was a difficult act, but one which the Iranian participants and beneficiaries of 28 Mordad thought they could perform.

---

³ FO 416/107, 7 January 1954.
⁴ FO 371/98602, 28 July 1952; Foreign Relations of the United States (FRUS), *Iran, 1952–1954*, vol. x, p. 754.

The events of 28 Mordad ushered in a psycho-political conundrum. Loyalty to the Shah, who was supposed to symbolize the national sovereignty, integrity and independence of Iran, came to be associated with betrayal of those very same principles. The Shah did not seem capable of ridding himself of his sense of obligation to foreign powers. The monarch was back in power but acted as though he had no legitimacy or popular support. Four months after the overthrow, Dennis Wright, the interim chargé d'affaires in Iran, wrote to Anthony Eden that "the Shah was thinking of dismissing [Hoseyn] Ala but would not wish to do so if this might be taken by us as an anti-British move".[5] Even though immediately after the overthrow of Mosaddeq the Shah publicly claimed that 28 Mordad proved that his people loved him, he sincerely believed that he owed his position to his "Western friends" rather than to "his people", and that he therefore needed to obtain their approval to change his Minister of Court. After ousting Mosaddeq, the Shah's dilemma was that he continued to derive his legitimacy and authority not from the Iranian people but from foreign powers, which, having put him on the throne, had assured him that he did not owe them anything.

On 17 March 1954 – some seven months after the ousting of Mosaddeq – Anthony Eden reported that through the intermediary of his ambassador, the Shah had asked him "the direct question as to what were our [British] desires for Persia's future".[6] By asking the British what their desires for Iran's future were, the Shah was again acknowledging British dominance and his own position of subordination. The Shah's servility towards the British betrayed his claim that "the people have shown their trust in me and it rests upon me to prove that their trust was merited".[7]

MOSADDEQ'S OVERTHROW ACCORDING TO THE SHAH

One way to present a summary of who played what kind of a role in the overthrow of Mohammad Mosaddeq on Wednesday 19 August (28 Mordad) is to review the exchanges between Mohammad Reza Shah Pahlavi and two key American figures after General Zahedi took power and the Shah returned to Iran. The Shah's conversations with Kermit Roosevelt and Loy Henderson provide a telling account of the Shah's perception of who returned him to power. Furthermore, it clarifies each side's assessment of its own role and contribution, as well as that of the other in the events leading to Mosaddeq's overthrow. With certain nuances, one could argue that the Shah's private perception of who had brought about the events was not different from that of the Iranian people. It even accorded with the perception of the foreigners who had intervened in Iranian affairs.

Kermit (Kim) Roosevelt was the enigmatic and somewhat bombastic chief of the combined Central Intelligence Agency (CIA) and Secret Intelligence

---

[5] FO 416/106, 23 December 1953. [6] FO 416/107, 17 March 1954. [7] FRUS, vol. x, p. 763.

Service (SIS) TPAJAX operation in Tehran. Kim was the grandson of US President Theodore Roosevelt. Roosevelt's mission in Tehran was to fine-tune the plan and execute the ousting of Mosaddeq. Loy Henderson was the discreet American Ambassador to Iran. He was a career diplomat who had entered the State Department in 1922, gradually climbed the ladder of success, served in Moscow between 1934 and 1938, and developed a deeply ingrained suspicion of Soviet foreign policy designs. By the time Henderson was appointed Ambassador to Iran, he had already served as Ambassador to Iraq and India as well as having been head of the Near Eastern Affairs Bureau; he was therefore a seasoned emissary whose diplomatic responsibility was to assure Mosaddeq's government as well as the international community that the US had no interest in intervening in the domestic affairs of any country. Both Kim Roosevelt and Loy Henderson were in Tehran during 28 Mordad.

The conversations between these two American high officials and the Shah tell the general story of the major actors in the 28 Mordad overthrow, even though they never discussed the details of who did what, on whose orders, when or how. It would be too naive to expect a conversation on the details of a covert operation when both sides were in an elated and festive mood, gloating over their victory; mutual compliments and niceties seemed more appropriate for the occasion. Yet the exchanges leave hardly any ambiguity that, at the time, the Shah did believe the Americans to have played a determining role in bringing him back to power; inter alia, this would imply that in his mind they were instrumental in overthrowing Mosaddeq. The Shah's own position in private at the time flies in the face of the public and official discourse of his supporters that 28 Mordad and the fall of Mosaddeq resulted from a "spontaneous" movement of Iranians (if spontaneous is understood as an unpremeditated, unmanaged and unplanned popular and endogenous surge of political energy).

The Shah returned to Iran on Saturday 22 August, three days after Mosaddeq's overthrow. Kermit Roosevelt met with him immediately after midnight on Sunday 23 August. Since 2 August Roosevelt had been meeting with the Shah secretly, at around midnight, in a car parked on the Royal Palace grounds. According to Western secret service sources, Kermit Roosevelt was the mastermind and coordinator of the 28 Mordad events – and the Shah knew this. Woodhouse, the head of MI6 in Tehran until the end of October 1952, goes so far as to say that without Roosevelt's "presence to direct events" during 28 Mordad, the overthrow of Mosaddeq would have been doubtful.[8]

The post-overthrow meeting between the two men obviously took place under very different circumstances. The two were no longer secret conspirators forced to meet clandestinely in the dark, but were victorious allies meeting inside the Royal Palace. Yet strangely, the time and manner of

---

[8] C. M. Woodhouse, *Something Ventured* (London: Granada, 1982), p. 130.

their meetings gave the impression that each man, for his own particular reason, was uneasy, if not almost embarrassed, about being seen with the other. On this particularly happy but circumspect occasion, the Shah told Roosevelt: "I owe my throne to God, my people, my army – and to you".[9] When later that day, on the evening of 23 August, at the Shah's request, Ambassador Henderson met him "privately and without publicity", the Shah greeted him warmly and "expressed deep appreciation of the friendship which the US had shown him and Iran during the period".[10] The Shah wept as Henderson read Eisenhower's message to him and asked the ambassador to "tell the President how grateful he was for the interest which the President and the Government of US had shown in Iran". The Shah added that "he would always feel deeply indebted for this proof of genuine friendship" and went on to present his view of the factors that had brought about the "miracle of saving Iran" on 28 Mordad.[11] The miracle, he said, was "due to the friendship of the West, to the patriotism of the Iranian people and to the intermediation of God".[12]

Between the very early hours of 23 August, when the Shah met with Roosevelt, and 6:00 p.m. in the afternoon, when he met with Henderson, almost all of the determining factors which in his mind had contributed to the "miracle" of 28 Mordad and needed to be credited were the same. The Shah did not refer to the role of his army in his meeting with Henderson, probably placing its contribution under the rubric of the "Iranian people". Furthermore, in his meeting with Roosevelt, the Shah owed his throne first to God; yet in his early evening meeting with Henderson he owed it first to "the friendship of the West". What is of importance to this study is that according to both accounts – that of Roosevelt (the show-off spymaster) as well as that of Henderson (the tight-lipped diplomat) – "the friendship of the West" is not only specifically acknowledged but is also singled out by the Shah as a significant explanatory factor for the "success" of what happened on 28 Mordad. Had the Shah even specifically thanked the CIA and SIS for their services during the clandestine operation, Henderson would not have reported this verbatim in his dispatch. Instead, in his tactful and prudent diplomatic manner, he would have cloaked such explicit references by the Shah in the allegory of "the friendship of the West".

In order to grasp the full importance of these conversations, the Shah–Roosevelt meeting of 23 August needs to be revisited from another angle. Roosevelt's response to the Shah, who had wholeheartedly thanked him for reinstating him on the throne, was as important as the Shah's statement. Roosevelt's response demonstrated the assessment and appraisal of the top foreign intelligence officer on the scene. Roosevelt repeated to the Shah what he had already said on the evening of 28 Mordad to General Zahedi, to his

---

[9] K. Roosevelt, *Countercoup* (New York: McGraw-Hill, 1979), p. 199.
[10] FRUS, vol. x, p. 762.   [11] FRUS, vol. x, p. 762.   [12] FRUS, vol. x, p. 762.

collaborators, and to his cabinet who were celebrating their victory at the Officers' Club in Tehran. In a professional and seemingly cordial manner, Roosevelt returned the Shah's statement of gratitude by saying: "Iran owes me – us, the Americans and the British who sent me – absolutely nothing. Brief thanks would be received gratefully, but there is no debt, no obligation. We did what we have done to help in our common interest. The outcome is full repayment".[13] The American and British administrations had sent him to do a job – the overthrow of Mosaddeq – which he believed to be in the common interest of the West and the Shah; the result – the removal of Mosaddeq – was sufficient reward for his efforts. The Shah's response to Kim Roosevelt's blunt comment was: "We understand. We thank you and will always be grateful. And we will be additionally grateful for your statement that there is no obligation. We accept and understand this fully".[14] Nevertheless, as a token of his personal appreciation and recognition of Roosevelt's efforts, the Shah offered him a large, flat golden cigarette case. To Roosevelt, it was "a souvenir of our recent adventure".[15]

Aside from the false niceties, the pretentious humility peppered with professionalism, Roosevelt encapsulated 28 Mordad in a nutshell. For him, a job was a job. The American and British administrations had sent their spooks and cash to boot out Mosaddeq. Through the efforts of their Iranian networks the foreign secret services concluded their task efficiently. The Shah was back on his throne. General Zahedi, who was favoured by the British and Americans and eventually by the Shah to replace Mosaddeq, was safely installed as the Prime Minister. Mosaddeq, along with most of his ministers, close collaborators and loyal top military brass, was arrested. As Roosevelt had plainly put it, the common interest of the Shah, the British and the Americans was well served.

Perhaps even more important was that an example was made of the "maverick" Mosaddeq, who had had the audacity to reclaim the wealth of his own country and break the monopoly of the "Seven Sisters". For a while, the world was made safer for the powers-to-be. A third-world nationalist leader, who had attained power peacefully and legally, was purged and his defiance towards old colonialism and new imperialism was successfully passed off as yet another Communist bid for power. The menace of Communism, which had come to encompass anything posing a threat to US and UK interests, was thereby contained, and Mosaddeq's "erratic" policies and "chaotic" rule were replaced with the Shah's "Western-friendly" and predictable reign of "law and order".

The secret of the foreign intervention that led to the fall of Mosaddeq – which came to be publicly known through Roosevelt, Woodhouse, the State Department, the Foreign Office, Wilber and other sources some 27 years after the events – had been widely whispered among Iranians and foreigners ever

---

[13] Roosevelt, p. 201.   [14] Roosevelt, p. 201.   [15] Roosevelt, p. 201.

since the evening of 19 August 1953 (28 Mordad 1332). In a dispatch to the Department of State only two days after the overthrow of Mosaddeq, Ambassador Henderson lamented that "unfortunately the impression was becoming rather widespread" that the American Embassy or the US government had "contributed with funds and technical assistance to the overthrow of Mosaddeq and the establishment of the Zahedi Government".[16] Concerned about the consternation that belief in a US-backed intervention could provoke and the damage it could cause the stature and image of US foreign policy, Henderson tried to contain the situation and manage it swiftly and intelligently. In 1953, the impression of ethical conduct in US foreign policy was still of great concern to US diplomats; furthermore, the overthrow of Mosaddeq through foreign intervention had to be sanitized and legitimized nationally and internationally, for the sake of both the Shah and his Western friends. Henderson therefore sought to erase any traces of foreign intervention by giving all of the credit to the Iranians involved in the overthrow.

Henderson advised the Department of State to launch a campaign stressing the "spontaneity" of the anti-Mosaddeq and pro-Zahedi movement.[17] Once the overthrow was seen as the outcome of a "spontaneous" and therefore "domestic popular" movement, then the suspicion of foreign intervention would dissipate. Henderson advised the spokesman for the Department of State to "stress in [a] factual way [the] *spontaneity* of [the] movement in Iran in favour of [the] new government".[18] Henderson wrote that he sincerely hoped that ways would be found so that the American and international public would "understand that [the] victory of [the] Shah was [the] result [of the] will [of the] Iranian people".[19] He reiterated that he needed this type of a campaign launched and propagated through private and public channels for its usefulness back in Iran. Henderson was intelligent enough to understand the incipient perceptions of the role of the US in the overthrow of Mosaddeq and was correctly worried about its long-term implications. Whereas the Shah labelled 28 Mordad "a miracle" composed of three elements that included his Western friends, Henderson wished to present it to the world as a spontaneous movement. Each man was addressing his own audience and using concepts that he believed would not require further explanations. The purpose served by calling 28 Mordad a "miracle" was the same as calling it a "spontaneous" revolution. Even though both men knew that they could not come clean, the Shah, Zahedi and his associates seem to have been more forthright than Henderson.

For some years after 28 Mordad, this day was commemorated as a special occasion during which state-sponsored festivities and demonstrations marked the so-called *popular uprising* (*qiyam-e melli*) of the people in favour of their beloved king. On this day an attempt was made to recreate the "great

---

[16] FRUS, vol. x, p. 759.   [17] FRUS, vol. x, p. 759.   [18] FRUS, vol. x, p. 760.
[19] FRUS, vol. x, p. 760.

demonstration" that ushered in the overthrow of Mosaddeq. Various government organizations and the latest state-propped political party of the day would "fill trucks and lorries with kids, construction workers and brick baking workers", dispatch them to the main streets of Tehran and – in the words of a mastermind of the events of 28 Mordad, Asadollah Rashidiyan – make a mockery of themselves.[20] For years, the official commemoration of 28 Mordad was devoutly observed. In 1959, Asadollah Rashidiyan explained that even though he had been invited to attend 27 different events on this day, he had refused them all as he had come to believe that "all those who made sacrifices during 28 Mordad were being wronged".[21] The events of 28 Mordad were supposed to symbolize the day on which Iranians proved their historical loyalty to the monarchy and renewed their oath of allegiance to the Shah.

In 1961 – or some eight years after the 28 Mordad events – in a book called *Mission for My Country*, the Shah presented the Iranian people with a revised and refined account of the participants of 28 Mordad, one more in line with Henderson's version than with his original view. The Shah still referred to this day as "the miracle of 28 Mordad". He wrote: "It is my firm belief that the toppling of Mosaddeq's government was the work of the ordinary people of my country in whose hearts blazed the Divine providence".[22] By this time the Shah had already side-lined some of the key "heroes" of 28 Mordad, notably General Zahedi. According to this version of the Shah's rendition of what happened on 28 Mordad, ordinary people of the streets acting as God's agents overthrew Mosaddeq: it was God's will that Mosaddeq was overthrown and the Shah returned. Within the framework of this historical narrative, all of the forces which cooperated to overthrow Mosaddeq were moved to do so by a power far beyond their control and for a good cause far beyond the comprehension of any mortal. Most importantly, all references to the involvement of his Western friends were omitted.

In February 1970, when the Shah was in the midst of heated negotiations over oil prices with the oil companies, and all the OPEC ministers (except that of Libya) had congregated in Tehran, the Ambassadors of the US and the UK began exerting pressure on the Shah to soften his position on oil price hikes.[23] Refusing to heed their messages and demands, the Shah angrily confided in 'Alam, his most trusted Minister of Court, that "These guys think they can for example spend one or two million dollars in Iran and stage a coup. The time for such things has passed".[24] Perhaps the Shah was thinking of what he

---

[20] Be Ravayat-e Asnad-e Savak, *Rashidiyanha*, vol. 1, (Tehran: Markaz-e Barrasiy-e Asnad-e Tarikhiy-e, 1389), p. 148.
[21] *Rashidiyanha*, vol. 1, p. 234.
[22] M. R. Pahlavi, *Ma'muriyat Baray-e Vatanam*, (Paris: 1366), p. 123.
[23] A. N. 'Alikhani, *Yaddashthay-e 'Alam*, vol. 2, (Bethesda: Iranbooks, 1993), pp. 156–158.
[24] 'Alikhani, vol. 2, p. 159.

Introduction 9

knew "these guys" had done on 28 Mordad: staged a coup d'état. The Shah's justification of his position and his explanation to 'Alam concerning the state of Iran's army and its top brass reinforces the hypothesis that the Shah believed that his old Western friends could no longer intervene in the affairs of Iran as they had done in August 1953. Interestingly, 'Alam did not agree with the Shah that the "foreigners" could no longer intervene and candidly presented his counter-position.[25]

In his diaries, 'Alam, a long-standing confidant of the Shah, refers to the events of 28 Mordad (19 August) in two different ways. In August 1969, he refers to 28 Mordad as *qiyam-e melli*, a national insurrection or a popular uprising under the leadership (*ze'amat*) of General Zahedi.[26] In August 1973, after visiting the graves of "the martyrs of 28 Mordad" and General Zahedi, 'Alam bemoans the opportunism of his countrymen and writes: "It was surprising that at the grave of Zahedi, the founder (*baniy-e*) of the 28 Mordad coup d'état, there was not even a fly to be seen".[27] Was this a slip of the tongue on the part of the man closest to the Shah, or was it a conscious and intended informal acknowledgement of the facts 20 years after the event? Was 'Alam becoming bolder in putting his beliefs into his diary as time went by? Whatever the reason, 'Alam could not shake off the thought that 28 Mordad was a coup d'état, just as the Shah, at the peak of his power, could not free himself of the spectre of a foreign-masterminded coup, similar to that carried out in August 1953. The Shah was privy to the intricacies of the foreign-initiated coup in August 1953. Seventeen years after the overthrow of Mosaddeq, the Shah continued to worry that the foreigners who engineered the coup in his support in 1953 could just as easily carry out another coup against him. Their power to intervene in the domestic affairs of Iran haunted him for the rest of his life, obsessing him with a conspiracy theory which paralysed him whenever he felt politically insecure.

The debate over whether the overthrow of Mosaddeq on 28 Mordad was the outcome of a planned CIA–SIS coup d'état implemented with the assistance of Iranian collaborators and their networks, a miraculous "spontaneous" and therefore thoroughly home-spun uprising, or, better still, a national resurgence (*rastakhiz*) of the popular masses, is as old as the event itself. One could argue that those Western politicians and diplomats (such as Ambassador Henderson) who wished to present the overthrow as a function of the "spontaneity" of the Iranian people sought to absolve the aggressive interventionist foreign policy of their countries from the accusations of meddling in the affairs of other countries, of imperialism and of making a sham claim to democratic ideals when it was their own narrow economic and political interests that were being threatened. The Iranians who promote the "spontaneity" theory are generally of three broad types, with different shades somewhere between these categories. First, there are those who

[25] 'Alikhani, vol. 2, p. 159.   [26] 'Alikhani, vol. 1, p. 247.   [27] 'Alikhani, vol. 3, p. 131.

empathized ideologically and politically with the world outlook and/or interests of the collaborationists and their foreign patrons and subsequently welcomed foreign intervention, yet who were are too shy and embarrassed to say so out loud lest they be seen as traitors. Second, there are those who believed that the people had grown tired of the economic hardships and domestic political instability that prevailed during the premiership of Mosaddeq, and who subsequently rebelled against him impulsively on 28 Mordad. Third, there are those who were ideologically opposed to foreign intervention but were unable to account for the details of what happened between the first and second coups, and who concluded that, to their chagrin, the second coup must have been "spontaneous" (even though they did not refute the existence of an overall CIA–SIS design to overthrow Mosaddeq).

In an official and secret CIA document, "The Battle for Iran", which was written in the mid-1970s by a CIA History Staff member whose name was excised, it is stated that: "The military coup that overthrew Mosadeq and his National Front cabinet was carried out under CIA direction as an act of US foreign policy, conceived and approved at the highest level of government".[28] Elsewhere, the author refers to the 19 August 1953 event which removed Mosaddeq from power as "a U.S.-assisted coup d'état".[29] In the foreword to this document, the author explains that his/her research had the support of the CIA, and that to arrive at his findings he benefitted from "personal interviews with a number of active and retired Agency officers who participated in the action, on Central Reference Service personality files, and on a variety of open sources". The CIA History Staff member also informs his/her readers that "the great bulk of the correspondence and traffic dealing with the operation was destroyed in 1962".[30] Denis Wright, who returned to Iran in December 1953, provides a more complete picture of what actually happened that August. He recalls that before being dispatched he talked to "people in the Foreign office", "met people like Prof. Lambton" and was "told that the British had been involved with the CIA in the coup in August 1953".[31]

---

[28] National Security Archives, C01384417, *The Battle for Iran*, p. 26. http://www2.gwu.edu/~nsarchiv/NSAEBB/NSAEBB435/docs/Doc%203a%20%283%29%20-%20CIA%20-%20Battle%20for%20Iran%20-%20Appendixes%20-%202013%20release.pdf.
[29] Ibid, p. 28; the underlining is in the original.   [30] Ibid, p. 28.
[31] Denis Wright, Iranian Oral History Collection, Harvard University, Transcript 1, p. 9.

I

The British reaction to Mosaddeq in power: "Mossie grabs Britain's oil – but Navy to the rescue" (*Daily Express*)

With fury, the British had closely observed how Mosaddeq, as the Chair of the 18-man Parliamentary Committee in charge of reviewing and studying the 1949 Supplemental Oil Agreement (better known among Iranians as the "Gass–Golshayan Agreement"), had gradually steered the parliament towards not only rejecting the Supplemental Agreement but also preparing the legal ground for nationalizing Iran's oil industry. With Mosaddeq in power, the British were no longer dealing with a politician whom they could impress, pressure, intimidate or bribe into accepting their terms. The British suddenly felt that they had a politician in power with whom they could not talk in a familiar language. As such, Mosaddeq was a wild card in a country that had been under the politico-economic influence of the British and in which they felt deeply invested. The Anglo-Iranian Oil Company (AIOC), 51 per cent of which belonged to the British government, was a highly lucrative business that contributed significantly to the British economy, and its loss could not be taken lightly. The British considered their investment in Abadan as the "greatest single overseas enterprise in British commerce", making a profit of £170,000,000 in 1950.[1] Furthermore, Mosaddeq had four characteristics that made him abhorrent to the British. He was a true patriot and believed in placing Iran's benefit above all else, irrespective of the risks. He was inflexible, relentless and stubborn. He was Western-educated, Westernized and familiar with Western ways of doing politics, yet, contrary to most in his position, he was not in awe of everything Western – he was rather firmly against foreign intervention in the affairs of his country. Finally, he believed that as long as the Iranian people supported him, he could move mountains without the help of colonial powers.

It was therefore not surprising that Francis Shepherd, the British Ambassador to Iran, deeply disliked Mosaddeq as a person and resented his

[1] W. R. Louis, *The British Empire in the Middle East 1945–1951* (Oxford: Clarendon Press, 1984), pp. 682, 689.

ideas about how Iran should manage its affairs. Shepherd, the suave and supposedly restrained British civil servant, could not resist showing his resentment towards Mosaddeq as Iran's Prime Minister in his official correspondence. On 28 April 1951, one day after Mosaddeq received his vote of confidence from the parliament, Shepherd wrote that Mosaddeq's premiership would only prove disastrous.[2] Subsequently he referred to the Iranian Prime Minister as a "lunatic", who was "both cunning and slippery and completely unscrupulous".[3]

The Iranian parliament ratified the law nationalizing Iranian oil on 29 April 1951. On 5 May, Herbert Morrison, the British Foreign Secretary, asserted that "it was open to us to retaliate economically or militarily against Persia".[4] The idea of a British military intervention to protect the oil fields of the Anglo-Iranian Oil Company and the Abadan oil refinery was raised in the British Cabinet in mid-May. By 21 May 1951, the idea of an indefinite military occupation of Southern Iran was shelved because of mobilization problems as well as "logistical and technical difficulties".[5]

In June, however, three inter-related ideas coincided with the view of British authorities eager to intervene in Iran: first, that it was not possible to "do business" with Mosaddeq; second, that concessions should not be made to him; and third, that undermining the Iranian Prime Minister was possible "by covert means", as championed by Ann K.S. Lambton.[6] By the end of June, British policy-makers were once again considering the use of force, arguing that while taking and holding on to the Persian oil fields was not realistic, the occupation of Abadan was another matter. From 23 July, the long-term occupation of Abadan was again considered by the British Cabinet as an option.[7] Operation Buccaneer, involving the direct intervention of the Royal Navy, the Royal Air Force and the Army, was conceived in late June to address the modality of the takeover.[8]

According to the minutes of the British Cabinet meeting of 19 July, "three brigades of airborne troops were flown to the base at Shaiba in Iraq and the Persian Gulf squadron was strengthened by three frigates and four destroyers from the Mediterranean".[9] Morrison believed that the intervention would not only teach the Persians a lesson but "might well result in the downfall of the Mussadiq regime".[10] Even though fliers in Persian for distribution among the residents of Abadan, instructing them not to put up any resistance, were prepared in advance of the attack, the operation was called off.[11] It was not until 27 September that Prime Minister Attlee completely abandoned the idea of a military operation, arguing that the US government's attitude prevented the British from using force.[12] Hence, it was the strong opposition of

---

[2] FO 371/91457, 28 April 1951.   [3] Louis, pp. 651–652.   [4] Louis, p. 663.
[5] Louis, p. 665.   [6] Louis, pp. 659–661.   [7] Louis, pp. 672–673.
[8] FO 371/91461, 23 June 1951.   [9] Louis, p. 674.   [10] Louis, p. 675.
[11] FO 371/91462, 22 July 1951.   [12] Louis, pp. 687–688.

President Truman and George McGhee, the Assistant Secretary of State, to the military operation that eventually convinced Attlee to abort the invasion of Abadan. After the evacuation of the British from Abadan on 4 October 1951, the British government felt humiliated, impotent and exposed to similar threats to their overseas economic and geo-strategic interests.

Exactly two months after Mosaddeq became Prime Minister, and about the time Operation Buccaneer was being conceived, Shepherd wrote to the Foreign Office: "In short I feel that we must now do all we can to hasten Mussadiq's departure".[13] Two weeks later, in mid-July, Shepherd had an audience with the Shah, on which he reported: "We discussed the political situation and the Shah said he was convinced that Mussadiq must be got rid of as soon as possible".[14] At this time, the British and the Shah came to share the opinion that Mosaddeq needed to be ousted. With the military option of invasion off the table, the British Foreign Office began exploring other possible scenarios for removing Mosaddeq by "whatever means possible short of force".[15]

In the meantime, the Shah was taking less reckless steps to unseat Mosaddeq. The Shah seems to have believed that Mosaddeq could be replaced through normal political channels and party politics played out in parliament. Following his conviction that Mosaddeq could be removed from power through legal means, the Shah encouraged Seyyed Ziaeddin Tabataba'i (Seyyed Zia), as early as 12 July 1951, to revive his National Will Party (Hezb-e Eradeh Melli) and challenge Mosaddeq openly.[16] The Shah was deeply preoccupied with Mosaddeq's popularity among the people. He therefore did not wish to show himself keen on ousting Mosaddeq by force or by challenging him directly, lest the final confrontation led to the people siding with Mosaddeq and against him. In late July 1951, the British were still seriously considering the option of direct intervention.

By December 1951, the Shah had undergone a dramatic change of heart about how to replace Mosaddeq. The Shah's conversation with Henderson on 26 December clearly indicates that eight months after Mosaddeq became Prime Minister, the monarch was thinking of removing him via a coup. Between July and December 1951 three important events had brought the nature of the stand-off between successive British governments and Mosaddeq into sharper focus. First, the US administration was opposed to any direct British military intervention in Iran. Second, Mosaddeq's power and popularity at home seemed unassailable. Third, the British were opposed to an oil agreement proposal acceptable to the US and Mosaddeq, believing

---

[13] FO 248/1514, 28 June 1951.   [14] FO 248/1514, 12 July 1951.
[15] R. Louis, "Britain and the Overthrow of the Mosaddeq Government", in M. J. Gasiorowski and M. Byrne (eds) *Mohammad Mosaddeq and the 1953 Coup in Iran* (Syracuse: Syracuse University Press, 2004), p. 132.
[16] FO 248/1514, 21 July 1951.

that Iran's nationalization of its oil – if not reversed – would set a precedent threatening all British overseas interests, ultimately leading to the demise of the British Empire. The details of a proposal on the oil issue were hammered out by the US administration while Mosaddeq was in the US between 6 October and 22 November 1951. On 10 November, faced with British intransigence, Dean Acheson, the US Secretary of State, wrote: "They [the British] will accept no settlement by which (a) it cannot be plainly shown to everyone that Mosadeq has not profited over rulers who abide by their contracts, or (b) Britain is humiliated and discriminated against".[17] According to Acheson, the British were not willing to make "specific proposals", except to boycott Mosaddeq and hope for his fall, while at the same time they were convinced that negotiations with Mosaddeq would help strengthen his hand.[18] The result of the deadlock between the UK and the US on how to deal with Iran in November 1951 forced the Americans reluctantly into a wait-and-see position, while the British pondered on how to replace Mosaddeq with a government more understanding towards their oil interests.

The confluence of these three factors must have convinced the Shah that he could depend on neither direct foreign military intervention nor the quick resolution of the oil issue; faced with an ever more emboldened Prime Minister, he needed to think of radical alternatives. On 26 December 1951, the Shah informed Henderson that "since there was no organized effective opposition to Mosadeq in [the] country, he did not see how any change could be effected except by [a] coup".[19] The Shah lucidly explained that a "successful coup must be followed, at least temporarily, by [a] dictatorial regime and he did not know who could be trusted to head such [a] regime". It seems clear that by the end of December 1951, the Shah was entertaining the idea of a coup to replace Mosaddeq. He informed Henderson that the problem with his idea was that he could not find a strong person whom he could trust to lead the coup. The Shah seems to have been afflicted by this problem even until a couple of weeks before 28 Mordad. However, he seemed to have an even bigger problem with operationalizing the idea of a coup: he may have earnestly wanted a coup to remove Mosaddeq, yet he was too scared of its unknown consequences. The Shah was very apprehensive about becoming implicated in a coup lest it failed. He wanted others to do all the dirty work for him and free him of Mosaddeq.

One of the architects of the adversarial position of the British with respect to the Mosaddeq government was Ann Katherine Swynford Lambton, known to Iranians as "Miss Lambton". From 1939 to 1945, Lambton was the press attaché at the British Embassy in Tehran. She spoke Persian, had travelled to the four corners of Iran and was an expert on the country. Lambton believed that through "covert means" the British could rally a

[17] FRUS, vol. x, p. 279. [18] FRUS, vol. x, p. 282. [19] FRUS, vol. x, p. 299.

segment of Iranians "who feared the risk of being denounced as traitors but whose idea of the Iranian national interest coincided with the British conception".[20] Lambton was of the opinion that, before the Mosaddeq regime could be overthrown, a public relations and educational campaign was necessary to break the Persian taboo that collaborating with the British constituted an act of treason.[21]

History was to prove that on the issue of seeking and finding Iranians who saw a perfect coincidence between their own national interests and those of the British, Lambton's knowledge and assessment of certain Iranian politicians and their social psychology was flawless. For Lambton, Seyyed Zia was the archetype of the audacious Iranian politician who was unabashed in his sincere belief that Iran's long-term welfare could only be secured through safeguarding and guaranteeing British interests. By June 1951, Lambton suggested that Robin Zaehner – an academic, scholar and SOE (Special Operation Executive) agent in Iran (1943–1945) – would be the ideal person to contact Iranians friendly to the British cause and create an atmosphere conducive to regime change.[22] For Roger Louis, the origins of a covert plan to undermine Mosaddeq, resulting in the 1953 coup d'état, can be traced to the "Zaehner mission" and Lambton.[23]

THE SWEET DISTANT FRAGRANCE OF A COUP

Less than two weeks after the Shah's conversation with Henderson about the virtues of a coup against Mosaddeq, Seyyed Zia broached the subject of a coup with George Middleton, the British chargé d'affaires. Seyyed Zia, who had been encouraged by the Shah to prepare for a political and a parliamentary battle against Mosaddeq, may have been the person who informed the Shah that organized political opposition to Mosaddeq, with the aim of removing him, was not really feasible. Seyyed Zia was close to the Shah and was supposed to become Prime Minister before Mosaddeq was nominated to this position by the Majles in late March 1951. As prospects for the removal of Mosaddeq by peaceful parliamentary manoeuvrings or contrived domestic crises were successively frustrated because of his charisma and public support, the option of using force was reinvoked as an alternative. This time, however, it was an Iranian pro-British politician who sought to convince the British that they needed to seriously consider the coup d'état option. As early as 10 January 1952 – or less than nine months after Mosaddeq became Prime Minister and 19 months before the two coups in 1953 – Seyyed Zia informed Middleton, the British Chargé D'Affaires in Tehran, that "there might be no solution except a coup d'état".[24] At this point Seyyed Zia did not suggest a

---

[20] Louis, p. 659. [21] Louis, p. 660. [22] Louis, p. 660. [23] Louis, p. 660.
[24] FO 248/1531, 10 January 1952. The underline is in the original text.

candidate for leading the coup. The proposal of the solution of a coup d'état to remove Mosaddeq by both the Shah and Seyyed Zia seems to be too concurrent to be accidental or random.

The radical and probably realistic conclusion of the Shah and Seyyed Zia was reached subsequent to Mosaddeq's ability to consolidate power both at home and abroad. Mosaddeq's successful trip to the US in October, his speech at the Security Council of the UN on the issue of Iran's nationalization of its oil and his meeting with President Truman and negotiations with Dean Acheson gave the international community the impression that Iran was being led by a reasonable, affable and wise politician who was interested in a solution to the oil issue and who trusted the Americans as intermediaries. This was an image which the British did not appreciate, especially since they felt that Mosaddeq was forcing a wedge between them and the US. On his return to Iran, in late November, Mosaddeq scored another political victory against his domestic opposition. Challenged by parliamentary opposition to his policies, the overwhelming majority of the members of parliament (90 out of 107 members) gave the Prime Minister a vote of confidence. Subsequent parliamentary challenges to his government throughout December failed to bear fruit and simply enhanced Mosaddeq's stature.[25]

It could be assumed that the Shah felt as though Seyyed Zia would be the most suitable person to follow through the idea of a coup, as the idea may originally have been Seyyed Zia's own. The use of the term "coup d'état" by Seyyed Zia, as a solution to the "Mosaddeq problem", should not be taken lightly. Seyyed Zia was well aware of what he meant by a coup and so was his British interlocutor, as he was the person, along with Reza Khan, who had successfully organized and executed the 1921 coup against Ahmad Shah Qajar. The 1921 coup d'état installed Seyyed Zia as Prime Minister and Reza Khan, who later became Reza Shah, as the Commander in Chief. Seyyed Zia was proud of his role in the 1921 coup, which he considered to be "a surgical operation to remove a pestering tumour" and necessary to "bring the people back in line".[26] Seyyed Zia openly confirmed that the British had financed the 1921 coup in Iran and that he was paid directly by them.[27] The success of the coup, Seyyed Zia believed, was sealed by his ability to "purchase" the services of influential military figures who could have opposed it.[28] So, when in January 1952 Seyyed Zia proposed that the time had come for a coup d'état against Mosaddeq, his British interlocutor and the Foreign Office knew full well that 31 years before, Seyyed had successfully planned and executed a coup d'état in Iran for them. Seyyed Zia was a man of many resources, whose strong connections ranged from the political right to the left, the Court to the commoners, the

---

[25] B. Aqeli, *Roozshomar-e Tarikh-e Iran*, vol. 1 (Tehran: Nashr-e Goftar, 1369), pp. 329–330.
[26] S. Elahi, *Seyyed Zia, Mard Aval ya Mard-e Dovom-e Coup d'état* (LA: Ketab Corp, 2011), pp. 92–93.
[27] Elahi, pp. 32, 59.   [28] Elahi, p. 84.

zealous "Devotees of Islam" to their targets of assassination. Seyyed was well connected with the landowners and the well-to-do, with influential military figures as well as with the thug leaders of Southern Tehran. Hence, when Seyyed Zia spoke about replacing Mosaddeq through a coup d'état, it was not mere speculation or swaggering by a middle-ranking Iranian politician who sought to endear himself to the British, but a concrete proposal by someone who was experienced in the business, trusted by his previous customers and who possessed the capacities that Lambton sought for the person who would remove Mosaddeq from office.

MOSADDEQ RESIGNS, BUT NO ONE ELSE CAN GOVERN

Almost six months after Seyyed Zia and the Shah spoke of a coup against Mosaddeq as the only way to oust him, Mosaddeq surprised his opponents by twice tendering his resignation. First, on 5 July 1952, after his return from the Hague, Mosaddeq presented the Shah with a letter of resignation of his government; however, 52 of the 65 members of parliament voted in his favour, returning him to power. Ten days later, on 16 July, Mosaddeq met the Shah and presented his new cabinet members, reserving the portfolio of the Minister of War for himself. At this meeting the Shah opposed the Prime Minister's constitutional right to appoint the Minister of War of his choice. Mosaddeq informed the young monarch that if he were to oppose the nomination of any member of his cabinet, he would be obliged to resign. The Shah responded that if he were to decide to accept Mosaddeq's cabinet members, he would give news of it by 8:00 p.m. that evening, and if he were to decide to oppose it, then Mosaddeq could do as he wished.[29] Appointing the Minister of War had become the prerogative of the Shah during previous governments, but Mosaddeq sought to establish a balance of power between the Shah and the Prime Minister on the basis of the constitution.

When Mosaddeq did not hear from the Shah by 8:00 p.m. he wrote a letter of resignation and sent it to the Shah. On 17 July the morning newspapers printed the letter and in that afternoon the parliament met in a closed session and, in the absence of 28 pro-Mosaddeq members, voted in favour of Ahmad Qavam's premiership. Effective from the evening of 17 July, Mosaddeq was removed and power was in the hands of Ahmad Qavam, who had the full support of both British and American administrations and their embassies in Tehran.[30] For the British, who had first supported the candidacy of Seyyed Zia and then agreed to Ahmad Qavam's appointment as Prime Minister, the main issue was to replace Mosaddeq with someone whom they could trust and who would cooperate to resolve the oil problem to their benefit. Once Mosaddeq resigned, the British felt their troubles were over.

[29] H. Makki, *Vaqaye' Siyom-e Tir* (Tehran: Entesharat-e 'Elmi, 1378), p. 101.
[30] FO 371/98601, 18 July, 20 July, 21 July 1952.

From Friday 18 July, crowds spontaneously gathered in front of the parliament at Baharestan Square, demonstrating in favour of Mosaddeq and demanding his return to power. Once Ayatollah Kashani came out in full support of Mosaddeq and the Tudeh Party followed suit, Qavam's fate was sealed. The Shah's wavering position did not help Qavam impose his authority. The Shah did not have the necessary conviction or courage to fully support Qavam in implementing his repressive policies of closing the parliament and arresting key opposition leaders, including Kashani.[31] Qavam's foreign supporters – especially the British, who stood to gain the most – did their utmost to prop up and maintain the unpopular Prime Minister in power. During the four tumultuous days of 18 to 21 July, Middleton, the British chargé d'affaires, did all in his power to convince Qavam to hold on to power despite the mounting opposition against him. The correspondence of British and American diplomats in Iran provides ample and implacable evidence of British and American intervention in the domestic affairs of Iran aimed at retaining Qavam and preventing Mosaddeq from returning to power.[32] Diplomatic representatives of both countries placed considerable pressure on the Shah to agree to Qavam's demands that parliament be dissolved, the opposition be imprisoned and the pro-Mosaddeq demonstrations be repressed.[33]

By the end of Monday, 21 July (30 Tir), the four-day national uprising against Qavam and in favour of Mosaddeq reached its culmination. At 5:00 p.m. Tehran Radio announced Qavam's resignation.[34] Earlier that day, 'Ala, the powerful Minister of Court, informed Middleton of the British Embassy that the British had underestimated Mosaddeq's popularity and that at that time only the resignation of Qavam and the return of Mosaddeq could calm public opinion.[35]

The events of 17 to 21 July 1952 initiated an interminable and agonizing nightmare not only for the British but also for the Americans and the Shah. The lessons to be drawn from this short experience of trying to replace Mosaddeq were depressing for all of Mosaddeq's opponents. The facts demonstrated that even if Mosaddeq were to resign and withdraw from political life, as he had done, Iranians would oppose his successor, oust him, and drag Mosaddeq back into politics. If the reign of public opinion meant the continued premiership of Mosaddeq, then ousting Mosaddeq necessitated stifling public opinion by force. The events of late July demonstrated that if Mosaddeq's opponents wanted him removed from power, the soft parliamentarian way would not suffice as the people would simply take to the streets and oppose it. Mosaddeq had become too popular, and any attempt at his removal united various political tendencies behind him. The Shah preferred the soft parliamentarian mode of getting rid of Mosaddeq. Yet

---

[31] FO 371/98601, 18 July 1952. [32] FO 371/98601, 18 July 1952.
[33] FO 371/98601, 20, 21, 28 July 1952. [34] Makki, p. 131.
[35] FO 371/98601, 21 July 1952.

his influential aids as well as his foreign friends came to the conclusion that the realistic option after 30 Tir was to impose their candidate for premiership on the people by force. Even though one scenario for removing Mosaddeq was dashed on 21 July, it revived the old coup scenario privileged by Seyyed Zia. Vacillation between the soft and hard approaches, or a combination of both, to put Mosaddeq out of office continued until the first coup.

FRESH COUP D'ÉTAT MURMURS

A few days after the Shah had reappointed Mosaddeq as Prime Minister, Sam Falle of the British Embassy met with Seyyed Zia. He found Seyyed in good spirits, in contrast to "his mood of philosophic depression" a few days before.[36] After the failure of Qavam, Seyyed Zia was adamant that reaching "a satisfactory agreement" with Mosaddeq was impossible and that any compromise or "co-operation" with him "would be tantamount to complete surrender" and would result in the "collapse" of British influence in Iran.[37] Seyyed Zia insisted upon a hard approach to Mosaddeq, and argued that "it was therefore necessary to get rid of him as soon as possible". Seyyed Zia seemed very hopeful, informing Falle that "it would be possible to use the army for what he described as 'a transaction'". In Seyyed Zia's opinion "a maximum of two months would be necessary to prepare the grounds for action".[38] Six months after his original proposal of a coup d'état against Mosaddeq, Seyyed Zia was repeating his original offer to the British.

On 27 July 1952, a day after meeting with Seyyed Zia, Falle met Seyyed's right-hand man Asadollah Rashidiyan, who was "in no way depressed by recent events" and was only interested in what was to be done next.[39] Rashidiyan proposed "a coup d'état in support of General Zahedi". He believed that the motor for the coup would be the political party which he was thinking of founding and the support which he had in the army and among "the mullahs".[40] Falle, who was in agreement with Rashidiyan's assessment, later wrote to his superiors that "I hope it will be possible to give Rashidiyan a clearer view of our policy fairly soon. I do not want to set him off working up a coup d'état and then have to call it off should we decide, which heaven forbid, to support Musaddiq".[41]

At nightfall on Sunday 28 July, Falle met with Seyyed Mehdi Mirashrafi in "a dark garden". Mirashrafi, the editor of the staunchly anti-Mosaddeq daily *Atash*, was another close associate of Seyyed Zia. Falle reported that Mirashrafi "wants to take rapid and violent action and is full of the idea of a coup d'état".[42] Even though Mirashrafi had spoken about leading the coup

---

[36] FO 248/1531, 28 July 1952.   [37] FO 248/1531, 28 July 1952.
[38] FO 248/1531, 28 July 1952.   [39] FO 248/1531, 28 July 1952.
[40] FO 248/1531, 28 July 1952.   [41] FO 248/1531, 28 July 1952.
[42] FO 248/1531, 28 July 1952.

himself, Falle believed that it was best to "enlist his help and get him to co-operate with Zahedi". Falle was confident that Mirashrafi was prepared to follow the advice given to him by the British, just as he had done in the past "even at great risk to his own life".[43] The return of Mosaddeq to power in spite of his resignation had convinced Seyyed Zia and the close circle of political activists around him that the only way to remove Mosaddeq was through a coup d'état.

THE ONE-WAY ROAD TO REMOVING MOSADDEQ

By the end of July 1952, the British concurred with the Iranians that a coup d'état seemed to be the only efficient way of getting rid of Mosaddeq. Based on Falle's report and his own interactions with anti-Mosaddeq Iranians, Middleton concluded that "It now looks as though the only thing to stop Persia [from] falling into communist hands is a coup d'état".[44] Middleton was so shocked and disgusted at the failure of Qavam's premiership and the return of Mosaddeq that, in an emotional and desperate telegram to the Foreign Office, he suggested an almost immediate "military coup d'état" to remove Mosaddeq again.[45] In his telegram, Middleton added that even though he did not rate the likelihood of the coup succeeding as very high, he believed that "such a coup d'état would in any case need active encouragement and possibly support from outside".[46] Middleton was repeating the proposal of Seyyed Zia and Rashidiyan. He was promoting a coup d'état similar to that which Seyyed had successfully engineered in 1921. At this time Middleton also believed that even though there were no outstanding candidates for leading the coup, General Zahedi was adequate for the job.[47]

The British learnt five important lessons from their failure to remove Mosaddeq, lessons which informed and shaped their political posture towards Iran from late July 1952 until the overthrow of Mosaddeq. First, the British became convinced that it was impossible to remove Mosaddeq through legal means, and that even if they were to do so, Mosaddeq's popularity would bring his supporters out onto the streets, just as had happened between 18 and 21 July. In the absence of a violent clampdown on his supporters, Mosaddeq would be returned to power. The hypothetical successor to Mosaddeq needed to be willing and able to violently repress Mosaddeq's supporters, should this prove necessary. Middleton therefore wrote to his superiors in London that a successor to Mosaddeq could not be found through "normal constitutional methods".[48]

---

[43] FO 248/1531, 28 July 1952. [44] FO 248/1531, 28 July 1952. Underline in the original.
[45] FO 248/1531, 27 July 1952. [46] FO 248/1531, 27 July 1952.
[47] FO 248/1531, 28 July 1952. [48] FO 416/105, 28 July 1952.

Second, according to Middleton's assessment of the events, "the only thing to stop Persia [from] falling into communist hands is a coup d'état".[49] The idea that the continuation of Mosaddeq's premiership would culminate in a Communist takeover was an important bogus construction, effectively employed by the British to drag the US into the anti-Mosaddeq camp. Middleton camouflaged his initially unabashed recommendation for a coup d'état to remove the barrier to British oil interests in Persia by presenting Mosaddeq's rule as tantamount to future Communist rule. The Communist scarecrow eventually played a key role in convincing the US that Mosaddeq needed to be overthrown by a coup d'état. As of 6 August 1952, a year before the coup, some highly placed British and US diplomats were in agreement over "the increasing dangers of Communism in Persia" – an expression which veiled the increasing danger of Mosaddeq and his oil-nationalization policy to the world order based on US and UK economic and political interests.[50] Furthermore, the association of Mosaddeq's rule with creeping Communism provided a compelling excuse for all domestic political forces which were opposed to Mosaddeq to ally themselves with the anti-Communist/anti-Mosaddeq/royalist bloc championed by the British and the Americans. The rallying call of this foreign-supported political opposition to Mosaddeq was anti-Communism and the preservation of the monarchy, with appeals to safeguarding Islam.

Third, disappointed by the performance of Qavam, the British started looking for military successors to Mosaddeq. Three days after the fall of Qavam, members of the British Embassy in Tehran referred to General Zahedi and General Hejazi as possible coup leaders against Mosaddeq.[51] A few days later, Middleton concluded that "there is no outstanding candidate though General Zahedi has apparently entered himself in the lists and might well be adequate".[52] Exactly two weeks after the Qavam fiasco, Anthony Eden, the British Deputy Prime Minister and Secretary of State for Foreign Affairs, wrote to Oliver Franks, the British Ambassador to Washington, on the situation in Persia. Eden wrote that he and Julius Holmes, the US minister in the UK, were discussing the need to find "a local Neguib" to resolve the problems in Persia.[53] This was a clear reference to the events in Egypt, where General Mohammad Neguib, with the help of Gamal Abdel Nasser and some one hundred officers, had staged a coup d'état against King Farouk on 23 July 1952 and had initially replaced him with the Crown Prince. Almost a year before the coup d'état against Mosaddeq, Eden wrote about what was to come: "if we could find a Neguib and Persia could set up an effective administration, we would be doing something to combat Communism".[54] If Seyyed Zia had paved the way for Reza Khan, a military figure, to take over power in

---

[49] The term "coup d'état" is underlined in the original dispatch, FO 248/1531, 28 July 1952.
[50] FO 416/105, 6 August 1952.   [51] FO 416/105, 6 August 1952.
[52] FO 416/105, 6 August 1952.   [53] FO 416/105, 6 August 1952.
[54] FO 416/105, 6 August 1952.

1921, he and 'Ala were to play a somewhat similar role in bringing Fazlollah Zahedi to power.

Fourth, the British learnt that they could neither rely on the Shah to remove Mosaddeq, nor could they trust him to make tough decisions. In his account of the events in Iran during Qavam's premiership, Middleton deplored the fact that: "The Shah hates taking decisions, and cannot be relied upon to stick to them; he has no moral courage and easily succumbs to fear; he is pre-occupied with his personal position on the throne and thinks to retain it by a policy of appeasement".[55]

Fifth, in view of the Shah's indecisiveness and wavering at critical moments when hard, fast and unpleasant decisions had to be made, the British came to the conclusion that they would need to take a more proactive and openly interventionist role in unseating Mosaddeq. They felt as though every detail of the coup had to be worked out by them and handed over to the Iranians only for execution. Less than one week after the failure of Qavam's attempt, Middleton continued to mull over the possibility of a coup d'état against Mosaddeq with "active encouragement and possibly support from outside".[56]

By the end of July 1952 there was a consensus among anti-Mosaddeq Iranians and the British Embassy in Iran that a coup d'état was necessary to remove Mosaddeq; that General Zahedi was not the best but an adequate choice for leading the coup; that Seyyed Zia and his circle of friends would support the coup idea by pooling all their resources and networks; and that foreign or outside encouragement and support were needed for the coup's success. Eleven months after the fall of Qavam and the return of Mosaddeq, the crude idea of a coup d'état began taking serious shape in the form of an initial agreement to intervene in Iran by the British and the Americans. The coup idea which had been broached by Seyyed Zia in January 1952 and which had obtained favourable reception among Mosaddeq's opponents, both foreign and domestic, in July 1952, was subsequently taken up by the CIA and the SIS and made operational in June 1953.

DISCONTENTED MILITARY OFFICERS RALLY AROUND ZAHEDI

On 23 August 1952, roughly one month after the July episode, Mosaddeq forced 136 officers of the Iranian armed forces into retirement.[57] Mosaddeq's purge of the armed forces seems to have been partly a response to his knowledge or intuition that the British were already thinking of a coup by officers sympathetic to their cause, and partly a reaction to the role the army had

---

[55] FO 416/105, 6 August 1952.   [56] FO 248/1531, 27 July 1952.
[57] J. Bozorgmehr, *Doctor Mohammad Mosaddeq dar Dadgah-e Tajdid Nazar* (Tehran: Enteshar, 1365), p. 117; G. Nejati, *Jonbesh Melli Shodan-e Naft-e Iran* (Tehran: Enteshar, 1366), p. 235.

played in repressing the people during the 21 July uprising. Irrespective of Mosaddeq's motives, this pool of discontented, side-lined, resentful and generally young army officers provided an ideal recruitment ground for Iran's anti-Mosaddeq ruling class. In the aftermath of the purge, two overlapping key military organizations – the "Retired Officers' Association" and the "Devotees of the Shah" – composed of active and retired military officers became highly active in the political life of the country, with the single aim of removing Mosaddeq. After September 1952, both of these organizations played a crucial role in all efforts to destabilize the Mosaddeq government, until they eventually succeeded in replacing him on 19 August 1953.

The "Retired Officers' Association" (*kanon-e afsaran-e bazneshasteh*) was an official and authorized organization which publicized its events. The "Devotees of the Shah" (*fadaiyan shah*), sometimes referred to as the "Devotees of the Shah and the Army", was a secret military apparatus which included active as well as retired military officers.[58] These two overlapping military organizations, one public and the other clandestine, became important anti-Mosaddeq vehicles once General Zahedi was considered as a serious alternative to Mosaddeq by the British and the Americans. As far back as March 1952, there was a report on the organization of a large group "of restless dissatisfied ex-officers and serving officers of the army", under the leadership of Colonel Ettehadiyeh.[59] Colonel Ettehadiyeh's group, possibly also associated with Zahedi, may have constituted the core of what some seven months later was to become the "Devotees of the Shah".

General Zahedi was the leader of the "Retired Officers' Association" and was successful in uniting and organizing the retired officers around an anti-Mosaddeq, pro-Shah and anti-Communist political platform. At the headquarters of the "Retired Officers' Association", Zahedi organized regular meetings on the current affairs of the country for the disgruntled and purged officers who bore a grudge against Mosaddeq and his policies.[60] From the summer of 1952, even before Qavam's short premiership, Zahedi had gathered two groups of civilian and military sympathizers around himself. He had formed a "shadow cabinet" of civilians and, more importantly, had organized a group of officers, the most notable of whom was General Gilanshah.[61] This military group, which probably constituted the nucleus of the "Devotees of the Shah", was supported by a group of between three and 40 army officers.[62] General Gilanshah, along with the "Retired Officers' Association" and the "Devotees of the Shah", was to play a key role in the events leading up to the coups (25 and 29 August) and the coups themselves in August 1953.

---

[58] *Ettela'at*, 22 Mehr 1331.   [59] FO 248/1531, 5 March 1952.
[60] A. Zahedi, *Khaterat-e Ardeshir Zahedi*, vol. 1 (Tehran: Ketab Sara, 1385), p. 74.
[61] FO 248/1531, 26 July 1952.   [62] FO 248/1531, 26 July 1952.

A COUP PLOT UNCOVERED: THE FOREIGN
AND DOMESTIC ALLIANCE

On 13 October 1952, a few months after the birth of the "Retired Officers' Association" and the "Devotees of the Shah", Hoseyn Fatemi, the Mosaddeq government's spokesman, confirmed the rumours in the Iranian press about an impending coup and announced that retired General Abdol-Hoseyn Hejazi, as well as Habibollah Rashidiyan and his sons Asadollah and Qodratollah, had been arrested in relation to this plot. The conspirators were accused of having been in collusion with a "foreign embassy". Other key figures involved in the plot – but who were not arrested because of their immunity as members of the upper (*sena*) or lower (*shoraye melli*) houses of parliament – were General Fazlollah Zahedi, Mozaffar Baqa'i, Ebrahim Khajehnouri and Mehdi Farrokh.[63] According to Iranian sources, Mosaddeq's government had received information about a series of meetings at Zahedi's house in Hesarak, at which seven senators, four members of the lower house of parliament and five high-ranking military personnel regularly met. Among those who regularly met were Hejazi, Ariyana, Haji Ansari and the Rashidiyan brothers. This group was said to be in contact with Seyyed Ziaeddin Tabataba'i, Amir Assadollah 'Alam, Ebrahim Khajehnouri and Middleton, the British chargé d'affaires in Tehran.[64]

A brief review of the events between end of July and late October 1952 is necessary to assess the validity of the Mosaddeq government's claim of having discovered a conspiracy involving notable military and political Iranians in league with a "foreign embassy". This claim constituted the basis upon which the Mosaddeq government decided to break diplomatic ties with Britain on 22 October. The British Embassy and its consulates in Iran were closed nine days after Iran's Minister of Foreign Affairs, Hoseyn Fatemi, disclosed the details of the plot. On 22 September 1952 Mosaddeq had warned that if the British government continued its policies it would become evident that its intentions towards Iran were not friendly, and that in this case there would be no alternative but to break diplomatic relations with Britain.[65]

In the aftermath of the 21 July uprising, the fall of Qavam and the resumption of power by Mosaddeq, and almost three months before the Mosaddeq government disclosed this plot and associated it with a "foreign embassy", the names of General Zahedi and General Hejazi were explicitly mentioned as possible coup leaders against Mosaddeq by the British in their internal correspondence.[66] Less than a week after the fall of Qavam, Zahedi, who had been waiting for an opportunity to make a bid for power, had

---

[63] A. Rahnema, *Niruhaye Mazhabi bar bastar Nehzat-e Melli* (Tehran: Gam-e No, 1384), pp. 694–697.
[64] M.A Safari, *Qalam va Siyasat* (Tehran: Namak, 1371), p. 669.   [65] Safari, p. 669.
[66] FO, 371/98602, 24 July 1952.

approached the British Embassy. John Fearnley of the British Embassy in Tehran reported that General Zahedi was "very anxious to co-operate with this Embassy" and that "he hoped that Mr Middleton would appreciate his (Zahedi's) genuine desire to co-operate with us".[67] Fearnley emphasized that Zahedi wished "to meet Mr Middleton privately as soon as possible".[68]

From August 1952, Zahedi was regularly in touch with the British Embassy. On 7 August Middleton reported to the Foreign Office in London that he had learnt from "General Zahedi himself that approaches have been made to him by Makki, Baqa'i, Ha'erizadeh and an emissary from Kashani".[69] Makki, Baqa'i, Ha'erizadeh and Kashani were one-time allies of Mosaddeq who had all, for different reasons, fallen out with him. On the same day, Sam Falle of the British Embassy in Tehran, who was General Zahedi's regular interlocutor, reported: "I saw General Zahedi yesterday. Zahedi claims that he has support in the army".[70] Two weeks later, on 21 August, Sam Falle met with General Zahedi.[71] On 3 September 1952, around the time when the two military organizations of the "Retired Officers' Association" and the "Devotees of the Shah" were becoming actively engaged in Iranian politics, Sam Falle reported that: "I saw General Zahedi today and found him full of the joys of Spring".[72]

On 20 September Henderson reported on a meeting with a person who had been in one of Mosaddeq's previous cabinets and who maintained close relations with Kashani. This "Iranian political leader" had commented that "Iran could now be saved only by some form [of] coup". In this report to the State Department, Henderson pointed out that "hints of coup d'état or resort to tactics of violence are becoming more open".[73] Almost two weeks later, or some ten days before the Mosaddeq government accused Zahedi of plotting against it in collusion with "a foreign embassy", Falle reported that the "Retired Officers' Association" was going to meet on that day and they were going "to take an oath that they will oppose the government".[74] This information was probably passed on to Falle by Zahedi, as in the same report Falle added that "Zahedi appears to be increasing his activity".[75]

One day before the plot was made public, Falle met with Zahedi again and found him to be "bubbling with optimism". According to Falle, "all opposition elements" were rallying around him and he was planning to have lunch with Kashani, Ha'erizadeh and Baqa'i during the week.[76] Falle summed up Zahedi's political prospects as follows: "Whatever his vices or virtues and chances of success, the General is performing quite a useful task in uniting the discouraged and dispersed opposition which, after the 30th Tir [21 July], went

---

[67] FO 248/1531, 26 July 1952. [68] FO 248/1531, 26 July 1952.
[69] FO 248/1531, 7 August 1952. [70] FO 248/1531, 7 August 1952.
[71] FO 248/1531, 21 August 1952. [72] FO 248/1531, 3 September 1952.
[73] FRUS, vol. x, p. 475. [74] FO 248/1531, 2 October 1952.
[75] FO 248/1531, 2 October 1952. [76] FO 248/1532, 12 October 1952.

underground".[77] This was probably the last time that Falle met Zahedi, as on the next day Zahedi and his colleagues were exposed, and ten days later (22 October) the British Embassy was closed and British diplomatic staff were gradually expelled.

Zahedi, his co-conspirators and the British learnt a lesson from this event that was important for their future endeavours. Even with evidence of a coup against his government, Mosaddeq was a legalist and not one who would forcefully move against, confront or repress any move against his government with an iron fist. His perception of running the country as the Prime Minister was not marked by a "security" perspective or approach. Mosaddeq's soft response to the conspirators significantly reduced the risk and cost of future coup attempts. While Zahedi and the other conspirators such as Baqa'i and Khajehnouri (who enjoyed immunity as senators or members of parliament) remained untouched, those arrested (such as the Rashidiyans) were released after some four months.

With the British expelled from Iran in late October, their everyday contacts with the Anglophile Iranian opposition to Mosaddeq naturally dried up and their dependence on their American colleagues for information, recommendation, guidance and analysis increased. As Middleton had concluded in late July, in order for a coup d'état to succeed in Persia, it needed active encouragement and possibly support from outside. Hoping that their collaborators and their networks in Iran would be able to continue destabilizing Mosaddeq, the British actively sought the support of the Americans for a coup in Iran.

REACHING CONSENSUS ON FOREIGN INTERVENTION

By November 1952, British intelligence agents had approached Kermit Roosevelt in London and informed him that they were thinking of "nothing less than the overthrow of Mosaddeq".[78] Seeing no point in wasting time, they wished to start immediately. Roger Louis provides a comprehensive and well-documented chronology of Britain's conspiratorial designs and activities against the Mosaddeq government, indicating how despite the initial policy differences with the British over Mosaddeq, the Americans warmed up to and eventually agreed to a joint covert operation against Mosaddeq.[79] Louis' account demonstrates that at each step, Mosaddeq's non-compliance with proposals made by the British, the Americans and the World Bank on the settlement of the oil issue, based on his assessment of Iran's interests, further enraged the British and also helped bring the Americans closer to the belligerent British position. According to Louis, Mosaddeq's rejection of the September 1952 Truman–Churchill proposal

---

[77] FO 248/1532, 12 October 1952.   [78] Roosevelt, p. 107.
[79] R. Louis in *Mohammad Mosaddeq*, pp. 126–177.

eventually convinced the Americans that Mosaddeq was not "negotiable" and had to be removed.[80]

Christopher Montague (Monty) Woodhouse, the MI6 head in Iran (mid-August 1951 to mid-October 1952), recounted that "The Shah would do nothing without prompting by the British government and the new British government under Churchill was reluctant to act without American support".[81] It was therefore not surprising that the comprehensive plans for the overthrow of Mosaddeq were not drawn up until the Americans were convinced that it was in their geo-political and long-term economic interests to put all their weight behind the idea of forcefully replacing Mosaddeq. Woodhouse explains how he had to reframe the justification for removing Mosaddeq so that the apprehensive American administration would come to support the idea of a joint venture in Iran. The Americans, he argued, were not necessarily interested in restoring the position of the AIOC in Iran and were therefore more likely to cooperate with the British if they were convinced that the removal of Mosaddeq would contain Communism in the region.[82] This was the Communist scarecrow that Middleton had conceived of after the Qavam fiasco in July 1952.

Between November 1952 – following the expulsion of the British from Iran – and late April 1953, the American opposition to British intervention in Iran yielded to a convergence of interests. Subsequently, the two governments colluded and planned a covert operation against Mosaddeq. Even before Eisenhower's inauguration on 20 January 1953, some key members of his future administration were in favour of intervention in Iran. The Dulles brothers in particular had discussed the idea and were inclined towards the British intervention plan: "Operation Boot". This plan was initially presented to the CIA and the State Department in mid-November 1952 during Montague Woodhouse's trip to Washington.[83] In January, the SIS was actively following up on the idea of a joint CIA–SIS operation in Iran.[84] After Eisenhower's inauguration, meetings between the CIA and MI6 intensified and resulted in authorizing the CIA to "begin planning a coup at some point in March".[85] On 18 March, British intelligence was informed that the CIA was in a position to discuss "detailed tactics".[86] Some two weeks later, on 4 April, Allen Dulles, the CIA director, authorized a budget of $1,000,000 to be used "in any way that would bring about the fall of Mosaddeq".[87] Subsequently, on 20 May 1953, the CIA Tehran station was authorized to spend "one million rials a

---

[80] R. Louis in *Mohammad Mosaddeq*, p. 158.
[81] C. M. Woodhouse, *Something Ventured* (London: Granada Publishing, 1982), p. 115.
[82] Woodhouse, p. 110.   [83] Woodhouse, p. 117.
[84] Louis in *Mohammad Mosaddeq*, p. 168.
[85] Gasiorowski in *Mohammad Mosaddeq*, p. 232.
[86] Louis in *Mohammad Mosaddeq*, p. 168.
[87] D. Wilber, *Clandestine Service History. Overthrow of Premier Mossadeq of Iran* (http://cryptome.org/cia-iran.htm). Wilber's substantial report was written in March 1954, some seven months after the second coup. The important appendices to his report, including the

week (rate of 90 rials to the US Dollar)" for the purpose of purchasing "the cooperation of members of the Iranian Majles".[88] Roosevelt maintained that the CIA Tehran station had about $1,000,000 in its safe, and during the operations in August $100,000 was spent.[89]

DOMESTIC REPERCUSSIONS OF FOREIGN COLLUSION

As the British and American positions on the necessity of political change in Iran converged and consolidated, between November 1952 and March 1953 the political situation in Iran became more polarized and the divisions between pro- and anti-Mosaddeq forces became more accentuated and hostile. External developments found their internal echoes. Subsequent to several confrontations in the Majles (parliament) between Mosaddeq and his opponents (in the process of which Mosaddeq's authority and popularity were strengthened), the anti-Mosaddeq opposition effectively abandoned the parliament as an arena of political opposition, struggle and negotiation, and chose to challenge the Mosaddeq government by resorting to violence.

The 28 February 1953 (9 Esfand 1331) attempt to intimidate and destabilize Mosaddeq's government and the subsequent murder of Lieutenant General Mahmud Afshartus, Mosaddeq's Chief of Police, in late April 1953, demonstrate that the domestic opposition to Mosaddeq was rehearsing violent scenarios for ousting him around the time when the British and Americans were agreeing on an anti-Mosaddeq coup d'état in Iran. It is not easy to determine with certitude whether the overlap between the plans of foreign anti-Mosaddeq forces and domestic ones were closely synchronized, were loosely coordinated or were purely coincidental. The fact that the Iranian opposition to Mosaddeq moved into a much more aggressive gear with the clear intention of destabilizing and, if possible, overthrowing his government after Eisenhower's inauguration as President in the US may be coincidental. However, between November and December 1952, or a few months before the unfolding of a string of events in late February 1953 aimed at destabilizing Mosaddeq's government, representatives of British intelligence – Montague Woodhouse, Samuel Falle and John Lockhart – met the representatives of the Near East and Africa (NEA) Division in Washington and invoked the proposal of a joint action to remove Prime Minister Mosaddeq. This fact necessitates further research aimed at evaluating whether or not the activities of the domestic opposition – especially during 9 Esfand, which predated the official US change of policy towards Iran – were linked to or supported by the foreign opposition (which at this time was mainly British).

various TPAJAX operational plans, will come under his name followed by the reference to the appendix.

[88] Wilber, pp. 18–19.   [89] Roosevelt, p. 166.

The London draft of Operation TPAJAX, drawn up on 15 June 1953 for the purpose of overthrowing Mosaddeq, clearly indicated that $50,000 had already been spent by the Rashidiyan Brothers in support of Zahedi and against Mosaddeq. This considerable sum was spent in Iran in the course of the "several months" leading to 15 June 1953.[90] This information is highly revelatory in three respects. First, it demonstrates that subsequent to Falle's meeting with Seyyed Zia, Rashidiyan and Mirashrafi after the Qavam fiasco (26 July 1952), and Middleton's dispatches at the same time proposing a coup d'état in support of Zahedi, the idea of a coup d'état was taken seriously by the British, and in preparation for it the Rashidiyans had spent $50,000 by 15 June. This money must have been made available to the Rashidiyans by the British Embassy in Iran, up to their departure in October 1952. Second, it lends credence to the Mosaddeq government's claim at the time that the coup uncovered in October 1952 involving Zahedi, the Rashidiyans and a number of other military and civilian pro-British figures was conceived of in collusion with a foreign embassy (British) and supported by it. Third, the revelation suggests that in the absence of the British after the closure of their embassy, CIA sources in the American Embassy in Iran may have been the source or intermediary of the funds. If British money was spent for the "9 Esfand" demonstrations, which seems likely, the Rashidiyans were the probable paymasters. The fact that the Rashidiyan brothers were arrested in October 1952 and were in a very low security prison at the police headquarters during "9 Esfand" does not rule out their ability to have managed the funds to which they had access.

Woodhouse provides a very interesting piece of information which sheds light on active British agitation against Mosaddeq after their abandonment of "Operation Buccaneer". In February 1953, almost three months after the British and the Americans initiated discussions on a coordinated operation against Mosaddeq, the British Foreign Office decided to "stand down all plans for action against Mosaddeq" until the Americans fully committed themselves to a joint plan.[91] This decision, which was accepted by Eden on 21 February 1953 (a week before 9 Esfand), had two important outcomes. First, the Rashidiyans were informed that "the subsidies which had been paid to them for the past 18 months would gradually taper off". Second, they were instructed "to give up their operational plans and devote themselves entirely to intelligence". This temporary change of course indicates that up until February 1953 the British did have "an operational" plan to destabilize Mosaddeq, and that for 18 months (from August 1951) the Rashidiyans were receiving money directly from the British. According to Woodhouse, the Rashidiyans refused to accept their instructions and decided "to carry on as before"; even though the sum they were to receive from

---

[90] Wilber, Appendix B, p. 2. [91] Woodhouse, pp. 117, 119, 120, 123.

the British "would gradually taper off", they committed themselves to paying "their active agents out of their own pockets".[92] Woodhouse suggests that the Rashidiyans were paid £10,000 a month, and thus if they had been receiving this sum for 18 months, they had received a total of £180,000 from the British by February 1953.[93] It would be reasonable to hypothesize that in February 1953 the Rashidiyans wished to demonstrate to the British that their money had been well spent, and that in spite of their instructions to stand down, the Rashidiyans had the organization and capability to actually destabilize Mosaddeq on their own initiative.

The decision by the Rashidiyan brothers to continue their clandestine anti-Mosaddeq operation despite directives to the contrary from the British demonstrated their resolve and also their relative financial and operational autonomy with respect to their direct superiors at critical moments. Their reaction to British instructions was not that of employees, but of engaged partners and stakeholders. The Rashidiyan organization, the activities of which probably dated back to 1940–1941, seems to have been a smooth network functioning under the auspices of the British secret service in Iran. In the absence of the British after their expulsion, the Rashidiyans acted as concerned guardians of British interests in Iran. Through their own independent initiative, vision and, when necessary, their own financial means, the Rashidiyans kept intact the efficient machine they had jointly created with the British.

THE DOMESTIC ANTI-MOSADDEQ COALITION

After the failure of Qavam to take the realm, Mosaddeq's political leadership was buttressed and consolidated, enabling him to exercise his premiership more strongly than before. Relying on his enhanced political popularity, Mosaddeq gradually moved to curb the irregular meddling and interventions of Ayatollah Kashani, who had been instrumental in returning him to power. Ayatollah Kashani and his allies Baqa'i and Makki, once staunch supporters of Mosaddeq, began to witness the erosion of their political influence, as they felt ever more side-lined and isolated. Subsequently, all three, who were members of the parliament (Majles), along with their handful of allies, formed a parliamentary group and tried to curb Mosaddeq's powers in the hope of eventually forcing his government to resign.

When on 10 January 1953 Mosaddeq requested the parliament to extend his "extraordinary legislative powers" (*ekhtiyarat*) for another year, the Kashani coalition in the parliament chose to flex its muscles by opposing him. These "extraordinary legislative powers" enabled Mosaddeq to

---

[92] Woodhouse, p. 123.   [93] Woodhouse, pp. 118, 123.

expedite his reforms and legislate with immediate effect, without the formalities of passing a bill through parliament. Displaying his usual self-confidence as well as his commitment to parliamentary rules and procedures, Mosaddeq reminded the members of the parliament that whenever they felt dissatisfied with his government they could simply give it a vote of no-confidence and rid themselves of the Prime Minister, his government and his "extraordinary legislative powers".[94]

Ayatollah Kashani, who was the Speaker of the Majles at the time, confronted Mosaddeq head-on and ruled that Mosaddeq's request was "contrary to the Constitution", forbidding discussion of it in the Majles.[95] Kashani's reaction backfired as cities across Iran went on strike and brought all activity to a halt, demanding that the Majles approve Mosaddeq's "extraordinary legislative powers".[96] At this time, almost exactly seven months before the coup, Mosaddeq was riding on a high wave of public trust and support. In Tehran, the bazaar closed and crowds gathered in Baharestan Square, in front of the Majles, chanting "Mosaddeq or death" and "death to hypocrites".[97] On the evening of 19 January 1953, the parliament echoed the general mood of the people. Fifty-nine of the 67 members of the parliament voted in favour of Mosaddeq's "extraordinary legislative powers".[98] This was a humiliating defeat for Kashani and his coalition, demonstrating Mosaddeq's popularity both inside and outside of the parliament. On the following day Mosaddeq replaced Colonel Kamal, the Chief of Police, who was close to Kashani, with Lieutenant General Mahmud Afshartus.[99] This was another blow to Kashani's personal and political prestige. Kashani's anti-Mosaddeq coalition in the parliament gradually came to realize that given the Prime Minister's popularity it was almost impossible to weaken or replace him through legal and constitutional means. By the end of January 1953, while enmity between Kashani's coalition and Mosaddeq's government became more pronounced, Kashani's coalition allied itself with General Zahedi, the Shah and Mosaddeq's old Anglophile circle of opposition.

Even though it was not until January 1953 that the divergences and disagreements between Ayatollah Kashani's coalition and Mosaddeq reached a culmination, leading to a public confrontation and split, this process of estrangement had been under way since November 1951. Concurrently, the gravitation of Kashani towards Zahedi, the Shah and their supporting foreign powers was also an ongoing incremental process. The Ayatollah and his friends had long been in contact with domestic and foreign forces dissatisfied with Mosaddeq's government. However, the accelerated rapprochement with anti-Mosaddeq forces was triggered by

---

[94] *Ettela'at*, 25 Day 1331.   [95] *Ettela'at*, 28 Day 1331.   [96] *Ettela'at*, 28, 29, 30 Day 1331.
[97] *Ettela'at*, 29 Day 1331.   [98] *Ettela'at*, 30 Day 1331.   [99] *Ettela'at*, 30 Day 1331.

domestic rivalries and power struggles, such as Kashani's annoyance with Mosaddeq over the latter's decision to prevent the Ayatollah from using his religio-political influence to arrange the election of the candidates whom he supported during the 17th parliamentary election.[100]

As far back as October 1951, or only six months into Mosaddeq's premiership, Ayatollah Kashani met Princess Ashraf and her husband at the Shah's behest, right before the Princess was sent to Europe.[101] At that time, Mosaddeq believed that Princess Ashraf and the Queen Mother were conspiring with anti-Mosaddeq members of the parliament and politicians. Kashani's meeting with Princess Ashraf as the Shah's envoy in October 1951 was therefore probably a less than innocent or casual encounter. In November, a month after Kashani had met Princess Ashraf, Middleton reported to the Foreign Office that Kashani "has put out his feelers in various directions and has established contact with the Court". Middleton added that Kashani "has also been in touch with the American Embassy, who told me in strictest confidence that his main thesis was the danger of Communism and the need for immediate American aid".[102]

By March 1952 Kashani and Zahedi were exchanging visits, and four months later Zahedi claimed that he "had come to an agreement with Kashani whereby if he came to power Kashani would support him on the condition that he would have a say in the appointment of certain ministers".[103] At the end of September 1952, or two months after the triumphant return of Mosaddeq to power, Middleton reported to Anthony Eden that in his assessment, "Kashani would like to see Mosaddeq removed".[104] In the same report, Middleton added that Kashani had visited Zahedi, and that the two men had discussed matters for three hours.

So, by the time the British were expelled from Iran in October 1952, Zahedi and Kashani were in contact with each other and Kashani had already mended fences with the Court and made contact with the American Embassy. More importantly, Baqa'i (Kashani's close ally) had already appealed to the Rashidiyan brothers and their network to help him out with his disintegrating Toilers Party.[105] Baqa'i's request for help from the Rashidiyans is very significant because of Baqa'i's very close ties to Kashani on the one hand, and the Rashidiyans' established reputation as the closest friends and assistants of the British Embassy on the other. It should also be remembered that it was Asadollah Rashidiyan who had mentioned Zahedi's name as the coup leader to Sam Falle of the British

---

[100] Rahnema, pp. 532–547; FO 248/1536, 18 February 1952.
[101] FO 248/1514, 1 October 1951.   [102] FO 248/1514, 14 November 1952.
[103] FO 248/1531, 11 March 1952; FO 248/1531, 26 July 1952.
[104] FO 248/1531, 30 September 1952.   [105] FO 248/1531, 3 September 1952.

Embassy in late July of 1952. One key and unresolved issue concerns whether the important Rashidiyan network and all their key resources and connections were placed at the disposal of the Americans and the CIA immediately after the departure of the British in October 1952, or later in mid-March 1953 once the Americans decided to join the British to overthrow Mosaddeq. In spite of their initial reticence to work with the Americans, the Rashidiyans finally complied with the British request that they do so.

2

Mosaddeq's opposition strikes: testing tactics

The events of 28 February 1953 (9 Esfand) and Afshartus' murder, which rocked the Iranian political scene and destabilized Mosaddeq's government, were ominous signs of how Mosaddeq was to be removed from power. These two cases also presaged the tactics and strategies that Mosaddeq's opponents were to use against him as well as the actors that were to be involved in the attempts against him. The string of events that culminated in the 9 Esfand upheaval, threatening Mosaddeq's government, started with the disturbing news about Abolqasem Khan-e Bakhtiyar's attack on a column of government troops in the oil-rich region of Khouzestan at Eizeh, close to Masjed Soleyman, on 14 February 1953.[1] Abolqasem Bakhtiyar's attack left 42 soldiers and officers dead. The news of tribal rebellion by the influential Abolqasem Bakhtiyar signalled the tightening of the noose around the neck of Mosaddeq's government.

Long before, the British-owned Anglo-Persian Oil Company (APOC), and later the Anglo-Iranian Oil Company (AIOC), had, with the aid of British diplomacy in Iran, entered into an agreement with the powerful Bakhtiyari tribes to protect their oil wells and pipelines in the region. Abolqasem Bakhtiyar's rebellion was therefore understood by Mosaddeq as a British plot against his government. The plot thickened as the very advanced weapons used by the Bakhtiyari tribesmen during the attack were said to have been furnished by the Court and the Retired Officers' Association. Members of the Retired Officers' Association were even said to have participated in the attack.[2] According to one account, General Zahedi's involvement in Abolqasem Bakhtiyar's revolt was undeniable.[3] Furthermore, the Rashidiyan brothers were said to have been thoroughly *au courant* of the attack.[4]

---

[1] *Ettela'at*, 25 Bahman 1331.
[2] Jami, *Gozashteh Cheraq Rahe Ayandeh* (Tehran: Entesharat Niloufar, 1362), p. 634; *Khandaniha*, 1 Farvardin 1332.
[3] Jami, p. 634.   [4] *Bakhtar Emrouz*, 7 Esfand 1331.

Five days after Bakhtiyar's attack, on 19 February, Mosaddeq sent word to the Shah that he could no longer tolerate his unfriendly posture and that of his court towards his government and was consequently going to inform the people of their plots against him and resign on 24 February 1953.[5] Worried about the political consequences of Mosaddeq's resignation and the people's response, the Shah dispatched the Minister of Court, Hoseyn 'Ala, to meet Mosaddeq and persuade him to change his mind. At a meeting on 21 February, 'Ala informed Mosaddeq that the Shah continued to support him and added that the Shah was prepared to leave the country and stay abroad for as long as Mosaddeq thought suitable. Mosaddeq responded that the Shah should not leave the country.[6]

On the same day 'Ala met with Kashani and informed him of the new political situation, the key elements of which were that Mosaddeq intended to resign and to publicly announce his reasons for doing so, and that the Shah planned to leave the country. Kashani is reported to have been quite satisfied with the new situation, as Mosaddeq's resignation would have peacefully removed him from power, yet the departure of the Shah must have worried him.[7] Kashani informed the Minister of Court that he would do all that was in his power to prevent the Shah's departure.[8] On the next day, the Shah dispatched 'Ala to Loy Henderson, the American Ambassador to Iran, to secretly inform him of the events. In this meeting, the Minister of Court talked about either Zahedi or Allahyar Saleh as a possible replacement for Mosaddeq.[9]

Instead of resigning and making his public declaration, on 24 February Mosaddeq met with the Shah for four hours and presented him with documents which he believed proved the existence of the plots.[10] In this important meeting the Shah informed Mosaddeq that he needed to travel abroad and that he felt such a trip would be to the advantage of the country. The Shah also insisted that his departure needed to be kept a secret.[11] On the same day, Ardeshir Zahedi, General Zahedi's son, met with a member of the American Embassy and reported that in the next few days his father would probably be nominated as Prime Minister and that the general had already decided on the members of his cabinet.[12] Did the Shah expect Mosaddeq to resign, as he had indicated that he would? And were there plans for the appointment of Zahedi as Mosaddeq's replacement? Both seem quite likely. Had Mosaddeq resigned and Zahedi been appointed Prime Minister, the objective of the anti-Mosaddeq opposition would have been easily and peacefully attained

---

[5] FO 371/104563, 23 February 1953.   [6] FO 371/104563, 23 February 1953.
[7] FO 371/104563, 23 February 1953.   [8] *Khandaniha*, 12 Esfand 1331.
[9] FO 371/104563, 23 February 1953.   [10] *Ettela'at*, 6 Esfand 1331.
[11] Mosaddeq, *Khaterat va Ta'alomat* (Tehran: 'Elmi, 1365), p. 263; *Ettela'at*, 17 Farvardin 1332.
[12] FO 371/104562, 27 February 1953.

and the Shah could have left for a holiday with relative peace of mind. Yet, as usual, Mosaddeq was full of surprises. He did not resign on 24 February, and instead ordered the arrest of Zahedi on the next day for his involvement in Abolqasem Bakhtiyar's revolt.[13] Had Zahedi been arrested and the Shah left the country, Mosaddeq's position would have further strengthened and the anti-Mosaddeq coalition would have become leaderless.

At this time, the British government asked the Americans to do all they could to prevent the Shah from leaving the country.[14] Loy Henderson informed the British that the Shah was at the end of his tether, welcoming the opportunity to escape from the country, and it would be impossible to prevent him from leaving.[15] Fully aware of the fact that it was the Shah who had decided to take a trip abroad with his wife Queen Soraya, the domestic and foreign anti-Mosaddeq coalition, fearing the political consequences of his departure, decided to compel the Shah to cancel his trip, but the Shah initially refused to do so. With the Shah out of the country, Mosaddeq's opposition had no legitimate and unifying symbol to rally around as a countervailing force against Mosaddeq.

MAKING WAVES, RIDING WAVES AND CRASHING ON MOSADDEQ'S SHORE

The Shah's insistence on leaving the country provided Mosaddeq's opposition with a golden opportunity to reverse the situation to its own advantage, by presenting itself as the defender of the young Shah against Mosaddeq the old bully and usurper. The opposition's simple plan, based on disinformation and dissimulation, was three-fold. First, they would present Mosaddeq as the power-monger responsible for trying to oust the Shah. Second, they would play on the emotions of the Iranian army and the traditional supporters of the monarchy by appealing to them to demonstrate their patriotism and love of Islam and the monarchy. Third, they would ensure that a substantial crowd would appear in front of the Royal Palace, which was practically adjacent to Mosaddeq's home.

Once the crowd was roused and a large pro-Shah and anti-Mosaddeq demonstration was underway, anything could have happened. Mosaddeq or his house could have been attacked and the angry mob could have attacked and occupied sensitive government buildings. Amidi-ye Nouri, one of Mosaddeq's staunch opponents, later commented on the significance of 28 February 1953. He said: "If only the people had occupied the radio station on 9 Esfand, things would not have dragged [on] until 28 Mordad and the issue would have been settled on that same day".[16]

---

[13] *Bakhtar Emrouz*, 7 Esfand 1331.   [14] FO 371/104562, 27 February 1953.
[15] FO 371/104563, 23 February 1953.   [16] *Ettela'at*, 27 Mordad 1353.

At 9:00 a.m. on 28 February 1953 (9 Esfand 1331), Mosaddeq was invited by the Minister of Court to come to the Shah's palace, to bring with him the passports of the courtiers accompanying the royal couple on their trip, have lunch there and officially see the Shah off on his trip. By this time all of the key players of the anti-Mosaddeq coalition, domestic and foreign, were aware of the fact that on that particular day the Shah planned to leave the country. Almost concurrently, as 'Ala, the Minister of Court, was inviting Mosaddeq to come to the palace, the Shah met with three of the senior members of the parliament, who were anxious about his departure. The Shah informed them that his departure in no way signified his resignation or abdication, but was primarily for the purpose of taking special care of the Queen; at the same time he hoped that his absence would help resolve some of the existing misunderstandings.[17]

One hour earlier, at 8:00 a.m., Ayatollah Kashani ordered all members of the parliament to gather at the Majles for important business.[18] His son Mostafa delivered the Ayatollah's early morning letter to the parliamentarians. In this letter to the Shah, which Kashani wished to share with members of the Majles, the Ayatollah assumed his position as the official Speaker of the Majles and voiced his concerns on behalf of the Iranian legislature. He argued that the Shah should not leave the country at such a sensitive moment, warning that his departure would heighten political tensions, causing a crisis. He suggested that he delay his trip.[19] Before noon, a high-powered delegation of parliamentarians met with the Shah, presented Kashani's letter to him, and beseeched him to change his mind and stay. The Shah insisted that he was leaving, and this time suggested that his trip was solely for medical reasons.[20] The parliamentarians returned to Kashani's home and reported on their unsuccessful meeting.

Between 1:30 p.m. and 3:00 p.m., growing more anxious about the Shah's departure, Kashani issued an important public communiqué. In this message, he addressed the Iranian people and spoke as a national political leader and the coordinator of all those forces opposing the Shah's departure. Kashani called on the people to cooperate with members of the parliament, with the *olama* (the clergy), as well as with other social classes to actively prevent the Shah's departure; failure to do so, he argued, would lead to regrettable national chaos. While calling on the "people" to help stop the Shah from leaving, Kashani thanked those who had closed down their shops in the bazaar and participated in the demonstrations against the Shah's departure.[21]

From early in the morning of 28 February, the homes of Ayatollah Kashani and Ayatollah Behbahani had effectively become the headquarters of the operations conducted on that day. The key idea disseminated from these

---

[17] *Ettela'at*, 9 Esfand 1331. [18] *Keyhan*, 9 Esfand 1331. [19] *Ettela'at*, 9 Esfand 1331.
[20] *Ettela'at*, 9 Esfand 1331. [21] *Ettela'at*, 9 Esfand 1331.

two well-coordinated centres was that the Shah had resigned and was leaving the country. The mob leaders who were invited, and subsequently congregated, at both Kashani and Behbahani's houses were given similar assignments. They were charged with closing the shops in the bazaar, by force if need be, thus sending the traditional signal that the commercial classes objected to the Shah's departure. Having closed down the bazaar, the ruffians were supposed to lead the shopkeepers to the Shah's palace for the anti-departure demonstrations.[22] After receiving his orders from Ayatollah Kashani, Sha'ban Ja'fari, a well-known ring-leader of Tehran's thugs, departed from Kashani's house to close the bazaar, rally the crowds, lead them to the Shah's palace and prevent the Shah from leaving.[23] The slogan the ruffians chanted in the bazaar as they smashed the shops of those pro-Mosaddeq shopkeepers who refused to close their business was "Close your shops, close your shops, the Shah has resigned".[24] This slogan was intended to spread the fear that the Shah was being forced to abdicate by Mosaddeq. The next important message that had to be widely circulated was that since Mosaddeq sought a regime change and was trying to overthrow the Shah, he had to be ousted before it was too late.[25] Both of these sensational themes were once again evoked and widely propagated between the first and second coups in August 1953.

While Kashani stayed put at his headquarters, and when necessary sent his emissaries to the parliament and the Court, the aged Ayatollah Behbahani, assisted by his son-in-law Ayatollah Bahaeddin Nouri and Seyyed Jalaleddin Firouzabadi, went to the palace. When Behbahani met the Shah for some five minutes around noon, the crowds which he, Kashani and their associates had mobilized were gradually swelling in numbers in front of the palace door. Once Behbahani left the palace to report on his talk with the Shah, the old man was lifted off the ground by the mob so that he could address them. Dissatisfied with the news that the Shah was intent on leaving, the mob informed the Ayatollah that they were not going to let the Shah leave his palace; they carried Behbahani on their hands and shoulders back to the door of the palace and pushed him in so that he could convey their message to the Shah. By the time the gasping Ayatollah climbed the stairs of the palace to talk to the Shah for a second time, the situation around the palace had evolved considerably, and Behbahani almost threatened the Shah that he could no longer control the mob.[26] The Shah's palace was effectively surrounded by between 1,000 and 3,000

---

[22] Jami, p. 636.   [23] H. Sarshar, *Sha'ban Ja'fari* (Los Angeles: Nashr-e Nab, 1381), p. 123.
[24] *Ettela'at*, 9 Esfand 1331.
[25] *Ettela'at*, 21 Esfand 1331, 5 Khordad 1332; R. Zohtabfard, *Ghoghaye Naft* (Tehran: Chap Akhtar Shomal, n.d), p. 303.
[26] Rahnema, pp. 827–828.

people mobilized by Kashani and Behbahani.[27] It was around 2:00 p.m. that the Shah decided that he would temporarily cancel his trip.[28] What the British had asked Henderson to do – and what he had failed to achieve – was successfully accomplished by the Behbahani–Kashani axis. Having attained their first objective, the Kashani–Behbahani coalition tried its luck at redirecting the mob towards Mosaddeq's house.

The political relationship between Behbahani and Kashani, who had united forces against Mosaddeq in early 1953, had been tumultuous. When Kashani returned to Iran in the summer of 1950, the two high-ranking clerics of Tehran formed a religious united front against the enemies of the faith.[29] Unable to rally Ayatollah Borujerdi to his political ambitions, Kashani secured the implicit support of Behbahani. However, relations between the two soured in late May 1952 over the attack by Kashani's partisans on Mohammad-Taqi Falsafi, a close associate of Behbahani.[30]

Behbahani was known as a pro-British Court cleric, loyal to the Shah and opposed to Mosaddeq. It was widely believed that Behbahani was very attentive to directives and suggestions emanating from the British Embassy.[31] He was in contact with the staff of the British Embassy, before their expulsion from Iran.[32] According to the biographical notes of leading personalities in Persia, compiled by the British Embassy in Tehran, Behbahani was "an aged divine wielding great influence in Tehran, especially among the old-fashioned type of bazaar merchants". He also had "the reputation of being quite unscrupulous and corrupt, ready to sell his influence on the bazaars to the highest bidder". Behbahani was "believed to have some close connection with the Shah and to accept monetary payments from him".[33] At this time, Ayatollah Behbahani's close friendship with the Shah was not a secret.[34] Kashani, by contrast, was a virulent anti-British cleric, who had fought against the British in Iraq and was imprisoned by them in 1944 for pro-German and anti-Allied activities. He was arrested after an assassination attempt on the Shah's life and exiled in February 1949. Both from exile and after his return, Kashani rallied to Mosaddeq's cause of oil nationalization and continued to support him until they fell out. Subsequently, he rapidly became Mosaddeq's steadfast enemy. Mosaddeq labelled the odd clerical coalition that challenged his authority on 28 February the "9 *Esfand olama*".

---

[27] In Sarshar, pp. 123, 125, Sha'ban Ja'fari refers to some 4,000 to 5,000 people in front of the Shah's house. This figure seems highly exaggerated. Eye-witnesses refer to around 900 people (correspondence with A. Anvar, 2013).
[28] *Ettela'at*, 10 Esfand 1331.   [29] Rahnema, pp. 140–141.   [30] Rahnema, pp. 607–614.
[31] BP Archive, University of Warwick, File 071068, 12 December 1950.
[32] FO 248/1531, 19 May 1952.   [33] FO 416/103, 1 June 1950.
[34] Musa Al-Musavi-Esfahani, Iranian Oral History Collection, Harvard University, Transcript 3, p. 14.

This group of clerical leaders did not represent the mainstream clergy in Iran, who were led by the Grand Ayatollah Borujerdi. Borujerdi remained silent and did not become involved in the anti-Mosaddeq campaign whipped up by Behbahani and Kashani during 9 and 10 Esfand. Relations between Kashani and Borujerdi had always been very cold at best. In October 1952, when Kashani was gradually shifting camps and making political overtures to Zahedi and the Shah, he also tried to enlist the support of Borujerdi, but seems to have failed.[35] The Behbahani–Kashani coalition had orchestrated the events on 28 February (9 Esfand) in order to drive an irreconcilable wedge between the Shah and Mosaddeq, presenting Mosaddeq as the Shah's adversary and exerting pressure on the people to choose the monarch over his Prime Minister. Uncomfortable with the tension resulting from 28 February (9 Esfand), Borujerdi tried hard to minimize and reconcile the differences between the two men. Whereas the Behbahani–Kashani coalition operated with an eye to removing Mosaddeq from power, Borujerdi acted on the grounds that the country needed both the Shah and Mosaddeq.[36]

THE OPPOSITION SHOWS TEETH: THE ABDUCTION AND MURDER OF MOSADDEQ'S CHIEF OF POLICE

The Afshartus affair occurred around a month after the SIS was informed that the CIA was ready to discuss the ousting of Mosaddeq, and about two weeks after "the [CIA] Director approved a budget of $1,000,000 which could be used by the Tehran Station in any way that would bring about the fall of Mosaddeq".[37] Ambassador Henderson and the Tehran Chief of Station were allowed to use part or all of the sum allocated so long as the two concurred on its use.

In late April 1953, or less than two months after 28 February (9 Esfand), the Iranian press reported that Mosaddeq's Chief of Police, Lieutenant General Mahmud Afshartus, had mysteriously disappeared on the evening of 20 April 1953. Afshartus was one of the four founding members of the pro-Mosaddeq organization of "Nationalist Army Officers".[38] On 26 April, Afshartus' rope-strapped body was unearthed in a cave in Tello, a hilly area north of Tehran. The military officers involved in Afshartus' abduction and murder were members of the two overlapping pro-Zahedi, pro-Shah and anti-Mosaddeq organizations, the "Retired Officers' Association" and the "Devotees of the Shah". These two organizations, active already in the events

---

[35] FO 248/1531, 2 October 1952.
[36] *Ettela'at Haftegi*, 22 Esfand 1331; *Ettela'at*, 13 Esfand 1331; Rahnema, pp. 874–879.
[37] Wilber, p. 3.
[38] Nejati, p. 270; Be Ravayat-e Asnad-e SAVAK, *Mozaffar Baqa'i* (Tehran: Markaz-e Barrasiy-e Asnad-e Tarikhiy-e Vezarat-e Ettela'at, 1382), p. 101.

of 28 February (9 Esfand), would also play a key role in the August 1953 events.

Similar to the 28 February (9 Esfand) show of force, the Afshartus Affair demonstrated that numerous intricately interwoven and well-coordinated anti-Mosaddeq networks were at work. The military perpetrators of the plot – Colonels Ali-asghar Mozayyani, Ali-akbar Monazzah, Nasrollah Bayandor and Nasrollah Zahedi, and Captain Fereydun Baluch Qara'i – were all members of the "Retired Officers' Association". This was the team of doers and actors. The planning and commandeering team was composed of two civilians: the enigmatic Hoseyn Khatibi and Mozaffar Baqa'i, both of whom were following a precise political agenda. They sought to destabilize Mosaddeq's government, eliminate a very effective and daring pro-Mosaddeq officer, demonstrate the government's vulnerability and ineptitude, disseminate fear among the military supporters of Mosaddeq, foster an atmosphere of insecurity, force Mosaddeq's resignation by arresting or liquidating other key supporters of his, and even eventually abduct or murder the Prime Minister.[39]

Khatibi firmly believed that subsequent to the abduction and concealment of Afshartus, Mosaddeq's government would fall. In his discussions with the conspirators he spoke of the premiership of Baqa'i and Zahedi.[40] The masterminds also aimed at two important ancillary objectives pertinent to their final goal of overthrowing Mosaddeq in the long-run. First, they hoped that, in the absence of Afshartus, General Mohammad Daftari (who later played a pivotal role in the "success" of 28 Mordad) would be appointed Chief of Police.[41] Second, in view of their failure to confront and intimidate Mosaddeq's supporters on the streets, they believed that by switching to such heavy-handed intimidation tactics against high-profile pro-Mosaddeq targets, they would be able to keep the pressure on Mosaddeq, while at the same time they hoped to raise the morale of the anti-Mosaddeq forces, which had been waning since 28 February (9 Esfand).

Whether Baqa'i and Khatibi were receiving their orders from elsewhere or were operating independently can be deduced with some degree of certainty. Hoseyn Khatibi was a member of Baqa'i's Toilers Party and collaborated with him in publishing his newspaper, *Shahed*.[42] In the 1940s Khatibi is said to have been friends with prominent Tudeh Party members, but later he established close relations with the Americans.[43] Khatibi was rumoured to have been the main contact person between the Shah and Baqa'i. Like Baqa'i, Khatibi was also in close league with Shams Qanatabadi, Ayatollah Kashani's

---

[39] M. Torkaman, *Tote'eh Robodan va Qatl-e Sarlashgar Afshartus* (Tehran : Rasa, 1363), pp. 25, 29, 41, 52, 55; *Ettela'at*, 12 Ordibehesht 1332.
[40] Torkaman, pp. 14, 29, 41. [41] Torkaman, p. 13. [42] *Ettela'at*, 7 Ordibehesht 1332.
[43] H. Abadiyan, *Doctor Mozaffar Baqa'i* (Tehran: Moaseseh Motale'at va Pajoheshhaye Siyasi, 1377), pp. 139–140.

right-hand man. Finally, Khatibi was Baqa'i's liaison person with prominent anti-Mosaddeq military figures such as Arfa', Zahedi and Akhavi, who were in turn connected with the troika of Zolfaqar, Ariya and SUMKA organizations.[44] Khatibi was also connected with members of the Retired Officers' Association. It was through Colonel Nasrollah Zahedi, a member of the Retired Officers' Association, that Khatibi recruited the other officers who participated in the abduction of Afshartus.

General Zahedi, the leader of the Retired Officers' Association, was directly implicated in the Afshartus plot. According to Nasrollah Zahedi, it was Ardeshir Zahedi, the General's son, who had given him a German gun, which he had then handed over to Captain Baluch Qara'i, who was accused of murdering Afshartus.[45] After the arrest of the officers involved in the affair and the discovery of the gun in the possession of Baluch Qara'i at the murder scene, Ardeshir Zahedi was questioned and responded that the gun belonged to his father (General Zahedi) and that he had borrowed it to go hunting.[46] The retired officers involved in the Afshartus plot were also connected with the troika organizations of Zolfaqar, Ariya and SUMKA, which were actively involved in the 28 February (9 Esfand) events. These officers were also affiliated with Ayatollah Kashani's "Society of Moslem Mojaheds" and Baqa'i's Toilers Party.[47]

Exactly two weeks before the abduction and murder of Afshartus, a police report indicates that circles around Baqa'i were talking about the mobilization of "a number of army sergeants in the SUMKA and Ariya organizations" to assassinate a group of influential pro-Mosaddeq figures.[48] "Dr Shourin" – probably the misspelt or misheard version of Dr Shervin's name – is quoted in the police report as saying that plans for terrorist activities were ready and lower-rank army members of Ariya and SUMKA organizations were its designated perpetrators.[49] At the time, Dr Shervin was very close to both Ayatollah Kashani and Baqa'i. This police report connects the circles around Baqa'i and Ayatollah Kashani with an assassination list and ipso facto with the murder of Afshartus. It also demonstrates that the masterminds of the plots against Mosaddeq regarded the military members of SUMKA and Ariya as a single operational unit, indicating the existence of some hierarchically superior command standing above the immediate leadership of Monshizadeh and Sepehr, the respective leaders of SUMKA and Ariya.

The presence of Amir Rostami, one of the two civilian participants in the abduction and murder of Afshartus, connects the Baqa'i-Khatibi conspiracy centre to a different and wider network than the military alone. Amir Rostami is said to have been one of the Haft Kachaloun brothers, an influential clan

---

[44] Abadiyan, p. 140.   [45] Torkaman, p. 93.
[46] H. Shahhoseyni, *An Suye Khaterehha* (Tehran: Samadiyeh, 1388), p. 88.
[47] Torkaman, pp. 89, 92.   [48] Azizi, pp. 217, 425.   [49] Azizi, pp. 217, 425.

of thugs in the south of Tehran.⁵⁰ Haft Kachaloun, a nickname, literally means "the seven bald ones". On the night of Afshartus' abduction Amir is said to have been a replacement for Ja'far Rostami (Shahmirzadi), one of Mozaffar Baqa'i's key thugs, whose main job was to beat up members and sympathizers of the Tudeh Party and tear up their newspapers. Ja'far, who was implicated in the planning of Afshartus' abduction and murder and was supposed to take part in the operation, was prevented from doing so by an unexpected family emergency.⁵¹ The fact that Amir Rostami was a last-minute replacement indicates that he must have been highly trusted by Baqa'i and Khatibi to be considered for such a sensitive and secretive operation. It is probable that Asadollah Rashidiyan, who was out of prison by this time, recommended Amir Rostami to Baqa'i and Khatibi. After 28 Mordad, Amir Rostami frequented Asadollah Rashidiyan's house.⁵² Rashidiyan and Amir Rostami knew one another, and Rostami was probably a member of Rashidiyan's vast Southern Tehran network. The coalescence and cooperation of the Southern Tehran thugs, the Retired Officers' Association, the troika organizations of Zolfaqar, Ariya and SUMKA, the Toilers Party and the Society of Moslem Mojaheds, at the behest of their leaders, which began in a systematic manner with the 28 February (9 Esfand) demonstration, repeated itself in the plot against Afshartus. This coalition of forces provided the backbone of the anti-Mosaddeq coup on 28 Mordad.

According to the confessions of the retired officers arrested in the Afshartus Affair, Khatibi was the mastermind of the plot, exploiting mysterious and very important connections inside the army and police force. Whatever information was made available to the army and police, Khatibi was said to be informed of it on the very same day.⁵³ Two unreliable reports link Baqa'i and Khatibi's plot to abduct and murder Afshartus to the Shah and General Zahedi. According to one report, the Shah was directly implicated in the abduction of Afshartus and was believed to have been instrumental in luring him into an ambush. During a routine meeting between the Shah and the Chief of Police, the Shah is said to have instructed Afshartus to attend a meeting at which he could act as a mediator, settling the differences between Mosaddeq and Baqa'i. Afshartus is believed to have gone to Khatibi's house, with the impression given to him by the Shah that there he would be able to act as a peacemaker between Baqa'i and Mosaddeq. At Khatibi's house Afshartus was subdued, drugged and later transported to a desolate place and murdered.⁵⁴ In his confessions, Lieutenant General Bayandor confirmed that

---

[50] A. Manzarpour, *Dar Koucheh va Khiyaban* (Tehran: Vezarat-e Farhang o Ershad-e Eslami, 1386), p. 79.
[51] Manzarpour, pp. 78, 79.   [52] *Rashidiyanha*, vol. 1, p. 139.
[53] For details on the "Afshartus plot" see Mohammad Torkaman's excellent, *Tote'eh Roboudan va Qatl Sarlashgar Afshartus* (Tehran : Rasa, 1363), pp. 13, 55, 63, 84.
[54] Shahhoseyni, 1388, p. 108.

Afshartus was invited to Khatibi's house under the pretext of mediating between Mosaddeq and Baqa'i.[55]

According to a second report, based on Lieutenant General Monazzah's confessions, after Afshartus was drugged at Khatibi's house, thrown into the boot of a car and dispatched to Telo, Ardeshir Zahedi, thinking that Afshartus was still at Khatibi's house, instructed the abductors to convince Afshartus to call Mosaddeq from Khatibi's house and urge him to go to General Fazlollah Zahedi's house to meet with the Shah. Once Afshartus was transported to Telo and regained consciousness, Baluch Qara'i promised him that he would be safely released and returned to Tehran if he agreed to call Mosaddeq and go along with the plan of luring him into a trap at General Zahedi's house. Afshartus is said to have realized that this was a ploy to murder Mosaddeq and refused to cooperate with his captors. It is said that Captain Baluch Qara'i then strangled him.[56]

THE MILITARY AND THE THUGS: SUBSTITUTES OR COMPLEMENTS?

Both the 28 February (9 Esfand) and the Afshartus Affair were projects to undermine and – if possible – remove Mosaddeq from power. An assessment of the failures and successes of both projects yields important information, especially with regard to the planning of 28 Mordad and the manner in which the fall of Mosaddeq was brought about. The 28 February (9 Esfand) episode was particularly successful in mobilizing and coordinating the three networks of thugs, anti-Mosaddeq army officers and militant members of organizations and parties closely associated with prominent clerical, civilian and military anti-Mosaddeq leaders. The key roles of Ayatollahs Behbahani and Kashani in mobilizing their small yet effective army of thugs was striking during 28 February (9 Esfand). The *"olama* of 9 Esfand" proved that if necessary they were perfectly capable of marshalling the principal strike forces in order to subdue the bazaar and control the targeted streets and areas in which they roamed and destroyed. The ability to take Mosaddeq by surprise and strike a first unexpected blow by rushing the thugs from the very early morning hours – first to the bazaar and then to the Shah's palace and Mosaddeq's house – guaranteed that the operation was a quick success. The morning blitzkrieg by the thugs crippled the government forces and their supporters, thereby assuring the coordinators of the anti-Mosaddeq strike of the upper hand in the morning operation.

On 28 February (9 Esfand) the two networks of officers (both retired and active) and the heterogeneous members of the political organizations were

---

[55] Nejati, p. 271.
[56] N. Shifteh, *Zendeginameh va Mobarezat Siyasiye doctor Mosaddeq* (Tehran: Koomesh, 1370), p. 141.

dispatched to the Shah's palace to stage a demonstration. Once they were joined and re-enforced by the thugs, the anti-Mosaddeq forces of some 1,000 to 3,000 gained full control of the theatre of operations, which then extended to Mosaddeq's house. More importantly, the mixing of different social elements through the blending of the members of the three different networks gave the semblance of a "popular" rather than an "engineered" demonstration of public discontent against Mosaddeq. Even though the anti-Mosaddeq forces continued their operations the next day (10 Esfand) and attempted to take over the radio station and the Majles, their initiatives on the second day of disturbances were far less successful.

The main forces engaged in the activities of 1 March (10 Esfand) were composed of the two networks of officers (retired and active) and political organizations.[57] From 2:00 p.m. on 1 March, the pro-Mosaddeq forces which had gradually become informed of what had happened on 28 February started organizing and taking to the streets. By 2 March, Tehran was fully under the control of pro-Mosaddeq forces. The anti-Mosaddeq newspapers, gloating that the "life of Mosaddeq's demagogic government had approached its end", were intensely disappointed.[58]

One key element that could explain the loss of momentum of the impressive anti-Mosaddeq show of force on 28 February, and the eventual dismal performance of 29 February, was Ayatollah Behbahani's important announcement on 29 February. Behbahani announced that his job of preventing the Shah from leaving the country was concluded and he invited the people to calm down, warning against extremists and rabble-rousers who might take advantage of the situation.[59] In effect, on 29 February (10 Esfand), Behbahani called his thugs off the streets. Without the thugs, the other partners – namely the members of Zolfaqar, Ariya, SUMKA, Toilers Party, Society of Moslem Mojaheds and even the members of the Retired Officers' Association, who, once the going got tough went whining and complaining to Kashani at their being mistreated – could not really be effective in bringing down Mosaddeq.[60] The events of 28 February demonstrated that a sudden and swift early morning operation led by the thugs and supported by the auxiliary forces of the other two networks could destabilize the pro-Mosaddeq forces. It also demonstrated the weakness of pro-Mosaddeq forces to respond rapidly in the face of a blitzkrieg. Only in time would the pro-Mosaddeq forces prevail. The pro-Mosaddeq forces were hampered by the fact that they did not receive their orders from a centralized and single leadership and were therefore slow to organize and retaliate.

The lesson learnt by the opposition was that the chances of overthrowing Mosaddeq would increase if military and civilian targets were speedily attacked and overrun; otherwise, attrition would play into the hands of the

---

[57] *Ettela'at*, 10 Esfand.   [58] *Khandaniha*, 12 Esfand 1331.   [59] *Ettela'at*, 10 Esfand 1331.
[60] *Ettela'at*, 11 Esfand 1331.

pro-Mosaddeq forces that, once informed of anti-Mosaddeq agitations and fully mobilized, outnumbered the plotters. In the final stage of a plan to overthrow Mosaddeq, the anti-Mosaddeq forces also needed fire-power and therefore the engagement of army units and personnel. Most importantly, the opposition learnt that Mosaddeq was dedicated to the due process of law and was not the type of politician to react categorically, rapidly and brutally against those who threatened his government. This realization allowed the conspiring opposition to act with impunity and without ever worrying about the consequences of their acts. Colonel Eskandar Azmudeh, a key player in the 1953 coup, recalled that the plotters against Mosaddeq were not at all fearful of him as he was not authoritative enough. Azmudeh believed that the events of 28 February (9 Esfand) and the murder of Afshartus clearly demonstrated that Mosaddeq was not a man of harsh or severe political reactions.[61]

The events of 28 February (9 Esfand) provided a great opportunity for the organized opposition to demonize Mosaddeq in the press and praise General Zahedi as his valiant and patriotic successor.[62] The content of Baqa'i and Kashani's indictment against Mosaddeq set the tone for the anti-Mosaddeq propaganda machine that was to continue repeating the same accusations until 19 August (28 Mordad). The picture painted of Mosaddeq as an anti-religious, anti-constitutional, anti-monarchic, anti-patriotic and pro-Communist extremist leader was very important in the campaign to convince the pious, the army and the patriots that Mosaddeq had to be overthrown by force. In Kashani's newspaper, 28 February (9 Esfand) was presented as a plot by Mosaddeq to change the regime and the constitution, exile the *olama* and dismantle the army. Mosaddeq was denounced as a traitor, a spy and a lackey of the Tudeh Party.[63] Iranians were warned that Mosaddeq was threatening their country, religion and constitution, and they were promised that the struggle against Mosaddeq would continue until the threat was removed.[64] Baqa'i's newspaper repeated the same allegations, accusing Mosaddeq of collusion with the Tudeh Party and paving the way for a Communist government. Baqa'i reminded Iranians of the fate of Edward Benes in Czechoslovakia and warned them about what awaited them if Mosaddeq remained in power – a Soviet Socialist Republic, under Soviet influence.[65] As of 28 February, Baqa'i and Kashani's hostility against Mosaddeq, whom they portrayed as a pawn in the hands of the Communists and therefore an enemy of religion and the monarchy, became blatant and antagonistic.

---

[61] M. Torbatiy-e Sanjabi, *Koudetasazan* (Tehran: Kavosh, 1376), p. 21.
[62] *Democrat-e Eslami*, 21 Esfand 1331.   [63] *Democrat-e Eslami*, 17 Esfand 1331.
[64] *Democrat-e Eslami*, 18 Esfand 1331.
[65] *Khandaniha*, 26 Esfand 1331; *Ettela'at*, 21 Esfand 1331 and 5 Khordad 1332.

In comparison to 28 February (9 Esfand), the Afshartus plot was unsuccessful, unless its sole aim was to eliminate Afshartus. With his abduction and murder, the Mosaddeq government did not fall, nor did either Baqa'i or Zahedi become Prime Minister. Not only was the operation reckless, but it proved to be careless and uncalculated at every stage of its preparation and execution. If anything, it demonstrated that the members of the Retired Officers' Association involved in the plot were incapable of executing a thoroughly secret operation. They panicked, were incapable of initiative and improvisation, and when their plan did not result in the expected outcome, they were at a loss. Once arrested, they talked. This pattern repeated itself almost identically during the first coup attempt on 16 August 1953.

The so-called political minds behind the operation, namely Baqa'i and Khatibi, also proved that they were incapable of planning and executing a multi-phase, multi-purpose operation, and were also inept at selecting efficient personnel. The conspirators were only successful in luring Afshartus, subduing him, drugging him and finally killing him. If they intended only to murder him they could have done so at Khatibi's house, thrown the body somewhere and minimized the risk of exposing their network. None of the political objectives of Afshartus' kidnapping and murder were attained, except for the momentary destabilization of Mosaddeq's government by the release of the news.

It is not surprising that, after the Afshartus Affair, Baqa'i and his friends realized that for the purpose of their political assassinations and campaigns of intimidation they were better off establishing closer ties with rogue elements of the Fadaiyan Eslam. After 20 months of imprisonment, Navvab Safavi was freed from prison on 3 February 1953, and intentionally kept out of politics. In a meeting on 12 May with the Vahedi brothers (Abdol-Hoseyn and Mohammad) and Khalil Tahmasebi, Baqa'i and Shams Qanatabadi discussed the importance of founding a "Vengeance Committee", and of the assassination of Abdol-Ali Lotfi (Mosaddeq's Minister of Justice) and Mosaddeq himself.[66] At this meeting two members of the retired officers, Colonel Hoseyn Yamani, his brother, the publisher of the newspaper *Adib* and Colonel Haji E'temadi were present.[67] From June 1953, if not earlier, the rogue elements of Fadaiyan Eslam under the leadership of Abdol-Hoseyn Vahedi entered into an alliance not only with Baqa'i and Kashani, but also with SUMKA and Ariya organizations.[68]

In retrospect, it can be argued that the murder of Afshartus did yield a long-term benefit for the foreign and Iranian conspirators intending to overthrow

---

[66] Be Ravayat-e Asnad-e, *Rowhaniy-e Mobarez Ayatollah Seyyed Abolqasem Kashani*, vol. 2 (Tehran: Markaz-e Barrasiy-e Asnad-e Tarikhiy-e Vezarat-e Ettela'at, 1379), p. 589; Ahmad Golmohammadi, *Jam'iyate Fadaiyan Eslam be Ravayat Asnad*, vol. 2 (Tehran: Markaz-e Asnad-e Enqelab-e Eslami, 1382), pp. 466, 468.

[67] Golmohammadi, vol. 2, pp. 466, 468.   [68] Golmohammadi, vol. 2, pp. 480, 484.

Mosaddeq. On 28 Mordad, the absence of a strong, daring and aggressive pro-Mosaddeq officer occupying a sensitive military position was deeply felt. Had Afshartus been alive and acting as Tehran's Chief of Police instead of Modabber and Daftari (who were secretly in league with Zahedi and the conspirators), the outcome might have been very different.

3

Who beckoned and who executed on 28 February (9 Esfand)?

The activities of the main anti-Mosaddeq actors and networks on 28 February (9 Esfand) and the coordination between them foreshadowed the events of 19 August (28 Mordad). Immediately after 28 February, the CIA prepared a memorandum for the US President. It maintained that "Mullah Kashani has been a key figure in promoting the pro-Shah demonstrations".[1] The memorandum correctly observed that even though Mosaddeq still enjoyed "greater strength" than Kashani, "Kashani's following however is better consolidated in the capital through a well-organized 'street machine', which Mosaddeq does not possess".[2]

On 28 February, the network of thugs operated in three locations: in the bazaar, in front of the Shah's palace and subsequently in front of Mosaddeq's house (which was a couple of hundred metres from the Shah's palace). The thugs carried short wooden clubs as they roamed round the bazaar, calling for the closure of the shops as an act of protest against the Shah's departure.[3] Sha'ban Ja'fari left Kashani's house at Pamenar around 9:00 a.m. and, along with his band of toughs, vandalized as many shops as was possible and intimidated the shopkeepers in the bazaar into closing down. He then proceeded with his gang to Naserkhosrow Street, where he joined a crowd that had congregated there, subsequently leading the bigger crowd to the Shah's palace.[4]

In addition to Sha'ban Ja'fari, other thug leaders such as Amir Zarrinkia (popularly known as Amir Moubur or Amir the Blond) and Ahmad 'Eshqi were also implicated in the events.[5] Like Sha'ban Ja'fari, Ahmad 'Eshqi and Amir Moubur were renowned thugs who were connected to the circle of Ayatollah Kashani, Shams Qanatabadi and Mozaffar Baqa'i.[6] A significant number of the 1,000–3,000 who congregated in front of the Shah's palace, as well as the 40–50 who were clad in their shrouds, were Ayatollah Behbahani's

---

[1] FRUS, vol. x, p. 690. [2] FRUS, vol. x, p. 690. [3] *Ettela'at*, 9 Esfand 1331.
[4] Sarshar, pp. 123–124. [5] Sarshar, pp. 123,125. [6] Rahnema, p. 580.

thugs who had come from Barforoushan Square, Esmaʻil Bazzaz Street and the Shoosh area. They too were instrumental in closing the bazaar.[7] It was reported that on that day the sum of 170,000 Tomans was paid out to the thugs.[8] At about 3:00 p.m. the thugs moved to Mosaddeq's house, trying to break into it and set fire to it. The assailants chanted "death to doctor Mosaddeq" and "death to Mosaddeq the traitor".[9] The culmination of the anti-Mosaddeq demonstrations on 9 Esfand was Shaʻban Jaʻfari's attempt to drive a jeep through the large gate of Mosaddeq's house.[10]

The second anti-Mosaddeq network operating on 9 Esfand was that of the retired and active army officers. On this day, members of Zahedi's Retired Officers' Association went to Ayatollah Behbahani's house, then congregated in front of the Shah's palace, and finally entered into action in front of Mosaddeq's house.[11] This same network also organized sporadic demonstrations in various parts of the city on 9 Esfand, and more targeted ones on 10 Esfand. It was reported that groups of agitators wearing their military uniforms were rallying the people to demonstrate in favour of the Shah and against Mosaddeq.[12] A good number of key retired army officers associated with General Zahedi participated actively in the demonstrations in front of the palace and Mosaddeq's house. Some of these officers, such as Generals Ali-Asghar Mozayyani, Ali-Akbar Monazzah and, Nasrollah Bayandor and Captain Fereydun Baluch Qara'i, later became directly implicated in Afshartus' murder.[13]

Three prominent retired generals, Shahbakhti, Amir Ahmadi and Garzan, also played key roles in the demonstrations on 9 Esfand.[14] Rahimi, Sadri and Khosrovani were among the active officers known to be involved in the agitations in front of Mosaddeq's house, which lasted from about 3:45 p.m. to about 7:00 p.m.[15] Five active military officers (Mohammad-Baqer Sadiq Mostowfi, Mohammad Naqdi, Nasrollah Hakimi, Azizollah Rahimi and Parviz Khosrovani), along with a few sergeants, were later arrested for their destructive activities in front of Mosaddeq's house.[16]

SECRET MILITARY ORGANIZATIONS ARE BORN

Parviz Khosrovani provides a revealing account of how on 28 February, members of his Taj (Crown) Athletic Club, which he characterizes as an "anti-Communist organization", along with thug leaders Tayyeb Haj Rezaʼi, Hoseyn Esmaʻilpour (Ramezoun Yakhi) and Shaʻban Jaʻfari, accompanied by

---

[7] Jami, p. 636; Sarshar, pp. 123, 125. [8] *Bakhtar Emrouz*, 13 Esfand 1331.
[9] *Ettela'at*, 17 Farvardin 1332; *Khandaniha*, 12 Esfand 1331. [10] Sarshar, pp. 126–128.
[11] *Bakhtar Emrouz*, 9 Esfand 1331. [12] *Khandaniha*, 12 Esfand 1331.
[13] Torkaman 1363, p. 41; Sarshar, p. 124. [14] Jami, p. 636. [15] Sarshar, pp. 124, 127.
[16] Parviz Khosrovani, Iranian Oral History Collection, Harvard University, Transcript 1, pp. 5–6; *Ettela'at*, 10 Mordad 1332.

their followers, were called upon and mobilized by Shahpur Ali-Reza Pahlavi, the Shah's brother.[17] From Khosrovani's account three conclusions can be drawn. First, there seems to have been prior coordination between the thug networks and the retired and active officers' network. Second, the thug networks active during the events of 9 Esfand were called upon during the second (and successful) coup of August 1953. Third, Ali-Reza Pahlavi, who played a key role in organizing the events of 28 February (9 Esfand) is said to have been deeply involved in the activities of a mysterious organization called "the Special Headquarters of Shahpur Ali-Reza".[18] Not much is known about this organization; however, it has been suggested that Ali-Reza Pahlavi, who resented his crowned brother's irresolute inactivity in the face of events during Mosaddeq's government, was the founder of the "Devotees of the Shah".[19] The reference to "the Special Headquarters of Shahpur Ali-Reza" may be an allusion to the "Devotees of the Shah". Unlike the Shah's other brothers, Ali-Reza seems to have been involved in organizing an active nucleus of pro-Shah elements, ready and able to deliver an effective blow to Mosaddeq's government, whenever necessary.

Based on Parviz Khosrovani's important recollections of how he was drawn into both the 28 February (9 Esfand) and 19 August (28 Mordad) events, it becomes evident that neither event was "spontaneous"; rather, on the contrary, each was well-organized, coordinated and engineered. All those who were mobilized by Ali-Reza Pahlavi to demonstrate in favour of the Shah and against Mosaddeq on 9 Esfand would go on to play similar roles on 28 Mordad. According to Khosrovani, he and the members of his Taj Athletics Club played an equally important part in the events of 28 Mordad.[20] Military officers with very strong connections with popular athletic clubs, such as Khosrovani, were in the ideal position to mobilize and coordinate the activities of the military and their own musclemen, who were not necessarily the traditional thugs of Southern Tehran. Khosrovani's skills in commanding and coordinating the two key pro-Shah networks of the army and the athletic clubs would prove to be very useful on 28 Mordad.

One of the important outcomes of the failed mini-putsch of 28 February (9 Esfand) was the birth of a secretive pro-Shah and anti-Mosaddeq military organization. The "Committee for Saving the Motherland" (*komiteh nejat vatan*), composed of some 250 devout pro-Shah officers of different ranks, is reported to have been born on the day after 9 Esfand.[21] This organization was founded with the objectives of overthrowing Mosaddeq, saving the country

---

[17] Parviz Khosrovani, Iranian Oral History Collection, pp. 6–7.
[18] A. Khameh'i, *Az Ensha'ab ta Kudeta* (Tehran: Hafteh, 1363), p. 411.
[19] H. Karamipour, *Khaterat-e Doctor Shervin* (Tehran: Markaz-e Asnad-e Enqelab-e Eslami, 1384), p. 136.
[20] Parviz Khosrovani, Iranian Oral History Collection, Transcript 1, p. 12.
[21] *Ettela'at Haftegi*, 13 Shahrivar 1332.

from anarchy and disorder and strengthening the monarchy and the army, which the Mosaddeq government was alleged to have weakened.[22] The officers involved in this organization did not hold regular meetings but were constantly in touch with one another, with a few among them in close contact with Generals Batmanqelich, Garzan and a few other senior army officers.[23] According to Major Zolfaqari, a member of this committee, a few weeks after 28 February (9 Esfand), Major Pahlavan and Colonel Vali Qarani met with the Shah to request his permission to overthrow Mosaddeq – which the Shah refused.[24] Preparing themselves for the day when the go-ahead for the overthrow of Mosaddeq would be given, some members of this committee asked for leaves of absence, making themselves available for mobilizing their forces and entering into action against Mosaddeq.[25] It would be safe to assume that unless the "Committee for Saving the Motherland" was not another name for the military organization of the "Devotees of the Shah", then most of their members were the same. Given the fact that the top brass in the two military organizations – namely Zahedi, Batmanqelich, Garzan and Gilanshah – were the same, the "Committee for saving the Motherland" and the "Devotees of the Shah" were one organization with two different names or two overlapping military organizations.

ANTI-MOSADDEQ POLITICAL ORGANIZATIONS: FASCIST, ROYALIST, MILITARIST AND RELIGIOUS

The third network of anti-Mosaddeq forces active on 28 February (9 Esfand) comprised a loose coalition of small organizations (Ariya, SUMKA and Zolfaqar) along with more well-established organizations such as Baqa'i's "the Iranian People's Toilers Party" and Kashani's "Society of Moslem Mojaheds". This network of political organizations and parties played an important part in the demonstrations in front of the Shah's palace and later Mosaddeq's house. The highly suspect organization of Zolfaqar was led by the enigmatic and beautiful Malekeh E'tezadi, who was an exceptional woman of her time, and Hoseyn-Ali Dowlatshahi.[26] At the time, Malekeh E'tezadi owned a luxury clothing boutique called *Taraneh*, on Villa Street, frequented by the well-to-do classes. The organization's name clearly indicated that its leaders had or pretended to have a religious predisposition, as Zolfaqar referred to Imam Ali's legendary double-edged sword. Zolfaqar's members were primarily composed of "tribal youths and sons of religious dignitaries".[27] Malekeh E'tezadi's social and political conduct at the time, however, was atypical and spectacular. On 9 Esfand, in the midst of an all-male crowd of pro-Shah demonstrators in front of the palace, Malekeh

---

[22] *Ettela'at Haftegi*, 13 Shahrivar 1332.   [23] *Ettela'at Haftegi*, 13 Shahrivar 1332.
[24] *Ettela'at Haftegi*, 13 Shahrivar 1332.   [25] *Ettela'at Haftegi*, 13 Shahrivar 1332.
[26] *Ettela'at*, 18 Farvardin 1332.   [27] *Khandaniha*, 30 Khordad 1332.

E'tezadi, holding a large framed portrait of the Shah, was lifted up by her supporters chanting pro-Shah slogans.[28] It was believed that the Zolfaqar Party received its orders from the Court.[29]

Police reports demonstrate how some three months after 28 February (9 Esfand), and soon after the CIA and SIS representatives drew up the TPAJAX operational plan for the overthrow of Mosaddeq in Nicosia, the three anti-Mosaddeq networks of thugs, retired army officers and pro-Shah and pro-British political organizations involved in the 28 February demonstrations continued to coalesce and interact in pursuit of their common objective of overthrowing the Mosaddeq government. According to these reports, the supporters of Sha'ban Ja'fari and Tayyeb Haj Reza'i, renowned thug leaders, were preparing for the opening of a branch of the Zolfaqar Party in the Southern district of Tehran around Mowlavi Street and Barforoushan Square. This initiative was at the behest of the retired army officers and had the objective of organizing broad anti-Mosaddeq activities.[30] The leaders of the Zolfaqar Party intended to designate a board of directors for this special branch that would be loyal to both the retired army officers and Tayyeb.[31] It may be surmised that the Zolfaqar Party was funded by the Court, but organizationally it seems to have been a creation of Seyyed Ziaeddin Tabataba'i and closely associated with Ayatollah Behbahani's son, Ja'far Behbahani. By the time of the second coup on 19 August (28 Mordad), in which both the leaders and the supporters of the Zolfaqar Party played a complementary role, this mini-party was well-integrated within Asadollah Rashidiyan's wider network. On the day of the second coup, E'tezadi, the leader of Zolfaqar Party, spoke on the radio, right after the radio station fell into the hands of Zahedi's supporters, and Dowlatshahi, her second-in-command, is reported to have been one of the most influential pro-Shah field players on 19 August (28 Mordad).[32]

The Ariya Party, also active during the pro-Shah and anti-Mosaddeq demonstrations of 28 February (9 Esfand), was officially led by Hadi Sepehr, but was generally believed to be the brain-child of the pro-British retired General Hasan Arfa'.[33] It has been suggested that Ariya was founded and organized by General Arfa', who was known for his anti-Communist tendencies.[34] The Ariya Party had a military branch run by Colonel Habibollah Dayhimi, a very close collaborator of General Arfa' and also a member of Mozaffar Baqa'i's security and military network, which preceded

---

[28] *Khandaniha*, 30 Khordad 1332. [29] *Ettela'at*, 26 Farvardin 1332.
[30] Be Ravayat Asnad-e SAVAK, *Azad Mard:Shahid Tayyeb Haj-Reza'i* (Tehran: Markaz-e Barrasiy-e Asnad-e Tarikhiy-e, 1378), p. 34.
[31] *Shahid Tayyeb Haj Reza'i Be Ravayat Asnad-e SAVAK*, p. 34.
[32] Felix Aghayan, Iranian Oral History Collection, Transcript 1, p. 7.
[33] *Ettela'at*, 10, 11 Esfand 1331.
[34] H. Fardust, *Zohur va Soqute Saltanat-e Pahlavi*, vol. 1 (Tehran: Entesharat-e Ettela'at, 1390), pp. 141, 144.

his Toilers Party.[35] A staff member of the British Embassy who met Dayhimi at dinner referred to him as a "close friend of General Arfa'".[36] The real mastermind of the military branch of the Ariya Party is said to have been Hasan Akhavi, who later played a key role in organizing the events that culminated in the second coup on 28 Mordad.[37] The Ariya Party and its subsidiary networks were known for their anti-Communist and pro-British politics.[38] The following day after the 28 February events, around 300 members of the Ariya Party, supported by members of SUMKA and the retired army officers, organized pro-Shah and anti-Mosaddeq rallies around the Majles and surrounded Tehran Radio Station.[39]

The militants of SUMKA constituted the third leg of the small but vocal triad of pro-Shah organizations active on 9 Esfand and later on 28 Mordad. SUMKA was the abbreviation for *Sosiyalist Melli Kargaran Iran*, or Iran's Nationalist Socialist Workers Party. This was a fascist organization founded in April 1951 by Davud Monshizadeh.[40] This political organization prided itself on emulating the rituals and principles of Hitler's Nazi party and considered its prime mission as waging a relentless battle against Communism.[41] Partisans of SUMKA wore black shirts and armbands with an insignia very similar to the fascist swastika; they were drilled into greeting one another according to the standard Nazi salute. SUMKA's shock troopers carried short-handled bats, which they used to assault their political rivals.[42] Their headquarters at Khaneqah Street was called the "Black House". There, they held practical, martial and ideological classes.[43] By August 1952, a year before the coup, SUMKA claimed some 600 registered members, though according to government reports only about 100 of them could be mobilized at any one time.[44]

From late June 1952, SUMKA's "assault group" (*gorouh-e hamleh*) openly attacked Tudeh Party members, set fire to Tudeh-associated bookstores, and even ransacked the Hungarian Trade Office and the Soviet Cultural Center (VOX) in Tehran. Violent scuffles between the members of the Tudeh Party and SUMKA, involving assault and battery, were a common scene in central Tehran on streets such as Lalehzar, Manouchehri, Syrus, Mowlavi and Baharestan Square. After a raid on SUMKA headquarters and the discovery of "weapons", Monshizadeh was arrested on 6 March 1953, a week after the 9 Esfand events.[45]

---

[35] Abadiyan, pp. 139, 171.   [36] FO 248/1514, 16 May 1951.   [37] Fardust, vol. 1, p. 141.
[38] Fardust, vol. 1, p. 141.   [39] *Ettela'at*, 10 and 11 Esfand 1331.
[40] G. Azizi, *Hezb-e Sosialist-e Melli-e Kargaran-e Iran* (Tehran: Markaz-e Asnad-e Enqelab-e Eslami, 1383), p. 175.
[41] D. Homayoun, *Man va Rouzegaram* (Hamburg: Nashre Talash, 1387), pp. 35–36.
[42] Fardust, vol. 1, 140.   [43] Azizi, p. 273.
[44] Azizi, p. 310; Homayoun, however, refers to a few hundred members: see Homayoun, p. 37.
[45] Azizi, pp. 408, 412.

The militants of SUMKA played an important role in the anti-Mosaddeq demonstrations of 28 February (9 Esfand).[46] It is highly probable that the raid on the "black house" and the arrest of SUMKA leaders was in retaliation for their involvement in the 9 Esfand disturbances.[47] Curiously, Monshizadeh was released from prison just one day before the second coup of 19 August (28 Mordad).[48] Both in Tehran and in the provinces, he and his partisans came out in full support of the anti-Mosaddeq coup on 28 Mordad and proudly referred to their active role on this day in their newspaper, speeches and declarations.[49]

The necessity felt by certain conservative and politically influential groups within the Iranian army and the Court to establish and support an extremist right-wing party which would stand up to and combat the Tudeh Party as well as Mosaddeq's National Front seems to have been the raison d'etre of SUMKA.[50] Therefore, it followed that from its inception SUMKA was reported to have had strong links with the army.[51] Daryoush Homayoun, a long-time member of SUMKA and a close associate of Monshizadeh, maintains that Monshizadeh was connected with General Arfa'.[52] Ebrahim Ranjbar, an expelled member, believes that SUMKA was the creation of Colonel Pakravan, the chief of the army's counter-intelligence office (*rokn do*).[53] As of late September 1952, when talk about the necessity of getting rid of Mosaddeq through a coup was gaining more momentum and Henderson informed the State Department that "Hints of *coup d'état* or resort to tactics of violence are becoming more open", a police report suggested that a few influential figures from SUMKA approached General Arfa, among others, to coordinate their anti-Mosaddeq activities.[54] Colonel Fateh, a retired Air Force officer who owned a pastry shop on Shahreza Street, was not only one of the key organizers and members of SUMKA, but was responsible for the training of the party's assault group and was also its official financial patron.[55] While Monshizadeh was in prison, it was the retired Colonel Sheybani who controlled and managed SUMKA.[56]

SUMKA was affiliated with other pro-Shah, anti-Communist and anti-Mosaddeq organizations, especially during the last year of Mosaddeq's government. Certain militants, such as Colonel Ariyana (Hoseyn Manouchehri), had dual membership in both SUMKA and the Ariya Party.[57] Also, simultaneous memberships in SUMKA and the Zolfaqar Party or close associations between members of the two groups must have been so prevalent that in April 1953 an attempt was made by SUMKA to place on probation those members who had established relations with the Zolfaqar Party.[58] By

---

[46] Homayoun, p. 44.   [47] Homayoun, pp. 43, 44.   [48] *Ettela'at*, 27 Mordad 1332.
[49] Azizi, p. 182, 500.   [50] Azizi, pp. 52, 53.   [51] Azizi, p. 212.   [52] Homayoun, p. 37.
[53] FRUS, vol. x, p. 475; Azizi, pp. 52–53.   [54] Azizi, p. 351.
[55] Azizi, pp. 220, 231, 232, 270.   [56] Azizi, p. 434.
[57] Fardust, vol. 1, p. 141; Azizi, p. 221.   [58] Azizi, p. 182.

June 1953, police reports indicate that members of SUMKA tried to establish contacts with Navvab Safavi's Fadaiyan Eslam organization, the majority of whom (with the exception of the Vahedi group) avoided involvement with the existing political alignments.[59]

SUMKA's precarious financial conditions forced Monshizadeh to seek assistance from different quarters. SUMKA's financial dependence on various sources may partly explain its political orientation and activities. After the 28 Mordad coup d'état, Monshizadeh received an allowance of 2,500 rials per month from the Iranian police and other security authorities (*maqamat-e entezami*).[60] When, in 1958, Monshizadeh decided to go to the US, the Minister of Court instructed General Bakhtiyar, the Chief of SAVAK, to pay him $7,000 from the following sources: The Pahlavi Foundation, SAVAK, the Ministry of Culture and the University of Tehran.[61] The generous compensation which Monshizadeh received after the coup was most probably related to the services which he and his party had offered to the destabilizing of Mosaddeq before and during the second coup.

SUMKA was also said to have been financed by foreign embassies in Tehran. According to reports by Iranian police agents, as of April 1952, Monshizadeh was seeking to meet officials at the British Embassy in order to secure financial support.[62] Apparently, through the mediation of Mostafa Fateh, such a meeting did take place in May, during which Monshizadeh succeeded in obtaining certain promises.[63] At this time, police reports indicate that SUMKA was connected with an Iraqi fascist organization also supported by the British, and that in Tehran Monshizadeh had established close links with a British merchant.[64] By June 1952, there are reports of SUMKA being supported by the US and even receiving orders from them.[65] Homayoun, a former member of SUMKA, suggested that Monshizadeh did receive money from CIA-connected Iranian journalists, who he believed to be the "Boscoe Brothers".[66] Even though Homayoun did not directly name the "Boscoe Brothers", he indirectly suggested that they were two journalists, Ali Jalali and Farrokh Keyvani.[67] The CIA is said to have funded the Pan-Iranist Party (the ultra-nationalist precursor to SUMKA) as well as the SUMKA through the TPBEDAMN organization in Iran.[68]

Based on the available evidence, it appears likely that Seyyed Ziaeddin Tabataba'i, Arfa' and Asadollah Rashidiyan were the spiritual leaders behind Ariya, SUMKA and Zolfaqar. They played a key role in all three organizations' major political decisions, while keeping away from their day-to-day concerns or ideological formulations and debates. In the spring of 1953,

---

[59] Golmohammadi, vol. 2, pp. 401, 480.   [60] Azizi, p. 519; Homayoun, p. 58.
[61] Azizi, p. 522.   [62] Azizi, p. 223.   [63] Azizi, p. 261.   [64] Azizi, p. 280.
[65] Azizi, p. 264.   [66] Homayoun, pp. 45, 46.
[67] N. Askari, *Shah, Mosaddeq, Sepahbod Zahedi* (Sweden: Arash, 2000), p. 333.
[68] Gasiorowski in *Mohammad Mosaddeq*, p. 236.

or shortly before 28 Mordad, Daryoush Homayoun was approached and paid money by one Tabataba'i, who, according to Homayoun, was a leading politician of those days – almost certainly Seyyed Zia – to publish SUMKA's anti-Communist and anti-Mosaddeqist newspaper, which had ceased publication due to insufficient funding.[69] Almost a year before this, police reports indicate that Monshizadeh had established relations with Seyyed Ziaeddin Tabataba'i, Seyyed Mehdi Farrokh, Arfa' and the Faramarzi brothers, all of whom were both staunch anti-Mosaddeq and pro-British elements.[70] Even after the coup, Seyyed Zia maintained his connection with Monshizadeh.[71]

The obscure and almost improvised anti-Communist and later anti-Mosaddeq troika of Ariya, SUMKA and Zolfaqar did not seem to have a veritable social base and were numerically rather insignificant. The Ariya and Zolfaqar organizations were crafted and put into action for a specific purpose; once the objective of overthrowing Mosaddeq was accomplished they died out as quickly as they had sprung up. SUMKA's evolution is somewhat different, but by 1953 it too was in the same single goal-oriented position of overthrowing Mosaddeq as the two other organizations. At this time, the SUMKA leadership was also as dependent on and subsequently subservient to the political wishes of its financial benefactors as were the other two organizations. In comparison to the manufactured troika of the Ariya, SUMKA and Zolfaqar organizations which participated in the 9 Esfand anti-Mosaddeq demonstrations, the political organizations affiliated with Baqa'i and Kashani-Qanatabadi enjoyed a longer history of political engagement and were more firmly implanted within certain social strata.

KASHANI'S MOSLEM MOJAHEDS AND BAQA'I'S TOILERS OF IRAN

On 3 February 1949, Shams Qanatabadi, with the assistance of Dr Mahmud Shervin, officially inaugurated the "Society of Moslem Mojaheds" (*Majma' Mosalmanan-e Mojahed*) at the behest of Ayatollah Kashani. This multi-task organization became Kashani's religious, political, cultural and social executive arm and mouthpiece once the Ayatollah decided that Navvab Safavi's "Devotees of Islam" (*Fadaiyan Eslam*), who were originally his militants, shock troopers and trouble-shooters, were too single-minded, inflexible and volatile to be politically dependable, consistent or useful. From 1948, the "Society of Moslem Mojaheds" became involved in organizing demonstrations in favour of Kashani-initiated action against the Ayatollah's political opponents. The Society was adept at mobilizing crowds, controlling the streets, recruiting muscle, engaging in political gang fights, intimidating

---

[69] Homayoun, p. 46.   [70] Azizi, p. 385.
[71] Be Ravayat-e Asnad-e SAVAK, *Seyyed Ziaeddin Tabataba'i* (Tehran : Markaz-e Barrasiy-e Asnad-e Tarikhiy-e Vezarat-e Ettela'at, 1381), p. 367.

political enemies and providing protection for political allies. The headquarters of the Society was at Sarcheshmeh, in the heart of Tehran's popular quarters and close to Ayatollah Kashani's house. At its inception, the Society boasted some 2,000 members, while according to police estimates it had anywhere between 50 and 200 members.[72] Irrespective of its official membership, Kashani and Qanatabadi's political network was quite wide and their associations and affiliations with such varied people as General Zahedi and Seyyed Ziaeddin Tabataba'i enabled them to mobilize a considerable crowd for special political demonstrations.[73] In Kashani's incessant opposition to Hajir, Razmara, Qavam and finally Mosaddeq, the Society and its militants acted as untiring fighters.

Mozaffar Baqa'i's political organization, the Iranian People's Toilers Party (*Hezb-e Zahmatkeshan-e Melat-e Iran*), was founded on 16 May 1951. Rumour had it that Baqa'i's party was founded at the behest of a British Labour Party activist, a Mr. Thomas, who travelled to Iran, resided at the posh and fashionable Hotel Darband located in the North of Tehran and held meetings with Baqa'i.[74] Baqa'i's newspaper *Shahed*, which later became the Toilers Party's official organ, had been in circulation, and had attained the reputation of a democratic and hard-line anti-dictatorial paper, well before the founding of the party. Initially, the Toilers Party was successful in attracting a considerable number of educated youths. Yet the party also included a nucleus of knife-wielding shock troopers, such as Amir Zarrinkia (better known as Amir Moubur), Hasan Arab and Ahmad 'Eshqi, whom Baqa'i had earlier befriended and recruited.[75] As far back as September 1949, when Dr Shervin (Kashani's trusted lieutenant) started collaborating closely with Baqa'i's newspaper *Shahed*, the distinction between Baqa'i's forces and those of the "Society of Moslem Mojaheds" became difficult. *Shahed*'s systematic attacks on Razmara, the Prime Minister, accusing him of being a foreign lackey and imposing a dictatorship through the bayonet, led to Razmara's attempt to close the paper.[76] Faced with the threat of closure, Baqa'i asked Kashani to send his toughs to protect his paper; the Ayatollah obliged, sealing a long-term alliance between them.[77] From this time until 28 Mordad, Kashani's "Society of Moslem Mojaheds" and Baqa'i's "Toilers Party" formed a united front, pooling their resources and coordinating their activities. Baqa'i's subordinates were known for their hatred of anything related to the Tudeh Communist party, whose members, demonstrations and newspaper sellers they attacked and injured whenever and wherever they could. The active and staunch anti-Communism of the Toilers Party was shared by SUMKA and the Ariya Party.

According to Middleton, the British chargé d'affaires in Tehran, Baqa'i's party and his newspaper were kept afloat in October 1952 by support from

---

[72] Rahnema, p. 508.   [73] Rahnema, pp. 43, 44, 509.   [74] *Ashofteh*, 12 Bahman 1334.
[75] Rahnema, p. 580.   [76] Rahnema, pp. 157, 158.   [77] Rahnema, pp. 163, 164.

the government, the Americans and the Court.[78] So by January 1953, when Baqa'i and Kashani openly confronted Mosaddeq over the latter's request for "extraordinary legislative powers", the Mosaddeq government's support for Baqa'i's organization and paper must have ceased. From this date, Baqa'i's benefactors must have been only the Americans and the Court.

[78] FO 371/98605, 13 October 1952.

4

TPAJAX: company (CIA) commanders and firm (SIS) functionaries operationalizing the coup idea

According to Kermit Roosevelt, the original proposal of TPAJAX – the clearly stated objective of which was the overthrow of Mosaddeq – had come from British intelligence. This was to be a three-way cooperative and clandestine operation involving the Shah; Churchill, Eden and other British representatives; Eisenhower, John. F. Dulles and the CIA.[1] Iran was the theatre of operation, where an absent and humiliated Britain acting through her deep-rooted, well-informed and loyal Iranian collaborationist networks and a relatively young and inexperienced, yet wealthy and gung-ho American intelligence agency were to cooperate in bringing down Mosaddeq.

Subsequent to initial British–US contacts in December 1952, the first official discussions of the plan to overthrow Mosaddeq were conducted between 13 and 30 May 1953 in Nicosia. The main participants in drafting this preliminary operational plan were Dr Donald Wilber, covert consultant to the Near East and Africa (NEA) Division, and Norman Darbyshire, an SIS officer. Darbyshire was in charge of SIS's Iran branch and had lived in Iran for several years and spoke the language fluently.[2] During these first, very cordial encounters the two agents discovered that they held similar views on the political situation in Iran; it became evident that "the SIS was perfectly content to follow whatever lead was taken by the Agency".[3]

On 25 June 1953, an assembly of highly distinguished US foreign policy-makers composed of politicians, diplomats, military and intelligence master-minds, officers and operatives met in Washington and heard Kermit Roosevelt's presentation on why and how to remove Mosaddeq. As Woodhouse had foreseen, the main justification for overthrowing the legal government of Mosaddeq was presented as the "Soviet threat to Iranian sovereignty", which was argued to be "genuine, dangerous and imminent".[4] All 11 American conspirators attending, including Allen Dulles, director of the CIA, agreed to give Operation TPAJAX the thumbs-up. The

---

[1] Roosevelt, p. 2.   [2] Wilber, pp. 1, 5.   [3] Wilber, p. 6.   [4] Roosevelt, p. 11.

Secretary of State, John Foster Dulles, adjourned the successful meeting by exclaiming "That's that, then let's get going".[5] By 11 July 1953, the directors of SIS and the CIA, along with Prime Minister Winston Churchill and President Eisenhower, had approved Operation TPAJAX.[6]

The TPAJAX plan was developed and refined over time. The final plan, which succeeded in executing the second coup of 28 Mordad, was a modified and adapted form of the original drafts. A review of the different documents drafted by the planners of Operation TPAJAX sheds light on the evolution of the project and on the main Iranian actors upon whom the plotters depended for its success. It is not clear what TPAJAX (the name of the operation) refers to or means; it could well be an acronym. In the absence of clarity it can be hypothesized that the term came to the minds of the planners as a combination of "TP", referring to "Target Practice" – implying the intention to eliminate a designated target – and "AJAX" referring to the famous US brand of detergent for washing away unwanted and unclean blotches or substances.[7]

As would be expected, the planners needed to provide a cost estimation of the coup operation in Iran. The initial operational plan drawn up in Nicosia in May 1953 allocated $60,000 to General Zahedi. Zahedi was to be "supplied" with $35,000 from the CIA and $25,000 from the SIS.[8] The London draft of 15–17 June 1953 clarified the estimated duration of these costs and in effect provided a prognosis for when the planners believed the coup d'état would take place. The London draft confirmed the initial figures and stipulated that starting from 1 June and "for an estimated two months maximum thereafter" the United States would provide $35,000 and the United Kingdom $25,000 towards the financing of the operations in Iran.[9] The sum of $60,000 per month seems to have been only part of the total budget. As the Nicosia draft suggests, this sum seems to have been earmarked only for Zahedi and his expenses. More was needed to "cleanse" the Iranian political scene of Mosaddeq and bring Zahedi to power by sometime in August.

The full projected budget of the Nicosia draft for the implementation of the plan was $285,000, of which $147,500 would be provided by the CIA and $137,500 by the SIS.[10] The monthly expense of $60,000, "supplied" to Zahedi for three months of preparation, brought this cost to $180,000. The CIA and SIS were clearly budgeting above this sum. In the absence of a detailed breakdown of expenditures, the main budgeted items mentioned in this draft reflected the particular domains in which the planners believed that

---

[5] Roosevelt, p. 18.   [6] Wilber, pp. 18–19.
[7] According to Mark Gasiorowski, TP "was a random prefix that the CIA used to designate covert operations carried out in Iran". He suggests that those who named TPAJAX and TPBEDAMN informally took it to mean "Tudeh Party", as in Tudeh party be damned (Gasiorowski, personal correspondence 2013).
[8] Wilber, Appendix A, p. 1.   [9] Wilber, Appendix B, p. 2.   [10] Wilber, Appendix B, p. 1.

monies had to be spent and the actors who needed to carry out specific duties in order for the plan to yield results. For example, a sum of $75,000 was earmarked for the Military Secretariat "to carry out its functions".[11] The job of the Military Secretariat (eventually composed of three Iranian officers: Farzanegan, Akhavi and Zand Karimi) was the selection and recruitment of reliable key officers "for action against the Mosaddeq government" and participation in staff planning sessions with appropriate CIA station personnel for Mosaddeq's overthrow.[12] A sum of $150,000 was budgeted for conducting "a massive propaganda campaign against Mosaddeq".[13] The anti-Mosaddeq campaign required the newspapers involved in the project to "hammer" at the three main themes highlighted by the CIA: Mosaddeq favoured the Tudeh Party and the USSR; Mosaddeq was an enemy of Islam; Mosaddeq was deliberately destroying the morale of the army.[14] The recipients of this considerable sum were in part the anti-Mosaddeq newspapers, some of which were traditionally Anglophile, some of which were not necessarily Anglophiles but had joined the anti-Mosaddeq coalition, and others that were connected with the American TPBEDAMN network of Jalali and Keyvani. Money was also allocated to the "purchase" of deputies in the Majles and for payments to parties such as Baqa'i's Toilers and SUMKA, even though the report correctly indicated that such parties could "supply only limited and probably ineffectual street gangs".[15]

The same report placed great hopes on the "up to approximately 3,000 street activists" whom the "British group" could muster.[16] Yet in the Nicosia draft no specific sum of money was earmarked for the services of such "street activists". The British had long been interested in organizing a special type of "street activist". From July 1951, when Seyyed Zia began reviving his National Will Party (*Hezb-e Eradeh Melli*) at the Shah's behest, Hillier-Fry of the British Embassy emphasized that "it was most important that the strong-arm or roughneck side of the party be organized as soon as possible".[17] On 14 September 1951 the new headquarters of Seyyed Zia's National Will Party were inaugurated. The British Ambassador, Francis Shepherd, reported on the occasion, emphasizing that 1,000 people attended and that "the strong-arm organization of the party" was very well represented "by two lorry-loads of '*pahlevanan*' (champions)".[18] The roughnecks whom Shepherd praised for their "physical power" were the ruffians recruited through Rashidiyan's network in the Southern Tehran. These same elements were recruited for the 9 Esfand demonstrations and the second coup of 19 August 1953.

---

[11] Wilber, Appendix B, p. 11. [12] Wilber, Appendix B, p. 11.
[13] Wilber, Appendix B, p. 15. [14] Wilber, Appendix B, p. 16.
[15] Wilber, Appendix B, p. 20. [16] Wilber, Appendix B, p. 20.
[17] FO 248/1514, 12 July 1951. [18] FO 248/1514, 15 and 18 September 1951.

Shortly after the leaders of the free world – the US and the UK – approved a coup d'état in Iran, the key US coup-makers were on their way to their target country. On 19 July Kermit Roosevelt, the field commander of Operation TPAJAX, arrived secretly in Tehran from Iraq. George Carroll, a CIA paramilitary expert responsible for the military planning of the operation, followed him on 21 July. Carroll was "a six-foot-four inch 200 pounder who had arrived in Teheran from Korea".[19] In Iran, the CIA station had already established covert contact with General Zahedi, who under the protection of Kashani had taken sanctuary in the Majles after he was summoned for his involvement in Afshartus' murder. Between 4 May and 20 July 1953, Zahedi was confined to the Majles' grounds; Ardeshir Zahedi, the General's US-educated son who spoke English and was trusted by both his father and the CIA, acted as the covert liaison person between General Zahedi and the coup planners.[20] General Zahedi left the Majles and went into hiding one day after the arrival of Roosevelt and one day before the arrival of Carroll. After General Zahedi left the Majles on 20 July, the CIA station in Tehran contacted him directly.[21] Joseph Goodwin, who would become Chief of the CIA Station in Tehran after the departure of Goiran, was already in place. Donald Wilber – a CIA consultant who had travelled to Iran in January 1952 to work with two Iranian CIA operatives, Jalali and Keyvani, and who was responsible for the important propaganda and psychological warfare aspect of Operation TPAJAX – must have also been in Tehran by 21 July.[22] Wilber's original assignment in Iran was for six months, and so he should have left Tehran around the end of July or the beginning of August, but certainly before the two coups.[23]

On the ground, two major covert collaborationist Iranian organizations, with a wide and readily operational network, were well in place. It was on the basis of the capabilities and potential of these two organizations that the British and American intelligence services constructed their original plan to launch and execute Operation TPAJAX. Woodhouse and Roosevelt had become convinced of the possible success of this plan because they both believed that the collaborationist Iranian organizations could be relied upon to carry out the task in a coordinated manner.[24] Each of these collaborationist Iranian organizations was originally connected to, funded by, and had their original allegiance to a different Western power. The expulsion of the British by Mosaddeq and the joint CIA–SIS effort to bring down Mosaddeq led to a pooling of these resources under the leadership of the Americans who were still in Iran. Woodhouse

---

[19] K. Love, *The American Role in the Pahlavi Restoration in 1953* (unpublished manuscript, Allen Dulles Papers, Princeton University Library, 1960), p. 37. I am grateful to Mark Gasiorowski for bringing this important manuscript to my attention and for kindly sending it to me.
[20] Wilber, p. 4. [21] Wilber, p. 4. [22] Wilber, pp. 20–21; Gasiorowski, p. 236.
[23] Gasiorowski, p. 236. [24] Woodhouse, p. 120.

refers to "*two different organizations or networks*", with a pair of brothers at the helm of each.[25] It is important to distinguish the initial individual contacts, friends, assets, informants and even employed agents of the SIS and the CIA from an organizational point of view. There were many Iranians who were in close contact with British and American Embassy personnel, providing information during their informal chats, even acting as liaison personnel or carrying out tasks and missions as personal favours, who were not necessarily field members of the covert collaborationist Iranian organizations that brought about the fall of Mosaddeq.

Yet those Iranians personally in contact with the CIA operatives dispatched to Iran to unseat Mosaddeq, or those who were members of the previously established SIS organization, constituted the main leads or the bridge-heads standing at the apex of the Iranian networks and organizations and handing down the decisions sent to them and their CIA colleagues. On 28 Mordad, the anti-Mosaddeq foot soldiers – the officers, soldiers, policemen, government employees, thugs, lumpen-proletariat and all those who took to the streets in favour of the Shah and against Mosaddeq because of an authoritative or religious order, a fee, an eye to career advancement, zeal, conviction, loyalty or a combination of the above – were receiving their action plans from their Iranian compatriots, who were either the bridge-heads, the network leaders or their intermediaries. Distinguishing between the British- and American-associated groups to the fullest extent possible provides for a clearer picture of how Mosaddeq's fall was conceived.

THE SIS-CONNECTED ORGANIZATION: THE RASHIDIYANS

In his account of the coup in Iran, Wilber refers to the Rashidiyan brothers as "the British Group".[26] These three brothers and their well-oiled hydra-headed network played a determining role in the successful overthrow of Mosaddeq. The Rashidiyan brothers had many virtues and assets from the point of view of their British and subsequently American patrons. Their ultimate strength, however, was "their avowed willingness to risk their possessions and their lives in an attempt against Mosaddeq".[27] Referring to those decisive and long hours between the early morning of Sunday 25 Mordad (16 August), when the first coup failed and the afternoon of Wednesday 28 Mordad (19 August), when the second coup succeeded, Wilber confirms that "the Rashidiyans did display such a willingness".[28]

The Rashidiyan family's close ties with the British went back to their father, Habibollah. Habibollah Rashidiyan is said to have worked as a stage-coach driver or a servant at the British Embassy in Iran before the bloodless February 1921 coup which brought Reza Khan (later Reza Shah)

---

[25] Woodhouse, p. 120. [26] Wilber, Appendix B, p. 2. [27] Wilber, p. 7. [28] Wilber, p. 7.

and Seyyed Ziaeddin Tabataba'i to power.²⁹ While the details, facts and circumstances of Habibollah's acquaintance and friendship with Seyyed Zia are not clear, a vague picture can be constructed. It is said that Habibollah Rashidiyan and Seyyed Zia met before the 1921 coup, and that it was Rashidiyan who introduced Seyyed Zia to Herman Norman (the British chargé d'affaires in Iran from 1920 to 1921) and acted as Seyyed Zia's liaison with the British authorities.³⁰ If this is true, it would mean that Habibollah Rashidiyan's friendship with the British pre-dates that of Seyyed Zia. It is also possible that Seyyed Zia was known to the British before this date and that Walter Smart, the Oriental Secretary of the British legation (diplomatic corps), would have brought him to the attention of Norman.

After the Reza Khan–Seyyed Zia coup, Seyyed Zia became Prime Minister for some three months, but was subsequently removed from office and exiled by the powerful Reza Khan. Seyyed Zia went first to Europe, and then eventually settled in British-mandated Palestine in the 1930s. From the beginning of his rule, Reza Shah imprisoned Habibollah Rashidiyan at the newly opened Qasr prison.³¹ It can only be surmised that Habibollah was imprisoned for his close contacts with both the British and Seyyed Zia, which made him a potential threat to Reza Shah. Habibollah Rashidiyan is said to have been a very respected prisoner at wing number two (*bande-e do*) of Qasr prison, where he had a room to himself.³² During his almost twenty years of captivity, he received weekly visits from the head warden of the prison and influential prison officers, his three sons (Asadollah, Seyfollah and Qodratollah), his daughter and his in-laws. Seyfollah, the eldest son, was born in 1915; Qodratollah was born in 1917; Asadollah, the youngest, was born in 1922.³³

Habibollah is said to have been released from prison after Reza Shah was exiled in September 1941. At this time, the three Rashidiyan brothers – probably at the behest of their father Habibollah and possibly of the British – travelled to Palestine to convince Seyyed Zia to return to Iran.³⁴ Asadollah Rashidiyan believes that their mission to Palestine was instrumental in Seyyed Zia's return in 1943.³⁵ Upon Seyyed Zia's returned to Iran, Habibollah Rashidiyan became his special counsellor and once Seyyed decided to re-enter politics and launched his anti-Communist "National Will Party" (*Hezb Eradeh Melli*) in 1945, he appointed the 23-year-old

---

²⁹ Rashidiyanha, vol. 1, p. Davazdah; Rashidiyanha, vol. 3, p. 419.
³⁰ Rashidiyanha, vol. 1, p. Davazdah; Ahmad Aramesh, *Haft sal dar zendan-e Ariyamehr* (Tehran: Bongah-e Tarjomeh va nashr-e Ketab, 1358), p. 18.
³¹ A. Khameh'i, *Panjaho Seh Nafar* (Entesharat Hafteh: Tehran n.d), pp. 214–215.
³² Khameh'i, pp. 214–215.
³³ Rashidiyanha, vol. 1, pp. Panzdah (15), Bist o Chahar (24), Bist o Hasht (28).
³⁴ Rashidiyanha, vol. 3, p. 249.
³⁵ Be Ravayat-e Asnad-e SAVAK, *Seyyed Ziaeddin Tabataba'i*, p. 342.

Asadollah Rashidiyan as its director.³⁶ During the Second World War, Habibollah Rashidiyan maintained his close ties with Seyyed Zia, while he also became the sole purchasing agent for British war needs in Iran, a job which proved to be highly lucrative.³⁷

Given the close relationship between Habibollah Rashidiyan and Seyyed Zia, it is not surprising that Seyyed Zia was also said to have been "a sort of a benevolent godfather" to his sons, the Rashidiyan brothers.³⁸ Asadollah Rashidiyan developed great admiration and love for Seyyed Zia and was proud to publicly announce his heartfelt loyalty and devotion to him. Asadollah would candidly declare that "Seyyed Zia was the only politician who had rendered the worthiest and greatest service to Iran, the Shah and the people without personal ambition or the expectation of a reward".³⁹ Asadollah Rashidiyan's loyalty towards Seyyed Zia, who was commonly known as one of the most – if not *the* most – Anglophile Iranian politicians at the time, was paralleled by his vaunting of proudly following, as well as guiding, British policies in Iran.⁴⁰ Asadollah Rashidiyan believed that British colonialism was the midwife of development, progress and welfare in less developed countries and that Iraq and India were proof of his theory.⁴¹

Asadollah Rashidiyan acted not only as a trustworthy counsellor, advisor and informant to the British Embassy, but also as a highly reliable intermediary between sensitive British Embassy personnel such as Zaehner and L.F.L Pyman and key Iranian political figures. When Qavam wished to meet secretly with Zaehner, it was Asadollah Rashidiyan who would take Zaehner to his house.⁴² When Qavam or Seyyed Zia met the Shah during a private audience, it was Rashidiyan who would report verbatim to Zaehner or Pyman on the precise content of the meetings.⁴³ When Kashani was threatened by the Fadaiyan-e Eslam and considered leaving the country, it was Rashidiyan who would give the details of the Ayatollah's reactions and plans to Zaehner.⁴⁴ His British Embassy liaisons were all well aware of Asadollah Rashidiyan's unquestionable loyalty to Britain and to Seyyed Zia.⁴⁵

In his conversations with them, Rashidiyan consistently hammered at the notion that Seyyed Zia should become Prime Minister and that only he "would be able to get the supplemental oil agreement as it stood passed by the Majles".⁴⁶ The very close relationship between the Rashidiyan brothers and the British Embassy in Iran was not a secret to those who knew of the inner

---

[36] Khameh'i, p. 215; Rashidiyanha, vol. 3, p. 476.
[37] *Tarikh Moaser-e Iran*, Sal-e Haftom, Shomareh 26, Tabestan 1382, p. 124.
[38] S. Falle, *My Lucky life* (Sussex: The Book Guild, 1996), p. 82.
[39] Rashidiyanha, vol. 3, p. 250.   [40] Rashidiyanha, vol. 3, pp. 325, 348.
[41] Rashidiyanha, vol. 1, pp. 16, 17, 107.
[42] FO 248/1514, 19 November 1951 and 7 November 1951.
[43] FO 248/1514; 28 November 1951; FO 248/1493, 14 January 1950.
[44] FO 248/1531, 16 February 1952.   [45] FO 248/1531, 28 July 1952.
[46] FO 248/1511, 2 January 1950.

intricacies and workings of British interest, lobby and pressure groups in Iran before Mosaddeq terminated the activities of the British Embassy in Iran and after it was reactivated in the post-28 Mordad coup d'état.[47] According to a police report, Asadollah Rashidiyan was known "for his support of British policies in Iran" and was "also considered as one of Britain's first class handymen".[48]

Besides being devoted to the British and Seyyed Zia, Asadollah Rashidiyan was also devoted to Mohammad Reza Shah. He would publicly claim that as an Iranian he was a lover of the Shah – indeed, was his "slave" (*gholam*).[49] Asadollah Rashidiyan was intimate with Mohammad Reza Shah and was almost completely trusted by him before, during and well after 28 Mordad, a predisposition that the Shah seldom demonstrated towards others. Asadollah was invited to the parties thrown at the Court and would accompany the Shah on his unofficial trips.[50] After 19 August (28 Mordad), Asadollah would brag about the fact that he and his wife regularly met the Shah and the Queen on Fridays and that he would meet with the Shah at least five times a week to discuss affairs of state.[51] When in 1973 Asadollah 'Alam, the Shah's trusted friend and Minister of Court, quipped about Asadollah Rashidiyan's meddling in foreign policy concerning India, to 'Alam's utter surprise the Shah retorted curtly that Rashidiyan was following his direct orders and that he wished that relations with Indira Gandhi (the Indian Prime Minister) be conducted through Rashidiyan and not the Ministry of Foreign Affairs.[52]

Asadollah Rashidiyan was closely connected not only with the Shah, but also – and more importantly – with Ashraf Pahlavi, the Shah's powerful twin sister whose resolve and tenacity made her an indispensable player on the Iranian political scene. When Asadollah Rashidiyan first met and started to befriend the Shah and Princess Ashraf remains a mystery, but there is no doubt that he was trusted by both.[53] It seems as though the relationship between Rashidiyan and Ashraf Pahlavi was based on their common political and (later) financial interests.[54] Immediately after the coup d'état, Ashraf Pahlavi, who remained in France, wrote a series of letters to Asadollah 'Alam, instructing him to send her money, sell her house and obtain the monies owed to her. In every letter she instructed 'Alam to consult Asadollah Rashidiyan, whom she claimed to be privy to her orders.[55] These letters clearly indicate the extent to which Ashraf Pahlavi and Asadollah Rashidiyan were not only politically but also financially associated.

Rashidiyan had other intimate and politically compatible friends who occupied highly sensitive positions at the Court. Soleyman Behboudi, an SIS

---

[47] Rashidiyanha, vol. 1, pp. 383, 399; vol. 3, p. 326.   [48] Rashidiyanha, vol. 3, p. 467.
[49] Rashidiyanha, vol. 1, p. 325.   [50] Rashidiyanha, vol. 1, p. 361.
[51] Rashidiyanha, vol. 1, pp. 338, 365.   [52] Alikhani, vol. 3, p. 57.
[53] Rashidiyanha, vol. 3, pp. 399, 420.   [54] Rashidiyanha, vol. 1, p. 383.
[55] *Tarikh Moaser-e Iran*, Sal-e Haftom, Shomareh 26, Tabestan 1382, pp. 290–298.

operator who was the Shah's Chief of Protocol at the Court during 28 Mordad, was also a friend of Asadollah Rashidiyan. The fact that both Rashidiyan and Behboudi were closely affiliated with the British may have been the reason for their association and friendship. After the fall of Mosaddeq, Behboudi would frequently visit Rashidiyan at his house and consult with him privately.[56] General Zahedi, the "hero" of 28 Mordad, also figured among Rashidiyan's influential friends and associates. Right before the plot of 13 October 1952 was uncovered by the Mosaddeq government and the Rashidiyans were arrested, General Zahedi, who was also implicated in the plot, was in hiding at the Rashidiyan residence.[57]

THE IRANIAN ENGLISHMEN

Asadollah Rashidiyan, who must have learnt well from his mentor and godfather Seyyed Zia, was an exceptional political facilitator and fixer. He was also a generous and caring mentor, patron and patriarch to a wide spectrum of his compatriots. The politically ambitious and financially greedy gravitated towards Rashidiyan, who offered them his political, economic and social protection and patronage, as did the socially and economically marginalized with no institutional recourse to an adjudicating body when confronted with everyday legal, social and bureaucratic predicaments. The cultivation and development of Rashidiyan's wide patron–client network had the political and financial support of his old mentor Seyyed Zia, as well as the Court and the British.

Asadollah Rashidiyan's role in the 1953 coup was unique. He was neither a collaborationist pawn taking orders from the British, nor was he a servile underling. However, his life-long proximity to British interests in Iran had turned him into an Iranian for whom it was evident that Iran's wellbeing was a function of Britain's economic benefit and active political presence in Iran. He was an Iranian Englishmen, for whom British interests were synonymous with Iranian interests; Iranian prosperity that jeopardized British gains could not be considered to be beneficial to Iran in the long-run. To Rashidiyan, the nationalization of Iranian oil and the subsequent policies of Mosaddeq were rash and unpatriotic. He felt at ease prompting and pushing the British when they failed to see their own interests in Iran. The British neither felt the pulse of various segments of society, nor could they understand the complexity of Iranian politics as well as Rashidiyan. No doubt the British were much more in tune with Iran and Iranian politics than the Americans, but they owed their insight into and understanding of Iran and Iranians to people such as Seyyed Zia and the Rashidiyans. These "Iranian Englishmen", reliant upon their extensive networks, would keep the British informed, providing them with welcome counsel when sensitive decisions needed to be made. During the

---

[56] Rashidiyanha, vol. 1, pp. 31, 35, 89, 98, 112, 182.   [57] Rashidiyanha, vol. 3, p. 469.

planning for 28 Mordad, it was the Americans who came to understand and appreciate how precious the advice of the "Iranian Englishmen" could be.

THE RASHIDIYAN NETWORK

The extent of Asadollah Rashidiyan's network can be inferred with a high degree of certainty from his known activities and connections after the coup d'état.[58] According to official security reports, Rashidiyan's house was the hub of all major national decisions and discussions, where key political decisions were first made, to be implemented later.[59] These reports shed a real light on the sheer power, influence and authority which Asadollah Rashidiyan wielded within various segments of Tehran society.

Asadollah Rashidiyan was an exceptional Iranian godfather with a formidably wide patronage network of vassals, disciples and clients from all walks of Iranian life. For the variety of favours he offered his clients through his connections he expected a well-oiled network of reciprocations when he demanded them. Rashidiyan never shied away from pulling strings. His contacts stretched from the apex of the British Embassy, the Shah, Princess Ashraf, the Court and the Anglophile members of parliament and politicians, to clerics such as Ayatollah Behbahani and Kashani, the army, the security apparatus, the police, the government bureaucracies, the judiciary, the guilds, the factory workers and Southern Tehran's under-classes and thugs. At all levels of the socio-political ladder – from the highest echelons of the British and American Embassies and the Shah and his Court, to the lowest of the commoners – somebody owed him something. After the coup, whenever Rashidiyan held court at his house on Anatole France Street (running along the eastern side of Tehran University), anywhere from 100 to 1,500 people would flock to pay their respects.[60] Rashidiyan held three open houses during the week. On Fridays he would receive anyone who wanted to see him; on Sundays and Wednesday mornings he entertained his friends, heads of guilds, politicians and notables.[61] Rashidiyan's supra-class reach and the informal but powerful "brotherhood" organization he had spawned made him very different from the other patriarchs who exercised political power in Iran. Since 1941, Rashidiyan had "been closely in touch with the people, knew of their everyday problems and had committed his life to serving them" in his own way.[62] It would be safe to assume that the establishment of

---

[58] In the important three-volume publication comprising SAVAK reports on the Rashidiyan brothers, a glaring and significant hole is perceptible: there are no documents between February 1953 and April 1956, even though we know they exist. Only once the documents pertaining to these three key years are published will the real significance and import of the role of the Rashidiyan brothers in the overthrow of Mosaddeq be fully known.
[59] Rashidiyanha, vol. 3, p. 369.   [60] Rashidiyanha, vol. 1, pp. 23, 206, 231, 316, 358, etc.
[61] Rashidiyanha, vol. 3, p. 469.   [62] Rashidiyanha, vol. 2, p. 109.

Rashidiyan's patron–client brotherhood dated back to 1941; by 1953, it had been in place for some 12 years.

In the post-28 Mordad period, Asadollah boasted of being host to some 5,000 to 6,000 people per week.[63] The great majority of these people were his clients from long before 28 Mordad. At these gatherings, his clients, friends and protégés, sometimes arriving in bus loads, would praise him for the sacrifices he made during 28 Mordad, thank him for his role in resolving their everyday problems, exalt him as their only hope after the Shah, compose and recite poems eulogizing him, kiss his hands, rant against his political enemies, and chant "long live the Shah and long live Rashidiyan".[64] His followers would come to him for a variety of reasons. Some came just to demonstrate their continued loyalty to him or just to be seen at his house. Some came to consult him, seeking his advice and counsel on political and economic issues as well as on labour-relation problems. The rest came asking him for favours, ranging from building social services in their neighbourhood; finding them jobs; returning them to jobs from which they had been fired; putting in a good word for them to chiefs of police stations, the SAVAK, judges or influential governmental officials; releasing a jailed family member or a friend; saving a person condemned to death by the judiciary; making right a presumed wrong done by various government bureaucracies; and controlling spiralling prices. The sum of all these requests reflected the perception of Rashidiyan's clients of the scope of the patriarch's power and influence in the country.

The guilds whose representatives, chiefs and employees frequented Asadollah Rashidiyan's house included those of fruits and vegetables, nuts, ice cream, bakers, slaughter houses, butchers, bath houses, brick makers, taxi drivers, bus drivers, locomotive drivers, and restaurants.[65] In addition to receiving these guild representatives, Rashidiyan received representatives of various factory workers: textile, tobacco, copper melting, cooking oil, chemical, milk, tea, cement, and glass.[66] Among his weekly visitors were a wide array of workers from various ministries, offices and municipalities; teachers; journalists; military personnel of all ranks (from soldiers and sergeants to generals); chiefs and members of Tehran's police stations; clerics and seminary school students; university students; members and heads of sports clubs; various well-known thug leaders; members of parliament; Haji Abtahi, Ayatollah Behbahani's special secretary; and influential notables of all kinds.[67]

---

[63] Rashidiyanha, vol. 1, p. 308.
[64] Rashidiyanha, vol. 1, pp. 28, 317; vol. 2, pp. 85, 153, 164.
[65] Rashidiyanha, vol. 1, pp. 23, 27, 31, 52, 79, 110, 206; vol. 2, p. 398.
[66] Rashidiyanha, vol. 1, pp. 56, 64, 69, 111, 117, 174, 206, 218, 355, 394.
[67] Rashidiyanha, vol. 1, pp. 39, 52, 66, 74, 79, 80, 90, 98, 101, 136, 140, 150, 298; vol. 2. p. 183.

The most telling aspect of Rashidiyan's contacts is not only their political, professional and social representation, but also the key roles they played during the preparation and execution stages of the four days of 25 Mordad to 28 Mordad. The individuals who would visit him during his open-door receptions constitute a veritable "who's who" of the active participants in and perpetrators of 28 Mordad. The military brass which remained in close contact with Rashidiyan after the 1953 coup included some of the first and second tier of officers who had played a significant role during the coup days. Whenever Rashidiyan wanted to consult his military friends and clients discreetly, the undercover agent surveying his house was somehow prevented from properly identifying them. According to one report, Rashidiyan's aides made certain that the secret-service agent surveying his house would be unable to identify the generals and the two colonels who rushed into Rashidiyan's house in their full military uniform for a secret meeting with him.[68] From those highly placed military personnel who were identified, Teymur Bakhtiyar and Ne'matollah Nasiri openly maintained contact with Rashidiyan and supported him.[69] The officers involved in the 25 and 28 Mordad coup who continued to maintain close ties with Rashidiyan were Daftari, Khal'atbari, Khosrovani, Hamidi, Rahimi, Pahlavan and Shoja'i.[70]

Aside from the military brass and newspaper editors and owners who frequented Rashidiyan's house, one group that was even more regularly present was the Southern Tehran musclemen, ruffians and thugs, most of whom had become "respectable" guild members or employees of various government bureaucracies after the 1953 coup. The profile and description of those who flocked to visit him makes evident that Rashidiyan's popular power-base was in the South of Tehran. The continued loyalty of members and clan chiefs of this community towards Rashidiyan provides sufficient evidence that he was and continued to be the real boss of this potentially volatile section of the capital.[71] Even after the 1953 coup, whenever Rashidiyan needed to flex his political muscle to obtain his political ends, all he needed to do was to remind the authorities of how easily he could unleash his devout Southern Tehran partisans on the city. His followers repeatedly responded with great zeal to his calls, while the authorities begrudgingly took heed.[72] Rashidiyan continued to rely on the services of the same key figures of Southern Tehran that he had called upon on 28 Mordad.

The bosses, owners, managers and facilitators of the main fruit, vegetable and meat market of Tehran – Arbab Zeinolabeddin, Haji Khodadad and

---

[68] Rashidiyanha, vol. 1, p. 140.
[69] Rashidiyanha, vol. 1, pp. 264, 271, 272, 304, 320; vol. 2, pp. 243, 307.
[70] Rashidiyanha, vol. 2, p. 66; vol. 1, pp. 39, 92.
[71] Rashidiyanha, vol. 1, pp. 110, 144, 149.   [72] Rashidiyanha, vol. 2, p. 252.

Hasan Behbudgar, who had played different but important roles in the "popular" demonstration of 28 Mordad – were always on Rashidiyan's side and ready to go into action on his behalf.[73] Back in October 1951, Pyman, the Oriental Counsellor at the British Embassy in Tehran, had reported on the influence and potential role of Khodadad Khan or Haji Khodadad. Pyman referred to Haji Khodadad as the person "who controls an important fruit and vegetable market" in Tehran, and suggested that he be coveted and befriended as he had and would stand up to the Mosaddeq government in the bazaar.[74] The four chiefs of Southern Tehran's thugs – Hoseyn Ramezoun Yakhi, Tayyeb Haj Reza'i, Boyouk Saber and Mahmud Mesgar – who led their bands of ruffians on 28 Mordad to the heart of Tehran, continued to be at Rashidiyan's service whenever he needed them.[75] Clearly, among these clan chiefs, Hoseyn Ramezoun Yakhi enjoyed a privileged position. His allegiance and loyalty to Asadollah Rashidiyan were implacable. In return, Rashidiyan would willingly intercede on Ramezoun Yakhi's behalf and on that of his friends.

On one occasion after the coup Ramezoun Yakhi requested that Rashidiyan intervene on behalf of an imprisoned friend charged with peddling opium. Rashidiyan voiced his displeasure at interceding on behalf of opium smugglers, but added that "for you, I will see to it".[76] After the coup d'état, Ramezoun Yakhi assiduously attended every open-house meeting at Rashidiyan's house, and when he showed up following a week or two of absence, Rashidiyan would reproach him in an almost paternal manner; Ramezoun Yakhi would sheepishly respond that he and his clan were ready to perform their duty whenever they were called upon.[77] The other influential ruffians who played decisive roles in 28 Mordad and continued to maintain their contact with Rashidiyan by frequenting his open-house meetings and paying their respects, as on the occasion of commemorating 28 Mordad, were the Abbasi brothers (Haft Kachaloun or the Seven Bold Ones), Sha'ban Ja'fari, Naser Jigaraki (Naser the Skewer), Mostafa Tarkeh (Mostafa the Skinny) and 'Eshqi.[78] Both CIA and SIS sources were correct in their assessment that the reach of Rashidiyan's organization was extremely wide and politically significant. Woodhouse was of the opinion that "They could influence opinion in the Majles and the bazaars; and more important they could mobilize street mobs".[79]

---

[73] Rashidiyanha, vol. 1, pp. 23, 25; vol. 2, pp. 23, 25, 256.
[74] FO 248/1514, 29 October 1951.
[75] Rashidiyanha, vol. 1, pp. 395, 438; Rashidiyanha, vol. 2, pp. 25, 252.
[76] Rashidiyanha, vol. 3, p. 56.   [77] Rashidiyanha, vol. 2, p. 75.
[78] Rashidiyanha, vol. 1, pp. 72, 153, 168, 173, 235, 222, 226, 237, 261.
[79] Woodhouse, p. 111.

RASHIDIYAN AND THE BRITISH EMBASSY IN IRAN

In his furthering of Britain's prime objectives in Iran, Rashidiyan was a man of persistence and action. Through his close connections with British officials at the embassy, he helped form and even "correct" British policy towards Iran. It seems that he was among A.K.S. Lambton's close circle of Iranian friends. It is reported that during the period of Mosaddeq's government Lambton travelled to Iran and, while in Tehran, stayed either at the home of Dr Alavi, the Anglophile ophthalmologist, or at Asadollah Rashidiyan's house.[80] On her visits to Iran after the 1953 coup, Lambton is said to have stayed with either Alavi or Rashidiyan.[81] Asadollah Rashidiyan not only patiently and consistently promoted the idea that Mosaddeq's government had to be overthrown, but when the idea needed to be implemented he and his brothers contributed at every step of the way. He was not only a mastermind, but a perpetrator who managed, negotiated and executed the fall of Mosaddeq. As resourceful as he was, however, Rashidiyan did not undertake any serious political initiatives without the consent and "green light" of the British.

Wilber, a participant in the planning of Operation TPAJAX and its chronicler, considered Asadollah Rashidiyan to be "the principle SIS agent".[82] Without naming them, Woodhouse refers to "the Brothers" (Asadollah and Seyfollah) as "the keystone of our plans".[83] In his book, Roosevelt gives Asadollah Rashidiyan the code name "Nossy" and Seyfollah Rashidiyan the code name "Cafron"; he also refers to them as "the principal representatives of British intelligence".[84] At the time, those Iranians who sought quick and unmerited political and economic power and status knew that the Rashidiyans, through their close association with the British, could facilitate attainment of their objectives. The Rashidiyans

> were true agents in the sense that they worked for the British government... and what made them distinctive and very important for their type of operation was that everyone in Iran knew this, and therefore when someone wanted to run for Parliament and wanted British help... everyone knew where to go.[85]

Zaehner, a British diplomat in Tehran with extensive knowledge of Britain's Iranian contacts, referred to the Rashidiyans as "our friends", and complained about their "excess of zeal" for bringing down Mosaddeq and replacing him with Seyyed Zia.[86] He referred to an episode in September 1951 during which, suspicious of warming relations between the Shah and Mosaddeq, the Rashidiyan brothers pressured the British Embassy to weigh upon the Shah to harden his position against Mosaddeq.[87]

---

[80] Rashidiyanha, vol. 3, p. 343.   [81] Rashidiyanha, vol. 3, p. 190.   [82] Wilber, p. 24.
[83] Woodhouse, p. 111.   [84] Roosevelt, p. 152.
[85] S. Dorril, *MI6 Fifty Years of Special Operations* (London: Fourth Estate, 2001), p. 571.
[86] FO 248/1514, 22 September 1951.   [87] FO 248/1514, 22 September 1951.

The Rashidiyan brothers had a long-term working relationship with Robin Zaehner, who was stationed in Iran during the Second World War as a covert British operator. It was at this time that the Rashidiyans must have befriended Miss Lambton. Zaehner, an academic who was fluent in Persian, was identified by Miss Lambton as "the ideal man" to develop a network of pro-British Iranians.[88] The Rashidiyans are said to have collaborated covertly with Zaehner on both anti-German and anti-Communist activities.[89] According to Woodhouse (the SIS station chief in Tehran), the Rashidiyans had kept "their organization" active and "in good repair" since the war days.[90] The Rashidiyans were also financed by the British for activities on their behalf.[91] From August 1951 – which coincided with the British abandoning their "Operation Buccaneer" – the Rashidiyans received £10,000 a month from the British for their anti-Mosaddeq activities.[92] This monthly payment, which amounted to around £180,000 by 21 February 1953 when the British decided to gradually decrease it, was paid uninterruptedly and was resumed in April 1953; it lasted until the coup. It has also been suggested that the Rashidiyans received "well over £1.5 million" for necessary expenses to protect British interests in Iran.[93] Up to June 1952, British money is said to have been handed directly to the Rashidiyans by Zaehner; they in turn allocated it to their cronies and those "respectable" Iranian figures whom they kept on their payroll for an eventual favour or pay-back.[94] During the last month before the coup, Ashraf Pahlavi is said to have organized a network which was supposed to act in favour of the Shah at the opportune time. Asadollah Rashidiyan was involved in this organization.[95]

When the CIA and SIS representatives met between 13 and 30 May 1953 in Nicosia to draw up a joint preliminary plan of action for the overthrow of Mosaddeq, they felt obliged to share information about their operations and networks in Iran.[96] As discussions moved to disclosing their respective assets, the SIS's centrepiece was the Rashidiyan Brothers, whose contacts spanned such fields as "the armed forces, the Majles (Iranian Parliament), religious leaders, the press, street gangs, politicians, and other influential figures".[97] According to the CIA, which inherited the SIS's network in Iran, the Rashidiyans had in their employment "the best of the British trained stay behind operators".[98] On 15 June, as the plan to overthrow Mosaddeq was advancing, the SIS handed the Rashidiyans over to the CIA. At a meeting in London, the SIS representatives informed Roosevelt and Wilber that "the Rashidiyans would be ordered to follow completely the orders of the CIA's Tehran Station".[99] Nevertheless, the Rashidiyans continued to remain in contact with their British liaison, Norman Darbyshire, at the SIS station in

---

[88] Louis, 1984, p. 660.   [89] Woodhouse, p. 111; Louis in *Mohammad Mosaddeq*, p. 138.
[90] Woodhouse, p. 111.   [91] Woodhouse, p. 112.   [92] Woodhouse, pp. 118, 123.
[93] Dorril, p. 564.   [94] Dorril, p. 564.   [95] Fardust, vol. 1, p. 172.   [96] Wilber, pp. 5, 6.
[97] Wilber, p. 7.   [98] Wilber, p. 10.   [99] Wilber, p. 14.

Nicosia through tri-weekly wireless exchanges.[100] The importance of the Rashidiyan organization to the TPAJAX operation was such that when one of the Rashidiyan brothers was absent from Tehran, some of the meetings between various branch leaders of the CIA Tehran Station and the representatives of the Iranian collaborationist organizations had to be cancelled.[101] To highlight the central role of the Rashidiyan brothers, Roger Louis maintains that "It is difficult to imagine how the 1953 operation against the Mosaddeq government could have taken place without the Rashidiyan network".[102] However, there seems little doubt that between the brothers, it was Assadollah who played the key organizational role.

Roosevelt and Carroll, the CIA operatives dispatched to Tehran in July 1953, could not begin the operational aspect of the coup d'état without contact with the Shah. The irresolute and suspicious Shah needed to be officially informed that the operation to oust Mosaddeq had started, with the full backing of the US and UK, and that he was quickly and actively to get on board. This did not prove to be an easy task as the Shah did not trust many people, especially in a sensitive situation such as this where he feared losing his throne if he were to make the wrong move. Through the good offices of Asadollah Rashidiyan, the first steps were taken to establish contact between Ashraf Pahlavi, who was in Europe at the time, and the coup-makers. The Shah's sister was to become the messenger of the foreign plotters, informing and briefing her brother about their impending coup in his favour.

The key person who arranged the meeting between Ashraf Pahlavi and the two CIA–SIS envoys in Paris was Asadollah Rashidiyan. More than a year before, in May 1952, Rashidiyan had thought of visiting Paris to persuade Princess Ashraf to return to Iran and had discussed his plan with Zaehner of the British Embassy. Rashidiyan and the Princess were close and Rashidiyan believed that her presence in Iran would substantially help the anti-Mosaddeq opposition. After his meeting with Rashidiyan, Zaehner reported to his superiors that "Rashidiyan is so well known as a friend of this Embassy that the Princess will no doubt interpret his visit as direct encouragement from us".[103] In her memoirs, Ashraf Pahlavi referred to Asadollah Rashidiyan's meeting with her in July of 1953, but chose to call him "Mr. B.", as at the time she did not wish to reveal his real name.[104]

Rashidiyan located the Shah's sister on the French Riviera and met with her on 15 July, whereupon he told her that "the United States and Great Britain were extremely concerned about the current situation in Iran and they had devised a plan to solve the problem and benefit the Shah".[105] Rashidiyan informed Ashraf Pahlavi that her assistance was needed before the "plan could be put into operation", and that she needed to meet with an

---

[100] Wilber, p. 10.   [101] Wilber, p. 10.   [102] Louis in *Mohammad Mosaddeq*, p. 141.
[103] FO 248/1541, 13 May 1952.
[104] A. Pahlavi, *Faces in a Mirror* (N.J: Prentice-Hall, 1980), p. 134.   [105] Pahlavi 1980, p. 134.

American and an Englishman, who would brief her.[106] On 16 July, Stephen Meade of the US Army (who was working for the CIA at the time) and Norman Darbyshire (the SIS officer heading the Iran station from Nicosia) met with and convinced Princess Ashraf to travel from Paris to Tehran. Her job was to inform the Shah of the plot and secure his participation.[107] Ashraf Pahlavi flew to Tehran on July 25 on board a commercial flight, ensuring that the first joint operation of the CIA, the SIS and their Iranian networks bore fruit.

RASHIDIYAN BABY-SITTING THE SHAH BEFORE THE COUP

Having put Princess Ashraf in contact with the SIS and CIA representatives, Asadollah Rashidiyan returned to Tehran to pursue his diplomatic task of gradually convincing the reluctant Shah to become involved in the coup that was being planned in his name. From 30 July 1953, Asadollah Rashidiyan met the Shah at least six times (30 and 31 July; 2, 7, 8 and 9 August). During each meeting Rashidiyan carefully and skilfully guided the very hesitant and almost petrified Shah to take baby-steps towards dismissing Mosaddeq and appointing Zahedi. Rashidiyan's role during these meetings was to brief the Shah on the process and stages of the operation against Mosaddeq and put all interested and involved parties in touch with the monarch. Rashidiyan sought to inform the Shah and draw him into the plot against Mosaddeq, without frightening him. This proved to be a difficult task. Rashidiyan's trump card was to comfort and assure the Shah that the Americans and the British stood behind him, supported him all the way, and had thought of everything. The Shah needed to be convinced that his participation as the symbol of national unity and the Commander in Chief of the army was indispensable to the success of the project. With the Shah implicated, the soldiers and officers that needed to be won over to the coup d'état could be convinced that the operation was a patriotic one in defence of the Shah and against a Communist takeover. Asadollah Rashidiyan's job was to give the over-cautious Shah the reassurance that for his own good he needed to become more involved with the project. The fact that this most sensitive mission was entrusted to Rashidiyan is indicative of the relation that he had with the Shah and the foreign powers plotting against Mosaddeq. With proper insight into the Shah's psychological condition, Rashidiyan took certain appropriate steps to accomplish his mission.

First, Asadollah Rashidiyan convinced the Shah that he was "the official spokesperson of the UK government" and their liaison person with the Shah.[108] Second, Rashidiyan briefed the Shah on General Norman Schwarzkopf's visit and alerted him to the key message which Schwarzkopf

---

[106] Pahlavi 1980, p. 134.   [107] Wilber, pp. 22–23.   [108] Wilber, p. 24.

was to deliver, further assuring the Shah of the close collaboration of the US and UK in their common effort to remove Mosaddeq.[109] Schwarzkopf, whom the Shah knew and trusted, arrived in Tehran on 26 July, one day after Princess Ashraf's arrival. He was sent by the American administration to obtain two royal edicts (*farman*): one appointing Zahedi as the Chief of Staff, and a second calling on all ranks of the army to support the Shah's newly appointed and therefore legal Chief of Staff.[110] Schwarzkopf's visit did not prove successful, however, as the Shah refused to sign the documents, arguing that he had no confidence in the loyalty of his army to himself.[111] Third, Rashidiyan presented the Shah with the specific details of how the operation to overthrow Mosaddeq would be carried out, and reported back to his foreign superiors that the Shah was ready to dismiss Mosaddeq and appoint Zahedi as both Prime Minister and Deputy Commander in Chief.[112] Fourth, Rashidiyan arranged for Kermit Roosevelt, the CIA-designated chief of the overthrow operation, to secretly meet with the Shah.[113] Fifth, Rashidiyan met the Shah on 7 August, when it was decided that "action should be taken on the night of either 10 or 11" of August.[114] It was probably at this meeting that Rashidiyan provided the Shah with the full list of officers involved in the coup.[115] Subsequent to Rashidiyan's important meeting with the Shah, Roosevelt met the Shah for a second time (on 8 August) and tried to convince him to actively back the coup. The Shah, intent on minimizing his risks, insisted that the army should act "without his official knowledge"; only if the plan succeeded would he name Zahedi as Prime Minister.[116] The plotters needed to keep the pressure on the Shah, who was in "a mood of stubborn irresolution".[117] Hence, on 9 or 10 August, Colonel Hasan Akhavi, probably through the intermediary of Rashidiyan, met with the Shah. This was the first meeting between the Shah and a member of the Military Secretariat in charge of planning and executing the coup. In a meeting, which "later proved vital to the success of the military phase of TPAJAX", Akhavi presented the Shah with "the name of the army officers who were ready to take action upon the receipt of an order from the Shah".[118] This list of army officers had already been given to the Shah by Rashidiyan. The Shah continued to refuse to sign the royal edicts, and Akhavi "registered a protest at this decision".[119] Sixth, Rashidiyan met the Shah at the latter's request and eventually succeeded in enjoining him to issue the two royal edicts.[120] By this time Rashidiyan had gained the confidence of the Shah. Without Rashidiyan's counsel, it seemed as if the Shah was almost incapable of thinking clearly. During this final meeting

---

[109] Wilber, p. 25.   [110] Wilber, pp. 25–6.   [111] Wilber, p. 29.   [112] Wilber, p. 33.
[113] Roosevelt, p. 154.   [114] Wilber, p. 35.   [115] Wilber, Appendix D, p. 15.
[116] Wilber, p. 35.   [117] Wilber, p. 35.
[118] Wilber, p. 35; Wilber, Appendix D, p. 14. In Wilber's report both 9 and 10 August are mentioned as the days on which Akhavi met the Shah.
[119] Wilber, p. 36.   [120] Wilber, pp. 35–36.

before the Shah's departure to Ramsar, which must have been on either 10 or 11 August, Rashidiyan informed the Shah that Roosevelt was becoming impatient and had threatened that if the Shah refused to sign the royal edicts he would leave the country "in complete disgust".[121] During this sensitive meeting Rashidiyan treated the monarch like an infant, finally convincing him to sign the edicts. The Shah informed Rashidiyan that once he had signed the papers and met with Zahedi, he would fly to Ramsar, a summer resort on the Caspian Sea.[122] On the day of the Shah's departure to Ramsar the two edicts were not prepared for his signature, and so after meeting Zahedi he left for his summer resort without having signed them. The final decision to have two distinct royal edicts – one dismissing Mosaddeq and another appointing Zahedi – had resulted from discussions between Rashidiyan and Roosevelt.[123] In the absence of the two edicts, and with the Shah's departure to Ramsar, Colonel Ne'matollah Nasiri, commander of the Imperial Guards, was dispatched to obtain the royal signatures.

According to Nasiri, at Ramsar the Shah did not personally write the contents of the two important edicts on the official letters brought back to Tehran, but placed his signature at the bottom of two blank official pieces of paper with the royal letterheads. Nasiri then flew to Tehran with two rough drafts, one in his own handwriting concerning the dismissal of Mosaddeq and one in someone else's handwriting regarding the appointment of Zahedi as Prime Minister. Upon arrival, Nasiri took the rough drafts and the signed blank letterheads to Rahim Hirad, chief of the Shah's Private Secretariat, and asked him to copy the content of the two rough drafts onto the official signed letters.[124] After 28 Mordad, Nasiri concurred that while in Ramsar, the Shah signed the two edicts, the contents of which were handwritten by Hirad in Tehran.[125] The "preparation" of the content of the two royal edicts is attributed to Behboudi, an established UK agent, and Rashidiyan.[126]

---

[121] Wilber, p. 36.   [122] Wilber, p. 36.   [123] Wilber p. 36.   [124] Nejati, pp. 514, 609.
[125] A. Baniahmad, *Panj Rooz Rastakhiz-e Mellat-e Iran* (Tehran: Chapkhaneh Artesh, n.d), p. 156.
[126] Wilber p. 36.

5

The CIA-affiliated organizations: propaganda and combat

It seems as though between 1948 and 1953, Roger Goiran, the CIA Chief of Station in Tehran, developed "station assets" who "proved valuable and necessary" in the preparation and execution stages of the two coups in August 1953.[1] Goiran, who himself believed that the CIA intervention in Iran was a mistake, left Tehran on 2 August 1953. The area(s) of activity, duties and responsibilities of these CIA assets are hard to establish. Were they active field operatives and agents, information gatherers, propaganda officers or infiltrators in state and governmental offices, such as the military? Ambiguity over the professional fields of activity or affiliation of these assets and their organizational structure poses a problem in determining how they operated during the first and second coups in August 1953.

Roosevelt refers to his Iranian team as being led by the "Brothers" whom he calls "the Boscoes", and he even insinuates that the idea of Operation TPAJAX originated with them.[2] The Boscoe Brothers were American assets while the British Brothers (or Rashidiyans) were originally British assets. Roosevelt's involvement with the Boscoe Brothers went back to the last months of 1950 when the Brothers reached out to American intelligence officers in Tehran.[3] This precedes the premiership of Mosaddeq. The Boscoe Brothers are said to have been prompted to approach the Americans primarily as a result of their anxiety over the growing power of the Tudeh Party, its potential allies and eventually the Soviet threat.[4] Roosevelt's assessment of the Boscoe Brothers was that they clearly had some sort of training in clandestine activity.[5] According to Roosevelt, they could be relied upon "to turn out the bazaar in support of H.I.M. (the Shah)" and that would be "the signal needed by the people and the army".[6] The Brothers were not willing to divulge the history of their affiliations, their associates or their operations. They "claimed to have an organization to

---

[1] Wilber, p. 21. [2] Roosevelt, pp. 16, 41. [3] Roosevelt, p. 79. [4] Roosevelt, p. 79.
[5] Roosevelt, p. 79. [6] Roosevelt, p. 16.

support them", yet once again they refused to throw any light on its structure, members, supporters or sympathizers.[7] To verify their claims, Roosevelt flew the Brothers to the US and put them through a polygraph test in order to "evaluate their capabilities thoroughly".[8] Convinced of the veracity of their claims, the Boscoe Brothers were enlisted "as working allies in support of the Shah".[9] According to Roosevelt, at least some of the violence during Averell Harriman's visit to Tehran in July 1951, which was attributed to the Tudeh Party and was domestically and internationally embarrassing to Mosaddeq, was provoked by the Boscoe Brothers.[10]

From Kermit Roosevelt's account it is not clear who the Boscoe Brothers actually were. He does provide a short biography of them, which may or may not be precise. Both, he says, were "quiet, business-like and very impressive". The elder was a large, solidly built, dark-looking lawyer. The younger, in his late twenties, was also dark, but shorter and more talkative, and a journalist by profession.[11] According to Woodhouse, Roosevelt "had been approached by two influential Iranians, who offered him the same kind of services as our Brothers [the Rashidiyans], provided us".[12] Woodhouse goes on to add that "by a strange coincidence, Roosevelt's two conspirators were also brothers".[13] For a while, both Roosevelt and Woodhouse worried that what they thought would be their respective and complementary assets would turn out to be the same; they were both relieved to discover that their respective sets of brothers were indeed different.[14]

In Woodhouse's opinion "both pairs" of brothers had good contacts with the bazaar, but "Roosevelt's pair" – namely the "Boscoe Brothers" – "had the edge in contacts with the armed forces", while the SIS's pair – namely the Rashidiyans – had the edge in terms of contacts connected to the Shah.[15] Whereas Roosevelt only refers to the influence of his pair of brothers (the Boscoes) in the bazaar, Woodhouse attributes their comparative advantage to their contacts in the military. Shedding light on the circumstances and unfolding of 28 Mordad requires familiarity with its actors, and so it is therefore important to try identify the "Boscoe Brothers".

THE ENIGMA OF THE BOSCOE BROTHERS

In Wilber's detailed and professional account of Mosaddeq's overthrow, there is understandably no reference to the "Boscoe Brothers", as this was Roosevelt's pseudonym for them. However, Wilber mentions that in the planning stage of Mosaddeq's overthrow, while the CIA and SIS were in the process of exchanging information about their assets on the ground, the CIA decided that the identities of two "vitally important principal agents of the

---

[7] Roosevelt, p. 80. [8] Roosevelt, p. 80. [9] Roosevelt, p. 81. [10] Roosevelt, p. 98.
[11] Roosevelt, p. 79. [12] Woodhouse, p. 120. [13] Woodhouse, p. 120.
[14] Woodhouse, p. 120; Roosevelt, p. 124. [15] Woodhouse, p. 120.

Tehran station, Djalili and Keyvani would not be disclosed to the SIS".[16] Wilber is clear on the fact that, to his knowledge, Djalili and Keyvani were not uncovered by the Rashidiyan brothers or any other SIS agents.[17] Aside from emphasizing that Djalili and Keyvani were purely CIA assets and not handed over to the CIA by the SIS or their Iranian collaborators, Wilber's statement indicates that these two were the "principal agents" of the CIA station in Tehran. Since Roosevelt writes about the "Boscoe Brothers" as the CIA's most important Iranian assets, could his brothers be Djalili and Keyvani? Several challenges make identifying the "Boscoe Brothers" as Djalili and Keyvani problematic, especially if Roosevelt's and Woodhouse's depictions of the "Boscoe Brothers" are to be taken as factual.

In his detailed report of the coup, Wilber does not refer to Djalili and Keyvani as brothers, yet he leaves little doubt that they were the CIA's two chief non-military Iranian agents. In real life, Djalili and Keyvani were not siblings. This would lead to an initial observation that Djalili and Keyvani, whom Wilber identifies as "vitally important principal agents of the Tehran station", cannot be Roosevelt's and Woodhouse's brothers, unless the reference to "brothers" was intended to be taken symbolically. Furthermore, according to Roosevelt, the "Boscoe Brothers" claimed to have an organization supporting them, they clearly had some sort of training in clandestine activities and they could be relied upon to turn out the bazaar in support of the Shah. Roosevelt and Woodhouse give the impression that the "Boscoe Brothers" were high-powered, well-connected and influential figures on the Iranian political scene. The comparisons made between the UK- and US-affiliated brothers by Roosevelt and Woodhouse imparts the sense that the CIA station's operatives were political heavyweights such as the Rashidiyans.

The identification of the two key CIA agents known as the "Boscoe Brothers" takes an interesting turn when Mark Gasiorowski, the academic expert on the CIA's involvement in the August coup, provides first names for them. Gasiorowski argues that it was Ali Jalali and Faruq Keyvani who approached Goiran in late 1950 or early 1951. Chronologically, this account corroborates Roosevelt's account of the "Boscoe Brothers" approaching the CIA station in Tehran in late 1950. For Mark Gasiorowski and Malcolm Byrne, therefore, Roosevelt's "Boscoe Brothers" were Ali Jalali and Faruq Keyvani in real life and their code names were Nerren and Cilly, respectively (not to be confused with Nossy and Cafron, the British Brothers).[18] Neither Gasiorowski nor Byrne explicitly states that Jalali and Keyvani were Roosevelt's "Boscoe Brothers", but the fact is systematically intimated. Yet Gasiorowski talks about Jalali, not Djalili;[19] throughout his report Wilber

---

[16] Wilber, p. 8, 47. [17] Wilber, p. 8.
[18] Gasiorowski, "The 1953 coup d'état against Mosaddeq", in *Mohammad Mosaddeq*, p. 236; Byrne, "The road to intervention", in *Mohammad Mosaddeq*, p. 217.
[19] Gasiorowski, in *Mohammad Mosaddeq*, pp. 236, 238, 239.

refers to a man called Djalili, not Jalali.[20] Even though the Persian spelling of Djalili/Jalali could imply two different people, it is certain that Wilber meant Jalali and that Gasiorowski is correct. However, whereas Gasiorowski refers to Faruq Keyvani, his real first name was Farrokh.

Who were Jalali and Keyvani? In September 1941, Ali Jalali was the Editor in Chief of Abbas Mas'udi's well-established daily *Ettela'at*. He made political waves when, in an article called "The People's Disappointment", he mildly criticized the Soviets and the British for violating Iran's neutrality by forcing Mohammad Ali Forughi's government to close down the German, Italian, Hungarian and Rumanian embassies in Iran.[21] This article is said to have given the British and the Soviets the excuse to depose Reza Shah Pahlavi, banish him and replace him with his son Mohammad Reza. At the time, Ali Jalali was a reserve officer and came to work in his military uniform.[22] Jalali was a graduate of Tehran University's Law School and was an expert in the governments and politicians of the post-constitution period.[23] At some point in his career, Jalali edited a publication called *Iran Parastan* or "The Worshippers of Iran".[24]

Farrokh Keyvani was also a journalist at the *Ettela'at* daily. His father was in the Iranian Ministry of Foreign Affairs and Farrokh is said to have accompanied his father on a diplomatic mission to India, where he learnt his excellent English. Keyvani was said to be a good journalist, eloquent, sociable and refined.[25] Keyvani also worked as a correspondent with the Associated Press and was said to be connected to the Americans.[26] It is also said that Keyvani was a part-time stringer for the *Daily Telegraph*.[27]

Jalali and Keyvani first worked together at *Ettela'at*, where their friendship matured into a very close partnership.[28] According to one account, Jalali and Keyvani were in Princess Ashraf Pahlavi's clique and had come to *Ettela'at* under the patronage of Ahmad Dehqan, who was said to be another protégé of Ashraf Pahlavi.[29] According to another account, both journalists had rightist political tendencies, were anti-Communist and were close to Seyyed Zia.[30] Subsequently, they both left Mas'udi's *Ettela'at* and followed Dehqan to the weekly *Tehran Mosavvar*, which was said to be close to the army's

---

[20] Wilber, pp. 8, 9, 49.
[21] A. Behzadi, *Shebh-e Khaterat*, vol. 2 (Tehran: Ata'i, 1388), pp. 234, 235.
[22] Behzadi, p. 235.
[23] Reza Marzban, personal interview, Paris, 9 April 2012. I am grateful to Shahram Ghanbari for arranging this interview.
[24] M. J. Mohammadi, *Raze Piruziye Kudetaye 28 Mordad* (Koln: Forough, n.d), p. 196.
[25] Marzban, personal interview, 9 April 2012.
[26] Ahmad Ahrar, personal interview, Paris, 15 March 2012.   [27] Mohammadi, p. 196.
[28] Ahrar, personal interview, 15 March 2012.
[29] Marzban, personal interview, 9 April 2012.   [30] Ahrar, personal interview, 15 March 2012.

counter-intelligence office or Second Bureau (*rokn do*).[31] *Tehran Mosavvar* was printed at the army's publishing house. The migration of Jalali and Keyvani to Dehqan's *Tehran Mosavvar* is also believed to have been at the behest of Ashraf Pahlavi.[32] In view of Ashraf Pahlavi's close connection with Asadollah Rashidiyan it is quite possible that Rashidiyan was fully aware of the activities of Jalali and Keyvani.[33]

Between 1941 and 1950, under the direction of Dehqan, *Tehran Mosavvar* followed an anti-Communist line. A series of semi-fictional articles entitled "I was a Russian Spy" that were published in *Tehran Mosavvar* were written under the supervision of Jalali and Keyvani.[34] When on 16 November 1949 Mohammad Reza Shah travelled to the US on his first official state visit, Keyvani is said to have accompanied him as a journalist. On his return to Iran, Keyvani repeated his favourite sentence: "Great food is to be found in Paris and dazzling women in the US".[35] After the assassination of Ahmad Dehqan on 27 May 1950, Jalali and Keyvani left *Tehran Mosavvar* and almost vanished from the public scene. Reza Marzban, a fellow journalist at *Tehran Mosavvar* during Jalali and Keyvani's employment there, recalled that the two were political agitators.[36] Jalali and Keyvani maintained a low profile and were unknown to their fellow journalists working at dailies and weeklies other than *Ettela'at* and *Tehran Mosavvar*. Some of Iran's veteran journalists of the same generation as Jalali and Keyvani do not recall the presence of these two in any of the known political milieus of Tehran.[37] The political discretion of the pair at a time when everyone took pride in displaying their political colours is probably a sign of their clandestine activities.

Matching the profile of the "Boscoe Brothers" according to Roosevelt and Woodhouse with the life stories and activities of Jalali and Keyvani reveals that it would be safe to conclude that the "Boscoe Brothers" were indeed Jalali and Keyvani. The fact that they were very close friends, that Jalali had legal training, that Keyvani went to the US in 1949, and that they both had a reputation for being anti-Communists corresponds to Roosevelt's account. The information provided by Wilber on the details of the activities of Jalali and Keyvani on the few days leading up to the second coup strengthens the hypothesis that Jalali and Keyvani were Roosevelt's "Boscoe Brothers". Daryoush Homayoun's testimony on the activities of two journalists, whom he indirectly acknowledges to be Ali Jalali and Farrokh Keyvani, leaves little

---

[31] Marzban, personal interview, 9 April 2012.
[32] Marzban, personal interview, 9 April 2012.
[33] This idea is based on a comment made to me by John Gurney.
[34] Marzban, personal interview, 9 April 2012.
[35] Marzban, personal interview, 9 April 2012.
[36] Marzban, personal interview, 9 April 2012.
[37] Ali-Asqar Haj-Seyyed Javadi, personal interview, Paris, 21 June 2012. I am grateful to Houshang Keshavarz-Sadr for arranging this interview.

doubt about the fact that Jalali and Keyvani were in fact Roosevelt's pair.[38] At the time, Homayoun was not only a highly influential member of the virulent anti-Communist SUMKA, but also a jingoist journalist familiar with the extreme-right political milieus.

According to Homayoun, the two journalists Jalali and Keyvani had founded a commercial company as a front for distributing CIA money to anti-Communist organizations and publications.[39] The leader of an anti-Communist student organization whose members had battled with Tudeh Party members on the streets of Tehran confided in Homayoun that he received money from Jalali and Keyvani.[40] Homayoun also thought that Monshizadeh, the leader of SUMKA, was a beneficiary of CIA money through Jalali and Keyvani. The principal activity of Jalali and Keyvani, according to Iranian sources, seems to have been the distribution of CIA money to anti-Communist individuals, organizations, activities and newspapers. Once the heavy propaganda of anti-Mosaddeq forces presented him as a pro-Communist, then all anti-Mosaddeq organizations and newspapers were eligible to benefit from the financial benevolence of the CIA through Jalali and Keyvani.

According to Wilber, the Jalali and Keyvani team did play a more operational and direct role in the preparation and execution of the second coup d'état. Their primary role was a logistical one, focused on reproducing and distributing the royal edict dismissing Mosaddeq and nominating Zahedi as Prime Minister. They coordinated the publication and dissemination of this sensitive news through friendly domestic and foreign journalists, most of whom had benefitted from CIA hand-outs through them. Subsequently, on the day of the second coup, Jalali and Keyvani took direct action by whipping up emotion and fervour among the ruffians, taking charge of them, guiding them towards their main strategic targets and inciting them to seize and destroy those objectives.

Even though it is evident that the Jalali–Keyvani team played a key role in the second coup, it would be wrong to assume that they constituted the most important CIA team. The Jalali–Keyvani team were primarily troubleshooters, facilitators and agitators responsible for propaganda, logistic support, provocations and street brawls. They may have been annoying gadflies, but they were not predator panthers. Yet the CIA came to organize and control an assault military network, without which the coup plan could not have succeeded. Woodhouse, the SIS station head in Tehran, and who had a firmer grasp of the Iranian political scene than Roosevelt and was involved in the various stages of planning the TPAJAX operation, distinguished his brothers, the Rashidiyans, from Roosevelt's pair by emphasizing the fact that Roosevelt's brothers had an edge in the army. There is no evidence that Jalali and Keyvani possessed any real army links or connections.

---

[38] Homayoun, pp. 45, 46; Askari, p. 333.   [39] Homayoun, pp. 45, 46.   [40] Homayoun, p. 46.

It seems unlikely that the main CIA-linked network in Iran belonged to Jalali and Keyvani, who were almost strangers to the broad Iranian political scene of the 1950s. Jalali and Keyvani may have been extremely agile foot soldiers and creative trouble-shooters, as they proved to be in the days before and during the coup, but they could not have been the well-connected leaders of an organization such as the one the Rashidiyan Brothers were running. A pair of relatively unknown protégés of Ashraf Pahlavi setting up a commercial front for distributing CIA money to anti-Mosaddeq and anti-Communist organizations, and buying influence, press coverage and public opinion with CIA money was one thing; wielding the kind of power, weight, connection and leverage that the Rashidiyans had built over the years was quite another. The second coup needed much more than an anti-Mosaddeq propaganda campaign and manipulated public opinion; it needed serious muscle and a show of military power backed by the willingness to use real bullets and tank shells – and these could be provided only by infiltrated and subverted army and police units.

The fact is not in dispute that Jalali and Keyvani, supported by their recruits and sidekicks mainly from the ranks of the Ariya, SUMKA, Toilers and Zolfaqar parties and perhaps the Society of Muslim Mojaheds, acted as streetwise agitators and leaders on 26, 27 and 28 Mordad. They used their network and its muscle ingeniously throughout the day before 28 Mordad in order to convince the people of Tehran that the city was insecure as it was being taken over by the Communists who had been egged on by Mosaddeq. As important as this type of activity was to the success of the coup, it should not be confused with the military plans and operations conceived and executed by the CIA-connected military collaborationist network. The Jalali–Keyvani team galvanized and directed the mob to vandalize, rampage and set fire to or occupy buildings on 28 Mordad. These activities were very different from the military activities that took place on the same day. Therefore, it may be useful to separate the propaganda, logistic and agitation aspects of the CIA network associated with Jalali and Keyvani from that of the CIA-related military and security network of the collaborationist army officers.

THE CIA'S OLD PROPAGANDA ORGANIZATION

In the late 1940s – which coincided with the date that Goiran, the Chief of the CIA Tehran Station, started developing his station assets – the CIA set up a covert organization under the code name "Operation TPBEDAMN" in Iran.[41] After the pro-Soviet semi-coup of February 1948 against Edward Benes in Czechoslovakia, fear of Soviet domination through parliamentary

---

[41] The information in this section is primarily based on the excellent works of M. Byrne, "Road to Intervention", in *Mohammad Mosaddeq*, pp. 216–117, and M. Gasiorowski, "Coup d'Etat Against Mosaddeq", in *Mohammad Mosaddeq*, pp. 235–236.

methods not just in Europe, but also in the Near and Middle East, increased in the US. To counter the perceived Soviet threat, Operation TPBEDAMN was launched in Iran. This operation seems to have been entirely focused on containing the Iranian Communist Tudeh Party and relied on psychological and propaganda warfare against Communism. The operation was a well-funded, comprehensive program aimed at undermining Communist influence in Iran. A good part of the $1,000,000 per year TPBEDAMN budget was spent on journalistic activities, countering the influence of Tudeh Party literature and Tudeh Party activities.[42] The main thrust of this operation was producing and propagating disinformation, defamation and "newspeak". TPBEDMAN was primarily an organization for conducting a psychological war and targeted assaults against Communist influences or interests in Iran. This was not a combat-oriented or military force, even though it could incite and engage in brawls, agitations and small-scale gang fights. TPBEDAMN's befriending and recruiting of anti-Communist elements connected it to a wide array of Anglophile and Americanophile elements, ranging from extremist and ultra-right fringe groups such as SUMKA to the up-and-coming social-democrats of Mozaffar Baqa'i's Toilers Party, as well as the more traditional conservative groups connected with Qavam, Seyyed Ziaeddin Tabataba'i and General Arfa'.

TPBEDAMN spent money to try to influence or control certain Iranian newspapers and plant anti-Tudeh articles and cartoons in them. The publication branch of TPBEDAMN also published "leaflets and books and had them translated into Persian by Iranians working under TPBEDAMN".[43] The TPBEDAMN budget was also spent on subsidizing, paying off and befriending both right-wing and anti-Tudeh extremist nationalist parties as well as religious figures. Another aspect of the operation was concerned with financing *agents provocateurs*, "provoking violent acts and blaming them on the Tudeh" as well as "hiring thugs to break up the Tudeh rallies".[44] This latter task was carried out by the anti-Tudeh organization and parties who were benefitting from the TPBEDAMN budget. The most well-known Iranian organizations actively and consistently involved in Tudeh-bashing were Baqa'i's Toilers Party, Sepehr's Ariya Party and Monshizadeh's SUMKA. From 28 February 1953 (9 Esfand), all three organizations meshed their anti-Communist vocation with an anti-Mosaddeq mission. According to Gasiorowski, it was the TPBEDAMN network which constituted "CIA's main political action network in Iran", and it was Ali Jalali and "Faruq" [*sic.*] Kayvani who were its Iranian coordinators or main agents.[45] Gasiorowski maintains that at the end of May 1953, "Jalali and Kayvani

---

[42] Byrne in *Mohammad Mosaddeq*, p. 217.
[43] Gasiorowski, in *Mohammad Mosaddeq*, p. 235.
[44] Byrne in *Mohammad Mosaddeq*, p. 217; Dorril, p. 566.
[45] Gasiorowski, in *Mohammad Mosaddeq*, p. 236.

had over one hundred sub-agents in their network".⁴⁶ It would be fair to assume that without any significant traditional political clout and connection, a couple of relatively unknown middle-ranking journalists were capable of running such a wide network only with the aid of generous hand-outs.

THE CIA'S NEW IRANIAN COMBAT ORGANIZATION

While Joseph Goodwin was the Chief of the CIA Station in Tehran, George Carroll was the key CIA field officer in charge of the military aspect of the TPAJAX operation. He was a paramilitary warfare expert dispatched to Tehran and placed in charge of military planning for the overthrow of Mosaddeq.⁴⁷ Roosevelt, Carroll and Goodwin constituted the CIA core in Tehran, around whom a web of Iranian military networks was gradually woven. It is therefore important to understand how the Iranian military network associated with the CIA began to take shape. Contrary to Woodhouse's assertion that Roosevelt's brothers had connections among the military, Wilber maintains that when the CIA started planning the TPAJAX operation (May 1953), it "did not possess any military assets".⁴⁸ It was therefore decided to train Colonel Abbas Farzanegan, a CIA station agent at Fort Leavenworth.⁴⁹ While in Washington, Farzanegan was given a lie detector test.⁵⁰ Roosevelt also recalled that the "Boscoe Brothers" were flown to the US and given tests in order to "evaluate their capabilities thoroughly".⁵¹ Colonel Abbas Farzanegan, who played an instrumental role in the events leading to 28 Mordad and the fall of Mosaddeq, had a younger brother, Azizollah. It was Azizollah who sheltered General Fazlollah Zahedi and 13 of his military and civil associates on the night of the failure of the coup on 15 August.⁵²

Captain Azizollah Farzanegan was 32 when he was retired from the army in 1952. He was a close friend of Colonel Hasan Akhavi and was a member of General Arfa''s National Movement Party.⁵³ In view of Abbas Farzanegan's key military role in approaching, infiltrating and subverting key officers and units in the Iranian armed forces and also preparing, planning and executing the coup in cooperation with Roosevelt and Carroll of the CIA, the hypothesis that the Farzanegan brothers were Roosevelt's "Boscoe Brothers" gains strength and seems plausible. This is especially the case if one accepts Woodhouse's observation on the military connections of the Boscoe Brothers. Gholamreza Nejati has already suggested that the "Boscoe Brothers" could have been the Farzanegan brothers in real life.⁵⁴

Abbas Farzanegan is probably the most important military link between the CIA station in Tehran and different groups of military personnel in the

---

⁴⁶ Gasiorowski, in *Mohammad Mosaddeq*, p. 236.　⁴⁷ Wilber, p. 21.
⁴⁸ Wilber, Appendix D, p. 4.　⁴⁹ Wilber, Appendix D, p. 4.　⁵⁰ Wilber, Appendix D, p. 5.
⁵¹ Roosevelt, p. 80.　⁵² Zahedi, pp. 116–119.　⁵³ Mohammadi, p. 158.　⁵⁴ Nejati, p. 359.

city and in garrisons throughout Iran. Farzanegan was sent back to Tehran from Washington in early July with the mission to "renew all of his old contacts within the Iranian army".[55] The main concern of the CIA headquarters was to develop a new "fighting force" in time to enter into action in case Mosaddeq disobeyed the Shah's royal edict dismissing him.[56] The CIA's concern was based on its assessment of an absence of "CIA and SIS military assets capable of being organized into an effective fighting force".[57] Naturally, before the first coup on 15 August, the CIA was prudently considering the possibility of Mosaddeq's non-compliance with the Shah's royal edict (*farman*) and was subsequently planning the necessity of a military riposte. The task of founding and organizing a new military organization was entrusted to Abbas Farzanegan and Carroll. They needed to start from scratch and "work quickly to find powerful friends among Iranian army troop commanders".[58]

In mid-July, Carroll, who was in London, panicked when he realized that General Zahedi did not control any of the five brigades – two armoured brigades and three mountain brigades – in Tehran.[59] The First Armoured Brigade, with its headquarters at the Qasr garrison, was commanded by Colonel Rostam Nowzari; the Second Armoured Brigade, at the Jay garrison, was under the command of Colonel Naser Shahrokh; the First Mountain Brigade, at Mehrabad, was commanded by Colonel Ali Parsa; the Second Mountain Brigade, at Jamshidabad, was under the command of Colonel Ezatollah Momtaz; and the Third Mountain Brigade, at 'Eshratabad, was commanded by Colonel Hoseynqoli Ashrafi. Zahedi believed that he could rely on his military contacts and friends in the Imperial Guards (headed by General Ne'matollah Nasiri), the police (headed by Colonel Nasrollah Modabber), the Armed Custom Guards (headed by Colonel Mohammad Daftari), and the Department of Army Transportation (*edareh motoriye artesh*) (headed by Colonel Hasan Akhavi).[60] Carroll believed that if the TPAJAX plan was to succeed, assets had to be developed within the five brigades in Tehran.[61]

Roosevelt arrived in Tehran on 19 July 1953, and Carroll followed on 21 July. On his arrival Carroll contacted Abbas Farzanegan and the two men set out to forge a new military organization to move against Mosaddeq. Two "old and good friends of Farzanegan", Major General Nader Batmanqelich and Colonel Hasan Akhavi, proved to be especially promising contacts.[62] Batmanqelich headed the Department of Army Transportation and Akhavi was his second-in-command, until the former left and the latter replaced him.[63] The two officers knew one another well and were also well connected to other influential army officers. Colonel Mohsen Mobasser, who headed the

---

[55] Wilber, Appendix D, p. 5.   [56] Wilber, Appendix D, p. 5.   [57] Wilber, Appendix D, p. 5.
[58] Wilber, Appendix D, p. 6.   [59] Wilber, Appendix D, pp. 6, 8.
[60] Wilber, Appendix D, p. 8; Mohammadi, p. 157.   [61] Wilber, Appendix D, pp. 8–9.
[62] Wilber, Appendix D, p. 9.   [63] Mohammadi, p. 157.

inspectorate of the Department of Army Transportation, was transferred in July 1953 by Akhavi to head the Inspectorate Office of the army's Counter-Intelligence Office (*ra'is sho'beh tajasos rokn dovom artesh*). Mobasser served in this highly sensitive post throughout the days leading up to and including 28 Mordad (19 August), all the while in league with the anti-Mosaddeq conspirators.[64]

According to Hoseyn Fardust, a close friend and confident of the Shah as well as being very knowledgeable about the Iranian political scene, Colonel Hasan Akhavi, Farzanegan's close friend, was the designer and planner of 28 Mordad.[65] Akhavi, who had served under General Arfa' as the head of the army's Counter-Intelligence Office, possessed a thorough knowledge of senior army officers: their personal and private files, their profiles and their political leanings. Akhavi was one of the few officers in the country with a vast and detailed database on the Iranian senior officer corps.[66] He had a retentive memory and knew almost 90 per cent of all Iranian officers.[67] After the ascent of General Haj Ali Razmara as the Chief of Staff, General Arfa''s protégés, including Akhavi, were purged from sensitive positions in the army. Akhavi was sent to the Department of Army Transportation, yet he continued to play an important role in promoting people to key positions, extending his circle of "client" officers. It was Akhavi who, employing his exceptional memory and knowledge of Iranian senior officers, suggested Colonel Nasiri as commander of the Imperial Guards when the Shah was searching for a reliable and loyal officer.[68] When the detailed planning of the coup against Mosaddeq began in Tehran, Akhavi joined Farzanegan and Carroll in the Military Secretariat, charged with the military aspects of Mosaddeq's overthrow. Akhavi's network and connections within the army seemed comparable to that of Asadollah Rashidiyan among the civilians.

In view of Colonel Akhavi's widespread connections with active military officers and Zahedi's lack of any real plan of action, as well as his "manifestly weak position among" the active military officers, the CIA decided to "seize the opportunity".[69] The CIA's new combat network of Iranian officers was thus forged on the already existing circles of acquaintances and patron–client relations of three key officers: Farzanegan, Akhavi and Batmanqelich. Initially, the CIA interacted with Akhavi through the intermediary of Farzanegan. Akhavi was charged with developing "a military plan" which would include the important task of identifying and recruiting collaborating "military forces".[70] By 30 July, Akhavi had drawn up and presented two plans, which seemed "pitifully inadequate" to the CIA operatives

---

[64] Mohsen Mobasser, Iranian Oral History Collection, Harvard University, Transcript 2, p. 5; Mohammadi, pp. 159–161.
[65] Fardust, p. 176.   [66] Mohammadi, pp. 132–133.   [67] Fardust, p. 181.
[68] Fardust, vol. 1, pp. 180–181.   [69] Wilber, Appendix D, p. 10.
[70] Wilber, Appendix D, p. 10.

in Tehran.[71] However, Akhavi's plans indicated that "he was in touch with three young colonels who might possess important strength within the Tehran garrisons".[72] Akhavi had also informed Carroll that "he had friends who could control the Second and Third Mountain brigades".[73] Akhavi's collaborationist friends were not the commanders of Tehran's brigades, but their deputy commanders and regimental commanders. Akhavi was alluding to Colonel Zand Karimi, who was Colonel Momatz's deputy at Jamshidabad, where the Second Mountain Brigade was stationed, and Colonel Rowhani, who was Colonel Ashrafi's deputy at 'Eshratabad, the base of the Third Mountain Brigade. Zand Karimi turned out to be an exceptionally important contact as he had "a long list of assets within the Tehran garrisons".[74] Through his contacts, Zand Karimi "was in touch with every infantry battalion commander in Tehran and with most of the company commanders.[75] The problem which remained was that these individuals needed to be "formed into an organization".[76]

News of Zand Karimi's network of military friends was the break that the CIA planners were waiting for in order to infiltrate and recruit allies within the five brigades in Tehran. This information enabled the military planners to overcome their main weakness of being cut off from operational military forces, by securing collaborators within the five army garrisons that commanded forces and fire-power. The time was now right for Carroll to meet Akhavi, who seemed to have certain concrete elements from which a military plan could be constructed. On 2 and 3 August, Carroll met Akhavi and Farzanegan and they "began staff planning".[77] At the next meetings, on 5 August, Carroll met Akhavi's friend, Zand Karimi, at the American Embassy.[78] At this meeting Zand Karimi presented Akhavi and Carroll with his list of contacts, "particularly among deputy commanders and regimental commanders".[79] In addition to friendly regimental and battalion commanders, Zand Karimi singled out as his "primary friends" colonels Hamidi of the Tehran Police, Ordubadi of the Tehran District Gendarmerie, and Mansurpour of the Third Mountain Brigade.[80] Zand Karimi was convinced that along with his accomplices – Rowhani, the deputy commander of the Third Mountain Brigade; Khosrowpanah, commanding officer of the Second Mountain Brigade's Infantry Regiment; and Yusefi, soon to be named commanding officer of the Third Mountain Brigade's Infantry Regiment – victory was assured.[81] On 6 August, Carroll, Farzanegan and Akhavi met at Batmanqelich's house in Karaj.[82]

---

[71] Wilber, Appendix D, p. 10. [72] Wilber, Appendix D, pp. 10–11.
[73] Wilber, Appendix D, p. 11. [74] Wilber, Appendix D, p. 12.
[75] Wilber, Appendix D, p. 12. [76] Wilber, Appendix D, p. 13.
[77] Wilber, Appendix D, p. 11.
[78] Wilber, Appendix D, p. 12; Nejati (Vasiyatnameh Sargord Doctor 'Elmiyeh), p. 524.
[79] Wilber, Appendix D, p. 12. [80] Wilber, Appendix D, p. 12.
[81] Wilber, Appendix D, p. 12. [82] Nejati (Vasiyatnameh Sargord Doctor 'Elmiyeh), p. 524.

The web that was being woven around Farzanegan, primarily through the intermediary of Akhavi, had now expanded considerably. On 9 August, Akhavi met the Shah and presented to him the names of all the officers cooperating with the coup. In his own way, the Shah confirmed that if he were to sign the royal edict dismissing Mosaddeq and appointing Zahedi, he would "desire military support".[83] Akhavi was delighted to hear this as he could then report back to the military conspirators that the Shah approved of the coup, thereby partially legitimizing their action. At this time, the only civilian aware of the list of collaborating officers seems to have been Asadollah Rashidiyan, who had presented their names to the Shah before Akhavi met the monarch.[84] The meetings between Carroll and his Iranian military collaborators continued throughout 11, 12 and 13 August. In these meetings "staff planning continued based upon the use of forty line commanders within the Tehran garrisons".[85] Reflecting on the TPAJAX coup operation in Iran after 28 Mordad, Wilber wrote that "In Iran we developed and recruited young colonels after very quick assessment".[86] This recruitment was made possible through the network of Farzanegan, Akhavi and Zand Karimi.

The concerted and persistent efforts of the core group of conspirators – namely Carroll and the Military Secretariat – had yielded a reliable operational network of some "forty line commanders" within the Tehran garrisons. If the collaborationist officers outside the five garrisons, such as the police and the Armed Custom Guards, are added to this number, it demonstrates the efficiency with which the conspirators succeeded in connecting with already semi-organized pro-Shah and pro-Zahedi military groups and rapidly establishing a viable military network. By 13 August, the date of the last meeting of the Military Secretariat with Carroll, it seems that Carroll and Goodwin believed that they possessed a solid military plan and commanded reliable and well-placed military personnel to carry it out.

What proved to be of great importance, in retrospect, was that Carroll had also meticulously drawn up a contingency plan in case his "first team" of officers was arrested. Carroll's main concern was that his "first platoon of young officers" may be arrested before the overthrow of Mosaddeq.[87] Along with Farzanegan and Zand Karimi, Carroll decided that the alert signal for all those involved would be the arrest of Zand Karimi and his closest friends, most probably Rowhani, Khosrowpanah and Yusefi.[88] If, for whatever reason, contacts between the masterminds and the executors were severed, the battalion and company commanders involved in the plot would adopt an auto-pilot system: whatever their directives had been would need to be carried

---

[83] Wilber, Appendix D, p. 15. [84] Wilber, Appendix D, p. 15.
[85] Wilber, Appendix D, p. 15. [86] Wilber, Appendix E, p. 15.
[87] Wilber, Appendix D, pp. 13, 14. [88] Wilber, Appendix D, pp. 13, 14.

out independently by the commanders involved.⁸⁹ As long as the "go" signal for the operation was given before the arrest of Zand Karimi and his closest friends, the military machine executing the coup plan was to follow through the course of action. Zand Karimi assured his friends that he was in the position of contacting lower unit commanders within 48 hours after the receipt of the Shah's royal edict dismissing Mosaddeq and replacing him with Zahedi.

From Wilber's account of the planning phase of the coup, it is evident that the full military plan drawn up by Carroll, Farzanegan, Akhavi and Zand Karimi involved officer teams from all of the infiltrated units.⁹⁰ By the end of July, Akhavi and Zand Karimi possessed assets in the Second and Third Mountain Brigades. As time went by, officers and operational teams from the other three brigades were drawn into the web. The military plan for the fall of Mosaddeq involved a broad range of military personnel from various garrisons and was not at all limited to the Imperial Guard, whose loyalty to the Shah was a given and who played a key role in the unsuccessful first coup d'état on 25 Mordad.

Akhavi and Zand Karimi had not been in direct contact with Zahedi for several months prior to the coup.⁹¹ Akhavi, in connection with Carroll and Farzanegan, operated independently from Zahedi. While Zahedi remained the military leader of the coup plan, he was purposefully not privy to the details of who was involved and how the plans were to unfold. According to Fardust, Zahedi's role in the success of the coup was minimal, while it was due to Akhavi's disciplined and widespread organization and his exceptional planning that the coup succeeded.⁹² It was only subsequent to Akhavi's meeting with the Shah on 9 August, and upon the Shah's suggestion that he should meet with Zahedi, that such a meeting took place.⁹³ At this time Zahedi was not involved in the details of the staff planning and military operation, but he was briefed about its important elements. It was not until 11 August, and following a three-hour discussion between Farzanegan and Zahedi, that Zahedi appointed Farzanegan as the "liaison officer between himself and the Americans for military purposes".⁹⁴ Ardeshir Zahedi referred to this meeting and wrote that at this time his father appointed Abbas Farzanegan as the liaison between him and "our friends in the military organizations".⁹⁵ On 12 August, Farzanegan accompanied Batmanqelich and Zand Karimi to meet General Zahedi. At this meeting, Zand Karimi reported to Zahedi on the progress of the military staff planning.⁹⁶

---

⁸⁹ Wilber, Appendix D, p. 14.   ⁹⁰ Wilber, Appendix D, p. 14.
⁹¹ Wilber, Appendix D, p. 15.   ⁹² Fardust, p. 180.
⁹³ Wilber, Appendix D, pp. 14, 15, 16.   ⁹⁴ Wilber, Appendix D, p. 16.
⁹⁵ Zahedi, p. 121.   ⁹⁶ Wilber, Appendix D, p. 16.

While information about the military phase of TPAJAX was being passed on to Zahedi, the general "did not know of the young officers involved and General Batmanqelich knew of only a few".[97] The junior officers were briefed on their responsibilities in the military plan once the signal was given to them by Zand Karimi, after the royal edict was in the hands of Zahedi and his supporters. On 13 August a final meeting was held between Carroll, Batmanqelich and the Military Secretariat composed of Farzanegan, Akhavi and Zand Karimi.[98]

By late evening on 13 August (22 Mordad), the royal edicts (*farmans*) signed by the Shah and written by Hirad were delivered to Zahedi by Nasiri.[99] Iranian sources set the time of Zahedi's receipt of the *farmans* at 11:00 p.m.[100] Since the Military Secretariat and Carroll had agreed that Zand Karimi needed 48 hours to contact the 40 implicated "line commanders", the time for commencing the military plan was set for the late evening of Saturday 15 August (24 Mordad).[101] After the receipt of the royal edict, the decision to start operations on the night of 15 August was made at Zahedi's hideout at Mostafa Moqadam's house, in the presence of Colonels Eskandar Azmudeh, Zand Karimi, Rowhani, Nasiri, Khosrowpanah, Reza Keynejad (a prominent merchant) and Mostafa Kashani (Ayatollah Kashani's son).[102] The CIA station in Tehran was informed of the exact time of execution on the evening of 14 August (23 Mordad).[103]

According to Zand Karimi's confessions, a meeting was scheduled for the night of Friday 14 August at Soheyli's house, which at the time was at Rashidiyan's disposal. At this meeting, Zahedi, Daftari and Dadsetan, in addition to a number of other officers and non-military personalities, were supposed to have been present. Suspecting that the house was under surveillance, this meeting was cancelled.[104] Another meeting was convened by Zahedi at Moqadam's garden at 8:00 a.m. on 15 August (24 Mordad), or some 16 hours before the first coup. Present at the meeting were Zahedi, his son Ardeshir, Batmanqelich, Farzanegan, Gilanshah, General Taqizadeh, Ha'erizadeh, Faramarzi and a few unnamed members of parliament.[105] At this meeting Zahedi spoke about the eventuality of Mosaddeq disobeying the royal edict that was to be handed to him by Nasiri, and informed those present of their responsibilities and obligations.[106] If Mosaddeq were indeed

---

[97] Wilber, Appendix D, p. 16.
[98] Wilber, Appendix D, http://www2.gwu.edu/~nsarchiv/NSAEBB/NSAEBB28/appendix%20D.pdf
[99] Wilber, pp. 37–38; for a different account see Baniahmad, p. 156.
[100] Nejati (Vasiyatnameh Sargord Doctor 'Elmiyeh), p. 516.
[101] Nejati (Vasiyatnameh Sargord Doctor 'Elmiyeh), p. 516.
[102] Nejati (Vasiyatnameh Sargord Doctor 'Elmiyeh), pp. 516, 524; Askari, p. 311; Torbatiy-e Sanjabi, p. 17.
[103] Wilber, p. 39.   [104] Nejati (Vasiyatnameh Sargord Doctor 'Elmiyeh), p. 516.
[105] Zahedi, p. 112; Baniahmad, p. 177.   [106] Zahedi, p. 112.

to resist, the military forces dispatched by Zand Karimi, Khosrowpanah and Azmudeh were supposed to arrest him.[107] At first, Mohammad Daftari was designated to present the royal edict to Mosaddeq; but apparently he was given a more sensitive responsibility, and therefore this task was conferred upon Nasiri.[108]

---

[107] Nejati (Vasiyatnameh Sargord Doctor 'Elmiyeh), p. 518.
[108] Nejati (Vasiyatnameh Sargord Doctor 'Elmiyeh), p. 518.

6

The precision coup flops: back to the drawing-board

As the hour of execution of the military plan approached, the activities of certain groups of collaborationist officers intensified. What actually happened on the evening of 24 Mordad (15 August) among the officers involved in the coup can be gleaned only through the very limited sources that have reported on these activities. From 7:30 p.m. until 11:00 p.m., when the first coup was launched, an important core of the conspirators composed of Farzanegan, Batmanqelich, Taqizadeh, Sha'ri, Aftasi, Kajehnouri and Navvabi gathered at Kashanian's house to discuss the final details of the operation with General Zahedi, who was himself constantly on the move to fend off the possibility of being arrested.[1]

Earlier that night, Colonel Mansurpour of the Third Mountain Brigade, Captain Nasrollah Sepehr of the Second Mountain Brigade, Majors Sepehr and Amanollah Safa'i of the Second Mountain Brigade and a group of other officers gathered at Tehran's Boat Club. Before they dispersed, Colonel Khosrowpanah of the Second Mountain Brigade joined them and issued their military orders.[2] This group of officers, led by Colonel Mansurpour and Khosrowpanah, who were on Zand Karimi's original list of collaborating officers, controlling platoons, companies and regiments within the Second and Third Mountain brigade, had taken a common vow to support the first coup. Whereas the commander of the Second Mountain brigade, Colonel Ezatollah Momtaz, was one of the few brigade commanders who remained undoubtedly loyal to Mosaddeq, his deputy, Zand Karimi, was the key to turning various officers in the five brigades in Tehran against Mosaddeq. The fact that Momtaz's brigade had, without his knowledge, been so widely and deeply infiltrated by pro-coup officers, does not come as a surprise since the inspectorate of the army's Counter Intelligence Office, headed by Colonel Mobasser, which was responsible for keeping an eye on such subversive

---

[1] Zahedi, p. 113.   [2] Nejati (Vasiyatnameh Sargord Doctor 'Elmiyeh), p. 525; Nejati, p. 392.

activities, was in league with the plotters. Momtaz's ignorance of what was going on amongst his direct subordinates may demonstrate that the plotting officers were successful in keeping the finer details of the coup secret, even though the general subject of an imminent coup was well publicized by the Tudeh newspapers a few days before the coup. It is also possible that Momtaz's additional assignment of defending Mosaddeq's house after the events of 28 February broke his close ties with his brigade.

At 10:30 p.m. Colonel Nasiri, the commander of the Imperial Guards, arrived at the Baghesha garrison accompanied by Major Fardust, Major Rokni, Lieutenant Jahanbin, Captain Salimi and Lieutenant Riyahi.[3] Nasiri and his companions had driven from the Sa'dabad garrison, the headquarters of the Imperial Guards, to meet the officers under the command of Major Hoseyn Atefi, who had joined their cause. The Baghesha garrison was strategically located in the neighbourhood of Mosaddeq's house and Nasiri wished to secure it before delivering the royal edict to Mosaddeq. At Baghesha, Nasiri read out the Shah's royal edict, underlining that Mosaddeq had been dismissed and informing the officers present that they needed to execute the Shah's orders.[4] Repeating his instruction at Sa'dabad garrison to the personnel of the Imperial Guards, Nasiri invoked the gravity of the political situation, reminding the officers at Baghesha that the Tudeh Party had gained control of the country, that sections of the army were collaborating with them, that the Shah had decided to dismiss Mosaddeq, and that he was himself executing the Shah's orders.[5]

While at the Baghesha garrison Nasiri consulted with General Gilanshah and Colonels Khosrowpanah and Azmudeh. The four officers coordinated the details of their final plans before the overthrow operation was put into motion.[6] Gilanshah briefed the officers and soldiers present at Baghesha garrison on their precise assignments and instructed two truck-loads of soldiers, fully armed and ready under the command of Lieutenant Askari, to escort Nasiri, Fardust, Jahanbin and Salimi – driving in two green Buicks – to Mosaddeq's house.[7] At 11:45 p.m., before Nasiri's departure on his mission, Lieutenant General Kiyani, Mosaddeq's deputy Chief of Staff, came to the Baghesha garrison unexpectedly. General Riyahi, who had been nervous about the rumours of a coup, had come to the Chief of Staff headquarters at that time of night and had dispatched Kiyani to the Baghesha garrison, which was also home to the Imperial Guards, the Shah's most loyal forces.[8] As a preventive measure, Nasiri, who believed

---

[3] *Khandaniha*, 27 Mordad, 1332. The Major Fardust accompanying Nasiri is Nosratollah Fardust, Hoseyn Fardust's brother, since at this time Hoseyn Fardust was in Paris; see Fardust pp. 171, 173, 174.
[4] *Khandaniha*, 27 Mordad, 1332.
[5] Nejati (Vasiyatnameh Sargord Doctor 'Elmiyeh), p. 518.
[6] Nejati (Vasiyatnameh Sargord Doctor 'Elmiyeh), p. 518; *Khandaniha*, 27 Mordad 1332.
[7] *Khandaniha*, 27 Mordad 1332.   [8] Baniahmad, p. 30.

that Kiyani would oppose the operation, arrested his superior officer, clearly displaying the intentions of the conspiring anti-Mosaddeq officers. At Bagheshah, almost certain of victory, Nasiri informed the officers present of the new appointments after the arrest of Mosaddeq and the instalment of Zahedi as Prime Minister. He announced that Batmanqelich was to be appointed as the new Chief of Staff and that Daftari was to become Zahedi's new Chief of Police.[9] Nasiri informed those present that once the operation had been successfully completed, Mosaddeq would be taken to the Officers' Club, and from there he would be exiled to a country of his choice. Tehran's radio station would broadcast the Shah's message to the people at 6:00 a.m. the following day – 16 August 1953.[10]

At around 11:00 p.m. on 15 August, a group of officers and soldiers stationed at Sa'dabad garrison descended on Hoseyn Fatemi's house, which had been under surveillance for some time, its telephone line having already been disconnected.[11] This assault team was under the command of Captain Shaqaqi and Lieutenants Naraqi, Ja'farbay and Mohsen Eskandari, and its members belonged to the Imperial Guards. Fatemi, the mercurial Minister of Foreign Affairs, was returning home from a party when he was arrested at his home near Sa'dabad. He and his wife were mistreated and Fatemi was immediately deployed to Sa'dabad garrison. Half an hour later, at 11:30 p.m., two truck-loads of soldiers commanded by the same officers who had arrested Fatemi (Captain Shaqaqi, Lieutenants Naraqi, Ja'farbay and Mohsen Eskandari), attacked and forcefully entered a house in Za'faraniyeh, a northern suburb of Tehran, where three of Mosaddeq's very close civilian and military associates lived. Unable to find Riyahi (Mosaddeq's Chief of Staff), they rounded up Zirakzadeh (a high-profile pro-Mosaddeq Member of Parliament) and Haqshenas (the Minister of Roads).[12] They too were arrested and dispatched to Sa'dabad garrison. Having become anxious about the rumours of an impending coup, Riyahi had gone downtown to his office at around 11:00 p.m. and was out of danger. Of the four officers responsible for the arrest of Mosaddeq's ministers, appointees and associates, three were members of the clandestine military network of the "Devotees of the Shah".

At around midnight, while at Bagheshah garrison, Colonel Eskandar Azmudeh dispatched two truck-loads of soldiers, under the command of Captain Belari, to assist Nasiri in his mission to arrest Mosaddeq.[13] At around 11:30 p.m., accompanied by one truck-load of his well-armed soldiers, Azmudeh, the commander of the Pahlavi Regiment, set out from Bagheshah garrison. He arrived at the telephone centre of the bazaar area,

[9] *Khandaniha*, 27 Mordad 1332.   [10] *Khandaniha*, 27 Mordad 1332.
[11] Baniahmad, p. 51.
[12] Nejati (Vasiyatnameh Sargord Doctor 'Elmiyeh), p. 517; Baniahmad, pp. 38–50.
[13] Nejati, p. 519; Baniahmad, p. 85; Torbatiy-e Sanjabi, p. 17.

his military target, at around midnight. The occupation, sabotage and neutralization of the telephone centre at the bazaar – which processed and serviced all of the calls to and from key governmental buildings such as the Ministry of Interior, the Office of Propaganda, the police headquarters, and the Chief of Staff headquarters – was crucial to the success of the first coup.[14] Colonel Azmudeh proceeded as planned, overcame the staff at the telephone centre and cut off the communication system by taking out the fuse box. At around 00:15 a.m. Azmudeh headed towards Mosaddeq's house as planned, and there he learnt of Nasiri's failure to arrest Mosaddeq. He then returned to the telephone centre, and at around 2:00 a.m. he replaced the fuse box and reconnected the telephone system.[15] In order to completely sabotage the city's communication system, Zand Karimi was assigned to occupy the telephone centre at Ekbatan. The extent to which he succeeded in carrying out his mission is not clear.

The military phase of the first coup, which started late at night on 15 August, and which according to the London Draft of the TPAJAX Operational Plan was supposed to culminate in the arrest of key government officials, was foiled in the early hours of Sunday 16 August.[16] Colonel Khosrowpanah, along with Azmudeh and Zand Karimi, were responsible for dispatching troops to Mosaddeq's house in case Mosaddeq were to disobey his own dismissal edict, as handed to him by Nasiri.[17] Therefore, military units from the First Mountain Brigade under the command of Azmudeh, from the Second Mountain Brigade under the command of Zand Karimi and Khosrowpanah, and from the Third Mountain Brigade under the command of Rowhani were assigned to assist Nasiri in the arrest of Mosaddeq. Shortly after Mosaddeq signed the receipt of the Shah's royal edict at 1:00 a.m., Colonel Nasiri, who had delivered the royal edict and planned to arrest Mosaddeq, was himself arrested by Colonel Momtaz.[18] With Nasiri's arrest and the high state of alert of forces loyal to Mosaddeq, General Batmanqelich, who was supposed to have occupied Riyahi's headquarters, thus paving the way for Zahedi's ascent to power, "lost heart and went into hiding".[19] The other forces converging on Mosaddeq's house to help Nasiri arrest Mosaddeq returned to their barracks when they witnessed the arrest of Nasiri. The first radio announcement of the aborted coup went on air at 7:00 a.m. on 16 August.[20]

At 6:00 a.m. Farzanegan entered the American Embassy, gave a report of the events and was rushed into hiding by the Embassy staff.[21] At 8:00 a.m. Ardeshir Zahedi gave news of his whereabouts and "[Kim] Roosevelt drove

---

[14] Torbatiy-e Sanjabi, p. 20; Nejati (Vasiyatnameh Sargord Doctor 'Elmiyeh), p. 519.
[15] Nejati (Vasiyatnameh Sargord Doctor 'Elmiyeh), p. 519.   [16] Wilber, Appendix B, p. 25.
[17] Nejati (Vasiyatnameh Sargord Doctor 'Elmiyeh), p. 518.   [18] Baniahmad, p. 86.
[19] Wilber, p. 42.   [20] *Ettela'at*, 25 Mordad 1332.   [21] Wilber, pp. 44, 45.

to Shemiran to hear that Ardeshir and his father felt that there was still hope in the situation".[22] Earlier, at 6:00 a.m., as Farzanegan was entering the American Embassy, General Mehdi Sepahpur (Iran's Air Force commander) called Mosaddeq to inform him that the Shah and Queen Soraya had taken off in a plane from Kelardasht and enquired what he should do about the situation. Sepahpur asked Mosaddeq whether he should force the airplane to land or shoot it down. Mosaddeq paused before responding *"begozarid beravad"* ["Let the plane go"].[23]

After the defeat of the first coup, Mosaddeq's close civilian and military associates, as well as his supporters, were overcome by a premature sense of relief. Mosaddeq, however, seemed more stunned, perplexed and uneasy. The peculiar issue that seems to have escaped many of Mosaddeq's military officers – or perhaps it did not, but they had insufficient time to examine it carefully and draw the necessary conclusions – was that a military coup carried out in the dark of the night, in a city under martial law, had effectively gone unhampered until the assailants were close to attaining their final objective. The coup forces were freely able to deploy truck-loads of soldiers and military vehicles – including jeeps transporting the belligerent officers and armoured vehicles – across the city without being stopped, checked, inspected or arrested. The police and military units responsible for maintaining martial law and guarding the city seemed to be blind, absent or complaisant. Equally as important as the infiltrated units whose commanders had actively joined the anti-Mosaddeq coup, were the complaisant and passive units and personnel whose commanders had adopted a neutral position of wait-and-see, thus increasing the coup's chances of success. By refusing to put up any opposition to the coup, they had in effect aided it. Many of the commanders who were active participants in the first coup were arrested, but the equally dangerous commanders who neither commited to nor counteracted the attempt were largely left untouched.

THE FIXED AND VARIABLE FACTORS OF TPAJAX

In the original British "Operation Boot", which later became TPAJAX, two British networks of Iranians were to play key roles in the ousting of Mosaddeq. This was because the British had two kinds of dependable resources or assets: first, an urban organization run by the Rashidiyan brothers; and second, a tribal organization led by a number of tribal leaders in the south.[24] The urban organization led by the Rashidiyan brothers "included senior officers of the army and police, deputies and senators, mullahs, merchants, newspaper editors and elder statesmen, as well as mob leaders".[25] According to "Operation Boot", it was the urban organization which would take the

---

[22] Wilber, p. 45.   [23] Davarpanah in *Ettela'at*, 28 Mordad 1358.   [24] Woodhouse, p. 118.
[25] Woodhouse, p. 118.

lead and seize control of Tehran and arrest Mosaddeq. Simultaneously, the tribal leaders would move towards the major cities in the south. As a backup plan, and in case of resistance to the seizure of Tehran by the Tudeh Party, the tribes would occupy key towns such as Esfahan and Abadan.[26]

In the spectacularly unsuccessful operations that took place late at night on 15 August (24 Mordad), it was only army units – and especially platoons and companies of the Imperial Guard – which played an active part. In the plan for action drafted by SIS and CIA in June 1953, two possible approaches for putting Zahedi in power were advanced: a) a "quasi-legal" operation, whereby the Shah named Zahedi as Prime Minister by royal edict (*farman*); or b) a military coup.[27] The June plan recommended that the "quasi-legal" method be tried first. It seemed that the operation that started on 15 August had elements of both approaches. Nasiri, supported by units of the Imperial Guard and anti-Mosaddeq army units, was to hand Mosaddeq's dismissal letter to him and, if possible, arrest him. This "quasi-legal" move was carried out within the context of a military plan, whereby designated units from the Mountain Brigades were responsible for rounding up influential pro-Mosaddeq officers and politicians, thus occupying and neutralizing sensitive communication and military centres. The June plan included an important provision. The "quasi-legal" operation required that "at least part of [the] machinery for the military coup will be brought into action".[28] The plan stipulated that if the "quasi-legal" approach were to fail, a "military coup will follow in matter of hours".[29] This implied that not all of the collaborative assets in the Iranian military could be committed to the first coup. On 15 August (24 Mordad), the "quasi-legal" method was combined with a limited military operation into a simultaneous thrust; when it failed, all was not lost as pre-planned alternatives were available. The availability of such pre-planned operations did not imply that they had to be followed to the letter.

As far back as late June 1953, when Roosevelt presented Operation TPAJAX for the first time to the high-powered US team in Washington, he was highly concerned with one issue. He believed in its plans, but was weary and nervous about becoming too committed to its finer details. Roosevelt believed that the "most" that could be done in terms of meaningful planning was to "define an objective".[30] Two months before the first coup, he wrote: "I did not want someone in Washington, London or wherever peering over my shoulder later on, saying 'wait this isn't what you said you would be doing'".[31] Woodhouse was in perfect agreement with Roosevelt on the fact that it was a "mistake to have too cut-and-dried a plan in advance".[32] Once Roosevelt and Woodhouse were convinced that Operation Ajax was "feasible", they both agreed that "everything" about the conducting of business to

---

[26] Woodhouse, p. 118. [27] Wilber, Appendix A, p. 3. [28] Wilber, Appendix A, p. 3.
[29] Wilber, Appendix A, p. 3. [30] Roosevelt, p. 1. [31] Roosevelt, pp. 1–2.
[32] Woodhouse, p. 120.

attain the objective of the operation "would depend upon a resourceful commander in the field".[33] Irrespective of what the SIS and CIA bureaucrats believed, for those who were putting it into action Operation Ajax was goal-driven; therefore, it was important that it would be able to shift from one plan to another almost automatically should insurmountable barriers in one plan obstruct the attainment of the final objective. As long as the lead operators controlling the major "assault" networks were free, and so was the Shah-approved alternative to Mosaddeq, only the fall of Mosaddeq would turn off the machine. The fixed objective was the overthrow of Mosaddeq, while the means to that end were variable. The idea of a single, one-time coup – a golden bullet that would attain its target with absolute certainty and would therefore not need a backup plan – was a reckless game for daredevils. The overthrow operation possessed an in-built self-adjustment mechanism that would enable it to change course immediately. As long as key assault units were not compromised, by decreasing or increasing the dosage of various political and military inputs that were to bring down Mosaddeq's government, the big plan remained intact.

Subsequent to the arrest of a number of officers after the first coup, the Military Secretariat proved capable of providing leadership for those units whose leading officers had been arrested, replacing the arrested officers by others and maintaining contact with and reorienting the large number of officers that remained unscathed from the original plan. Looking back on both the first and second coups, Wilber pointed out that in the planning phase of an operation it was important to factor in the possibility that "some elements within our friendly forces will be exposed".[34] Based on how the second coup was planned and executed, Wilber suggested that "danger signals should be included which automatically call for movement from one phase to the other depending upon who or what units have been exposed to the hostile government".[35] In his assessment, Wilber revealed the value of allowing for possible changes in the plan in case an attempt was compromised or foiled. As if providing an explanation for how the failure of 15 August was transformed into the success of 19 August, Wilber remembered that "In Iran there was good reason to believe that danger signals so noted prior to the change of government were instrumental in keeping alive an operation which, to an outsider, appeared to have failed".[36]

WHY DID THE FIRST COUP FAIL?

Two main arguments can be presented for the failure of the first coup. It has been argued that the delaying of the military action, while the word was out that a coup was under way, was partially responsible for its failure.[37]

---

[33] Woodhouse, p. 120.   [34] Wilber, Appendix E, p. 19.   [35] Wilber, Appendix E, p. 20.
[36] Wilber, Appendix E, p. 20.   [37] FRUS, vol. x, pp. 747–748.

The scheduling and subsequent postponing of military action may have had adverse consequences. The plotters had first decided on 10 or 11 August as "D-Day". They subsequently postponed it to the night of 14 August and finally decided to carry it out late at night on 15 August. Pro-Mosaddeq officers knew of these delays and changes before the Tehran CIA station.[38]

The most commonly agreed-upon reason for the failure of the first coup is that its plan of action was betrayed.[39] Military personnel from the Tudeh Party's Officer Organization had their ears and eyes wide open at this time. Some of them had successfully infiltrated various pro-Shah organizations. Major Mehdi Homayouni, a member of the Tudeh Party's Officers Organization, was also a member of the conspiratorial organization of officers plotting the first coup.[40] On 8 August, Colonel Azmudeh, who was recruiting anti-Mosaddeq officers, informed Homayouni of the details of the coup.[41] Azmudeh assumed that Homayouni, a member of the conspiratorial organization of the "Devotees of the Shah", was loyal to the Shah and opposed to Mosaddeq. By 7 August, Rashidiyan had met the Shah and it was agreed that "action should be taken on the night of either 10 or 11 of August". As soon as the details of the coup plan were discussed with junior and senior officers, the Tudeh Party knew about it; this is why the Tudeh newspapers were writing about a coup days before the first coup occurred.

According to one account, Mohammad-Ali Mobasheri, the Secretary of the Tudeh Party's Officers Organization, was tipped off by a member of his organization and called Mosaddeq directly, informing him of the impending coup.[42] According to another account, during the day of 15 August, it was Ali-Asghar Fouladvand, a pro-Mosaddeq commander of the Imperial Guards, who informed Mosaddeq of Nasiri's planned coup.[43] After the coup, Fouladvand's role in exposing the first coup is said to have become known, and he was exiled to Esfahan, where he soon died – reportedly of food poisoning.[44]

The role of nationalist and Communist pro-Mosaddeq officers is clear: on being informed of the coup, they informed Mosaddeq of its imminent occurrence. The vast and often open recruitment effort of the plotting officers exposed their plans to the threat of being uncovered. However, the abundance of rumours about a coup had almost rendered Mosaddeq insensitive to the news, thus freeing the hands of the plotters. Coup stories and scenarios flooded the public sphere through newspapers and provided the plotters with a shield of normality, as the topic had become almost a burlesque tale. It is therefore quite possible that the specific and detailed information provided by

---

[38] Wilber p. 39; B. Amir-Khosravi, *Nazar az Darun be Naqshe Hezb Tudeh Iran* (Tehran: Ettela'at, 1375), p. 527; Nejati (Vasiyatnameh Sargord Doctor 'Elmiyeh), p. 520.
[39] Wilber, p. 38; FRUS, vol. x, p. 747.   [40] Amir-Khosravi, p. 526.
[41] Amir-Khosravi, p. 526.   [42] Amir-Khosravi, pp. 528–529.
[43] Nejati (Vasiyatnameh Sargord Doctor 'Elmiyeh), pp. 520–521.   [44] Nejati, p. 606.

Hoseyn Ashtiyani on troop movements in Tehran during the night of 15 August constituted the last straw compelling Mosaddeq to take the coup threat seriously and prepare against it.

At 11:30 p.m. on 15 August, while returning to his home at Nahr-e Karaj (later known as *Boulvar-e Elizabet*), Ashtiyani observed a few tanks and armoured vehicles, accompanied by five jeep-loads of officers, driving from the Bagheshah garrison and parking in front of his house.[45] The fact that the officers spoke very softly amongst themselves and began blocking the street by turning away anyone who approached their military column made Ashtiyani more suspicious. He called Mosaddeq's house and gave details of what he had observed. Acting on this information, Mosaddeq placed the officers in the house on alert; when he tried to contact the army headquarters he realized that the phone had been cut off, which in turn convinced him that the coup was underway.

One of the reasons for the failure of the first coup was that at the last minute Mosaddeq acted on the information he had previously received from the Tudeh Party, nationalist circles and other concerned private sources, and ordered Momtaz to arrest Nasiri and disarm the Imperial Guards. There is no record of Mosaddeq being warned by his intelligence, security or counter-intelligence services, or by the office of his Military Governor. Their silence was ominous as it indicated their utter inefficiency, their voluntary insensitivity or their collaboration with the conspirators.

The Tudeh Party's infiltration of pro-Shah military organizations was important as it allowed them to obtain information about plots against the government and pass it to their leadership; their leadership subsequently shared this information with Mosaddeq. In the first coup, due to the long time-lag between the decision to execute the coup and its actual execution date, the pro-Mosaddeq officers had enough time to learn about the coup and report it, and for the government to take the minimum necessary precautions. The plotters were to learn from this error. In the second coup, the time lapse between the decision to launch the coup and the launch itself was so short, and the operational information so tightly guarded, that the Tudeh Party and the nationalists were upstaged. Ironically, some pro-Mosaddeq officers actually ended up taking part in the anti-Mosaddeq military operations.

URGENTLY RETHINKING TACTICS

Whereas the broad picture of the second coup, composed of the planning and execution phase, can be outlined with relative clarity, the finer details between the plan and the execution phase are more difficult to discern. In contrast to the first coup plan, which was prepared and formulated by the Military Secretariat composed of the Iranian military and CIA advisors, the planners

---

[45] Baniahmad, p. 25–27.

of the second coup were different in composition. The coup plan of 19 August (28 Mordad) was drawn up by key civilian and military Iranian conspirators and the CIA coordinators of the coup in Tehran. In the second coup, the perpetrators were individuals taking orders from civilian and military Iranian ring-leaders, while in the first coup the civilians hardly played any executive or operational role. Understanding the happenings and details between the planning by the masterminds and the execution by the perpetrators requires knowledge of how, when and where the masterminds contacted their subordinates, passed them their assignments and explained to them their objectives, parameters and timetable. When necessary, a detailed description of the unfolding of the second coup may be used as a proxy for the assignment, objectives, parameters and timetable given to the perpetrators by the masterminds. However, such a description fails to shed light on either the degree to which the perpetrators deviated from, innovated, botched or improvised upon their exact briefs, or on how, when or where they received their brief. One could argue that if all these missing parts were systematically documented and made available, then the operation could not be considered a coup, given that a coup requires secrecy for its success.

By their very nature, coups d'état are not supposed to leave behind any detailed traces that might compromise the conspirators after their accession to power. This is especially so when they are managed and administered by foreigners whose interests are deemed by the majority as running contrary to national interests. Coups are secretive, clandestine operations, with minimum traceable evidence and documentation on the finer details of how the "job" was carried out. Here, transparency is anathema to coups. The flow chart of the chain of command – namely who planned and who implemented, who took and who gave orders, who was a military and who was a civilian actor – is neither supposed to be clear, nor is it supposed to be discussed after the event. By definition, if researchers on coups wish to penetrate beyond generalities and beneath the surface, they would enter very murky waters, with all the attendant hazards and rewards. Yet, an attempt needs to be made to bring clarity to these muddy waters, wherever possible.

If Mosaddeq was to be overthrown, a plan of action different from the one of 15 August had to be put into place and lessons from the former misadventures had to be quickly learnt. The anti-Mosaddeq collaborationist army officers had failed to overthrow Mosaddeq by themselves. Their plan had been compromised and part of their assets exposed. Some of those officers arrested or in danger of being arrested had been involved in recruiting and networking from day one; they risked exposing the conspiratorial network within the army. Carroll (the paramilitary expert) and Roosevelt (the CIA agent in charge of TPAJAX) must have known that unless they were to move very quickly, what remained of their military network would be totally jeopardized by the confessions of the arrested officers. Just as the nationalist officers had their moles amongst the conspirators, the collaborationists must

The precision coup flops: back to the drawing-board

have had their discreet ears and eyes among the nationalist officers who started interrogating the arrested officers from 10:00 a.m. on 16 August.[46]

From 17 August, Zand Karimi, the officer in the Military Secretariat most connected with and therefore knowledgeable about the identity of the young collaborationist officers, started to confess. His interrogator was Captain Siyavosh Behzadi.[47] Less than one month after the second coup, the same Captain Behzadi was appointed as an interrogator in the high-profile team that was convened and approved by the Shah to prosecute Mohammad Mosaddeq.[48] Behzadi, whose credentials were approved for appointment to the sensitive position of interrogator during Mosaddeq's trial, must have been a trusted figure of the post-coup military brass – and perhaps he was in collusion with the collaborating officers from before the coup. Later, Behzadi became a three-star general and the Chief Prosecutor of Iran's military courts.[49] It can be surmised that whatever incriminating information Zand Karimi divulged during interrogations was immediately passed on to the collaborating officers planning for the second coup, enabling them to take whatever precautionary measures were required.

In his 17 August confessions, Zand Karimi mentioned Akhavi, who had conveniently become "very sick". As evidence mounted against Akhavi, on 18 August (one day before the second coup) Akhavi staged a most dramatic show in front of Riyahi, the Chief of Staff, confessing that he had betrayed Mosaddeq, but not divulging any useful information.[50] When on August 18 Zand Karimi was confronted by Akhavi in the presence of Riyahi, Akhavi encouraged Zand Karimi to tell all that he knew; there was no reason to hide the truth as Riyahi had promised that if they were to cooperate they would be granted amnesty.[51] Zand Karimi confessed to approaching certain key brigade commanders of Tehran, such as Colonel Ashrafi, the commander of the Third Mountain Brigade and the acting Military Governor of Tehran, to ask for their collaboration. Zand Karimi informed his interrogators that Ashrafi had promised him that even though he could not openly support the operations against Mosaddeq, he would not oppose any such actions and would surrender at the right time.[52] Zand Karimi's confessions from 17 August confirmed that the army brigades had been heavily infiltrated and had participated in the coup, that a number of the key military ring-leaders of the coup were at large, and that the conspirators were in cahoots with the staff of the American Embassy.

Even though by 8:30 p.m. on Tuesday 18 August (27 Mordad) the main outline of the first coup, including its actors, had been divulged, it was not until the morning of 19 August, when the second coup was well under way,

---

[46] Nejati, p. 599.   [47] Nejati, p. 599.
[48] Be Ravayat-e Asnad-e Savak, *Jebhey-e Melli* (Tehran: Markaz-e Barrasiy-e Asnad-e Tarikhiy-e, 1379), p. 9.
[49] Nejati, p. 598.   [50] Nejati, p. 600.   [51] Nejati, p. 600.   [52] Nejati, p. 601.

that Colonel Alinaqi Shayanfar, the nationalist Martial Law Prosecutor in charge of the arrested officers' case, reported on the full scope of the first coup to Mosaddeq.[53] It was at this point that Mosaddeq became aware of the full complicity of the Americans and the collaboration of Ashrafi (his Military Governor and martial law administrator).[54]

Given the extent to which Mosaddeq's military system had been infiltrated by collaborationist officers, it is safe to assume that the unscathed collaborationist officers had received word about the confessions of the arrested conspirators, in which case they knew that no sensitive information had been divulged concerning the uncompromised officers in their network. They may also have known that Mosaddeq was not informed of these findings by the time the second coup was launched and that their co-conspirators could safely continue to pursue their plans while occupying their sensitive positions in the military. For the conspirators, speedy action was of the essence if they were to use the remnants of their military network for another anti-Mosaddeq operation. Mosaddeq's followers, as well as the military officers loyal to him, had to be taken by surprise, just as they had been on 9 Esfand. The anti-Mosaddeq forces knew that the popular and unorganized pro-Mosaddeq supporters were slow to mobilize and react.

Foremost, a different, more imaginative, multi-dimensional plan was needed. Such a plan had already been drawn up by SIS and CIA during their joint mid-June meeting in London. The "Operational Plan" of TPAJAX envisaged three possible "situations" for the overthrow of Mosaddeq. According to "Situation A", action on the coup day would involve "a massive religious protest against the Mosaddeq government... followed immediately by military action".[55] Based on this operational plan, a hybrid course of action, employing the abundant resources of the conspirators – the ruffians – was selected: a loosely coordinated two-pronged paramilitary–military stratagem in Tehran.

THE MODIFIED HYBRID MULTI-PHASE PLAN

According to the newly modified plan, pure military action played second fiddle to a loosely but well-coordinated initial "great demonstration". The galvanizing spur of this new operation was to be a well-staged pro-Shah and anti-Mosaddeq show of force by the underclasses, the socio-economic marginals, the poor, the petty vendors, the *meydan* (Tehran's main fruit and vegetable market) errand boys, the racketeers and the hoodlums. The direct organizers of this anti-Mosaddeq and pro-Shah outpouring of rage and zeal were to be the influential and powerful thug leaders of Southern Tehran. This "popular demonstration" of patriotism needed to be clerically endorsed and

---

[53] Nejati, p. 604; Nejati (Vasiyatnameh Sargord Doctor 'Elmiyeh), p. 524.
[54] Nejati, p. 602.   [55] Wilber, Appendix B, p. 13.

promoted. Most importantly, it was to be financed by CIA–SIS funds earmarked for this purpose through the good office of Asadollah Rashidiyan and his network, which had for years cultivated this milieu. As it swept across the south–north axis of the city, this "popular demonstration" was intended to create a snowball effect within the larger population.

A key complementary component of this plan was the entrance of a phalanx of previously informed and collaborating army, police and Custom Guard military personnel on the side of the pro-Shah and anti-Mosaddeq demonstrators. This important phase would occur gradually once the demonstrators had occupied, secured and sealed off their targeted perimeters within Tehran. The injection of the armed military personnel into the civilian demonstrators would take various shapes and forms, culminating in scenes of "fraternizing" with the pro-Shah demonstrators. The initial waves of the military joining the crowd would have symbolic and numerical significance, demonstrating the unity between the "masses and the army" for ousting Mosaddeq. The occupation of lightly defended government buildings was made possible by the joint effort of thugs, the police and army personnel. The seizure of the more sensitive and heavily defended centres such as the headquarters of the Chief of Staff, the police headquarters and the Military Police's prison required more powerful arms.

The success of the operation depended on a modicum of coordination and collaboration between the two key actors (who were not necessarily acquainted with one another): the southern Tehran ruffians and the infiltrated military units. This task of coordination, crowd management, leadership, improvisation, problem-solving and innovation on 28 Mordad (19 August) was assigned to the Jalali–Keyvani network and their domestic anti-Mosaddeq political organizations. From the early morning hours, the forces under the command of the TPBEDAMN organization were gradually to infiltrate the demonstrators at various points of their march. Their job was to manipulate the crowd by delivering fiery speeches, to direct them towards particular targets, and to encourage them to move on to the next target once their sacking, looting, vandalizing, burning down, or occupying and neutralizing of buildings had been completed. Members of this important auxiliary force were to play a key role in feeding the crowds with information and misinformation throughout the day of the overthrow, as well acting as facilitators whenever snags threatened the success of the second coup. The Jalali–Keyvani team and the associated political organizations which they controlled under the umbrella of TPBEDAMN were to act as political commissars and shock troopers as well as match-makers between the thugs and the collaborating army and police personnel.

The "great demonstration" would jump-start the operation. Tehranis, who had witnessed three days of lawlessness through demonstrations, would initially be neither shocked nor surprised by another demonstration. The planners of the operation hoped that by the time the infiltrated military units entered in force, strengthening the momentum of the coup by brandishing their guns and occupying certain symbolically important targets, Mosaddeq's followers would be so confused and disoriented that they would be totally paralysed. This comprehensive plan of action had its own backup plan. The conspirators were to seek military support from garrisons in Kermanshah, where Colonel Teymur Bakhtiyar was the commander of the Armoured Brigade, and from Esfahan, where Colonel Amirqoli Zargham was the deputy of the Esfahan Army. There was also talk of the conspirators establishing their base in a "liberated zone" if the coup were to fail.[56]

Contrary to the 15 August (24 Mordad) late-night coup attempt, during which the conspirators had placed all their faith in primarily American-planned efficient military operations, on 19 August (28 Mordad) the full capacity of the British and American networks was being tapped. In the modified plan the conspirators drew upon the talents and strengths of all the assets and collaborators they had developed in Iran over the years. One of the key elements which sealed the success of the 19 August coup plan is found in Wilber's reflection on the lessons learnt from the military planning aspect of the coup d'état. Wilber writes that "The basis of a <u>coup d'état</u> is security which permits us to exercise operational surprise".[57] The speed and surprise with which the second coup struck – only four days after the failure of the first – hypnotized and subdued the pro-Mosaddeq forces: they became mere bystanders of the demise of their hard-won political achievements. A British source, reporting to the US Department of State a week after the coup, attributed the success of the 19 August coup d'état "to the fact that it was well planned, that it was kept secret and that plenty of money was made available to carry it out".[58]

Whereas the first coup was almost advertised and publicized, the second coup was conducted under air-tight security conditions. On 13 August (22 Mordad), the Tudeh Party newspapers had started reporting on an imminent coup led by prominent military figures such as Zahedi, Batmanqelich, Garzan, Shahbakhti, Dadsetan and a few others.[59] Warnings of a coup were repeated on 14 August. The plans for the second coup were conducted under maximum security and executed less than 36 hours later. The decision to initiate the second coup with a hired mob was informed by the fact that neither the Tudeh nor the nationalists, who had informed Mosaddeq of the first coup, had any connections with the thugs and ruffians of Southern Tehran. It was Rashidiyan, Qanatabadi, Behbahani and Kashani who were familiar with this social category.

---

[56] Wilber, p. 52; Zahedi, p. 134.   [57] Wilber, Appendix E, p. 18. The underline is Wilber's.
[58] FRUS, vol. x, p. 786.   [59] Jami, pp. 650–651.

THE STARS ARE ALIGNED FOR THE COUP-MAKERS

The unfolding of events from Sunday 16 August (25 Mordad) played directly into the hands of the conspirators. It seemed as though everything was working in their favour. The sense of relief, elation and empowerment following the defeat of the first coup, and the arrest of a handful of military officers and Court officials, resulted in the government's lowering of its guard. The disarmed Imperial Guard soldiers who had been involved in the first coup were not arrested, but at 11:00 a.m. on 16 August five truck-loads of them were sent packing from their base at Sa'dabad to the Baghesha garrison.[60] The general feeling among Mosaddeq's partisans was that the heralded coup had taken place and had been defeated. Over-confidence in Mosaddeq's government spawned irreparable laxity. Who could believe that the conspirators could and would strike again within three days? The official announcement of the referendum dissolving the 17th Majles, on Sunday 16 August (25 Mordad), and the news of the Shah's flight in the afternoon of the same day caused political uncertainty and concern. Foreign Minister Fatemi's fiery speech on the same day, against the monarchy in Iran, delivered at the huge pro-government demonstration held in Baharestan at 5:45 p.m., added consternation and disquiet to a state of anxiety amongst those Iranians who until that moment did not think of their support for Mosaddeq as an anti-Shah choice. The destruction of the statutes of Reza Shah Pahlavi the next day (Monday 26 Mordad) did not sit well with many Iranians and gave the impression of lawlessness.[61] The anti-Shah agitations, demonstrations and street battles of the Tudeh Party and their call on 27 Mordad for the establishment of a "Democratic Republic" evoked a state of general chaos; this in turn played into the hands of the anti-Mosaddeq propaganda that the Prime Minister was a pawn, manipulated by the Communists.

In this muddled political atmosphere, those military personnel who had sworn allegiance to the Shah and who were also loyal to Mosaddeq were left in a difficult bind. The three days that highlighted the Mosaddeq–Shah dichotomy weakened the Mosaddeq camp. Iranians did not seem at ease with the choice of *either* the Shah *or* Mosaddeq, a choice that the Tudeh Party and the anti-monarchist, republican circles around Mosaddeq were presenting. Perhaps they would eventually have opted for Mosaddeq and rejected the Shah and the monarchy. But to make that choice, three days were clearly insufficient and therefore they became withdrawn. The fact that, between Sunday and Wednesday, the public had become used to an atmosphere of disorder desensitized them to what was to happen in Tehran on Wednesday 19 August.

---

[60] Baniahmad, p. 49.
[61] On the dismantling of Reza Shah's statues, see Bozorgmehr, p. 357; K. Sanjabi, *Omidha va Naomidiha* (London: Nashre Ketab, 1968), p. 142.

7

Second coup capabilities of the military networks

Following the first coup, of the three Iranian members of the Military Secretariat involved in the planning and recruitment process of the operation, Zand Karimi was the first to be arrested. He began revealing sensitive information during his interrogation at 20:30 p.m. on 18 August (27 Mordad). In his preliminary confessions Zand Karimi simply provided information on the planning of the first coup and, except for Farzanegan and Zahedi, all of the other collaborationist officers whose identities he revealed had already been arrested. Later, after being informed that Colonel Azmudeh – who had also been arrested – was accusing him of organizing the coup, Zand Karimi provided important background information and some leads on the conspirators.[1] Had there been more time, and had Zand Karimi continued to reveal the collaborationist network of officers, his confessions could have led to the dismantling of the military network. The second member of the Military Secretariat, Akhavi, was in hospital and was not even questioned until the day of the second coup.[2] Riyahi, the Chief of Staff, had full confidence in Akhavi and worried that if Akhavi was arrested he would commit suicide; he therefore prevented his official arrest and interrogation. On the day of the second coup, Riyahi briefly questioned Akhavi in the presence of Zand Karimi. But Akhavi's shrewd role-play as the sick and repentant officer enabled him to not divulge any important information about his connections.[3] The third Iranian member of the Military Secretariat, Farzanegan, remained free, and as of the morning of August 16 he was in the safe custody of the Americans and "concealed" by the CIA station in Tehran.[4] Farzanegan, an official US agent and the primary ring-leader of the plotting officers, had effectively constructed the military network; along with Carroll he was privy to all information about assets and collaborators in all military

---

[1] Nejati (Vasiyatnameh Sargord Doctor 'Elmiyeh), p. 524.
[2] Nejati (Vasiyatnameh Sargord Doctor 'Elmiyeh), p. 525.
[3] Nejati (Vasiyatnameh Sargord Doctor 'Elmiyeh), p. 525.   [4] Wilber, p. 50.

and police branches. As much as the capture of Zand Karimi was an important blow to reactivating the military network for the second coup, there was no relevant, valuable or essential information about remaining assets, their backup plans, their garrisons, functions or the forces that they commanded that was not known to Farzanegan, who had from the outset participated in all staff planning sessions.

Another key player who was deeply involved in various stages of the coup and who was in the leadership group of the "Devotees of the Shah" was General Hedayatollah Gilanshah, the commander of the Iranian Air Force before he was retired by Mosaddeq. After the failure of the first coup, Gilanshah, who was also free and under American protection, was appointed by Zahedi as the coordinator of the overthrow operation in Tehran.[5] He was the only Iranian officer who was known to John Foster Dulles before the coup. At the June meeting, the Secretary of State had directly asked Kim Roosevelt about the role that Gilanshah was to play in the overthrow operation.[6] From the confessions of the arrested officers after 15 August, it was evident that Gilanshah was in contact with various military groups involved in the coup project.[7] The fact that Farzanegan and Gilanshah were both at liberty and each had sufficient information about the respective military networks which they controlled guaranteed that the military could actively participate in a second strike against Mosaddeq.

Most importantly, General Zahedi, the figurehead in the whole overthrow operation, remained untouched. Zahedi was the symbolic leader of opposition around whom the military and civilian forces had gathered. He was the emblem of the anti-Mosaddeq forces, the one to whom the conspiring officers had pledged their allegiance, and without whom the second coup would not have had anyone to replace Mosaddeq as Prime Minister. The process by which the British, the Americans, the Shah and the anti-Mosaddeq Iranians came to agree on Zahedi as a viable alternative to Mosaddeq had been a lengthy and laborious one. Had Zahedi been arrested, the anti-Mosaddeq forces would have lost their authority, cohesion and legitimacy. The first and second coups were both in the name of installing Zahedi as the Shah-appointed Prime Minister.

Even though a handsome reward was put on Zahedi's head following the first coup, he remained in the safe custody of the CIA station in Tehran. According to Roosevelt, Zahedi was taken to "Fred Zimmerman's house close to the Embassy".[8] Fred Zimmerman is probably a code name Roosevelt was using for Theodore Hotchkiss, a staff member of the US Embassy in Iran. Even though a General Zimmerman, who was attached to the American Embassy, did actually live in Tehran at the time, according to

---

[5] Zahedi, pp. 120–121. [6] Roosevelt, p. 15.
[7] Nejati (Vasiyatnameh Sargord Doctor 'Elmiyeh), pp. 518, 520, 522, 526.
[8] Roosevelt, p. 178.

Hotchkiss General Zahedi was hiding in the basement of his house, a few hundred metres away from the American Embassy on Takht-e Jamshid Street, from late Monday night on 26 Mordad until 1:00 p.m. on Wednesday 28 Mordad.[9]

Key inner-circle figures such as Gilanshah, the Rashidiyan brothers and Ardeshir Zahedi – axial contacts with the military networks that needed to be reactivated for the 19 August coup – had found sanctuary at the CIA station since the morning of Sunday 16 August (25 Mordad).[10] According to Wilber, "These people had to be concealed by the station, both in order to secure them from arrest and also have them in places to which Americans could logically and easily go".[11] In the absence of the sanctuary provided by the US, the whole Iranian inner circle of the coup might have been hunted down and arrested. American hospitality alleviated them of the necessity of being constantly on the move to avoid arrest, providing them with the necessary respite time to think, scheme and reorganize.

On the morning of 16 August (25 Mordad) some 20 officers were arrested or detained, creating lacunas within the established network involved in the first coup. The arrests that followed the first coup did not impair, still less cripple, the anti-Mosaddeq military network. The key Iranian plotters – Farzanegan, Gilanshah, General Zahedi, the Rashidiyan brothers and Ardeshir Zahedi – were free, safe and able to meet and confer with the CIA organizers and their Iranian contacts. The brain of the collaborationist military network was perfectly capable of reassessing, readjusting, reassigning and replanning.

The arrests did not interrupt the communication channels between the collaborationist junior officers, almost all of whom were out of danger, and the Military Secretariat in charge of the coup d'état. Farzanegan, who had been present throughout the planning and was the official liaison between Zahedi and the officers involved in the coup, knew the collaborationist officers, their military units and their garrisons. He knew whom to contact to re-establish links and send word to about future plans. Rashidiyan was also privy to some information, but it is unclear to what extent he knew of the details of the chain of command or the brief of each officer involved within each garrison. The arrests did not disrupt the chain of command and authority within military and police units, nor did they render subordinate junior officers, or soldiers already infiltrated, disoriented and dysfunctional. The more senior collaborationist officers at the apex of power remained safely in place, transferring and reallocating the responsibilities of the junior officers arrested.

---

[9] Ahmad Ashraf's interview with Theodore Hotchkiss (1926–2001), the CIA Station Operative at the US Embassy in Tehran on 22–23 December 1990 in Spencer (West Virginia); FRUS, vol. x. p. 686.
[10] Wilber, p. 50.   [11] Wilber, p. 50.

THE COMBAT STATUS OF COLONEL ZAND KARIMI'S CIRCLE OF OFFICERS

By reviewing the status of Colonel Mahmud Zand Karimi's list of six officers within various military and police units ready to cooperate with the coup against Mosaddeq, it may be possible to assess the real impact of the arrests after the first coup upon the capability of the conspiring officers to mobilize for the second. From Zand Karimi's list of three "primary friends", Esma'il Hamidi of the Tehran Police and Mansurpour of the Third Mountain Brigade were arrested, while Ordubadi, of the Tehran Gendarmerie Brigade (the third person on Zand Karimi's list), remained free.[12] As a result, the military network's ability to re-establish contacts within the Gendarmerie and mobilize its personnel remained intact. As important as Colonel Hamidi of the Tehran Police may have been in the first coup, the fact that the highest authorities in the police force were among the conspirators rendered the arrest of Hamidi insignificant for the plotters: these were Nasrollah Modabber, Tehran's Chief of Police until the morning of 19 August, and Mohammad Daftari, the commander of the Armed Custom Guards, who replaced Modabber as Tehran's Chief of Police on 19 August. Therefore, after the first coup, the police and the Armed Custom Guards remained firmly under the command and control of the conspirators.

Based on the confessions of the officers arrested after the first coup, Nasrollah Modabber (Mosaddeq's Chief of Police) was implicated with the conspirators, and the forces under his command had widely collaborated with the plotters.[13] Yet he was not arrested until midday on 19 August, when it was too late and he had already served the second coup. He ordered his forces to accommodate and cooperate with the conspirators. By the time Daftari, who was also Zahedi's appointed Chief of Police, took over from Modabber, the coup d'état was half-way through its course and the policemen on the streets of Tehran were actively cooperating with the coup forces. Throughout the day, the police at first stood by and watched, and later cheered the ruffians who were converging on their target perimeters brandishing sticks and clubs, attacking, destroying and burning property; later still, the police joined in with the thugs as they attacked the government buildings, before attacking Mosaddeq's house.

The arrest of Mansurpour of the Third Mountain Brigade had equally as little an impact upon the organization and execution of the second coup. His arrest did not breach the chain of command between the conspirators and the operational military units. According to a military report on the activities of officers who had participated in the coup, prepared after 28 Mordad (19 August), Mansurpour had done an excellent job of installing in the

---

[12] Wilber, Appendix D, p. 12.
[13] Nejati (Vasiyatnameh Sargord Doctor 'Elmiyeh), pp. 517, 521.

company under his command the belief that they should engage in all kinds of sacrifices for king and crown. Mansurpour was so successful in the indoctrination of his soldiers that, according to this report, on the day of the second coup, even though he was in prison, the doors of Tehran Radio's Broadcasting Station were opened to the assailants with the help of the company he commanded.[14] Furthermore, Mansurpour's commanding officer, Hoseynqoli Ashrafi (the commander of the Third Mountain brigade) was very strongly suspected of being in league with the conspirators. Ashrafi was not only at large, but remained the all-powerful Military Governor of Tehran. In the absence of Mansurpour, whatever contacts were to be made and military directives to be given for executing the second coup could have been issued by Ashrafi, who was perfectly free until noon on 19 August, when Mosaddeq belatedly ordered his arrest. After the success of the second coup, Ashrafi was immediately released from prison by General Zahedi, the new Prime Minister.[15]

In their first assessment of collaborationist assets in the Iranian military, the SIS believed that Ashrafi "could be relied upon".[16] The CIA and the SIS assumed "that Ashrafi was a controlled British agent and that his Third Mountain Brigade would follow his commands".[17] Later, doubts were raised regarding the degree to which the CIA and the SIS could rely on Ashrafi.[18] This may have been because the CIA and the SIS came to learn that Ashrafi was a member of the Organization of the Nationalist Officers, known for their particular loyalty to Mosaddeq. Little did they know that membership in the Nationalist Officers did not automatically mean unswerving loyalty to Mosaddeq. There were staunch pro-Shah and anti-Mosaddeq officers who were concurrently members of the pro-Mosaddeq Organization of Nationalist Officers *and* of the 'Devotees of the Shah" (an ardent anti-Mosaddeq organization), such as Colonel Azmudeh.[19]

Those Iranians involved and familiar with the files of the collaborationist officers were convinced that Ashrafi was closely in league with the conspirators and active in the two coups. According to 'Elmiyeh, who had access to the confessions of the arrested officers after the first coup, Ashrafi was in collusion with the conspirators and did play an important role in the first coup by allowing the military units involved to move freely and deploy their strike forces in a city supposed to be under strict martial law and curfew.[20] Shayanfar, who also had access to all the interrogation files of officers arrested after the first coup, was convinced that Ashrafi, who had sworn

---

[14] *Tarikh-e Moaser-e Iran*, Sal-e Haftom, Shomareh 26, Tabestan 1382, pp. 320, 322.
[15] *Khandaniha*, 3 Shahrivar 1332.   [16] Wilber, Appendix D, p. 3.
[17] Wilber, Appendix D, p. 7.   [18] Wilber, Appendix D, p. 3.
[19] G. Mossavar Rahmani, *Kohneh Sarbaz* (Tehran: Rasa, 1366), p. 213; Shahhoseyni, p. 100–102.
[20] Nejati (Vasiyatnameh Sargord Doctor 'Elmiyeh), p. 517.

allegiance to Mosaddeq and was a member of the Nationalist Officers, had colluded with the conspirators and had paved the way for their assault.[21] Since Ashrafi was free until noon of 19 August, when Mosaddeq personally ordered his arrest, he is said to have been instrumental in the military success of the coup.[22] Colonel Eskandar Azmudeh, well informed of the details of the coup and actively involved in it, confirmed that "it is perfectly true that the officials of the Military Governance (*farmandariy-e nezami*) did cooperate with the insurrectionists during 28 Mordad".[23]

Around 11:00 a.m. on 19 August (28 Mordad), Sadiqi, the Minister of the Interior, called Ashrafi, the Military Governor of Tehran. Sadiqi had received reports of small groups of anti-government and pro-Shah demonstrators freely roaming around the town, supported by truck-loads of soldiers and police chanting anti-Mosaddeq and pro-Shah slogans. He had also observed the commotions from his office at the Ministry of Interior and called Ashrafi for an explanation as to why the activities and movements of these groups were not being curtailed. Once Ashrafi informed Sadiqi that he did not trust his own soldiers, since those he had dispatched to scenes of disturbance had joined in with the demonstrators, Sadiqi suspected a ploy.[24] It must be remembered that Ashrafi had promised Zand Karimi that even though he could not openly support the operations against Mosaddeq, he would not oppose any such actions and would surrender at the right time. According to Riyahi, the Chief of Staff, Ashrafi was not a neutral accomplice but a double agent.[25] Without directly naming Ashrafi, Mosaddeq was also of the opinion that his Military Governor – Ashrafi – was in collusion with the colonialists.[26] During his trial after the coup, Mosaddeq lamented that his Military Governor and martial law administrator did not prevent the wide circulation of tanks, trucks and troops which came to arrest him and his colleagues in the very early hours of 25 Mordad. Mosaddeq explained to those prosecuting him that: "I was working with a system which was under the yoke of colonialism".[27]

Ashrafi could have also given the green light to the flexible yet focused military plan of 28 Mordad. In retrospect, Sadiqi's comment that Ashrafi was also present at his 7:00 a.m. meeting on 19 August with Mosaddeq becomes very revealing. At this meeting Mosaddeq sought a solution for the legal vacuum that was created by the departure of the Shah, asking Sadiqi to prepare for the formation of a Regency Council through a referendum.[28] Assuming that Ashrafi was in league with the conspirators, at 7:00 a.m. he knew and could inform his fellow officers that the Mosaddeq government had

---

[21] Nejati, p. 601.   [22] Nejati (Vasiyatnameh Sargord Doctor 'Elmiyeh), p. 527.
[23] Torbatiy-e Sanjabi, p. 18.
[24] Nejati (Goftogo ba Ostad Doctor Gholamhoseyn Sadiqi), p. 541.   [25] Nejati, p. 442.
[26] Mosaddeq (1365), pp. 271–272.   [27] Mosaddeq (1365), p. 272.
[28] Nejati (Goftogo ba Ostad Doctor Gholamhoseyn Sadiqi), p. 540.

absolutely no intimation of an impending coup and that the stage was clear for the execution of the second coup. If there had been any doubts or worries in the minds of the coup-makers that the plans for the second coup had been compromised, Mosaddeq's meeting with his Minister of Interior and his Military Governor, during which he was only preoccupied with the referendum and the Regency Council, would have convinced them that their plans were secure. The "old man" was planning how to involve the Iranian people in sensitive political decisions and was certain that his Military Governor would protect the government. Ashrafi may have been the officer who gave the final thumbs-up to the military conspirators, as early as 7:30 a.m. and concurrent with the movement of the mob.

Zand Karimi had three other dependable accomplices: Rowhani, Khosrowpanah and Yousefi. All three had contacts within the military that could have been reactivated for a second attempt.[29] The news of the arrest of Ali-Mohammad Rowhani and Ali-Farhang Khosrowpanah came on 26 Mordad.[30] Rowhani was the deputy commander of the Third Mountain Brigade; Khosrowpanah was the commanding officer of the Second Mountain Brigade's Infantry Regiment. Khosrowpanah's close associates – Captain Nosratollah Sepehr, Major Sepehr and Major Amanollah Safa'i, all of whom were implicated in the first coup – had not been arrested and therefore their chain of command and contacts within their units remained intact. Captain Sepehr, a company commander in the Second Mountain Brigade, had been active in the anti-government demonstrations in front of the Majles which followed the 9 Esfand plot against Mosaddeq.[31] The third trusted accomplice of Zand Karimi – whose name, unlike those of Rowhani and Khosrowpanah, appeared neither in the interrogations nor in the register of officers suspected of collaboration with the coup – was Yousefi.[32] Yousefi may have been active during the second coup, or may have decided not to collaborate with the first or the second coup. In any case, from Zand Karimi's list of six close contacts in the army, four were arrested and two were free and possibly active. Yet those knowledgeable about the contacts and confidants of those arrested were at large. These were either officers of the same rank or of superior rank within the same brigade.

Surprisingly enough, however, on 28 Mordad, along with Zand Karimi himself, two of the four arrested officers within Zand Karimi's close circle of friends – Khosrowpanah and Rowhani – managed to actively participate in the coup. At 2:00 p.m. Rowhani was freed from detention at the headquarters of the Military Police. A military eye-witness reported Rowhani directing the collaborationist tanks towards their designated targets at around 3:00 p.m.[33] He then led a group of armed soldiers to the 'Eshratabad garrison

---

[29] Wilber, Appendix D, p. 12.   [30] *Bakhtar Emrouz*, 26 Mordad 1332; Safari, p. 849.
[31] Nejati, p. 520.   [32] Wilber, Appendix D, p. 12; Nejati, p. 344–345.
[33] F. M. Javanshir, *Tajrobeh 28 Mordad* (Tehran: Entesharat Hezb Toudeh Iran, 1359), p. 309.

and freed some of the royalist officers of the Imperial Guard imprisoned there.[34] Only then did Rowhani proceed towards the final objective of the coup planners: Mosaddeq's house.[35]

By contrast, Khosrowpanah was actively assisting the royalist forces in front of the Majles at Baharestan on the *morning* of 28 Mordad.[36] He then participated in the battle in front of Mosaddeq's house during the evening.[37] On the day of 28 Mordad, Zand Karimi was at the headquarters of the Second Mountain Brigade at Jamshidabad, recruiting members of the Imperial Guard for the final stages of the coup. He too then proceeded to Mosaddeq's house.[38] While Rowhani was certainly detained at the Military Police headquarters, Khosrowpanah was almost certainly free on the day of 28 Mordad. Three explanations may clarify why some of the officers arrested after the first coup re-surfaced on 28 Mordad and played key roles in coordinating and directing the anti-Mosaddeq forces. First, some of those arrested were freed from the Military Police headquarters (*dejban*) at 2:00 p.m. on 28 Mordad, when their detention centre fell to the anti-Mosaddeq forces. Second, a number of those arrested officers were freed on 26 Mordad after a brief interrogation.[39] Third, some of them, such as Colonel Hamidi of the police and Colonel Khosrowpanah, were very loosely detained in the corridors of the Military Governor's headquarters.[40] With the chaos and confusion that reigned from about 10:00 a.m. on 28 Mordad and, in view of the fact that the Military Governor's office was collaborating with the conspirators, those detained in the corridors could have easily slipped out.

THE NETWORK OF THE DEVOTEES OF THE SHAH: FORTY LINE COMMANDERS

Wilber's report of the CIA operation in Iran clearly refers to 40 "line commanders" within Tehran's garrisons upon whom the entire process of staff planning for Operation TPAJAX relied.[41] In the US armed forces, the term "line commander" or "line officer" refers to a commissioned officer trained for combat and commanding such a unit. Wilber neither directly divulges the names of these line commanders nor sheds light on their organization, but he does emphasize the importance of these line officers in the execution of the overthrow operation. Operation TPAJAX was not dead once the first coup failed. It was revisited after the first coup by the Iranians and Americans who had participated in its conceptualization, and was converted into a plan much better adapted to the resources available.

---

[34] *Tarikh-e Moaser-e Iran*, Sal-e Haftom, Shomareh 26, Tabestan 1382, p. 322.
[35] *Tarikh-e Moaser-e Iran*, p. 322.   [36] Wilber, p. 67.   [37] *Tarikh-e Moaser-e Iran*, p. 322.
[38] *Tarikh-e Moaser-e Iran*, p. 322.   [39] Baniahmad, p. 108.   [40] Baniahmad, pp. 108, 109.
[41] Wilber, Appendix D, p. 15.

From around September 1952, or almost a year before August 1953, Zahedi's opposition to Mosaddeq had become public.[42] On 13 October 1952, retired General Hejazi and the Rashidiyans (father and sons) were arrested on charges of plotting with General Zahedi to overthrow Mosaddeq's government. It was probably between September and October 1952 that a group of disenchanted high-ranking officers – active and retired – including Nasiri, Gilanshah, Bakhtiyar, Rowhani, Batmanqelich, Mozayyani, Bayandor, Sha'ri, Taqizadeh and Aftasi, secretly contacted one another, met and organized.[43] Such a time-frame also coincides with Henderson's report to the State Department stating that hints of a coup d'état were becoming more open. To these discontented officers, General Zahedi was the only viable opposition to Mosaddeq and the only person who had proven his courage as well as his desire for change by challenging Mosaddeq and putting himself up as an alternative. Zahedi and the dissatisfied officers around him "formulated a plan" to counter what they identified as the two immediate dangers threatening the country. To them, Mosaddeq's policies endangered the monarchy and assisted an impending takeover by the Communist Tudeh Party.[44] To dispel what they believed were imminent dangers to the country and the king, they saw no alternative to the overthrow of Mosaddeq. To that end they founded the clandestine society of the "Devotees of the Shah" (*jam'iyat-e fadaiyan shah*).[45] The creation of the "Devotees of the Shah" coincided with Zahedi's regular meetings with the staff of the British Embassy, and Falle reports that Zahedi was intensifying his activities.

This network of the "Devotees of the Shah" was composed of pro-Shah "teams" (*ekip*) of three or four officers. Each officer in a team occupied a sensitive position in the military, the Ministry of War or the office of the Chief of Staff. Each team was connected to a liaison officer trusted by General Zahedi. The officers entering this clandestine and conspiratorial military organization against Mosaddeq took a ceremonial oath to willingly sacrifice all that was required for the defence of homeland and monarchy.[46] Zahedi and Batmanqelich stood at the apex of the organization, while Nasiri, Gilanshah, and Teymur Bakhtiyar, along with a few of their trusted collaborators, acted as liaisons between the leadership and the teams.[47] The officers in a team knew only of their own team commanders. The liaison superior officers alone were knowledgeable of other teams. The network was organized in such a way that in the event that any of the superior officers – such as Zahedi, Batmanqelich, Bakhtiyar, Nasiri, Gilanshah, or Rowhani – were arrested, other trusted officers stood in reserve and could step in and replace their arrested colleagues, continuing to coordinate the activities of the teams within the network.[48]

---

[42] Rahnema, pp. 688–698.   [43] Baniahmad, pp. 159, 161.   [44] Baniahmad, p. 159.
[45] Baniahmad, p. 161; Shahhoseyni, p. 104.   [46] Baniahmad, p. 161.
[47] Baniahmad, p. 161.   [48] Baniahmad, p. 162.

The "Devotees of the Shah" was composed of an initial nucleus of officers. At around the time of the second coup a large number of officers joined this nucleus.[49] The original network of the "Devotees of the Shah" was composed of at least 35 officers: General Fazlollah Zahedi, Lieutenant General Nader Batmanqelich, Lieutenant General Hedayatollah Gilanshah, Colonel Teymur Bakhtiyar, Colonel Ne'matollah Nasiri, Ali-Mohammad Rowhani, Colonel Amirqoli Zargham, Colonel Ali-Farhang Khosrowpanah, Colonel Mehdi Hey'at, Colonel Najmeddin Mar'ashi, Colonel Naser Hojabr Kiyani, Colonel Ali Moradiyan, Colonel Mahmud Zand Karimi, Captain Javid(pour), Captain Amanollah Safa'i, Major Asadollah Kavousi, Colonel Mansurpour, Major Majlesi, Major Habib Balari (Baladi), Major Mehdi Homayouni, Major Esma'il Yavari, Major Sepehr, Major Ali-Akbar Mowlavi, Captain Razaqi, Captain Naraqi, Lieutenant Vakili, Lieutenant Mo'ezzedin Daneshfar, Lieutenant Riyahi, Lieutenant Ghaffari, Major Khalil Sayyadiyan, Major Jalili, Captain Eskandari, Captain Ja'farbay, Captain Asgari and Captain Abbas Bahrami.[50] In compiling this important list, Baniahmad was assisted by the Iranian army after the coup. Even though it may not be exhaustive, Baniahmad's list does shed light on the composition of an important anti-Mosaddeq conspiratorial organization that had long stayed in the shadows. Colonel Shayanfar, a sympathizer of the pro-Mosaddeq Nationalist Officers' Organization (*Sazeman-e Afsaran-e Nasiyounalist*) and the Prosecutor of the Military Governor's courts before the second coup, recalled that he was approached by the "Devotees of the Shah", requesting that he join their group. He was told by the person who approached him that Colonel Azmudeh wished him to join this pro-Shah officers' organization.[51] The officer who approached Shayanfar referred to Habibollah Jahangiri and Mr. Zare' as other members of the "Devotees of the Shah".[52]

The existence and operation of the conspiratorial organization of the "Devotees of the Shah" is corroborated by other sources. Major Mehdi Homayouni, a member of the Tudeh Party's Officers Organization, whose name also appears on the initial list of the "Devotees of the Shah", recalled being a member of an organization of 25 officers whose contact person with the leadership of the plotting officers was Nasiri. Homayouni does not provide a name for this organization. According to Homayouni, the leadership team was composed of Gilanshah, Batmanqelich, Nasiri and Eskandar Azmudeh, while Baniahmad intimates that it comprised Zahedi, Batmanqelich, Bakhtiyar, Nasiri and Rowhani.[53] Homayouni recalled the names of 14 other officers in his team, which seems to have been one of the branches of the "Devotees of the Shah". Those whom Homayouni remembered were Safa'i, Ordubadi, Zand Karimi, Akbar Zand, Shaqaqi, Sepehr, Sa'idi, Javidpour, Kavusi, Balari, Mar'ashi, Ra'isiyan, Khosrowpanah and Majlesi. The information

---

[49] Baniahmad, p. 162.   [50] Baniahmad, pp. 162–167.   [51] Shahhoseyni, p. 102.
[52] Shahhoseyni, p. 102.   [53] Amir-Khosravi, p. 526; Baniahmad, p. 162.

provided by Homayouni about the conspiratorial officers' organization he belonged to is crucial as it corroborates accounts of this clandestine organization, better known as the "Devotees of the Shah", given by others.[54] During the first coup, under the command of Azmudeh, Homayouni participated in occupying and neutralizing the telephone centre at the bazaar.[55]

Homayouni accounted for 15 officers (14 plus himself) from a military organization which he claimed to be composed of 25 officers. Of the 15 officers that he remembered (including himself), 5 were arrested or provisionally detained after the first coup, while ten remained at large. Zand Karimi, Khosrowpanah, Shaqaqi, Balari and Homayouni were detained, while Safa'i, Ordubadi, Akbar Zand, Sepehr, Sa'idi, Javidpour, Kavusi, Mar'ashi, Ra'isiyan, Majlesi and Rahimiyan remained free.[56] Ten names mentioned in the two rosters of Baniahmad and Homayouni overlap. Homayouni's list includes five officers who are missing from Baniahmad's and could therefore be added to obtain a more complete list of the "Devotees of the Shah". The five officers on Homayouni's list include: Ordubadi, Eskandar Azmudeh, Akbar Zand, Ra'isiyan and Sa'edi.[57] Once these five names are added to Baniahmad's list of 35 members of the "Devotees of the Shah", we arrive at 40 officers, which corresponds perfectly with the magic number of 40 collaborationist "line commanders" referred to by the CIA report as the backbone of Operation TPAJAX. Taking into consideration that Homayouni had forgotten the names of ten other officers, some of whom may have been on Baniahmad's list, we are faced with some 40 to 50 collaborationist "line commanders".

From this network of 40 to 50 officers (including General Zahedi and all his top brass), only 11 were arrested or provisionally detained after the first coup.[58] After the arrest of Nasiri, Batmanqelich, Zand Karimi and Eskandar Azmudeh the danger of a full disclosure of the conspiratorial network of the "Devotees of the Shah" in time, if the Mosaddeq government was to stay in power, increased the resolve of the conspirators to strike the final blow as rapidly as possible. On 28 Mordad, some 29 to 39 known members of the "Devotees of the Shah", in addition to members of associated cells, openly and actively operated against Mosaddeq.

Less than two weeks after the successful coup d'état of 28 Mordad, on the recommendation of Chief of Staff Batmanqelich, by endorsement of Prime Minister Zahedi, and with the final approval of the Shah, 43 officers were promoted for their exceptional services.[59] From the common Baniahmad–Homayouni list of the 40 "Devotees of the Shah", 32 were promoted. From

---

[54] Baniahmad, p. 161; Shahhoseyni, p. 102.   [55] Amir-Khosravi, p. 527.
[56] Amir-Khosravi, p. 526.   [57] Amir-Khosravi, p. 526.
[58] These officers were Nasiri, Batmanqelich, Eskandar Azmudeh, Rowhani, Khosrowpanah, Zand Karimi, Mansurpour, Baladi/Balari, Naraqi, Eskandari and Ja'farbay. See Baniahmad, pp. 71, 86; Wilber, p. 54.
[59] *Shahed*, 9 Shahrivar 1332.

the list of promoted officers known to have been members of the "Devotees of the Shah", nine were among those who had been arrested after the first coup, including Zand Karimi, Rowhani, Azmudeh, and Mansurpour; this implies that the remaining known 23 members promoted were free and active during the second coup.

First on the list, promoted to the rank of Lieutenant General, was Hasan Akhavi, whose name does not appear on the common list but who, along with Farzanegan and Zand Karimi, was probably one of the most important officers in the "leadership team" recruiting for, creating, and connecting the collaborationist military network. His name was followed by those of Dayhimi, Bakhtiyar, Zargham and Izadpanah, who were also promoted to the rank of Lieutenant General. Only two of these four (Bakhtiyar and Zargham) are mentioned in the Baniahmad–Homayouni common list of the "Devotees of the Shah". Zand Karimi was not only promoted, but was also appointed to the highly prestigious position of the Shah's Special Adjutant.[60] Habibollah Dayhimi, who was promoted after the second coup, was the same Dayhimi who had headed the Ariya Party's military branch; he was a close associate of the pro-British General Arfa' as well as a collaborator of Mozaffar Baqa'i.

An invisible protective shield that extended to key military turncoats largely facilitated the second coup. Certain highly placed collaborationist officers, occupying extremely sensitive military and security positions – such as Daftari, Ashrafi, Siyasi (the head of *rokn dovom*, the army's Counter Intelligence Office), Modabber and Mobasser – benefitted from the almost unrestrained trust of either Mosaddeq or Riyahi.[61] Their privileged position enabled them to remain unmolested between 15 and 19 August, while considerable evidence suggested that they were either in league with or were themselves personally active members of the conspiring organizations. As such, they could coordinate the overthrow operation of 19 August with great ease from within Mosaddeq's military apparatus and under the cover of loyal Mosaddeq officers. According to Mohammad Daftari's adjutant, Captain Amirqahari, "between 25 and 28 Mordad, Daftari reported on all activities at Mosaddeq's house to General Zahedi".[62] Ashrafi, Modabber and Mobasser remained in their highly sensitive military posts until noon on 19 August when the coup had entered its final phase. They were then arrested by Mosaddeq, and subsequently released later that same day after Zahedi came to power.[63] Colonel Mobasser was arrested for encouraging demonstrators to assail the headquarters of the Military Police where Batmanqelich, Zahedi's appointed Chief of Staff, was being held prisoner.[64] Mobasser has

---

[60] *Shahed*, 9 Shahrivar 1332.
[61] Nejati, p. 393; Nejati (Vasiyatnameh Sargord Doctor 'Elmiyeh), pp. 527.
[62] Javanshir, p. 307.   [63] Nejati (Vasiyatnameh Sargord Doctor 'Elmiyeh), p. 528.
[64] Nejati (Vasiyatnameh Sargord Doctor 'Elmiyeh), p. 528.

candidly confirmed the fact that on 28 Mordad he was in league with the coup officers. In his opinion he was arrested because he constituted a viable opposition force to Mosaddeq's rule on 28 Mordad.[65] According to Mobasser, at 5:00 p.m on 28 Mordad, when the political situation turned in favour of his camp, "the people poured out and freed" him.[66] At around the same time, acting as the new Chief of Staff, General Batmanqelich reinstated Mobasser in his previous position as Head of the Inspectorate office of the army's Counter-Intelligence division.[67]

Mobasser is said to have been one of the main participants in the secret meetings of anti-Mosaddeq officers plotting the first coup. Other officers present are said to have included Nasiri, Batmanqelich and Eskandar Azmudeh.[68] These secret meetings started around 8 August and were held at the headquarters of the Military Governor (*farmandariy-e nezami*).[69] According to Homayouni, who was present at these secret meetings, in addition to the conspiring officers, two civilians were also present: one was Rashidiyan, and the other was a foreigner whom Homayouni believes was Kermit Roosevelt.[70] The fact that Mobasser was involved in the coup plan and was free until noon on 28 Mordad implies that as the Head of the Inspectorate Office of the army's Counter-Intelligence he could have prevented the communication of any intelligence report on the coup to Mosaddeq and could have shielded the activities of the plotters.

Even though the military network organized by the Military Secretariat did take a beating after the arrests that followed the foiled first coup, it was by no means deactivated, dismantled or destroyed by either the arrest of all of its key figures or by the loss of contact between the masterminds of the overthrow project and its perpetrators in the armed forces. So long as Zahedi, Farzanegan, Gilanshah and key members of their military networks and subnetworks familiar with intact collaborating officers within the army and the police were at large, and so long as the royal edict appointing Zahedi in Mosaddeq's place was at hand and Mosaddeq was not overthrown, the military network had unfinished business and possessed the capability to carry out its objective. This time, however, it needed the support of other American and British-controlled Iranian assets. Reflecting on the reason why

---

[65] Mohsen Mobasser, Iranian Oral History Collection, Harvard University, Transcript 2, p. 5.
[66] Mohsen Mobasser, Iranian Oral History Collection, Transcript 2, p. 5.
[67] Mohsen Mobasser, Iranian Oral History Collection, Transcript 2, p. 5; Mohammadi, pp. 161–162.
[68] Homayouni interview with RAIOH, http://www.iranianoralhistory.de/cxy43/4662cs/28_mordad-60years.html.
[69] Homayouni interview with RAIOH, http://www.iranianoralhistory.de/cxy43/4662cs/28_mordad-60years.html.
[70] Homayouni interview with RAIOH, http://www.iranianoralhistory.de/cxy43/4662cs/28_mordad-60years.html.

the conspirators pushed ahead with a second coup despite their failure on 16 August, the CIA report on the second coup maintained that: "The station continued to feel that the 'project was not quite dead' since General Zahedi, General Gilanshah, the Rashidiyan brothers and Colonel Farzanegan were still determined to press action".[71]

---

[71] Wilber, p. 52.

8

A viable home-spun coup

One of the factors which led to the failure of the first coup was that particular military operations, such as the arrest of Mosaddeq, Riyahi and other key political figures, as well as the attack on the headquarters of the Chief of Staff and the communication centres, needed to be coordinated to the minute. The first coup was a precision military operation, tightly planned and finely tuned to almost the smallest detail. It anticipated no room for glitches or mishaps. It was also wanting in backup plans. Whereas the coup planners had thought of Mosaddeq not accepting the royal edict dismissing him, they do not seem to have contemplated Nasiri's arrest. When confronted with unexpected situations due to mishaps or incoordination among different actors of the plot, the coup-makers panicked and froze. As one key actor in the coup stalled, missed a deadline or suspended planned operations, the taut military plan constructed on the timely success of each integral part jammed and failed. When events did not go as planned the military personnel involved were incapable of initiative.

Upon arrival at Riyahi's headquarters, Batmanqelich, who was supposed to occupy the key location, "saw tanks and troops in readiness," lost heart, shirked the responsibility of carrying out his orders, and turned back.[1] Nasiri is alleged to have blamed the failure of the first coup on Zand Karimi. Nasiri believed that had Zand Karimi and his two truck-loads of soldiers arrived at Mosaddeq's house "two minutes" earlier, he would have been able to neutralize the guards at Mosaddeq's house and arrest the Prime Minister.[2] Zand Karimi and Azmudeh were supposed to occupy the telephone centres at Ekbatan and Bazaar before converging on Mosaddeq's house.[3] If Nasiri's reproach is justified, Zand Karimi must have taken longer on his first assignment than planned, jeopardizing the coordinated implementation of his second mission and causing the failure of the plot.

---

[1] Wilber, p. 42; Zahedi, p. 115. [2] Wilber, p. 42.
[3] Nejati (Vasiyatnameh Sargord Doctor 'Elmiyeh), p. 519.

Batmanqelich and Zand Karimi were not the only ones blamed for what went wrong during the first coup. Colonel Khosrowpanah was also chided for having arrived half an hour late in front of Mosaddeq's house.[4] According to another report, during the first hours of his arrest early on Sunday morning, Nasiri had blamed Khosrowpanah for not having neutralized the forces around Mosaddeq's house, and for having arrived at Mosaddeq's house with reinforcements later than planned, thereby preventing Nasiri from engaging the forces around Mosaddeq's house and arresting him.[5]

Irrespective of the veracity of these allegations, Roosevelt and Carroll must have concluded that the Iranian collaborationist officers were incapable of carrying out operations which required precision, coordination and efficient execution. Frustrated by the failure of the first coup, Wilber wrote: "most of the participants proved to be inept or lacking in decision at the critical juncture".[6] Instead of being a taut military plan, swiftly executed within a specific time period, with clearly delineated and assigned responsibilities for each main actor, the second coup had a broad overall framework of objectives, main actors, coordinators, general assignments and approximate timeframes of operation. Most importantly, the second coup no longer relied solely upon the military and as such was not a classic military coup.

The new plan was based on the cooperation of the unruly thugs with the military. Even though a lot was left to the initiative and improvisation of each participating force, their trajectories and assembly points were made known to them, as was their final objective of attacking Mosaddeq's house. Therefore, while the coup process was left purposefully adjustable and malleable, its objectives and goals were planned, clear and fixed.

THE "COUNCIL OF WAR" ON AMERICAN SOIL IN IRAN

On the evening of 17 August (26 Mordad), inside the US Embassy compound, Kermit Roosevelt and George Carroll held a "council of war with the heads of their team". At this prolonged "council of war", which lasted some "four hours", the Iranian "team leaders" present were General Zahedi, Ardeshir Zahedi, General Gilanshah, Colonel Farzanegan and the three Rashidiyan brothers.[7] Less than a few hundred metres away, US Ambassador Henderson, who had returned to Tehran on that same day, along with General Robert McClure, the commander of the US military assistance mission in Iran, were "out in the garden in front of the residency".[8] McClure was a pioneer of psychological warfare in the US Army before being posted to Iran. At the end of this sensitive emergency meeting, "it was decided that some action would be taken on Wednesday the 19th" of August 1953.[9] In preparation for the 28 Mordad operations, a division of labour among the

---

[4] *Tehran Mosavvar*, 6 Shahrivar 1332. [5] *Ettela'at*, 27 Mordad 1332. [6] Wilber, p. 39.
[7] Wilber, pp. 56–57. [8] Wilber, pp. 56–57. [9] Wilber, p. 57.

CIA–SIS assets was planned: in the words of Wilber, "several specific activities were to be undertaken".[10] It is in the context of the decisions made during the key "council of war" on 17 August that Roosevelt's cryptic comment on the date for the execution of the second coup should be understood. Roosevelt, who at the time of writing his book, tried hard to provide information without divulging details and names, wrote: "We advised the Boscoes that Wednesday August 19 must be the day. In reply they sent out word that they were ready, that they would act".[11] The fact that the Boscoes were informed and that they sent back word strengthens the argument that they were indeed Jalali and Keyvani and not the Farzanegan brothers, as Colonel Farzanegan was present at this historically determining secret meeting. According to both Wilber and Roosevelt, the coup on 28 Mordad was planned and engineered in advance.

The broad plan contained one over-arching activity to trigger the overthrow operation of Wednesday 28 Mordad. This was the civilian and popular "great demonstration".[12] It would be reasonable to argue that in view of the failure of the first coup, the Rashidiyan brothers had realistically suggested a new approach, primarily based on the abundant resources that they always controlled: the Southern Tehran ruffians. Contrary to what is commonly repeated, the main actors of 28 Mordad were not from the traditional Tehran bazaar located north of Mowlavi Street, which housed various craftsmen and guilds, but from the fruit, vegetable and meat market of the Aminosoltan, Bagh Ferdows and Sahebjam streets south of Mowlavi. This was Rashidiyan territory, while the Tehran bazaar of the craftsmen was mostly pro-Mosaddeq territory. The idea of the great demonstration was crucial as it gave direction and a final objective to this political action. The "council of war" decided to focus on the pressing fact that "it was time for loyal army officers and soldiers and the people to rally in support of their religion and the throne".[13] The plan was for one huge demonstration composed of so-called pious and religiously motivated loyal subjects of Mohammad Reza Shah, who would be joined by their Shah-loving military brothers of all ranks, creating a religious, royalist and anti-Communist flood which would wash away Mosaddeq. The success of this broad plan rested on two separate but ultimately overlapping components, one civilian and the other military.

The new plan neither specified a precise schedule for the completion of its various phases on 28 Mordad nor did it stipulate a deadline for the termination of activities; it was therefore to be an open-ended operation, continuing until the objective of overthrowing Mosaddeq was realized. The most important aspect of the operation was that "people" needed to be mobilized to start the initial march, which would allow for the unfolding of the subsequent phases of the new overthrow plan. As the "people" converged on

---

[10] Wilber, p. 57.　[11] Roosevelt, p. 180.　[12] Wilber, p. 57.　[13] Wilber, p. 57.

their pre-determined assembly points of strategic and symbolic significance, the second phase of the operation, namely the gradual appearance of "loyal army officers and soldiers" fraternizing with the people at the assembly points, would begin. The successful completion of the second phase required mobilizing the soldiers and officers and moving them from their barracks to the strategic points of assembly, without the impression being given that the troop movements were intended against the Mosaddeq government. The movement of groups and crowds in Tehran was not particularly alarming, as the previous two days had seen many such commotions; until the crowds began chanting slogans, no one would be able to tell whom they were supporting. Whereas the movement of troops could and did cause suspicion, the movement of crowds provided the best disguise, until they stated their position through their slogans and fraternized with the military. During the third phase of the plan, the patriotic "people" and the soldiers would be joined by tanks, successfully concluding the overthrow operation.

The plan needed to prepare public opinion and neutralize, to the greatest possible extent, any potential opposition to the "great demonstration". The "people" and the soldiers had to be convinced that if a pro-Shah and patriotic demonstration got underway, they should either support it or remain neutral to it – or at least not oppose it. To attain this end, two key and inter-related ideas had to be widely publicized. First, the public needed to be convinced that the "great demonstration" was in support of Islam and the monarchy; and second, that Iran was on the precipice of falling into godless Communist and Soviet hands if the Shah's newly appointed Prime Minister, Zahedi, did not take power immediately. The coup forces needed to foster the idea that opposition to a pro-Shah movement was tantamount to acting against Islam, the monarchy and the motherland. The adoption of this formula sowed confusion and hesitation among Mosaddeq's more naïve supporters, diminishing the force of the backlash that his traditional followers could cause. By highlighting God, Shah and the motherland (*khoda, shah, mihan*) the importance of defending Mosaddeq and the oil nationalization movement was minimized in the minds of the common folk. Instead the principle binaries of Islam against atheism and the Shah against Communism were emphasized and aggrandized. On the one hand, the radical anti-monarchic words and deeds of the Tudeh Party and pro-Mosaddeq forces on 17 and 18 August, and, on the other, the activities of Jalali and Keyvani's network in wreaking havoc on the city in the name of the Tudeh Party, facilitated the task of the coup forces.

At the "council of war" it was decided that Ayatollah Seyyed Mohammad Behbahani should shoulder two key responsibilities. In the absence of Behbahani at the "war council", it would be reasonable to assume that Asadollah Rashidiyan played the interlocutor between the Ayatollah and the plotters. Behbahani was to "build up" the "great demonstration" of 19 August and to travel to Qom to "try and persuade the supreme cleric,

Ayatollah Borujerdi, to issue a fatwa calling for a holy war against Communism".[14] In order to present the "great demonstration" of 28 Mordad, the spearhead of the overthrow operation, to the public as a "national Islamic uprising" inspired by Islam and nationalism, and therefore a legitimate and popular quest, the masterminds of the coup needed the approval of Ayatollah Borujerdi, the most respected religious dignitary of the land. Those present at the "council of war" must also have remembered that, a few months earlier, on 9 Esfand, Behbahani and Kashani had played an important role in dispatching some 1,000 to 3,000 thugs to the Shah's palace, thereby preventing his departure.

Behbahani was a man of great resources and initiative with a wide network of smooth politicians, intermediaries, hired hands and ruffians. It would be safe to say that his network and that of Rashidiyan overlapped. Behbahani's services, according to British sources, could be easily obtained for the right compensation.[15] Some seven months after the fall of Mosaddeq, Behbahani paid a visit to the Shah. In the midst of his criticism of the Zahedi government, the Ayatollah reminded the monarch that "on 9 Esfand and then on 28 Mordad we fulfilled our obligation and revolted".[16] Behbahani insinuated that Zahedi was corrupt and complained that after Zahedi became Prime Minister "whatever [money] was in the country or came into the country went into the accounts of various people".[17] Ironically, according to CIA files, on 26 September 1953 Zahedi gave Behbahani 10,000 Tomans (approximately $1,200), followed by a further 5,000 Tomans (approximately $600) on 3 October.[18] The real reason for the estrangement between Behbahani and Zahedi seems to have been rooted in the former's insistence that his son Ja'far should be given the portfolio of the Minister of National Economy and Zahedi's refusal to satisfy the Ayatollah's wish.[19]

One of the key components of the "great demonstration" was the active participation and show of force of loyal army officers and soldiers side by side with the "people". The task of pursuing the contacts already established and issuing new military assignments to the approximately 30 line officers left intact after the first coup was left primarily to Farzanegan and Gilanshah, who were present at the "council of war". General Zahedi and his son, also present at the "council of war", were to assist Farzanegan and Gilanshah in assuring that word was sent out to collaborationist officers about the operation on Wednesday and their particular task within it. General Zahedi was

---

[14] Wilber, p. 57. [15] FO 416/103, Biographical notes, No. 39, 1 June 1950.
[16] *Ashofteh*, 24 Farvardin 1334. [17] *Ashofteh*, 24 Farvardin 1334.
[18] National Security Archives, C01384417, from Roosevelt, 9 October 1953. http://www2.gwu.edu/~nsarchiv/NSAEBB/NSAEBB435/docs/Doc%2018%20-%201953-10-09%20Zahedi-Makki-Behbehani.pdf.
[19] National Security Archives, C01384417, from Roosevelt, 9 October 1953. http://www2.gwu.edu/~nsarchiv/NSAEBB/NSAEBB435/docs/Doc%2015%20-%201953-09-21%20Intrigues%20-%20Behbehani%20son%20-%20etc.pdf.

also in contact with some of the retired army officers, especially General Shahbakhti. These had their own trusted contacts within the army to whom they could pass on the necessary instructions.

The assignment of the military with regards to the specifics of the demonstration on 28 Mordad was three-fold. First, they were to contact their safe collaborationist contacts in the military and police apparatus, informing them that another attempt was being made to oust Mosaddeq. Second, the officers in control of regiments, battalions, squadrons and companies needed to gradually inject truck-loads of military and police personnel amongst the marching demonstrators. These troops would gradually blend with the "people", fraternizing and chanting pro-Shah, anti-Communist, and (eventually) anti-Mosaddeq slogans. They would finally form a single wave moving toward Mosaddeq's home. The third responsibility of Farzanegan and Gilanshah was more specific. At some point, preferably once the "people" and the soldiers had joined forces, as many tanks as could be mustered needed to be made available to the conspirators to support the mixed civilian–military pro-Shah and anti-Mosaddeq demonstrators. Possession of these tanks by the conspirators was crucial. Tanks were the ultimate visible symbols of military power and authority. Chanting pro-Shah slogans and displaying the Shah's portrait from the top of growling and threatening heavy tanks would give the strong impression that the Shah's partisans held absolute power. The tanks were also necessary to engage with military and police forces loyal to Mosaddeq and, if necessary, to finish the job by blasting his house, which was also the Prime Minister's office.

The last asset of the conspirators that needed to be tapped and put into motion was the TPBEDAMN organization associated with Keyvani and Jalali and its sub-networks, which had already been active in feeding the collaborationist newspapers with propaganda material. In addition to the usual black propaganda used against Mosaddeq in TPBEDAMN's network of newspapers, it was also crucial for the conspirators to disseminate the news of the royal edict – *farman* – appointing Zahedi as Prime Minister, giving them some semblance of legitimacy, on the eve of the coup day.

The plotters also planned to leave a strong psychological impression on the people of the capital city right before the coup. They hoped that throughout the anti-Mosaddeq operation of 28 Mordad the people would remember the insecurity and anarchy that had reigned during the previous few days. The task of rousing the people against Mosaddeq's alleged pro-Tudeh position was conferred upon the organization of Keyvani and Jalali. On the eve of 28 Mordad, Tehranis had to experience and witness "the Tudeh Party's" gratuitous violence, rage and destructiveness. They had to be made scared of the terror that would follow the impending Communist takeover which Mosaddeq was said to be ushering in. The people had to feel that Mosaddeq's overthrow would save them from insecurity, Communism and chaos. Tehranis also needed to be shown a preview of what was planned for the next day. They needed to witness and digest the fact that once the royalist army and the pious people bonded, they could resist, subdue, and overcome the Communists and their accomplice, Mosaddeq. According to Wilber, Keyvani and Jalali, the CIA's principal agents were "given their instructions" as what to do and how to prepare for and support the "great demonstration" by all means possible.[20] One of their main tasks was to disguise themselves as Tudeh members while ransacking and looting shops on the evening before 28 Mordad.[21]

The "council of war" also decided on an auxiliary plan to ensure the success of the second coup. The conspirators knew that this was their last chance and that if they failed, not only would Mosaddeq's position be strengthened, but the various conspiratorial networks would in time become exposed, with their members facing retribution. It was therefore decided that direct contact would be made with dependable regional commanders who were loyal to the Shah and had the courage to march on Tehran, so that if by the night of 28 Mordad Mosaddeq had not been overthrown by the "great demonstration", the full might of the collaborationist regional units would seal the success of the coup. Wilber writes that "in the field of military action, support from outside of Tehran seemed essential".[22]

Farzanegan, along with a CIA station agent, Gerald Towne, were immediately dispatched to Kermanshah, 530 kilometres from Tehran, to summon Colonel Teymur Bakhtiyar, commander of the Armoured Brigade, to march on Tehran.[23] Ardeshir Zahedi, accompanied by Carroll, was sent to Esfahan, 450 kilometres from Tehran, to make the same demand on Colonel Amirqoli Zargham, the deputy commander of the 9th Division. The CIA station provided the "messengers" with well-forged identification and travel documents in addition to "station-prepared curfew passes", which according to Wilber "stood up under inspection".[24] In his memoirs, Ardeshir Zahedi does not mention the "council of war" at all. He maintains that he went to Esfahan alone (no mention of Carroll) and on his own initiative subsequent to a meeting at Seyf-al-Saltaneh Afshar's house on the evening of Sunday 16 August, at which only his father and his close circle of friends were present.[25] It is therefore not surprising that Ardeshir Zahedi "categorically" maintains that "the fall of Mosaddeq was not the result of a CIA conspiracy".[26]

The British Memorandum, dated 2 September 1953, is devoid of Wilber's details, yet it concurs with his report on the planning of the second coup and adds certain revealing points. It states that on 17 August "it was also established that a second attempt would shortly be made to overthrow Mosaddeq's government".[27] On this same day, General Zahedi is reported to have

---

[20] Wilber, p. 56. [21] Wilber, pp. 63, 65. [22] Wilber, p. 57. [23] Wilber, p. 57.
[24] Wilber, p. 58. [25] Zahedi, vol. 1, pp. 128–135, 145–146. [26] Zahedi, vol. 1, p. 179.
[27] FRUS, vol. x, p. 783.

succeeded in winning over the commander of the motorized regiment as well as the Chief of Police.[28] On 17 August, the Chief of Police was Modabber. According to the memorandum, "the plan for the events of the 19th of August were put into operation" after Henderson's meeting with Mosaddeq on the afternoon of 18 August.[29] The same British source maintains that the plans which were being put into operation were known to only a few outside the immediate circle of plotters. "On this occasion only the commanders of regiments, the Chief of Police, and Ayatollah Bihbahani [Ayatollah Behbahani], who was responsible for organizing demonstrations, knew of the plan, and the Tudeh had therefore no chance of discovering the plot beforehand".[30] However, it would be safe to assume that beyond the seven Iranians and two Americans present at the "council of war" and who were knowledgeable about all the details of the overthrow plan, the others, including Behbahani, Modabber and commanders of regiments, were privy only to the specific parts of the plan which required their input.

AN IRANIAN INSIDER'S ACCOUNT OF THE PLAN

Hoseyn Fardust's account of the coup plan is based on what he claims to have heard directly from Akhavi, one of the three Iranian members of the Military Secretariat.[31] After the first coup, even though the evidence against Akhavi was overwhelming, he was not arrested because of Riyahi's friendship with him. Akhavi remained in hospital due to his so-called "sudden illness". Fardust's report is a more substantive and systematic account of Wilber's broad outline of the "great demonstration", connecting the missing dots in his report and providing a more complete picture of the overthrow plan. The "great demonstration" is broken down into detailed specific steps, with assigned responsibilities and 11 clearly delineated steps from the start to the overthrow of Mosaddeq. Fardust divides up the plan of action for the second coup as follows.[32] First, groups of demonstrators would assemble in precisely pre-determined locations in Tehran; the approximate number of participants in each group and their respective leaders were also determined. Second, each group was assigned to move along a pre-determined route towards Shah and Naderi streets; these different groups of demonstrators were expected to arrive simultaneously at different points of Shah and Naderi streets. Third, members of athletic clubs (such as Taj) were designated to move their cortège of demonstrators in such a fashion that they too would arrive concurrently at Shah and Naderi streets. Fourth, the assigned slogans chanted by all groups of demonstrators were to be in support of the Shah's monarchy. Fifth, members of the Imperial Guard were assigned to join the demonstrators, arming the crowd. Sixth, a fully armed tank squadron, ready

---

[28] FRUS, vol. x, p. 783. [29] FRUS, vol. x, p. 784. [30] FRUS, vol. x, p. 784.
[31] Fardust, p. 176. [32] Fardust, p. 176–182.

to engage in battle, was designated to join the demonstration. Seventh, all of the above groups would merge and join forces in Shah and Naderi streets in a highly disciplined manner and, while chanting pro-Shah slogans, would move towards Mosaddeq's house, surround it, and arrest Mosaddeq. Eighth, a small military unit would occupy the radio station. Ninth, having occupied Mosaddeq's house, his arrest would be announced over the radio. Tenth, accompanied by a tank squadron, Zahedi would proceed to the new office of the Prime Minister, install himself, and announce his cabinet. Eleventh, subsequent to the overthrow of Mosaddeq by the Shah's appointed Prime Minister, the government in place would request that the Shah return to the motherland, and upon his arrival he would be escorted with pomp and ceremony to his palace.[33] Fardust's recollection of Akhavi's account of the plan, after some 35 years, may well have been mixed with other accounts that he must have heard. The "great demonstration" did not go exactly according to the specifics of the plan recounted by Fardust, but the plan's structure, objectives, the key actors and the sequencing of the phases overlapped neatly with the events of 28 Mordad.

CREATING THE PSYCHOLOGICAL CONDITIONS CONDUCIVE TO THE COUP

By Wednesday 28 Mordad, the political events that followed the announcement of the first failed coup on Sunday morning had rendered Tehranis of all sorts edgy and nervous. Different individuals had different reasons to feel agitated. Prior to the second coup the conspirators followed three objectives. First, they sought to encourage those who opposed Mosaddeq to actively engage in overthrowing him. Second, they hoped to push those who were bystanders to become disenchanted with his government and join the "great demonstration". Third, they wished to convince or intimidate Mosaddeq's supporters into not opposing the coup. Rallying the clergy, who were influential among the common folk against Mosaddeq, was important to the success of the coup. Consequently, Ayatollah Borujerdi, Seyyed Mahmud Taleqani and numerous other clerics received threatening letters written in red ink, warning them that they would soon be hanging by their green shawls from street lamp posts.[34] The letters were signed by the Tudeh Party, giving the impression that once the Tudeh Party came to power its first victims would be religious dignitaries. These letters were forgeries written by scribes at Ayatollah Behbahani's house and mailed from there to various religious figures.[35] One of these scribes, busy writing the letters to the clergy at Behbahani's house

---

[33] Fardust, p. 182.
[34] B. Afrasiyabi and S. Dehqan, *Taleqani dar Tarikh* (Tehran: Niloufar, 1360), p. 121; B. Afrasiyabi, *Khaterat va Mobarezat-e Doctor Hoseyn Fatemi* (Tehran: Sokhan, 1366), p. 65.
[35] Afrasiyabi and Dehqan, p. 121.

during the days leading to the second coup, later confided in Ayatollah Taleqani that even after 28 Mordad their fingers were still hurting from the inordinate number of letters they had written and sent.[36] Ayatollah Behbahani used his religious reputation and influence to run a very effective propaganda machine, sowing fear and anxiety among the pious common folk of a coming atheist government if Mosaddeq was not removed and the Shah was not returned.[37]

Behbahani's house – close to Syrus Street and adjacent to Sarpoulak and the main Tehran bazaar – was ideally situated for the dissemination of "grey and black" propaganda concerning the imminent threat of a Communist takeover among the clergy, the traditional bazaaris, the government employees and, most importantly, the roughnecks and knife-wielders of Southern Tehran. It is most probable that Behbahani was receiving his cue for the propagation of fear-sowing propaganda from the TPBEDAMN network. Both grey and black propaganda are directed at deceiving the public and making them believe in false and fabricated information. Grey propaganda refers to false information without any identifiable source, while black propaganda usually applies to information believed to come from one source, while in fact it is from another.

Another propaganda machine connected to the central command post of the conspirators was at work launching a major psychological assault against Mosaddeq. On 17 August (26 Mordad) the account of an interview with General Zahedi, typed on very thin paper and accompanied by photostats of the Shah's royal edict appointing Zahedi as Prime Minister, was dropped in the mailbox of Tehran's newspapers.[38] In this fictive interview, General Zahedi claimed to be the legal Prime Minister of Iran, as appointed by the Shah, who he maintained had employed his constitutional prerogatives to put an end to the chaotic state of the country under Mosaddeq's rule. In this interview, Zahedi reiterated that Mosaddeq had seen the Shah's royal edict and knew that he no longer held any official position, and he warned Iranian officials that following the deposed Prime Minister's orders would have dire consequences. In this concocted interview General Zahedi accused Mosaddeq of staging a coup on 15 August by ordering the arrest of the Shah. Zahedi claimed to be very ill, running a high fever and promised to resume his soldierly activities of implementing the law and the royal edict as soon as he had regained his health.[39] This forged text, which played an important role in justifying and legitimizing the position of the pro-Zahedi camp, was published along with the royal edict in anti-Mosaddeq Tehran newspapers on 18 August (27 Mordad). In fact, General Zahedi did not give an interview between the first and second coups. The trumped-up interview was in fact

---

[36] Afrasiyabi and Dehqan, p. 121. [37] Nejati, p. 429. [38] Baniahmad, p. 89.
[39] Baniahmad, pp. 89–91.

conducted by Ardeshir Zahedi, who met with the foreign correspondents while General Zahedi remained in hiding.[40]

Kennett Love, the *New York Times* correspondent in Iran, recalled that shortly after 7:00 a.m. on 16 August, Joe (Joseph) Goodwin, the CIA Station Chief in Tehran, called him at the Park Hotel and enquired if he wished to meet Zahedi and hear the real account of the events from the general.[41] Arrangements were made to conduct Love and Don Schwind of the Associated Press to "the residence of an American Embassy official in Shemiran", where instead of Fazlollah Zahedi they met with Ardeshir Zahedi. At this meeting, in the presence of Goodwin, Ardeshir Zahedi spoke about the two royal edicts (*farmans*) and handed Love and Schwind a handful of copies of the edict appointing Zahedi. Love recalled distributing his copies at the Park Hotel.[42] According to Love, it was Joe Goodwin, the CIA Station Chief in Tehran, who served as the "communication channel" between the foreign correspondents (Schwind and Love) and General Zahedi's team.

The native and foreign conspirators differ on three important issues related to this key text. First, the real identity of the author of the text which came to be known as the so-called interview; second, the organizer of the meeting between Ardeshir Zahedi and the foreign correspondents; and third, the distributor and circulator of the so-called interview and the royal edict. Ardeshir Zahedi maintains that the text of his interview was based on the notes that his father dictated to him, while Wilber suggests that the text was prepared by the CIA station in Tehran and was the result of teamwork based on the "direct advice" of Ardeshir Zahedi, the Rashidiyan brothers, and Colonel Farzanegan.[43] Ardeshir Zahedi claims that the idea of meeting with foreign press correspondents and presenting the royal edict to them belonged to his father. According to Ardeshir Zahedi, he himself organized the meeting with the foreign correspondents through the intermediary of his old classmate Parviz Ra'in, the Associated Press correspondent in Tehran.[44] Wilber, however, suggests that the 11:00 a.m. meeting with "two correspondents of the New York Times" on Sunday 16 August (25 Mordad) at Shemiran was arranged by the CIA station.[45] Ardeshir Zahedi claims that the distribution and circulation of the royal edict and the interview were carried out by a five-man team of General Zahedi's close associates.[46] Roosevelt maintains that it was the Boscoe Brothers who were responsible for the distribution of the bulk of the royal edicts.[47] Woodhouse, in turn, credits Roosevelt with circulating copies of the Shah's edict to the press.[48] The account of Love, who was personally involved, is similar to that of Wilber.

---

[40] Zahedi, vol. 1, pp. 125–127; Wilber, p. 48.   [41] Love, p. 31.   [42] Love, p. 32.
[43] Zahedi, vol. 1, p. 125; Wilber, p. 45.   [44] Zahedi, vol. 1, p. 125.   [45] Wilber, p. 48.
[46] Zahedi, vol. 1, p. 131.   [47] Roosevelt, p. 179.   [48] Woodhouse, p. 128.

Only one day after the failure of the first coup was announced, the anti-Mosaddeq papers published articles on the royal edict deposing Mosaddeq and appointing Zahedi as Prime Minister. In its second edition of 16 August/ 25 Mordad, Abbas Maso'udi's afternoon newspaper *Ettela'at* was the first to report on the royal edict which had been issued in Zahedi's name and the news that Nasiri was the officer responsible for handing the edict to Mosaddeq.[49] On Monday 17 August, Abolhasan Amidiy-e Nouri's anti-Mosaddeq newspaper, *Daad*, speculated that there had been no intention of a coup against Mosaddeq, but that in view of the dissolved parliament, the Shah had simply decided to depose Mosaddeq.[50] Amidiy-e Nouri's newspaper informed the public that on 13 August the Shah had signed three edicts in Ramsar: the first dismissed Mosaddeq; the second appointed General Zahedi as Prime Minister; and the third appointed General Batmanqelich as Chief of Staff.[51]

On Tuesday 18 August, *Daad* took the political offensive and openly made the case for the anti-Mosaddeq forces by arguing that if there had been a coup, it had been engineered by Mosaddeq against the Shah. *Daad* referred to Zahedi's fictive press interview and asserted that Zahedi did possess a royal edict appointing him as Prime Minister and that he was the legal Prime Minister while Mosaddeq was dismissed, and that Mosaddeq intended to arrest the Shah.[52] This was an important turning of the tables against Mosaddeq, as *Daad* was arguing that, according to the constitution, the appointment and dismissal of ministers was within the legal prerogative of the Shah, and in the absence of the parliament the Shah was entitled to appoint and dismiss the Prime Minister. Whipping up support among the anti-Mosaddeq forces, Amidi-ye Nouri's newspaper rhetorically concluded that "since Iran's constitution has not changed yet and the Shah has not resigned as the monarch, Mosaddeq's rule is provisional, relying on a coup".[53] On the same day Baqa'i's newspaper, *Shahed*, published a typewritten version of the Shah's royal edict appointing Zahedi as Prime Minister and argued that Mosaddeq's government was illegal and all foreign embassies had ceased to recognize his outlaw government.[54] *Shahed* argued along the same lines as *Daad*, maintaining that the Shah had the legal right to appoint and dismiss Prime Ministers.

On the morning of the second coup, *Shahed* published the handwritten royal edict on its front page, along with Zahedi's fabricated interview. *Shahed* wrote: "People of Iran, your independence, freedom, constitution and ethnicity is exposed to the most barbaric and treacherous attacks. Foreign agents of all shades with the aid of Mosaddeq-ol-Saltaneh have pushed Iran to the precipice of annihilation".[55] On the same day *Daad* published the full text of

---

[49] *Ettela'at*, 25 Mordad 1332.　　[50] *Daad*, 26 Mordad 1332.　　[51] *Daad*, 26 Mordad 1332.
[52] *Daad*, 27 Mordad 1332.　　[53] *Daad*, 27 Mordad 1332.　　[54] *Shahed*, 27 Mordad 1332.
[55] *Shahed*, 28 Mordad 1332.

Zahedi's proclamation, which constituted an open call to insubordination and rebellion against Mosaddeq. In the name of Iran's legal Prime Minister, Zahedi called on the people – especially soldiers, officers, and military commanders – to heed his commands and follow his instructions aimed at securing the freedom and independence of the country, or to prepare themselves for the dire consequences of treason.[56] In his open letter published on the day of the second coup, Zahedi warned that the monarchy, Iran's independence, and the holy religion of Islam were all endangered by foreign-worshippers (*biganeh parastan*) and the godless and that *today* was the day when the soldiers and officers had to perform their military duty towards the motherland.[57] After the second coup, Abolhasan Amidi-ye Nouri was fully compensated with a ministerial portfolio in the Zahedi government for his efforts to mobilize and boost the morale of anti-Mosaddeq forces with his sensationalistic journalism. Less than a week after the coup, Amidi-ye Nouri was appointed the Prime Minister's political undersecretary (*moaven siyasi*) and the spokesperson of the government.[58] Wilber was also delighted with *Daad*'s "remarkable efforts" in disseminating the news about the Shah's dismissal of Mosaddeq.[59]

Before sunrise on the morning of 19 August (28 Mordad) Ja'far Behbahani, Ayatollah Behbahani's son, called on Mehdi Ha'eri Yazdi and asked him to join the Ayatollah at his home for breakfast.[60] Mehdi Ha'eri Yazdi was the son of Ayatollah Abdol-Karim Ha'eri, the prominent founder of the Qom Seminary School and a confidant of Ayatollah Borujerdi. Sensing the urgency of the matter, Ha'eri Yazdi – who lived on Syrus Street, in the vicinity of the Ayatollah's house – immediately walked over and met Behbahani in his library. Behbahani expressed his anxiety over the departure of the Shah, and was particularly concerned about the danger of the country becoming a republic and subsequently falling behind the Iron Curtain.[61] The Ayatollah asked Ha'eri Yazdi to leave Tehran immediately, taking a message to Ayatollah Borujerdi, who was at Veshnaveh where he and his close circle of students resided during the summer. The message was that due to the imminent danger of Iran becoming a Communist republic and slipping behind the Iron Curtain, Ayatollah Borujerdi needed to issue a religious decree informing the people to come out and prevent the country from going to the Communists. Ayatollah Behbahani reiterated that the country, its religion and the religious institution of *marja'iyat* (according to which the Shi'i followed a cleric of their choice as their source of religious practice) were all faced with imminent demise.[62] Faced with Ha'eri Yazdi's reticence to take

---

[56] *Daad*, 28 Mordad 1332. [57] *Daad*, 28 Mordad 1332. [58] *Shahed*, 3 Shahrivar 1332.
[59] Wilber, p. 60, 65.
[60] Mehdi Hairi-Yazdi, Iranian Oral History Collection, Harvard University, Transcript 2, p. 3.
[61] Mehdi Hairi-Yazdi, p. 4. [62] Mehdi Hairi-Yazdi, p. 4.

this message to Borujerdi, and with his counter-arguments, Behbahani decided against dispatching Ha'eri Yazdi to Borujerdi.

Ha'eri Yazdi's account demonstrates that Behbahani was acting according to the decision reached during the "council of war" on 17 August, according to which Behbahani was assigned to obtain a *fatwa* against Mosaddeq from Ayatollah Borujerdi. It is highly probable that other emissaries with the same message were dispatched by Behbahani to Ayatollah Borujerdi, since on 28 Mordad the CIA station operatives Keyvani and Jalali were eagerly awaiting Ayatollah Borujerdi's pro-Shah, anti-Communist and anti-Mosaddeq *fatwa* – which never arrived. Early in the morning, Jalali and two of his associates, Afshar and Majidi, were hanging around the bazaar area, close to Behbahani's house, with "a jeep and trucks ready to set out for Qazvin", where they hoped to reprint Borujerdi's *fatwa*.[63] Borujerdi, the highest source of religious authority in the land, demonstrated that he would have nothing to do with the anti-Mosaddeq coup.

---

[63] Wilber, p. 65–66.

9

The crucial last-minute preparations

MOBILIZING "THE PEOPLE" IN TEHRAN'S ROUGH DISTRICTS

In the afternoon of 18 August (27 Mordad), Ghaffari, a police officer assigned to Tehran's old railway station situated in the Southern neighbourhoods of Tehran, invited Asadollah Khodayeki (also known as Asadollah Kachal or Asadollah the Bald) to a house on Qazvin Street.[1] When Asadollah Khodayeki arrived, the other guests were busy drinking alcohol. At this gathering some of the more prominent ruffians of the Javadiyeh district (located adjacent to the railway station) were present. Among them were Khalil Torkeh (Khalil the Turk), Qasem Sarpoly, Esmaʻil Shaleh (Esmaʻil the Lame), Mohammad Dakho (Mohammad the Simpleton), Ali Bolandeh (Ali the Tall One) and (Boyouk) Saber. That night, Ghaffari handed over a purse of money to Qasem Sarpoly.[2] Ghaffari was a member of the clandestine network of the "Devotees of the Shah".[3] He instructed the ruffians to mobilize a group and gather in front of a cinema in Javadiyeh before 9:00 a.m. the following day (28 Mordad).[4] They were given exact instructions on the following: how they would be transported by trucks to Amiriyeh; when they were to display the pictures of the Shah that they were provided with and which were hidden in brown canvas bags; and where they were to join forces with one of the main groups of ruffians on the move, led by Tayyeb and Taher Haj Reza'i. After combining forces with members of Tayyeb and Taher's gang, they were instructed to fan out in various directions: Kakh, Naderi, Eslambol, and Shahabad streets, as well as Baharestan.[5]

Later that night (18 August/27 Mordad) Hasan Saʻlehi (Hasan Behbudgar), a politicized gang leader of Southern Tehran, claimed to have played host to Ardeshir Zahedi and another group of thug leaders.[6] In his

---

[1] Torbati-ye Sanjabi, p. 18. [2] Torbati-ye Sanjabi, p. 18. [3] Baniahmad, p. 164.
[4] Torbati-ye Sanjabi, p. 18. [5] Torbati-ye Sanjabi, p. 19. [6] Manzarpour, p. 195.

Southern Tehran neighbourhood, Hasan Behbudgar went by his popular ruffian name of Hasan Seh Kalleh (Three-Headed Hasan) and was renowned for his fanatical love of and devotion to the Shah.⁷ Behbudgar was probably connected to Asadollah Rashidiyan's network of South Tehran ruffian leaders. Later, accompanied by other leaders of and participants in 28 Mordad's "great demonstration", Behbudgar attended Rashidiyan's gatherings at his house.⁸ After the coup, Behbudgar became Secretary of the "Society of the 28 Mordad National Uprising".⁹

According to Behbudgar's report, the pre-arranged meeting between the thugs and Ardeshir Zahedi was held at Behbudgar's house on Esma'il Bazzaz Street (Mowlavi), one of the main centres of the Southern Tehran roughnecks (*gardan koloftha*) and knife-wielders (*chaqu keshan*).¹⁰ Most of these roughnecks and knife-wielding thugs had trained in traditional athletic clubs (*zourkhanehs*) and were musclemen who usually got embroiled in neighbourhood brawls and rivalries, using brass knuckles, jack-knives and clubs – and often ending up in jail. The main sources of livelihood for these thugs were extortion and racketeering; intimidation and shakedowns of individuals, shop keepers and craftsmen in the neighbourhood; and providing protection to and/or running gambling houses, opium dens and brothels.¹¹ Some of them were petty traders, workers at stalls and shops, owners of small stalls and shops and, often, workers at the Tehran granary and the fruit, vegetable and meat markets (*meydan*) at Aminosoltan and Bagh-e Ferdows. Others were unemployed day labourers, prepared to do almost anything to feed themselves and their families, and often to support a habit or an addiction. The Southern Tehran ruffian world had its own social hierarchy and chain of command, running vertically from chiefs to foot soldiers.

The reason for this socially incongruent but politically compatible meeting between Ardeshir Zahedi and the gang leaders of Southern Tehran was that certain details relating to the activities planned for 19 August (28 Mordad) had to be clarified. Hasan Behbudgar had received instructions that on 28 Mordad the gang leaders and their roughnecks should "cause disorder in the city and loot Mosaddeq's house".¹² In return the thugs were promised good money from Ardeshir Zahedi. This instruction, as well the promise of money, probably came from Asadollah Rashidiyan or his intermediaries and was probably confirmed by Ayatollah Behbahani. Behbudgar had tried to secure the participation of the thug leaders but had not been very successful. Verbal promises of rewards for a hazardous job such as taking to the streets, defying the government and ransacking the Prime Minister's house did not

---

⁷ *Shahid Tayyeb Haj Reza'i be Ravayat Asnad SAVAK*, p. 133.
⁸ *Rashidiyanha*, vol. 1, pp. 261, 298.   ⁹ *Rashidiyanha*, vol. 1, p. 199.
¹⁰ Manzarpour, pp. 134, 164.   ¹¹ *Hamshahri*, 13 Dey 1382; Manzarpour, p. 84.
¹² Manzarpour, p. 196.

suffice. Suspicious of being hoodwinked, the gang leaders had asked Zahedi to pay them before they entered into action.

According to Behbudgar, on the night of 27 Mordad Zahedi showed up with the promised money. Fearing that the ruffians would take the money and not show up on the next day, Behbudgar informed them that he would keep the money until the task was successfully completed on the next day, and only then he would distribute the sums. The gang leaders accepted the deal.[13] According to Zahedi, he returned to Tehran from his mission to Esfahan at around 3:30–4:00 a.m. on Tuesday 27 Mordad.[14] He would, therefore, have had time to be present at Behbudgar's house on the night of 27 Mordad.

THE ORGANIZERS OF THE "GREAT DEMONSTRATION"

It has been widely claimed that the Rashidiyan Brothers, through their South-of-Tehran network of thugs, organized the "great demonstration" on 28 Mordad.[15] According to Fardust, the Rashidiyan Brothers were two of the most important actors in the 28 Mordad coup. Fardust maintains that on this day the Rashidiyan Brothers mobilized some 5,000 to 6,000 people from "non-military and guild groups".[16] This number seems rather exaggerated. Fardust believes that Malekeh E'tezadi and her political party, Hezb-e Zolfaqar, which actively participated in the 28 Mordad coup, were also under the command of Asadollah Rashidiyan.[17] On that day, Malekeh E'tezadi's gang gathered at Naderi Street and then moved on to Mosaddeq's house at Kakh Street.[18] Sha'ban Ja'fari, an influential gang leader of Southern Tehran who was imprisoned for his anti-Mosaddeq activities on 9 Esfand and who lingered in prison until the early afternoon of 28 Mordad, believed that Asadollah Rashidiyan "had a hand" in the turmoil of 28 Mordad, as he knew all of the roughnecks and thugs.[19]

Asadollah Rashidiyan was closely associated with Ayatollah Behbahani and his son Ja'far Behbahani. After the coup, and probably in recognition of the services rendered by Ayatollah Behbahani for the successful implementation of the second coup, Ja'far Behbahani became a member of the Iranian parliament on three successive occasions. There is ample evidence of Asadollah Rashidiyan's close political collaboration with both the Ayatollah and his son after 1953, strongly indicating that Rashidiyan must have also been close to the two before 1953.[20] The fact that Seyfollah Rashidiyan would refer to Ja'far Behbahani as "one of ours" seems to indicate the close

---

[13] Manzarpour, p. 196.   [14] Zahedi, p. 148.
[15] *Tarik-e Moaser-e Iran*, Sal-e Haftom, Shomareh 26, Tabestan 1382, pp. 140, 224.
[16] Fardust, vol. 1, p. 182.   [17] Fardust, vol. 1, p. 182.   [18] Fardust, vol. 1, p. 182.
[19] Sarshar, p. 167.
[20] Rashidiyanha, vol. 1, p. 328, 359; vol. 2, pp. 65, 74, 133, 237, 246, 264, 265, 297; vol. 3, p. 8.

The crucial last-minute preparations 141

relationship between the Rashidiyans and the Behbahanis.[21] Numerous sources, both domestic and foreign – including Queen Soraya, who at the time was married to the Shah, and Haj Manian, who was close to the Tehran bazaar and Richard Cottam – have maintained that Ayatollah Behbahani was instrumental in mobilizing the mob on 28 Mordad.[22] In fulfilling the assignment conferred to him for August 19 by the "council of war", Ayatollah Behbahani is said to have distributed large sums of money, even in Dollars, among the roughnecks of Southern Tehran. Mehdi Karimi, better known as Mehdi Qassab (Mehdi the Butcher), a traditional (*zourkhaneh*) athlete and butcher, was one of Ayatollah Behbahani's key contacts among the mob of Southern Tehran.[23] Mehdi Qassab was well known for his religiosity, charitable activities and the mourning processions which he organized.[24] Mehdi Qassab also frequented female singers of the day, such as "Rouhangiz", who performed for him and his friends privately.[25] Mehdi Qassab lived in Sarpoulak and was a neighbour of Ayatollah Behbahani.[26]

Other accounts from different sources corroborate the key role of Ayotallah Behbahani in the organization of the "great demonstration". Ayatollah Gerami is also of the opinion that it was common knowledge that Ayatollah Behbahani had a hand in the events of 28 Mordad.[27] Mostafa Alamuti, who was initially a supporter of Mosaddeq but then fell out with him, maintains that he did not know much about what the foreigners were doing during the days leading to 28 Mordad, but with regard to the domestic opposition's activities against Mosaddeq, Alamuti acknowledges the key role of Ayatollahs Behbahani and Kashani.[28]

PREPARING THE BIG GUNS

On the night of 18 August (27 Mordad), Captain Ali-Mohammad Arbabi was the officer on guard at the Saltanatabad garrison.[29] This garrison was organizationally attached to the First Armoured Brigade headed by Colonel Rostam Nowzari, yet it had its own independent commander, Colonel Dabirsiyaqi. At the time, it was home to two squadrons of tanks (a total of 24 tanks) composed of M-4s (Shermans), M-24s and M-32s.[30] According to Arbabi, on the eve of 28 Mordad, Nowzari, who seemed "frightened and

---

[21] Rashidiyanha, vol. 2, p. 270.
[22] Nejati, p. 468; Shahhoseyni, p. 145; R. W. Cottam, *Iran and the United States* (Pittsburgh: University of Pittsburgh Press, 1988), p. 106.
[23] Sarshar, p. 125; S. Mirza'i, *Tayyeb dar Gozar-e Lutiha* (Tehran: Madiya, 1381), pp. 40, 98.
[24] Mirza'i, p. 89. [25] Manzarpour, p. 175. [26] Mirza'i, pp. 88–89; Sarshar, p. 125.
[27] M. R. Ahmadi, *Khaterat-e Ayatollah Gerami* (Tehran: Markaz-e Asnad-e Enqelab-e Eslami, 1381), p. 119.
[28] Mostafa Alamouti, Iranian Oral History Collection, Harvard University, Tape 1, p. 8.
[29] Mohammadi, p. 33. [30] Mohammadi, pp. 29, 33, 36, 38.

perturbed", entered the garrison and lectured the military personnel present. He urged those under his command to follow the instruction of their superiors and to serve their country – without mentioning the Shah's name.[31] Half an hour after Nowzari's departure, Arbabi, the officer on guard, and Captain Madani, the superior officer on guard, were both relieved of their posts through a mysterious phone call. This call appointed Captains Iravani and Jahanbani as their respective replacements.[32]

On 28 Mordad, during the morning ceremonies of the garrison, which were usually held at about 6:00 a.m., Arbabi heard that four M-4 tanks had left the garrison under the command of Captain Iravani and a few other officers.[33] Arbabi thought that the tanks had been dispatched to restore order in the town and repress the anti-Mosaddeq demonstrators, especially since they had been assigned to move towards Mosaddeq's house.[34] After the coup, it became known that captains Arbabi and Iravani were both members of the Tudeh Party's Military Organization.[35] In view of his political allegiance, if Iravani had known that his tanks were to be used in a coup against Mosaddeq he would have been on his guard, even though there was not much he personally could have done. The winning card of the military conspirators was to give to the military personnel loyal to Mosaddeq the appearance of a normal tank deployment, while their true intentions were quite different. This camouflage operation was essential to getting the required tanks to the city centre. While for Arbabi and Iravani the tanks were going to guarantee the safety of Mosaddeq's house, the plan was for the tanks to be driven to sensitive areas of the town already occupied by the demonstrators, where they would be surrounded by the ruffians and eventually hijacked with the help of collaborationist military personnel manning the tanks. By the time Iravani discovered that the real mission of the tanks under his command was to join the "great demonstration", and eventually to attack Mosaddeq's house, it was too late as his tanks were no longer under his authority. Exactly the same scenario was replayed with the tank units commanded by Lieutenant General Ataollah Kiyani, a loyal pro-Mosaddeq officer.

According to Captain Mohammadi, who was also a member of the Tudeh Party's Military Organization at the time, a few months before 28 Mordad, anticipating a military coup, the tank units at Saltanatabad garrison were put on full military alert and were therefore fully maintained and constantly prepared for action, ready for their personnel to mount them and depart in a few minutes.[36] Mohammadi believes that it was the fire power and preparedness of these tanks at Saltanatabad that made them the ideal targets for the conspirators. He argues that since the direct commander of the Saltanatabad garrison was Colonel Qodrat Dabirsiyaqi, only he was

---

[31] Mohammadi, p. 33. [32] Mohammadi, p. 33. [33] Mohammadi, p. 34.
[34] Mohammadi, p. 34. [35] Mohammadi, p. 66. [36] Mohammadi, p. 43.

The crucial last-minute preparations

authorized to change the officer and the superior officer on guard. According to Mohammadi, the fact that Colonel Nowzari ordered Captain Hamid Jahanbani to replace Madani was irregular and signalled the first phase of the military plan of the second coup. Mohammadi maintains that Hamid Jahanbani was one of the collaborationist officers, and that in the absence of the commander of the garrison during the night of 18 August, Jahanbani, the superior officer on guard, had full military control over the garrison.[37]

Jahanbani's involvement in the tank attack on Mosaddeq's house on the afternoon of 28 Mordad is documented in a quasi-official post-coup account of the events.[38] Mohammadi was convinced that Colonel Nowzari's highly irregular appointment of Jahanbani as the superior officer on guard followed the coup plan, by which full control of the tank units was placed in the hands of the conspirators.[39] Immediately after the second coup on 28 Mordad, Zahedi changed all of the Mosaddeq-appointed garrison commanders but one. Colonel Nowzari, the commander of the Second Armoured Brigade, was the only Mosaddeq-appointed garrison commander, who was first arrested and then immediately reinstated in his former position after the second coup.[40] The fact that Nowzari was reinstated in his position demonstrates the degree to which Zahedi and Batmanqelich trusted him. The four Sherman tanks and their personnel of Mosaddeq loyalists as well as collaborationist infiltrators left the Saltanatabad garrison some time between midnight and 5:00 a.m. on 28 Mordad and made their way towards the centre of Tehran.[41]

SOWING INSUBORDINATION IN THE BARRACKS

During the afternoon of Monday 17 August, Taqi Riyahi issued a circular to all military units informing them that henceforth all references to the Shah's name during the morning and evening prayers at the flag ceremonies were to be deleted.[42] This controversial measure had been suggested by Brigadier Zangeneh, supposedly to prevent unrest in the garrisons after the Shah's departure, and had been approved by Mosaddeq.[43] In his trial after the coup Mosaddeq argued that since it was believed that the Shah would prefer the longevity of Iran to that of his own name he ordered the soldiers to pray for the endurance and preservation of the motherland.[44] Traditionally, the officer on guard during these ceremonies would pray for the Shah's health and say "to the Shah's health, hurray", and the soldiers would demonstrate their approbation by also yelling "hurray".[45] According to the new circular, the

---

[37] Mohammadi, pp. 38, 55, 57, 60. [38] Baniahmad, p. 235. [39] Mohammadi, pp. 55, 60.
[40] *Tehran Mosavvar*, 30 Mordad 1332. [41] Mohammadi, p. 63.
[42] Bozorgmehr, p. 536; Baniahmad, p. 192. [43] Bozorgmehr, pp. 353, 388, 536.
[44] Bozorgmehr, p. 354. [45] *Tehran Mosavvar*, 6 Shahrivar 1332.

slogan of "to the Shah's health" was to be replaced with "to the nation's health".[46] During the morning flag ceremonies of Tuesday 18 August, after no reference was made to the Shah's name at the Third Mountain Brigade located at 'Eshratabad, a secret meeting was held at the house of a few officers. These officers decided to incite the personnel of the Third Mountain Brigade against Mosaddeq and in favour of the Shah. At 4:00 p.m., 45 sergeants and sergeant majors congregated at the stables of the Third Mountain Brigade and pledged allegiance to the monarchy, whatever the sacrifices necessary to assure its preservation.[47]

At 6:30 p.m. as the evening prayers of the flag ceremony came to an end and the Shah's name was not mentioned, a sergeant unsheathed his bayonet, stepped forward, and shouted "to the Shah's health, hurray".[48] The soldiers, who had previously been spurred on by the pro-Shah activists, cheered for about 15 minutes.[49] At 7:30 p.m. the acting commanding officer of the Third Mountain Brigade phoned Colonel Hoseynqoli Ashrafi, the Military Governor of Tehran and the commander of the Third Mountain Brigade, to report on the unrest and insubordination at the garrison. Ashrafi did not give him a chance to explain, but instead kept repeating that troops needed to be dispatched immediately to Eslambol and Naderi Streets as well as Toupkhaneh (Sepah) Square to quell the Tudeh Party demonstrators.[50] Similar acts of insubordination incited by small groups of pro-Shah officers occurred during the evening of 18 August (27 Mordad) at the Shamsabad camp where some 500 sharpshooters of the Iranian army had gathered to compete, and also at Saltanatabad garrison.[51] Faced with a well-coordinated campaign of insubordination and defiance at the garrisons around the capital city, Ashrafi, who occupied the very sensitive position of Tehran's Military Governor, did not take any measures to control or quell the disturbing tide. He seems to have purposefully ignored the clear signals of simmering military disobedience against Mosaddeq. There are no records of Ashrafi reporting these disturbances to Riyahi or to Mosaddeq. During these days and up to midday on 28 Mordad, at which time Mosaddeq ordered his arrest, Colonel Ashrafi continued to claim that he had the situation well under control.

THRASHING THE ANTI-MONARCHISTS AND INTIMIDATING MOSADDEQ'S SUPPORTERS

The events of the evening of Tuesday 18 August (27 Mordad) should be considered the opening act of the second coup. When at 7:30 p.m. Colonel Ashrafi ignored the disturbing news of insubordination at 'Eshratabad

---

[46] *Tehran Mosavvar*, 6 Shahrivar 1332. [47] Baniahmad, p. 192.
[48] *Tehran Mosavvar*, 6 Shahrivar 1332.
[49] Baniahmad, p. 193; *Tehran Mosavvar*, 6 Shahrivar 1332. [50] Baniahmad, p. 193.
[51] Baniahmad, p. 193; Mohammadi, p. 34.

garrison and instead called for immediate reinforcements to break up and subdue Tudeh Party demonstrators, two platoons from the Naderi Battalion, under the command of Major Akbar Zand (not to be confused with Zand Karimi), were dispatched to Eslambol Street.[52] The commander of the Naderi Battalion was Colonel Ali-Mohammad Rowhani, the deputy commander of the Third Mountain Brigade, a high-ranking collaborationist officer. Colonel Rowhani and Major Zand had been in close contact with one another and had sworn allegiance as participants in pro-Shah activities that were being planned; they had also pledged the full engagement of the units and personnel under their command.[53] Rowhani was one of Zand Karimi's trusted friends and collaborators, and Zand Karimi was in turn directly connected with Carroll and Farzanegan, the CIA operatives in Iran. With the imprisonment of Rowhani after the first coup, the collaborating officers continued their newly planned activities unhampered. In the absence of Rowhani, Major Zand carried out his part of the activities in the second coup meticulously.

Major Zand, whose nickname was *Akbar Lati* (Akbar the ruffian), was assigned to command two platoons into action late on the evening of 27 Mordad. He must have been on some sort of standby alert and must have been given this important operation because of the trust of his superior commander, Colonel Ashrafi, and of the military network of the coup officers.[54] Akbar Zand had solid credentials for this important operation. He was one of the collaborating "line commanders" and a member of the "Devotees of the Shah". Zand handpicked his best soldiers and most royalist officers, took them outside the garrison and lectured them on their responsibilities. He spoke of the Tudeh Party demonstrators as agitators whom they were going to discipline, informing his troops that: "they [the demonstrators] want to dethrone the Shah and hand over the government to the Communists"; he added that, "those among you who are supporters of the Shah come with me and those who are not can return to the barracks".[55]

Major Zand played the usual card of first describing the situation as a war between pro-Shah forces and Tudeh Party supporters, and then placed the pro-Mosaddeq forces in the same category as the Tudeh Party supporters. The discourse of the collaborationist officers on the alignment of political forces and the identification of chief enemies of the state hinged on the notion that Mosaddeq was the cause of the republican, Communist and atheist threat. Zand's reference to the fact that "they want to dethrone the Shah" applied to all anti-Shah forces, including pro-Mosaddeq and Tudeh supporters. This opposition of Mosaddeq and Tudeh to the Shah and Islam, long hammered at by the anti-Mosaddeq newspapers, constituted a powerful argument within the military network of the conspirators. The anti-Shah

---

[52] Baniahmad, p. 193; *Tehran Mosavvar*, 6 Shahrivar 1332.
[53] *Tehran Mosavvar*, 6 Shahrivar 1332.   [54] Nejati, p. 648.   [55] Baniahmad, p. 193.

and anti-monarchist activities of Sunday 25 and Monday 26 Mordad played into the hands of anti-Mosaddeq forces and heightened the pro-Shah and anti-Mosaddeq sentiments among the soldiers and officers. All Zand's hand-picked military personnel agreed to go into action with him and "having kissed the butt of their rifles they pledged to do their utmost for the *Shahanshah* (king of kings), even if it meant sacrificing their lives".[56]

Upon their arrival at Eslambol and Ferdowsi streets the angry soldiers, who had been fully briefed by Major Zand on what to do, disembarked from their trucks and hurriedly began attacking the demonstrating Tudeh Party sympathizers, wounding some, sending some running, arresting approximately 70, and leaving two dead.[57] Feeling triumphant, the soldiers started to chant slogans in favour of the Shah.[58] On the same night a group of soldiers entered a cinema, stopped the screening of the movie, ordered the lights to be turned on, and commanded that the royalist national anthem (which was customarily played at the beginning of the film) be played again. Those who refused to stand up in honour of the Shah were arrested.[59]

That Tuesday night (18 August), Tehran seemed more feverish than usual. The shops around Shahabad, Eslambol, Naderi, Lalehzar, Ferdowsi and Saadi had closed down earlier and people were standing around to discuss and chat in small clusters; at times the Tudeh partisans would clash with different pro-Mosaddeq political tendencies. What was also unusual was the disposition of the forces of law and order. While between Sunday, when the failure of the first coup was first announced, and Tuesday, the forces of law and order had mainly looked on as groups clashed on the streets or the Shah's statues were dismantled, on the eve of the second coup the army showed its full might and enjoyed its military prowess and superiority. On Tuesday evening the demonstrating crowds were surprised – shocked, even – at the intensity and magnitude of police and army violence, attacked as they were not only with rifle butts and batons but with tear gas and live rounds (shot mostly in the air).[60] The hit-and-run street battles in Tehran on that Tuesday night lasted until 11:00 p.m. During these bloody engagements the army and the police were on the offensive and the anti-Shah protesters were clearly on the defensive.[61]

The significant consequences of the army's well-calculated spree of violence during that night upon the behaviour of Mosaddeq's supporters on the day of the coup is well documented in an article written on 19 August and published on 20 August 1953. Kennett Love, the young *New York Times* correspondent in Tehran, referred to the evening offensive of the army against anti-Shah protesters on 18 August as the "spark" of the events on 19 August. He wrote:

---

[56] Baniahmad, p. 193. [57] Baniahmad, p. 194. [58] *Tehran Mosavvar*, 6 Shahrivar 1332.
[59] Baniahmad, p. 194. [60] *Taraqi*, 2 Shahrivar 1332. [61] *Taraqi*, 2 Shahrivar 1332.

The street revolution began last night when police and soldiers shouting "long live the Shah" and "death to Mossadegh" smashed into pro-Government rioters. The rioters were Tudeh partisans and Pan-Iranists, who had often fought each other though both at this time were supporting Dr. Mossadegh. The troops beat the rioters unmercifully, forcing them to repeat their slogans at bayonet point.

Love opined that: "After the last night's fighting, the soldiers and police returned to their barracks only to join the pro-Shah crowds this morning. Apparently the boldness of the troops in shouting for the Shah last night had given courage to the populace".[62] After the coup, Love revealed how he had been manipulated to write about the important royal edicts by a CIA officer working under cover as the US Embassy's Press Office. Later, Love asserted that: "It is probable that the American role [in the coup] was decisive". He maintained that "It is doubtful that the coup would have been attempted without American cooperation".[63]

THE STREETS ARE CLEARED FOR THE "SHAH-LOVING PEOPLE"

At 11:00 a.m. on Tuesday 18 August (27 Mordad), a meeting was held by the Central Council of the Anti-Colonial Society (*jam'iyat zed-e este'mar*), one of the Tudeh Party's numerous organizations. During this extraordinary meeting, members unanimously agreed to issue a communiqué expressing their view on the necessity of changing the monarchical regime and establishing a democratic republic, based on a referendum.[64] From the afternoon of Sunday 16 August (25 Mordad), Tudeh Party demonstrators who had gathered at Baharestan Square to celebrate the defeat of the first coup and the Shah's departure were chanting "down with the Monarchy" and "long live the Democratic Republic".[65] The term "Democratic Republic" denoted a system of government adopted by the Soviet Union's client states. The Tudeh Party encouraged its members to demonstrate against the Shah and the monarchy, and in favour of a "Democratic Republic".[66] Tudeh Party demonstrations were usually countered by pro-Mosaddeq and anti-Tudeh organizations such as Khalil Maleki's Third Force Party and Daryoush Foruhar's Iranian People's Party (*Hezbe Mellat Iran*).

On 27 Mordad, Tudeh Party supporters hoisted banners of "long live the Tudeh Party of Iran", distributed the party newspaper *nameh mardom* and

---

[62] *New York Time*, 20 August 1953.
[63] W. Dorman and M. Farhang, *The U.S. Press and Iran* (Berkeley, University of California Press, 1987), p. 51.
[64] Baniahmad, p. 182.   [65] *Taraqi*, 2 Shahrivar 1332.
[66] Wilber, p. 60; Amir-Khosravi, p. 572.

staged demonstrations and rallies on the crowded downtown streets of Tehran. The extent to which they entered government offices and shops to dismantle the Shah's pictures, ransacked the offices of their political opponents, provoked scuffles with ordinary people of the street and engaged in looting shops and damaging property is not clear. Wilber credits CIA's Keyvani, Jalali and their confederates with a lion's share of the subversive activities, such as attacking the headquarters of the Iranian People's Party.[67] According to Wilber, "Keyvani and Jalili [Jalali] had gangs of alleged Tudehites on the streets with orders to loot and smash shops on Lalehzar and Amiriyeh streets whenever possible, and to make clear that this was the Tudeh in action".[68] Creating an atmosphere of insecurity and fear, in the name of the Tudeh Party, and then blaming the Mosaddeq government for its inability to deal with the situation, was an important aspect of the psychological plan of pushing the nerve-wrecked Tehranis to join the pro-Shah demonstration of the next day (28 Mordad).

While the CIA's domestic employees, in the guise of Tudeh supporters, were causing havoc on 27 Mordad, Zahedi's message to the Iranian army officers and people calling on them to sacrifice their lives for independence, the monarchy and the holy religion of Islam, which was threatened by the Communists, was dispatched by an Associated Press correspondent and was being prepared for publication in *Daad* for the morning of 28 Mordad.[69] Zahedi's proclamation, which was a directive for 28 Mordad, stated that "God willing, my government is decided on putting an end to the chaos that has been imposed on this country by foreign agents".[70] The planners of the second coup had intelligently taken advantage of the excessiveness of the Tudeh slogans: by sending their own agents into action, they had planted the seeds of suspicion in the hearts of the common folk, while at the same time providing hope for law and order if the pro-Shah demonstration of 28 Mordad were to succeed.

The activities of authentic Tudeh Party members chanting anti-Shah slogans and calling for a "Democratic Republic" were compounded with the destructive and hooligan acts of the make-believe Tudeh members of Keyvani and Jalali's organization, and lasted until around 8:00 p.m. At around this time, trucks filled with policemen and soldiers suddenly entered Sepah Square (Toupkhaneh) and warned the demonstrators to disperse. The reporter of the daily *Keyhan* wrote that the military and police personnel attacked the crowds every few minutes, chasing them away and beating up those who stayed behind, using their rifles, bayonets and batons. The forces of law and order also used tear gas, gravely injuring demonstrators.[71] According to one

---

[67] Wilber, pp. 59, 63. [68] Wilber, p. 63. [69] Wilber, p. 60; *Daad*, 28 Mordad 1332.
[70] *Daad*, 28 Mordad 1332. [71] *Keyhan*, 29 Mordad 1332, quoted in Javanshir, p. 299.

eye-witness, the quantity of tear gas used was such that breathing was difficult.[72] Raising their rifles, while giving chase the soldiers chanted "long live the Shah, death to the traitors and death to the Tudeh party". Anyone uttering a slogan against the Shah was arrested or beaten. Down the streets of Lalehzar, Eslambol, Naderi, Ferdowsi, Manouchehri and Shahabad, groups of soldiers and policemen pursued the demonstrators, chanting "long live the monarchy".[73]

In response to the disorder of 16, 17 and 18 August (25, 26 and 27 of Mordad), the Military Governor of Tehran issued a decree on 18 August (27 Mordad) commanding its forces to prevent any activity or demonstration that would undermine the peace.[74] The Military Governor of Tehran's communiqué referred to the lawlessness that had been prevalent during the past few days, attacks on shops by certain reckless elements, and the growing discontent of ordinary citizens. It strictly prohibited any demonstration without prior permission from the authorities, and ordered law-enforcement personnel to arrest anyone breaking the law.[75] One direct consequence of this ban on demonstration was the fierce repression of the Tudeh Party and pro-Mosaddeq sympathizers on the evening of Tuesday 27 Mordad.

The other important consequence of the ban on demonstrations was that pro-Mosaddeq nationalist parties were also obliged to keep their partisans off the streets. As of the afternoon of 18 August (27 Mordad), members of the pro-Mosaddeq Third Force Party of Khalil Maleki were officially ordered, through a directive in the daily *Bakhtar Emrouz*, to avoid clashing with Tudeh supporters roaming the streets of the city.[76] According to Hoseyn Sakaki, a member of the Third Force Party, the directive to avoid clashes with Tudeh supporters, which is said to have come from Mosaddeq himself and was intended to calm the tension on the streets, played a key role in the absence of pro-Mosaddeq forces on the next day, the day of the coup d'état.[77] The events of the night of 27 Mordad, orchestrated by two different networks of the conspirators – military and Keyvani–Jalali – in effect helped clear the streets of Tehran of any pro-Mosaddeq or anti-Shah supporters and militants on the following day, when the big demonstration was to take place. On 28 Mordad, the Keyvani–Jalali network staged chaos and mayhem, while the collaborationist military network unleashed their wrath to intimidate potential pro-Mosaddeq demonstrators.

The prelude to the second coup was successfully set in motion during the afternoon of 18 August. Reports from both Iranian and foreign sources clearly indicate that, as of the evening of 18 August, Tehran began to witness an unprecedented excess of zeal on the part of security forces dispatched to confront Tudeh Party demonstrators. As the bloody evening dragged on, the

---

[72] Amir-Khosravi, p. 589.   [73] *Keyhan*, 29 Mordad 1332 quoted in Javanshir, pp. 299–300.
[74] *Bakhtar Emrouz*, 27 Mordad 1332.   [75] *Ettela'at*, 27 Mordad 1332.
[76] Shahhoseyni, pp. 65–66.   [77] Shahhoseyni, p. 66.

rage of the military and the police turned against anyone who was not actively pro-Shah or pro-Zahedi. The conspiratorial officers used Riyahi's circular ordering the dropping of the Shah's name from the morning and evening flag ceremonies to the best interest of their cause. They fanned the great fear that the Mosaddeq government was committed to erasing any sign of the Shah. The well-concocted plan galvanized and inflamed the army personnel of the garrisons against any sign of disrespect towards the Shah. Even more important was the fact that by the end of 18 August the anti-Mosaddeq officers and soldiers were further emboldened by the fact that their insubordination during the evening flag ceremonies was left un-reprimanded, giving them the signal that either Mosaddeq's top military brass were in favour of his overthrow or that they would stand by, watch and wait. The chasm between Mosaddeq and the Shah was purposefully deepened in the army right before the launching of the second coup.

The ferocity with which the soldiers repressed the anti-Shah demonstrators bolstered the morale of the conspirators and heartened the collaborating "line commanders" preparing for the main operations the next day. It also intimidated and confused the militant rank and file of the Tudeh Party, who may have considered their anti-Shah actions as compatible with their pro-Mosaddeq stance, and who were subsequently baffled by the violence of government troops against them. Those who were being beaten up by the military and the police were under the impression that Mosaddeq had ordered the unprecedented intensification of violence.

In addition to the glaring indecision of the Tudeh Party's leadership over whether its members in Tehran should take any action on 19 August, the bloody repression of their members on the evening of 18 August must have dissuaded many of their rank and file from taking to the streets on the day of the second coup.[78] The effective intimidation campaign of the conspirators on the eve of the second coup, in addition to Mosaddeq's anxiety over keeping peace on the streets by banning demonstrations, also convinced the militant sympathizers of Mosaddeq and the political organizations supporting him to stay put, keep a low profile, and avoid confrontations during the days to come. Consequently, the political forces capable of countering the coup on 28 Mordad were effectively neutralized and pacified before the coup.

SUSPICIOUS GOINGS-ON

During the afternoon of 27 Mordad, Anvar Khameh'i, a young Communist who along with a group of his like-minded friends had splintered from the Tudeh Party, approached Mohammad-Hoseyn Ardeshiri to request 100 Tomans to publish the group's newspaper, *Sobh-e Enqelab* ("The Dawn

---

[78] M. Keymaram, *Rofaqaye Bala* (Tehran: Shabaviz, 1374), pp. 279–280; Javanshir, pp. 302–303; Amir-Khosravi, p. 552.

of Revolution") on the following day. Ardeshiri was the owner of Aftab pharmacy on Naderi Street. Aftab pharmacy was also the gathering place of Ardeshiri's friends, who represented a rainbow of political views and affiliations. A generous man, Ardeshiri had never refused assistance, but now he counselled the young man not to publish his radical and anti-Shah newspaper on 28 Mordad. One of Ardeshiri's old friends, a die-hard opponent of Mosaddeq and a "trusted and confirmed functionary" of the British, had passed by the pharmacy right before Khameh'i's arrival and they had discussed the country's political situation. Ardeshiri's "white-haired and tanned" friend had informed him that "Mosaddeq's fate will be sealed tomorrow".[79] The young Khameh'i responded that his friends knew that a coup was being planned, but that Mosaddeq would foil it. Referring to the mysterious visitor, Ardeshiri reminded him that "the chap seemed very hopeful and certain, it seems as if this time, they are coming full force" (*in bar sombeh kheyli por zour ast*).[80] Ardeshiri eventually did lend the 100 Tomans to the young activist, and Mosaddeq's fate was indeed sealed the next day.

Mashallah Varqa, Head of the Surveillance Office (*sho'beh moraqebat*) of the Bureau of Investigation, claims that on the morning of 18 August (27 Mordad) he informed his superior officer, Colonel Houshang Naderi, of a new coup pending against the Mosaddeq government. Varqa's source of information was a relative of his who worked with the American Military Attaché in Tehran.[81] After Varqa reported to Naderi, the latter left the office, giving Varqa the impression that he was on his way to Mosaddeq. Late in the afternoon of 28 Mordad, when the coup officers sought to arrest Mosaddeq's military brass, they came for Colonel Naderi, Mosaddeq's Head of the Bureau of Investigation. Faced with his potential captors at his office, Naderi is reported to have said "Zahedi knows me and is fond of me".[82] During Mosaddeq's trial after the coup, Naderi was called to the court as a source of information. He informed the court that between 25 and 27 Mordad he had reported the very sensitive information that his office had gathered to the Chief of Police (Modabber) and Tehran's Military Governor (Ashrafi).[83] It may be surmised that the Surveillance Office had received news of the preparation of the second coup and that Naderi had decided to share it only with Modabber and Ashrafi, both of whom were suspected of collusion with the anti-Mosaddeq conspiring officers. Naderi's comment after the coup – about Zahedi knowing him and being fond of him – supports the hypothesis that even though information about the impending coup was available to key individuals at strategic positions, the coup forces were

---

[79] Khameh'i, 1362, p. 437.   [80] Khameh'i, 1362, p. 437.
[81] M. Varqa, *Nagoftehha'i Piramoun-e Fororiziye Hokumat-eMosaddeq va naqsh-e Hezbe Tudeh-e Iran* (Tehran: Baztabnegar, 1384), pp. 41, 154.
[82] Varqa, p. 41.   [83] Varqa, p. 159.

successful at containing it and keeping it from getting into pro-Mosaddeq hands.

On the eve of 28 Mordad (19 August), all the groundwork for the "great demonstration" leading to the overthrow of Mosaddeq was prepared. So were the actors. A close circle of trusted Anglophiles, Americophiles and pro-Shah elements were informed that something important was in the air. The degree to which the coup agents and their collective effort were to succeed also hinged on the vigilance, preparedness and loyalty of the military forces defending Mosaddeq's government.

MOSADDEQ'S INFILTRATED DEFENCES

The military master plan for protecting Tehran and the government from potential turmoil and danger relied on four key military units.[84] This preventive plan first relied on the Military Governor of Tehran, Colonel Hoseynqoli Ashrafi (who was also a brigade commander). According to Riyahi, Mosaddeq's Chief of Staff, Colonel Ashrafi had special units of his Third Mountain Brigade always on standby alert. The zealous pro-Shah and anti-Mosaddeq Major Zand, and his equally zealous sergeants and soldiers of the Naderi Battalion, belonged to the Third Mountain Brigade and must have been a part of the special units on constant standby for the defence of the government. Ashrafi, who constituted Mosaddeq's first line of defence, was strongly suspected of being in league with the plotting officers. Had he not been implicated, he would have reacted appropriately as early as 7:30 p.m. on 27 Mordad, having been informed of insubordination in the garrisons, which he did not. After the coup, Ashrafi was arrested and accused of being complicit with Mosaddeq to overthrow the regime.[85] He was, however, released before he was ever put on trial.[86]

The second key officer responsible for the protection of Tehran was the Chief of Police, who was obliged to place units of his force at the disposal of the Military Governor of Tehran. On 18 August (27 Mordad), Tehran's Chief of Police was Colonel Nasrollah Modabber, a collaborator, who was dismissed and imprisoned by noon on 28 Mordad, as was Ashrafi. At 1:00 p.m. on Monday 17 August (26 Mordad), Modabber assembled all the commanders of Tehran's police stations and lectured them on the importance of keeping the public peace during the forthcoming days.[87] He ordered them to repress all demonstrations, and especially those by Tudeh Party members. Confidentially, he gave the police station commanders the go-ahead to crush all demonstrations by those who could be considered anti-Shah

---

[84] Nejati, p. 500. [85] Be Ravayat-e Asnad-e Savak, *Jebhey-e Melli*, p. 11.
[86] B. Aqeli, *Sharh-e Hal-e Rejal Siyasi va Nezamiy-e Moaser Iran* (Tehran: Goftar, 1380), p. 129.
[87] Baniahmad, p. 116.

demonstrators (both Tudeh and non-Tudeh pro-Mosaddeq forces).[88] On the afternoon of Tuesday 27 Mordad, Modabber participated in the National Security Council held at Mosaddeq's house.[89] The highly confidential national and security matters discussed and decided by this high-powered body must have become known to the conspirators through Modabber. It seems as though, through Modabber, the conspirators had a secure inside informant who could report on exactly how well-informed or uninformed the highest officials of Mosaddeq's government and military apparatus were with regard to the overthrow plan.

The third key military unit responsible for the protection of Tehran was the motorized units at Bagheshah garrison. At the time, this important garrison was under Colonel Mohammad Daftari's thumb.[90] In the summer of 1953, some 400 cadets of the Armed Custom Guards were being trained at Bagheshah under the direct command of Daftari, who was Zahedi's prospective Chief of Police even before the first coup was carried out.[91] Riyahi believed that if someone other than Mohammad Daftari had been in command of the units at Bagheshah, the events of 28 Mordad would not have taken place.[92] There is ample evidence to show that the Bagheshah garrison was thoroughly infiltrated by the coup-makers. Captain Parviz Khosrovani, who mobilized the members of his Taj Athletics Club on 28 Mordad and actively participated in the overthrow of Mosaddeq, recalled that he had been informed in advance that certain operations had been planned for 28 Mordad by an officer of the Imperial Guards at Bagheshah – an officer he does not name.[93] On 28 Mordad, the main protective shields against a possible coup – namely the forces at the disposal of the Military Governor, the Chief of Police of Tehran and the commander of the Armed Custom Guards – were placed in the single hands of Mohammad Daftari (Zahedi's accomplice) by Mohammad Mosaddeq himself.

The fourth and last protective shield of Tehran and Mosaddeq's government was the Second Armoured Brigade of Colonel Naser Shahrokh.[94] After the second coup d'état Colonel Shahrokh chided Colonel Momtaz for having resisted the coup and told him that on 19 August he had ordered the telephone lines of his garrison at Jay to be cut.[95] Tank units of this same brigade did play a role on 28 Mordad, and Wilber maintains that "the Second Battalion of the Second Armoured Brigade was originally committed to the operation".[96] However, it is unlikely that Colonel Shahrokh was a collaborationist officer. The way in which Jay garrison, the base of the Second Armoured

---

[88] Baniahmad, p. 116.   [89] Baniahmad, p. 118.
[90] Mohammad Daftari, Iranian Oral History Collection, Harvard University, Transcript 2, p. 13.
[91] *Tehran Mosavvar*, 22 Khordad 1332.   [92] Nejati, p. 501.
[93] Parviz Khosrovani, Iranian Oral History Collection, Transcript 1, p. 12.
[94] Nejati, p. 500.   [95] Nejati, p. 448.   [96] Wilber, p. 67.

Brigade, capitulated to pro-Zahedi forces on 28 Mordad rather demonstrates that Colonel Shahrokh remained neutral, even if he was complaisaent and all too ready to surrender his post (which from the plotters' point of view was the second-best attitude in a brigade commander). If the conspirators could convince all of the brigade commanders to stand by and watch while the collaborationist line commanders carried out the coup, then the success of the military aspect of the coup was guaranteed. Therefore, all four military units that were supposed to provide Tehran and the Mosaddeq government with a solid protective shield against military plots and conspiracies were compromised. They were either in the hands of collaborationist officers, loyal to the CIA–SIS operation of overthrowing Mosaddeq, or in the hands of effectively neutralized commanders. Of all of the military units in Tehran, only those under the command of Colonels Momtaz and Shahrokh were not in league with the collaborationist officers. Given Shahrokh's complaisance, it is fair to say that only Momtaz himself, and not his entire brigade, stood by Mosaddeq.[97]

---

[97] *Tehran Mosavvar*, 6 Shahrivar 1332.

10

The second coup begins with the pincer movement of the thugs

In the early hours of 28 Mordad, Tehran was split into two different worlds: that of the calm, almost dead centre of the town, and the bustling south. In the southern neighbourhoods of the city (the Mowlavi axis and below), forces were on the move. In and around Meydan Barforoushan (the vegetable market), Aminosoltan, Esma'il Bazzaz Street, Shoosh, Sar Qabr Agha, Bagh Ferdows, Javadiyeh and Robat Karim, ragtag groups of the lumpenproletariat, the ruffians and their followers (*lat o lut-ha*), as well as unemployed day labourers, ready to be hired, were being mobilized. From the eve of 28 Mordad, those living in these neighbourhoods could feel the hustle and bustle of preparations for something momentous. Manzarpour, a resident of Esma'il Bazzaz Street (Mowlavi), recalled that from the night of 27 Mordad there was a feeling in the air that something was under way. In the neighbourhood, he witnessed many of the roughnecks scurrying back and forth.[1]

One of the centres from which the ruffians of 28 Mordad started the "great demonstration" belonged to Seyyed Kamal, a neighbour of Manzarpour. Seyyed Kamal had been imprisoned and after his release had opened up a *zourkhaneh* – a traditional athletic club – as he was some sort of an athlete.[2] He subsequently became an organizer of religious passion plays (*ta'ziyeh*), and his house was frequented by the idle and those who forcefully collected protection money from shopkeepers. When mourning groups had their regular processions during *Moharram*, members of his gang would greet them. Financed by the Shah's state apparatus, Seyyed Kamal had established many headquarters around Tehran under the pretext of founding religious groups, traditional athletic centres, passion play centres and coffee houses.[3] From 26 Mordad, the people under his protective umbrella were mobilized, well fed and entertained. On the day of 28 Mordad, they were directed from Seyyed Kamal's "headquarters" towards the centre of the city and Mosaddeq's house; on their way they looted whatever they could. After the second

---

[1] Manzarpour, p. 164. [2] Manzarpour, p. 164. [3] Manzarpour, p. 165.

coup, Seyyed Kamal became rich.[4] There are numerous accounts of empty-handed individuals in Southern Tehran, whose humble material lives were "miraculously" transformed for the better after the coup, in recognition of services rendered on 28 Mordad.[5] Many of those ruffians who led small groups in the "great demonstration" of 28 Mordad became respectable government functionaries and were given regular salaries from the secret budget of state organizations, such as the Tobacco Company (*edareh dokhaniyat*), the Railroad Company (*rah-ahan*), the Sports Organization (*tarbiyat badani*), and the City Council (*shahrdari*).[6]

Mirza Abdollah Jandaqi (better known as Mirza Shahriyari), who worked in the main wholesale fruit and vegetable market (*meydan*) of Southern Tehran, remembered how the "great demonstration" of 28 Mordad took shape and started. Jandaqi recollected that four main columns or processions of roughnecks set off from four different areas in Southern Tehran. These four areas were scattered along the axis of Mowlavi Street. The leaders of these four groups were infamous thugs of Southern Tehran, known for their police records of assault, battery and stabbing, but also for their generosity to the needy and their central role in organizing religious mourning processions, especially during the month of *Moharram*.

Jandaqi clearly outlines the trajectory of these groups on 28 Mordad. At strategic points in the city, gang leaders of lesser status at the head of their own small packs of *chaqu keshan* (knife-wielders) joined the main four groups, swelling their size as they moved to previously ascribed strategic points.[7] The route taken by some of the groups which set out early in the morning of 28 Mordad to march on Mosaddeq's house was similar to the trajectory of the mourning groups which these same individuals led during the regular *Moharram* religious ceremonies. An interesting common denominator among the four clan chiefs who moved their foot soldiers into the heart of Tehran on 28 Mordad was their close acquaintance and client–patron relationship with Asadollah Rashidiyan, who was present at the "council of war" held on the evening of 17 August inside the US Embassy compound.

TAYYEB AND TAHER HAJ REZA'I

The first main column of ruffians was under the leadership of two brothers, Tayyeb and Taher Haj Reza'i. This group started off from *Sar Qabr Aqa*, moving north along Aminosoltan Street, crossing Mowlavi Street, and continuing straight north through Syrus Street to Baharestan Square (Majles). The key confederates in this group were: Ali Reza'i, better known as Qadam; Naser Hasan Khani, better known as Naser Jigaraki (Naser the Skewer); Asghar Ostad Alinaqi, better known as Asghar Seski; Asghar Bana'i, better

---

[4] Manzarpour, pp. 165–166. [5] Manzarpour, pp. 81, 195, 196, 263, 276, 279.
[6] Manzarpour, p. 81. [7] Torbatiy-e Sanjabi, pp. 104–106.

known as Asghar Shater (Asghar the Baker who puts the dough in the oven); Reza; Haj Ali Nuri, better known as Mard-e Ahanin (Man of Iron); Habib Mokhtarmanesh; Ahmad Zowqi; and Haj Mazlum Nahavandi, better known as Haji Sardar (Haji the Commander).[8] The total number of participants in this group was about 300.

After the coup, Tayyeb is said to have publicly announced that "We were responsible for 28 Mordad, if there was bad-mouthing of Mosaddeq we did it, we did all this and we accept it".[9] When Tayyeb Haj Reza'i was arrested after participating in the June 1963 uprising against the Shah, and before his execution, it is said that the authorities informed him that just as he had served his Majesty in the 28 Mordad coup, he should once again oblige his royal wish and do as he was told. Tayyeb is reported to have responded thus: "Yes, I did do all those things against Mosaddeq and now if I were punished for my past misdeeds, justice would be rendered".[10]

Tayyeb was born in 1913 and was five years younger than his brother, Taher.[11] He recalled having been a wrestler at a very young age and having also been involved in street brawls and fights. Tayyeb was imprisoned more than once. During one of his prison terms, while the partisans of the Tudeh Party and Ja'far Pishehvari (President of the separatist Communist Azerbayejan People's Government 1945) were tattooing pictures of Pishehvari and Stalin on their arms and chests, Tayyeb tattooed a picture of Reza Shah Pahlavi, clad in his military uniform, on his stomach. He proudly displayed his tattoo to a journalist interviewing him in 1954.[12] After a bloody ethnic prison fight with the Turkish-speaking prisoners at Qasr prison over a gambling racket, Tayyeb and his three close friends, Hoseyn Ramezoun Yakhi, Qadam and Ali-Sadeq, were banished from Tehran to Bandar Abbas.[13]

Tayyeb was a popular figure of Southern Tehran, admired by the young streetwise urchins for his reputation as a fearless fighter, skilled in the use of knives and clubs. He was respected and loved by his supporters and cronies for his generosity and charity, whilst being feared and despised by those who crossed him. At the time he lived on Khorasan Street, close to the intersection of Khorasan Street and Rey Street, south of Mowlavi Street.[14] He was a traditional *zourkhaneh* athlete who woke up at 5:00 a.m. to do his prayers, ate his special breakfast (*dizy*) at a particular coffee house, and then went to work at *Meydan Aminosoltan*, the main fruit and vegetable wholesale market of Southern Tehran.[15]

In 1947, when Tayyeb was freed from prison, Haj Khan Khodadad, who owned the *Meydan Aminsoltan* market, employed him, and later it was again

---

[8] Torbatiy-e Sanjabi, p. 104.   [9] Mirza'i, p. 179.   [10] Mirza'i, p. 177.
[11] *Ashofteh*, 11 Azar 1333.   [12] *Ashofteh*, 11 Azar 1333.
[13] *Ashofteh*, 11 Azar 1333; *Shahid Tayyeb Haj Reza'i be Ravayat Asnad SAVAK*, pp. 1, 4, 9, 10.
[14] Mirza'i, p. 31.   [15] Mirza'i, pp. 59, 85.

Haj Khan Khodadad who helped him buy his fruit store.[16] From 1948 Tayyeb became known for the religious mourning processions which he organized from the first of *Moharram* to the day of *Ashura*. His mourning group had the reputation of being the largest in Tehran.[17] During these special religious nights, Tayyeb was reputed to serve 5,000 free dinners at his own *takiyyeh* or mourning centre located next to *anbar-e gandom*, Tehran's granary.[18]

Tayyeb recalled that until 9 Esfand he was not interested in politics and kept away from it. Then on 9 Esfand, when he heard about the Shah's intention to leave the country, he went to demonstrate in front of the Shah's palace.[19] In the aftermath of 9 Esfand, along with Sha'ban Ja'fari, Hasan Moharrer, Hoseyn Esma'ilipour (Ramezoun Yakhi), Ahmad 'Eshqi and Mohsen 'Adl Tabataba'i, Tayyeb was arrested and put on trial.[20] According to Tehran's newspapers of 1 August (10 Mordad), while Moharrer, Sha'ban Ja'fari and 'Eshqi were given prison terms of six months to a year, the court acquitted Tayyeb and Hasan Esma'ilipour (Ramezoun Yakhi).[21] In prison and awaiting their trial, the above six ruffians constantly claimed that they were innocent and had been arrested for the crime of loving the Shah and demonstrating in his favour.[22] In his interrogations, Tayyeb divulged his relation with General Abbas Garzan, the Chief of Staff, who was forced to retire by Mosaddeq after the summer of 1952. According to Tayyeb, Garzan had prompted him to play an active part in the pro-Shah demonstrations in front of the palace.[23] Garzan was one of General Zahedi's staunch supporters and a participant in the 9 Esfand demonstrations in favour of the Shah.

According to his disclosures, Tayyeb was also ordered and prompted by Ayatollah Behbahani to mobilize his troops and demonstrate in favour of the Shah on 9 Esfand.[24] Again, in the case of 28 Mordad, Tayyeb is believed to have been in contact with Ayatollah Behbahani and to have been instructed by him to mobilize his men on the orders of Hoseyn Kalantari, who worked for Ayatollah Behbahani.[25] It can be surmised that even though on 28 Mordad Tayyeb was acting on the orders of Ayatollah Behbahani and Asadollah Rashidiyan, he may also have been approached by Ayatollah Kashani and Qanatabadi to organize his supporters for the "great demonstration" of 28 Mordad.

On 22 Khordad (12 June) – or about two months before the 28 Mordad coup – a police report indicated that Shams Qanatabadi, Ayatollah Kashani's

---

[16] Mirza'i, p. 70.   [17] Mirza'i, p. 87.   [18] Mirza'i, p. 71.   [19] *Ashofteh*, 11 Azar 1333.
[20] *Shahid Tayyeb Haj Reza'i be Ravayat Asnad SAVAK*, pp. 20, 22.
[21] *Ettela'at* and *Keyhan*, 10 Mordad 1332.
[22] *Shahid Tayyeb Haj Reza'i be Ravayat Asnad SAVAK*, pp. 20, 22.
[23] *Shahid Tayyeb Haj Reza'i be Ravayat Asnad SAVAK*, p. 33, 36.
[24] *Shahid Tayyeb Haj Reza'i be Ravayat Asnad SAVAK*, pp. 33, 37, 38.
[25] *Tarikh Mo'aser Iran*, Sale Haftom, Shomareh 26, Tabestan 1382, p. 234.

right-hand man, was contacting a group of Tayyeb's friends to organize a demonstration against Mosaddeq's government.[26] Shams Qanatabadi was a staunch proponent of Zahedi, a member of the general's close circle of friends while he was in hiding, and involved in the highly secretive planning of the coup.[27] According to a police report in 1958, Tayyeb also frequented Ayatollah Kashani's house and was on friendly terms with him.[28]

On 16 June 1953 (26 Khordad 1332), the police reported that a group of retired army officers had contacted and prompted the supporters of Tayyeb to establish a branch of the Zolfaqar Party at Shah Square and enter into anti-governmental activities.[29] Assuming that Malekeh 'Etezadi's Zolfaqar Party was financed by Princess Ashraf, the retired army officers were probably trying to get Tayyeb's supporters organized and financed by one of the Court's many fronts for the opportune time when the physical presence and muscle of the mob would be required, as they were to do on 28 Mordad. The almost perfect coincidence of timing between approaching Tayyeb's supporters in Southern Tehran by the representatives of the retired army officers and that by the anti-Mosaddeq clergy indicates a high degree of coordination and planning between them, as well as by the Court. Yet it seems as though the real boss of Tayyeb's clan, as well as of almost all ruffian clans in the South of Tehran, was Asadollah Rashidiyan.

The police reports of people frequenting Rashidiyan's house during his regular gatherings after the coup indicate that Tayyeb was a habitué.[30] When Tayyeb needed Rashidiyan to peddle his influence with the police and governmental authorities, he would go to Rashidiyan's house asking for pay-back for services rendered during 28 Mordad. When, some six years after the coup, Tayyeb found himself in trouble with the Chief of Police of Tehran's 6th precinct, he went to Rashidiyan and, in an almost threatening tone, informed him that the following week he would come back to the main fruit, vegetable and meat market with all of his clan and settle his problem with the Chief of Police.[31]

According to Tayyeb, on the morning of 16 August 1953 (25 Mordad), Gholamhoseyn Mosaddeq, the Prime Minister's son, sent for Tayyeb and sought to appease him. Tayyeb claims to have refused Gholamhoseyn Mosaddeq's offer of 50,000 Tomans in return for remaining politically neutral in the days to come.[32] Tayyeb believes that on 26 and 27 Mordad, Tudeh Party sympathizers (Communists) and Mosaddeq's partisans entered into an alliance to disturb the peace in Tehran.[33] He claims to have heard

---

[26] *Shahid Tayyeb Haj Reza'i be Ravayat Asnad SAVAK*, p. 35.
[27] Torbatiy-e Sanjabi, p. 61.   [28] *Shahid Tayyeb Haj Reza'i be Ravayat Asnad SAVAK*, p. 4.
[29] *Shahid Tayyeb Haj Reza'i be Ravayat Asnad SAVAK*, p. 34.
[30] *Rashidiyanha*, vol. 1, pp. 359–360, 382, 400, 422.
[31] *Rashidiyanha*, vol. 1, p. 359–360.   [32] *Ashofteh*, 11 Azar 1333.
[33] *Ashofteh*, 11 Azar 1333.

murmurs from around the city on the morning of 28 Mordad and to have decided to free his friends from prison. Tayyeb recalls that "I immediately sent for the purchase of ten truck-loads of sticks (*dah bar-e choob kharidam*), we already had a few machetes and knives, we gathered all the boys and came to town in trucks and jeeps".[34] Tayyeb boastfully tells his interviewer that "you know what we did on that day or rather everyone knows what happened and what did not happen [on 28 Mordad]".[35]

Most members of Tayyeb's group on 28 Mordad, named by Jandaqi, were well known in the circle of roughnecks, athletes and unruly gallant knife-wielders. Ali Reza'i (Qadam) was well known for his strength and his powerful grip in the neighbourhood of Sampaz Khouneh (*sabounpaz khouneh*) and beyond.[36] Qadam had a long history of fighting alongside Tayyeb and of spending time in jail with him. He also had a reputation for being a mischievous rogue and (according to Tayyeb) was a drunk.[37] Naser-e Hasan Khani (Naser Jigaraki) was the president of the butchers' guild and was succeeded by Asghar Ostad Alinaqi (Asghar Seski), another of the confederates in Tayyeb's group.[38] Naser Jigaraki is among the many thugs who maintained his relationship with Asadollah Rashidiyan after the coup. When the band of brothers of Southern Tehran involved in 28 Mordad gathered at Asadollah Rashidiyan's house on Fridays after the coup, Naser Jigaraki, along with Hasan Behbudgar, would be among them.[39] Naser Hasan Khani (Naser Jigaraki) was also friends with Sha'ban Ja'fari.[40] Asghar Bana'i (Asghar Shater), yet another confederate, was born into a well-off pious family and held firm religious beliefs.[41] Bana'i was also a traditional athlete and a wrestler who owned a bakery, a restaurant, coffee houses and, most importantly, an athletics club called Shah Mardan, on the Anbar Gandom street.[42] He too managed and organized his own mourning group during the month of *Moharram*.[43] Haj Ali Nouri worked in the *Aminsoltan* market and since he had spent years in prison he was nicknamed the Iron Man (*mard-e ahanin*).[44] It was Ali Nouri's space on Anbar Gandom street that was used by Tayyeb as a *takiyyeh* (a mourning place) during the month of *Moharram*.[45] According to Sheykh Hasan Abdollahi, who was close to Tayyeb and Taher Reza'i, "on 28 Mordad, the *lutis* and *jahels* [roughnecks and ruffians] became scared of the government in place, since members of the Tudeh Party [Communists] had taken over all positions of responsibility. [On that day], they engaged in certain activities, because of their religious zeal".[46]

After the coup, the special committee that was formed to reward the civilian elements who had rendered exemplary service through their special

---

[34] *Ashofteh*, 11 Azar 1333.   [35] *Ashofteh*, 11 Azar 1333.   [36] Mirza'i, p. 34.
[37] *Ashofteh*, 11 Azar 1333.   [38] Mirza'i, p. 35.   [39] Rashidiyanha, vol. 1, p. 261.
[40] Sarshar, p. 200.   [41] Mirza'i, p. 45.   [42] Mirza'i, pp. 45–6.   [43] Mirza'i, pp. 19, 46.
[44] Mirza'i, p. 29.   [45] Mirza'i, p. 71.   [46] Mirza'i, p. 153.

activities on 28 Mordad, presided over by General Gholam-Hoseyn Afkhami, decorated Tayyeb and 19 of his collaborators with the Second Class Medal of Rastakhiz (or resurgence).[47] Hoseyn Ramezoun Yakhi was also a recipient of the Medal of Rastakhiz.[48] Subsequently, Tayyeb became a member of, and then the elected President of, the Southern Tehran branch of "The 28 Mordad Uprising and Resurgence Organization".[49] Ten years later, when Tayyeb was arrested and condemned to death for his involvement in the 5 June 1963 pro-Khomeyni uprising against the Shah, his family and friends wrote letters to the Shah pleading for his pardon. In their letters they reminded the Shah of all that Tayyeb had done for him and of the fact that Tayyeb had put his life on the line for him on 9 Esfand and 28 Mordad.[50] Hasan Behbudgar (*Hasan Seh kalleh*), who was closely involved with the preparation and coordination of the part played by the thugs in 28 Mordad and knew both the perpetrators of the "great demonstration" and its masterminds (Asadollah Rashidiyan and Ardeshir Zahedi), also pleaded with the Shah to pardon Tayyeb in recognition of his role in the 28 Mordad uprising.[51]

HOSEYN AND NAQI ESMAʻILPOUR

According to Mirza Abdollah Jandaqi, a second column of ruffians set off from south of Mowlavi Street, led by Hoseyn Esmaʻilpour (popularly known by his nickname, Ramezoun Yakhi) and his brother Naqi.[52] Ramezoun's nickname, which literally meant Ramezoun the Ice-Seller, had its origin in the fact that Hoseyn's father was an ice-seller. He was born in 1914, and by the time of the second coup he had spent a total of ten years in jail and three years in banishment at Ahwaz, Kerman and Bandar Abbas.[53] He was first imprisoned at the age of 22 for having knifed and killed someone in a night brawl.[54] After serving his prison sentence, Ramezoun Yakhi recalled having been recruited by Hasibi and Zirakzadeh, of Mosaddeq's National Front, to campaign for their candidates to the Majles in Tudeh strongholds.[55] Ramezoun Yakhi confided to an interviewer that it was on the eve of 28 February 1953 (*qoroub-e 9 Esfand*) that he "heard that the Shah intended to leave the country in reaction to the disorder caused by Tudeh Party sympathizers".[56] On the day of 9 Esfand, he was among those thug leaders who congregated in front of the Shah's palace and demonstrated in his favour. After he returned home on that night, he was arrested for his activities

---

[47] *Shahid Tayyeb Haj Reza'i be Ravayat Asnad SAVAK*, p. 42,
[48] A SAVAK report dated 18/3/38: http://tavakkol23.mihanblog.com/post/71.
[49] *Shahid Tayyeb Haj Reza'i be Ravayat Asnad SAVAK*, pp. 43–45, 175.
[50] *Shahid Tayyeb Haj Reza'i be Ravayat Asnad SAVAK*, pp. 163, 175.
[51] *Shahid Tayyeb Haj Reza'i be Ravayat Asnad SAVAK*, p. 169.
[52] Torbatiy-e Sanjabi, p. 104.   [53] *Ashofteh*, 18 Azar 1333.   [54] *Ashofteh*, 18 Azar 1333.
[55] *Ashofteh*, 18 Azar 1333.   [56] *Ashofteh*, 18 Azar 1333.

in front of Mosaddeq's house. Ramezoun Yakhi told an interviewer that the fact of having been forcefully separated from his sick child, who had died a few days later while he was in prison, turned the night of 9 Esfand into a nightmare for him.[57]

The issue of Ramezoun Yakhi's personal leadership of the second column from early in the morning of 28 Mordad remains rather muddled and uncertain. Mirza Abdollah Jandaqi (Mirza Shahriyari), who was from the main market place (*meydan*), knew the leaders of the thug clans and was an eye-witness to the events of 28 Mordad; he claims that the second main group of ruffians was led by Hoseyn Esma'ilpour (Ramezoun Yakhi) and his brother Naqi. However, it seems certain that Ramezoun Yakhi was in prison until the eve of 28 Mordad. Hoseyn Esma'ilpour (Ramezoun Yakhi), Tayyeb Haj Reza'i, Hasan Moharrer, Sha'ban Ja'fari, Ahmad'Eshqi and Mohsen Adl Tabataba'i were the ruffian leaders arrested for their involvement in the disturbances of 28 February.[58] On 1 August, the daily *Ettela'at* reported that Tayyeb Haj Reza'i and Hoseyn Esma'ilpour (Ramezoun Yakhi) were acquitted after their trial.[59] Even though Tayyeb seems to have been released from prison at this time, Ramezoun Yakhi continued to linger in prison because of a previous conviction. Ramezoun Yakhi and Tayyeb had been involved in a brawl, probably before 28 February 1953, during which Ramezoun Yakhi had stabbed Tayyeb and had been condemned to 18 months in prison.[60] Hoseyn Ramezoun Yakhi maintained that he was in prison until the eve of 28 Mordad.[61] His statement may indicate that he was freed on the night of 27 Mordad, which would have enabled him to directly participate in the morning activities of the ruffians.

Sha'ban Ja'fari, a well-known thug leader and a staunch follower of Ayatollah Kashani who was in prison on the day of 28 Mordad but did play a direct role from the afternoon of that day, insists that Ramezoun Yakhi was in prison with him until noon on 28 Mordad.[62] Ja'fari's recollection enforces the hypothesis that Ramezoun Yakhi could not have personally led the second column. In an attempt to minimize the role of other thug leaders in the events of 28 Mordad, Ja'fari also insists – incorrectly – that Tayyeb did not play a role on this day. Ramezoun Yakhi's own account of this day does not completely dissipate the confusion over his direct involvement with the mob on the morning of 28 Mordad. In an interview, he stated that "I have no recollection more satisfying than the fall of Mosaddeq's government on the eve of which (*ghoroubash*) we were freed from prison"; elsewhere he has reiterated that "I was

[57] *Ashofteh*, 18 Azar 1333.
[58] *Shaheed Tayyeb Haj Reza'i* be Ravayat-e Asnad-e SAVAK, p. 22; Ettela'at, 22 Tir and 10 Mordad 1332.
[59] Ettela'at, 10 Mordad 1332.
[60] *Keyhan*, 29 Ordibehesht 1332; *Shaheed Tayyeb Haj Reza'i* be Ravayat-e Asnad-e SAVAK, p. 33.
[61] *Ashofteh*, 18 Azar 1333.   [62] Sarshar, p. 163.

freed from prison on the eve (*ghoroub-e*) of 28 Mordad".⁶³ Was Ramezoun Yakhi freed on the eve of 28 Mordad (on the night prior to 28 Mordad) or around sunset on 28 Mordad? The latter time would coincide with the time when Mosaddeq's house fell. When recounting his memories of 9 Esfand, Ramezoun Yakhi uses the term "eve of" or "*ghoroub-e*" 9 Esfand to refer to the night before 9 Esfand. If it is assumed that by the eve of *or ghoroub-e* 28 Mordad he once again meant the night before 28 Mordad, then his account conflicts with Sha'ban Ja'fari's account that "Hoseyn [Ramezoun Yakhi] was in prison until the noon (*zohr-e*) of 28 Mordad".⁶⁴ What is known is that by early afternoon – or around 2:00 p.m. – on 28 Mordad all the prisons in Tehran where military or civilian opponents of Mosaddeq were detained were opened and the prisoners were released.

The enigma of Ramezoun Yakhi's direct and personal involvement in the morning activities of the mob during 28 Mordad becomes even more complicated. Some five and a half years after the coup – March 1959 – a participant at the weekly gatherings in Asadollah Rashidiyan's house identified as Esma'ili – who must have been Hoseyn Ramezoun Yakhi, as he was also known as Esma'ilipour or Esma'ili and regularly attended Rashidiyan's open-house meetings – is reported to have bemoaned the treatment of the foot soldiers who had served the Shah in the past. Ramezoun Yakhi is reported to have said:

> On the day of 9 Esfand they sent for us (*ma ra mikhahand*), on the day of 28 Mordad they sent for us, [then] they sent for us to self-flagellate [during Moharram] and when the job was over and they had reaped their benefits, they cut us loose and since then we realized that they call on us only for their own benefit [so now] we demand that they let us be.⁶⁵

Ramezoun Yakhi, therefore, acknowledged the fact that he was called upon to actively participate in the events of both 9 Esfand and 28 Mordad against Mosaddeq and confirmed that he did what he was asked to do. Ramezoun Yakhi also lamented a lack of gallantry (*morrowat*) on the part of the Shah and suggested that once he, other clan chiefs and their thugs saved the king's crown, they were neglected and abandoned.

Even if it is assumed that Ramezoun Yakhi was in prison on the day of 28 Mordad, it is still highly possible that his thugs did participate in the morning events of 28 Mordad, as in those days it was easy for prisoners to have contact with the outside world. According to Sha'ban Ja'fari, Roqiyeh Azadpour (better known as Parvin Ajdanqezi), a pro-Shah participant in the 9 Esfand demonstrations who was said to be from Tehran's red-light district, came to visit him in prison on the day of 28 Mordad, at around 10:00 a.m.⁶⁶ Ajdanqezi sought a message or a note from Ja'fari to the "boys", which she would deliver, encouraging them to participate in the "great demonstration". Ja'fari responded that "the boys know what they are supposed to do", yet he

---

⁶³ *Ashofteh*, 18 Azar 1333. ⁶⁴ Sarshar, p. 163. ⁶⁵ Rashidiyanha, vol. 1, pp. 200–201.
⁶⁶ Sarshar, p. 160.

agreed to send another message to his thugs through Ajdanqezi.⁶⁷ Sha'ban Ja'fari came to be known as the "crown-giver" or *tajbakhsh* for the role he played in the events on 28 Mordad, even though he did not get out of prison until noon. Just as Sha'ban Ja'fari had mobilized, managed and commanded his troop of thugs from prison, Hoseyn Ramezoun Yakhi and his brother Naqi could have done exactly the same thing. Given the lax conditions of the prison in which they were held, Ramezoun Yakhi could have also sent out word to his thugs and the other clan chiefs to participate in the morning events of 28 Mordad, as Mirza Abdollah Jandaqi claimed they did. According to Sha'ban Ja'fari, "the Rashidiyan brothers were in league with all the thugs (*jahel mahelha*) of the fruit and vegetable market (*meydan*)".⁶⁸ Therefore, Asadollah Rashidiyan could easily have instructed the clan chiefs in prison to send word to their troops, or he could have directly contacted their confederates – such as the Taheri brothers, in Ramezoun Yakhi's case – to secure their presence and participation on the morning of 28 Mordad for an agreed fee.

For years after the coup, Hoseyn Ramezoun Yakhi, along with all other thug leaders, would devotedly visit Asadollah Rashidiyan's house and pay their respects to the patron of the fruit and vegetable market (*meydan*) ruffians.⁶⁹ After Tayyeb's arrest for his alleged involvement in the 6 June 1963 revolts against the Shah, Ramezoun Yakhi, who continued to place the muscles of his clan at Rashidiyan's disposal, pleaded with him to use his influence in the Court to free Tayyeb.⁷⁰ Ramezoun Yakhi privately reminded Rashidiyan that Tayyeb Haj Reza'i had spent a lot of money mobilizing people to chant "long live" and "death to" during the past governments, and warned him that Tayyeb's arrest had disenchanted the people of Southern Tehran.⁷¹ Even though Rashidiyan promised to seek Tayyeb's release, the Shah refused to spare Tayyeb's life. By executing Tayyeb, Mohammad Reza Shah Pahlavi was effectively signalling that after ten years of being under the shadow of and in debt to the ruffians, their chiefs, the Rashidiyans, Ayatollah Behbahani and General Zahedi, he felt as though he was finally the real boss and was taking over the realm. The only other two key actors of 28 Mordad whom he could not do away with – namely the British and the American governments – continued to haunt him until the end of his reign.

Ramezoun Yakhi's group started their march on 28 Mordad from Bagh Ferdows, the principal cradle of Tehran's ruffians.⁷² Bagh Ferdows was to the south of Mowlavi Street and ran parallel to it. It was perpendicular to Aminosoltan Street, another hub of the ruffians, and an important south–north artery. Aminosoltan Street became Rey Street as it went to the south of Tehran and Syrus Street as it turned northwards. The main figures in Ramezoun Yakhi's group were the famous roughneck family of the Taheri

---

⁶⁷ Sarshar, p. 161.   ⁶⁸ Sarshar, p. 166.
⁶⁹ Rashidiyanha, vol. 1, pp. 27, 79, 81, 144, 149.   ⁷⁰ Rashidiyanha, vol. 3, pp. 24, 31.
⁷¹ Rashidiyanha, vol. 3, p. 31.   ⁷² Torbati-e Sanjabi, p. 104; *Hamshahri*, 13 Day 1382.

brothers: Mashallah Ebram Khan, Houshang Ebram Khan, Akbar Ebram Khan and Amir Ebram Khan. The Taheri brothers were also close to Tayyeb and to Abbas Kavousi, an associate of Sha'ban Ja'fari.[73] Even though Mirza Abdollah Jandaqi does not mention the Haj Abbasi brothers (*haft kachaloun*) as participants in Ramezoun Yakhi's group, one of the Abbasi brothers, Mahmud, claims that Ramezoun Yakhi's clan and that of the Abbasi brothers were one and the same.[74] The Abbasi brothers (*haft kachaloun*), along with three of the Taheri brothers – Mashallah, Amir and Houshang – were known to be Hoseyn Ramezoun Yakhi's most intimate friends (*rafiq garmabeh o golestan*).[75] It would logically follow that the Haj Abbasi brothers, along with the Taheri brothers, were also involved in the Ramezoun Yakhi column. The fact that Abbas Abbasi would later accompany Ramezoun Yakhi to Assadollah Rashidiyan's house after the coup indicates that the patron–client relationship between the two thug leaders and their boss, Assadollah Rashidiyan, continued even after 28 Mordad.[76] It may be posited with a high degree of certainty that the Abbasi brothers also participated in Ramezoun Yakhi's group.

THE STICKS AND CLUBS OF THE THUGS

Not all of those demonstrating on 28 Mordad were armed with sticks and clubs. Inequalities existed even among Tehran's ruffians: some were more equal than others! According to Mirza Abdollah Jandaqi, Ramezoun Yakhi's group was equipped with special metre-long clubs.[77] The homogeneous and unusually long clubs brandished by a good number of the ruffians on 28 Mordad are of great importance as they demonstrate that the "great demonstration" was well planned and prepared in advance. In his account of the events of 28 Mordad, a journalist from the daily *Keyhan* remarked on "the crowd who were equipped with long clubs" as they joined the groups congregated at Sepah (Toupkhaneh) Square.[78] The photographs of the mob during 28 Mordad confirm the fact that a good number of the demonstrators were equipped with standardized long sticks or clubs that must have been issued from a single source.[79]

After the coup, Tayyeb was explicit about the fact that he had purchased ten loads of sticks (*dah bar-e choob*) to be used on 28 Mordad.[80] It has been suggested that Haji Khan Khodadad, the powerful owner of the main fruit and vegetable wholesale market of Southern Tehran at *Meydan Aminosoltan*,

---

[73] Mirza'i, pp. 27, 109; Sarshar, pp. 80, 200.   [74] Mirza'i, pp. 58, 146.
[75] Mirza'i, p. 109.   [76] Rashidiyanha, vol. 1. 204.   [77] Torbati-e Sanjabi, p. 105.
[78] *Keyhan*, 29 Mordad 1332.
[79] See http://www.iichs.org/docimages/M_28Mordad_13.jpg. See also 15jpg, 20.jpg, 22.jpg, 23.jpg, 25.jpg; http://www.iichs.org/magazine/bahar/68/68_BeRevayat_03.jpg.
[80] *Ashofteh*, 11 Azar 1333.

had paid for the standard long clubs used on 28 Mordad.[81] Since 1947, Haji Khodadad had been Tayyeb's mentor and sponsor, acting as his spiritual father.[82] So it would seem natural that Tayyeb would be the one carrying out the transaction, picking up and distributing the sticks, while Haji Khodadad would be the one who paid for them. From where did Haji Khan Khodadad receive his orders and his compensation? Haji Khodadad was also connected with Asadollah Rashidiyan and would visit his house after 28 Mordad. It is telling that, according to police reports, Haji Khan Khodadad attended Rashidiyan's house along with Tayyeb Haj Reza'i and Sha'ban Ja'fari.[83] It could safely be posited that Asadollah Rashidiyan had such close ties with Haji Khan Khodadad that he could ask him for favours whenever he required them, in return for his peddling influence for Haji Khodadad's interests in the market place.

Since Jandaqi maintains that members of Ramezoun Yakhi's group were armed with long sticks – which were in fact used by the thugs on 28 Mordad, as the photos of that day demonstrate – and given that Tayyeb insists that he purchased ten loads of sticks, leaving the impression that the members of his column were equipped with these special sticks, a few questions are in order. Were some of the sticks bought by Khodadad and Tayyeb distributed to members of Ramezoun Yakhi's column as a good number of them were also very close to Tayyeb? Were the metre-long sticks of Ramezoun Yakhi's column which Jandaqi was talking about different from the ten loads of sticks bought by Tayyeb and Haji Khodadad for the activities of 28 Mordad? Was it possible to distinguish between Tayyeb's and Ramezoun Yakhi's groups and the sticks they carried given that the two columns merged into one at Mowlavi Square, a short block away from their initial points of congregation and departure? Irrespective of the answers to these questions, it is certain that serious preparations had been made for the "great demonstration".

The fact that a considerable number of the anti-Mosaddeq thugs demonstrating on 28 Mordad, as clearly established by the photographs taken on that day, possessed standard issued sticks and clubs in addition to what they could lay their hands on; that they were transported at some point on their march from the south with trucks and lorries, some military and some civilian; and that they possessed pictures of the Shah and his father and were equipped with loudspeakers, which they used on the cars and from the balcony of the City Council (*shahrdari*) at Sepah Square, all demonstrate that considerable preparation had gone into the organization of the "great demonstration" on 28 Mordad. Tayyeb recalled that, once the "boys" (*bachehha*) were gathered on 28 Mordad, "we came to the city centre on trucks and jeeps".[84] He added that "when we came to the city centre we saw that people from

---

[81] Ahmad Ashraf, personal telephone interview, 16 December 2011.   [82] Mirza'i, p. 70.
[83] Rashidiyanha, vol. 2, p. 25.   [84] *Ashofteh*, 11 Azar 1333.

other neighbourhoods were also swarming in, everyone knows what we did on that day and what happened".[85]

THE TAYYEB–RAMEZOUN YAKHI JOINT COLUMN

Once Tayyeb's group of some 300 petty employees of the marketplace (*meydan*) merged with Ramezoun Yakhi's column of a few hundred ruffians and lumpen-proletariat at Mowlavi Square, they headed north on Syrus Street, along the eastern wing of Tehran's main bazaar, and arrived at Sarcheshmeh (another fruit and vegetable market).[86] There are no reports of bazaar employees or craftsmen joining the column of ruffians coming from the fruit and vegetable market (*meydan*) south of Mowlavi Street. As the original Tayyeb and Ramezoun Yakhi group swelled in numbers, it moved further north on Syrus Street, giving the impression that the demonstrators were marching towards Ayatollah Behbahani's house, which was also on Syrus Street, right above Bouzarjomehri Street.[87] The column did not go towards Behbahani's house, however – it moved straight to Sarcheshmeh (*sabzehmeydan*), where they were joined by another group of roughnecks (Abbas and Akbar Laleh, Mirza Ali Shafi'i and Akbar Zaghi), who were also employed at the local fruit and vegetable market (*meydan*).[88] From Sarcheshmeh, the reinforced column headed towards its first designated strategic target: Baharestan Square.

Baharestan was very strategically located as it housed the Majles (parliament) and, most importantly, a good number of pro-Mosaddeq organizations, parties and newspapers had their offices, clubs and headquarters around Baharestan. The occupation of Baharestan Square, where pro-Mosaddeq forces often displayed their political superiority during huge demonstrations in front of the parliament, was a clear signal to the common people that on the morning of 28 Mordad the tide had turned and the coup forces were in control of the parliament building – even though there were no reports of them entering it. The Majles was probably Iran's most symbolic building of political authority and legitimacy, and Baharestan Square was the most symbolically paramount space in the city. The decision by the coup planners to take possession of Baharestan early in the day was an astute and well-calculated military decision. It inflicted an early psychological defeat on the supporters of Mosaddeq by sending the message that the people's house – the Majles – had new landlords. Ironically, the new landlords of Iran's parliament were Tehran's ruffians.

From Baharestan the mob – which up to this point had been chanting pro-Shah and anti-Tudeh slogans and putting up a show of force – began smashing the centres of pro-Mosaddeq parties, organizations and newspapers. The crowd

---

[85] *Ashofteh*, 11 Azar 1333.   [86] Torbatiy-e Sanjabi, pp. 104–105.
[87] Shahhoseyni, p. 145.   [88] Torbatiy-e Sanjabi, p. 105.

then moved westward along Shahabad Street towards Mokhberodowleh Square, where they were joined by Mostafa Koliya'i, better known as Mostafa Zaghi (Mostafa the Blue Eyed) and a group of Armenian ruffians.[89] Mostafa Zaghi, who was an athlete and a devoted follower of Tayyeb, had killed an assailant of Tayyeb and had been imprisoned for it.[90] After the coup, Mostafa Zaghi was among those who accompanied Ramezoun Yakhi to Assadollah Rashidiyan's house.[91] From Mokhberodowleh Square, the ruffians moved westward, towards Eslambol, Naderi, and Shah Streets, and then descended Lalehzar, Ferdowsi, Hafez, and Pahlavi Streets to their other designated targets, thus half-circling and surrounding the administrative (including the police and military) and bureaucratic core of the city.

MAHMUD MESGAR AND BOYOUK SABER

Mirza Abdollah Jandaqi maintains that he heard of a third group who marched on Tehran on 28 Mordad. This group was led by Mahmud Mesgar, who was yet another traditional athlete and moved his followers from Shahr-e no, the official red-light district of Tehran at the time.[92] Mesgar was Hoseyn Ramezoun Yakhi's brother-in-law. He was yet another one of those influential South-of-Tehran thugs whom Assadollah Rashidiyan had cultivated and patronized for his political purposes. Similarly to Hoseyn Ramezoun Yakhi, Tayyeb, the Abbasi brothers (*haft kachaloun*) and others, Mesgar remained a loyal member of Rashidiyan's circle of thug leaders after the coup.[93] Mahmud Mesgar was also associated with Sha'ban Ja'fari, Abbas Kavousi and Hasan Arab.[94] This group must have started their march from Qazvin Street; from there they moved east, to Meydan-e Qazvin, then north on Pahlavi Street, from where they could fan westward towards Mosaddeq's house or eastwards towards Sepah Square.

Finally, the fourth column is said to have marched under the leadership of Boyouk Saber from the Javadiyeh neighbourhood, west of Rah-Ahan Square (Tehran's old railway station).[95] Aside from Mesgar's group, the other confederates congregated and started their invasion of the city centre from south of Mowlavi Street. Saber, who first published a newspaper called *Ki be Kiyeh* ("what is going on/who is who") and then one called *Siyasi* ("political"), had long commanded a group of roughnecks intervening in political disputes in favour of the Court and pro-British politicians.[96] Saber had close relations with some of Southern Tehran's well-known ruffians, such as Mostafa Dadkan, better known as Mostafa Divouneh (Mostafa the Madman), Hoseyn Aqa Mehdi, Hoseyn Ramezoun Yakhi and Mehdi

---

[89] Torbati-e Sanjabi, p. 105.   [90] Mirza'i, p. 106.   [91] Rashidiyanha, vol. 3, p. 185.
[92] Torbatiy-e Sanjabi, p. 105.   [93] Rashidiyanha, vol. 1, p. 395.   [94] Sarshar, p. 80.
[95] Torbatiy-e Sanjabi, p. 105.   [96] M. Araki, *Nagoftehha* (Tehran: Rasa, 1370), pp. 54–56.

The second coup begins with the pincer movement of the thugs 169

Qassab (Mehdi the Butcher).[97] Saber was close to pro-British politicians such as Jamal Emami.[98] Along with a number of pro-British journalists, some of whom were retired army officers, Saber had demonstrated his allegiance to the Rashidiyan family by publishing an open letter in October 1952 strongly condemning their arrest.[99] Saber was also a member of Asadollah Rashidiyan's coterie of well-organized southern thugs and continued to remain loyal to him after the coup.[100] While it may be surmised that Saber had connections with Ayatollah Behbahani, there is no doubt about his affiliation with Ayatollah Kashani and his son Mostafa Kashani.[101] Saber was contacted on the eve of 28 Mordad and participated in a gathering at Qazvin Street, where instructions were given and money paid out by Captain Ghaffari to the ruffians of the Javadiyeh and Koshtargah (Tehran's main slaughterhouse) neighbourhood for their activities on the next day.[102] Boyouk Saber participated in the morning events of 28 Mordad and the beating-up of Mosaddeq's partisans.[103]

Pro-Tudeh sources concur with certain aspects of Mirza Abdollah Jandaqi's account of the composition of the groups which marched on the centre of Tehran, their leadership and the organizational masterminds behind this "great demonstration". It is reported that on the orders of Ayatollah Behbahani, Mahmud Mesgar (one of the administrators and leaders of Shahr-e No, Tehran's red-light district), Tayyeb and Ramezoun Yakhi, along with a group of their supporters, first poured into Lalehzar and Naderi Streets on the evening of 27 Mordad (18 August) and demonstrated in favour of the Shah. On the next day, these same elements, in addition to groups under the leadership of Sha'ban Bimokh ("brainless") or Sha'ban Ja'fari, continued their demonstrations, armed with sticks and clubs and supported by military units.[104]

OTHER BROAD-CHESTED TRADITIONAL ATHLETES

Other than the four major groups which marched from around Mowlavi Street and onto the city centre, there are certain individuals whose names have also been associated with the organization of the mob on 28 Mordad. Karim Owliya'i, better known as Karim siyah (Karim the Black), held numerous championship titles in various fields of traditional athletics (*varzesh bastani*) and was a well-known ruffian. Owliya'i had entered politics during the Mosaddeq period and believed that, had the idea of a republic not been broached or supported by Mosaddeq and his entourage, 28 Mordad would

---

[97] Araqi, p. 56. [98] Safari, pp. 504, 590. [99] *Ettela'at*, 6 Esfand 1331.
[100] Rashidiyanha, vol. 1, p. 438.
[101] Be Ravayat-e Asnad-e, *Rowhaniy-e Mobarez Ayatollah Seyyed Abolqasem Kashani* vol. 1 (Tehran: Markaz-e Barasiy-e Asnad-e Tarikhiy-e Vezarat-e Ettela'at, 1379), p. 307.
[102] Torbatiy-e Sanjabi, p. 18. [103] Torbatiy-e Sanjabi, p. 65. [104] Jami, pp. 665–666.

not have occurred.[105] The notion that Mosaddeq was intent on changing Iran's political system from a monarchy to a republic was widely propagated between 25 and 28 Mordad by the coup planners and it seems to have been quite effective. Owliya'i recalled that on the morning of 28 Mordad, he, Haj Mohammad Sharif and a friend were the first ones to raise the picture of the Shah at Baharestan Square.[106] From there, he recalled heading towards Tehran's Radio Broadcasting Station. After the fall of Mosaddeq, Karim was awarded a Second Class Medal of Rastakhiz (*resurgence*) for his exceptional services rendered on 28 Mordad.[107]

Richard Cottam, a CIA officer under cover as a political officer at the American Embassy in Tehran between 1956 and 1968 and familiar with the goings-on during the coup (even though at the time of the coup he was in the US), maintains that Kashani and Baqa'i had de-facto alliances with the British but were "not the direct instruments of the Anglo-American effort".[108] He reiterates that: "Strong-arm leaders, especially Hasan Arab and Sha'ban Ja'fari and conservative religious leaders, especially Seyyed Mohammad Behbahani, served this function".[109] Cottam suggests that while Kashani and Baqa'i were not direct agents of the Anglo-American coup, Arab, Sha'ban Ja'fari and Ayatollah Behbahani were. Irrespective of the degree of validity of this statement, Cottam seems to have conflated the person, position and influence of the likes of Arab and Sha'ban Ja'fari with Ayatollah Behbahani, which seems inappropriate. Ayatollah Behbahani was in a league of his own. He was one of the key spiritual authorities and organizers of 28 Mordad, closely in touch with the nine masterminds (two American and seven Iranian) who re-designed and re-planned the coup in the grounds of the American Embassy in Tehran on 17 August. He belonged to the second circle of the masterminds of the second coup, while Arab and Sha'ban Ja'fari were mere footmen and perpetrators.

After the occupation of Iran by the Allies on 25 August 1941 and the departure of Reza Shah, the British founded a centre called the Victory House. The main function of this centre was the production and distribution of propaganda published in Persian, Arabic and English. The Victory House was headed by A.K.S. Lambton.[110] Hasan Arab is said to have become closely associated with Miss Lambton and to have accompanied her on her criss-crossing of Iran, as she inspected branches of the Victory House in the provinces, met tribal leaders and visited holy shrines wearing the *chador* (veil).[111] This may be a rather exaggerated account of actual events. At the time, Arab was also the owner of a publishing house called *Piyadehro* ("the side-walk"), located on Naderi Street; he had obtained the monopoly on

---

[105] *Ashofteh*, 18 Azar 1333.   [106] *Ashofteh*, 18 Azar 1333.   [107] *Ashofteh*, 18 Azar 1333.
[108] R. Cottam, 1988, p. 106.   [109] Cottam, 1998, p. 106.   [110] Torbatiy-e Sanjabi, p. 28.
[111] Torbatiy-e Sanjabi, p. 30.

distributing English publications.[112] The offices of *Piyadehro* are also said to have been used by Miss Lambton for her meetings with some of Iran's notable politicians such as Hajir, Movarekhodoleh Sepehr, Taheri, Malekmadani and Gholamhoseyn Ebtehaj.[113]

After the war, Arab entered politics and became a member of Seyyed Zia Tabatab'i's *Hezb-e Eradeh Melli* (The National Will Party). Along with a man called Sani' Hazrat, who was one of Tehran's ruffians, Arab became a member of Seyyed Zia's shock troopers and his bodyguard.[114] He subsequently organized a group of ruffians and knife-wielders from Southern Tehran and employed them in confrontations with Tudeh Party supporters.[115] Hasan Arab was known to the British Embassy in Tehran as a "political tough" who took orders from Dr. Baqa'i. He was also known for roughing up "news-vendors selling Communist and near-Communist papers and burning their supplies".[116] Arab was believed to be a British agent and was very well connected with Baqa'i, Sha'ban Ja'fari and Mahmud Mesgar.[117]

Whereas Sha'ban Ja'fari, very much like Tayyeb and Hoseyn Ramezoun Yakhi, was directly connected with and respected by the traditional athletes and ruffians of Southern Tehran, Arab did not really belong to that milieu. He had become a more well-to-do political knife-wielder, without solid ties to the athletic clubs. He frequented established political circles and was said to be close to the Shah. The extent to which Arab could have directly participated in 28 Mordad is uncertain, yet, like Ja'fari, he could well have commanded his followers without actually being present. In the early morning of 25 Mordad (16 August), Arab, in Beirut at the time, was ordered to go to Baghdad and place his services at the Shah's disposal. Arab arranged for the Shah to meet with Ayatollah Shahrestani, who performed a divination for him, and then saw the Shah off to Rome on 26 Mordad (17 August) and returned to Beirut from Baghdad.[118] In the absence of reports on Arab's activities in Tehran on 28 Mordad it can be deduced that he played a secondary role in the events, not comparable to that of Sha'ban Ja'fari.

THUGS MEETING THE SHAH

The importance of the services rendered by at least five key thug leaders during 28 Mordad is well reflected and documented in two photographs. These photographs provide further support for Mirza Abdollah Jandaqi's account of the four main organized groups of thugs involved in the morning of 28 Mordad, as well as for Manzarpour's account of Behbudgar's role. The first photograph – which has been amateurishly tampered with – shows five

---

[112] Torbatiy-e Sanjabi, p. 29.   [113] Torbatiy-e Sanjabi, p. 29.
[114] Torbatiy-e Sanjabi, p. 30.   [115] Torbatiy-e Sanjabi, p. 30.
[116] FO 248/1514, 9 July 1951.   [117] Shahhoseyni, pp. 16–17; Sarshar, pp. 80, 415.
[118] Torbatiy-e Sanjabi, p. 34.

men in elegant suits standing very respectfully in line, all looking in the same direction in a seemingly outdoor area. They seem to be attending a very official occasion and their posture reveals the probable presence of important dignitaries in front of them. The caption at the bottom of the photograph identifies the gentlemen from right to left as: Hasan Behbudgar (*Hasan Seh Kalleh*), in a smart, dark double-breasted suit with a tie; Mahmud Mesgar, in a light-coloured double-breasted suit, holding a large bouquet of flowers; Hoseyn Ramezoun Yakhi, in a dark suit; Haj Akbar Gilgili, in a dark suit and holding a bouquet of flowers; and finally Tayyeb, in a dark suit.[119] Haj Akbar Gilgili was a traditional athlete, a wrestler and a inseparable friend of Tayyeb; the two men were like brothers.[120] Three other figures, two of whom are military officers, can be distinguished standing at a distance behind the five key thug leaders.

A second photograph, which has not been tampered with, shows the same five men standing in the same suits and in the same order as the first photograph, along with three unidentified men, probably other prominent thug leaders involved in 28 Mordad, standing to the left of Hasan Behbudgar.[121] In this picture, Mesgar and Gilgili are no longer holding their bouquets of flowers and therefore it was presumably taken after they had presented them. This second photo shows Mesgar addressing the dignitaries in front of him. The figure in the photograph attentively listening to Mesgar and facing the confederates of the "great demonstration" of 28 Mordad is the young Mohammad Reza Shah, flanked by two civilians and a military man standing behind him. If the three other ruffians standing to the left of Behbudgar are ever identified, it will become clear who other than the five thugs were considered by the Court to be the key mobilizers of the mob on 28 Mordad. The two photos have no dates, but it can be strongly surmised that they were taken soon after 28 Mordad and the return of the Shah from Rome. It must have been on the occasion of a celebration ceremony during which the Shah wished to convey his gratitude and appreciation to the thug leaders who paved the way for his triumph.

After 28 Mordad, official ceremonies recognizing the contribution of ruffians in ousting Mosaddeq and returning the Shah were not taboo. Ten days after 28 Mordad General Zahedi threw a splendid party at his private estate in Jamaran in honour of Tayyeb, Ramezoun Yakhi, the leaders of the fruit and vegetable market (*meydan*) and all the prominent thug leaders who participated in 28 Mordad.[122] All those lined up in front of the Shah in the two pictures, as well as many more, must have attended Zahedi's party. During the first week of September 1953, or less than a month after the coup, the Shah played host to a number of "athletes", including Parviz

---

[119] Mirza'i, p. 25.　[120] Mirza'i, p. 143.
[121] *Shahid Tayyeb Haj Reza'i be Ravayat Asnad SAVAK*, p. 261.
[122] Torbatiy-e Sanjabi, p. 106.

Khosravani, owner of the Taj Sport Club.[123] On this occasion the Shah renewed his covenant with the "athletes" and told his visitors that "I would never forget the dear Iranian people's uprising (*qiyam*) during the great jihad (*jahad-e akbar*) of 28 Mordad".[124] He asked those present to convey this message to the people, and emphasized that they should in particular inform the "athletes" (*varzeshkaran*) that "we will always support them". The two pictures with the known thug leaders of 28 Mordad may have been taken on this occasion.

---

[123] *Ettela'at Haftegi*, 27 Shahrivar 1332. [124] *Ettela'at Haftegi*, 27 Shahrivar 1332.

11

Coup agents occupying the city centre

On Wednesday 28 Mordad there were no clouds in the skies of Tehran and the dry feverish heat of the day was typical of this summer month. Before Tehranis woke up on that day at least eight anti-Mosaddeq dailies were ready to inform their readers that Zahedi was the legitimate Shah-appointed Prime Minister of Iran.[1] One of these newspapers, *Mellat Ma*, the mouthpiece of Ayatollah Abolqasem Kashani and Shams Qanatabadi, also sent a clear message to Mosaddeq. It bluntly wrote: "Mosaddeq get lost (*Mosaddeqolsaltaneh gurat ra gom kon*)".[2] In line with the propaganda theme emphasizing the imminent threat of Communism and the collusion of Mosaddeq with the Communists, on 28 Mordad *Mellat Ma* wrote: "based on information received, a large statue of Stalin will be placed in the middle of Sepah Square, one of Marx will stand at Baharestan Square ... the 24 Esfand Square will house Lenin's statue and Malenkov's bust will be situated at Rah-Ahan Square".[3] Kashani's newspaper was whipping up patriotism and anti-Communism among its readers by falsely claiming that, subsequent to the dismantling of Reza Shah and Mohammad Reza Shah's statutes on Monday 26 Mordad, the symbols of Iran's monarchy were going to be replaced with heroes of Soviet Communism. *Mellat Ma* warned that "Those who consider themselves Muslim and Shi'i and those who think they are followers of the Qur'an, [should know that] helping Mosaddeq is synonymous with aiding *kofr* (unbelief) and waging war against religion".[4]

On 28 Mordad, everything was ready to put maximum psychological pressure on the people to passively accept, if not side with, the coup d'état – everything except word from the highest authority of Shi'i Islam. Jalali and Keyvani's employees were assured that "the first of the many thousand broadsheets which carried a photostatic copy of the Shah's royal edict and the text of the Zahedi statement" was available on the streets.[5] Jalali and Keyvani,

---

[1] Wilber, p. 65.   [2] *Mellat Ma*, 28 Mordad 1332.   [3] *Mellat Ma*, 28 Mordad 1332.
[4] *Mellat Ma*, 28 Mordad 1332.   [5] Wilber, p. 65.

who were supposed to receive, reproduce and distribute some kind of text from Borujerdi condoning the "great demonstration", were disappointed as Borujerdi made sure that no document undermining the authority of Mosaddeq would appear in his name on that day.

In the early morning hours, the four main groups of ruffians and their acolytes congregated at Gomrok Square and Mowlavi Square, two principal points on Mowlavi Street, the west–east artery of Southern Tehran. They then moved up north along the four almost parallel main streets of Pahlavi, Shahpour, Khayyam and Syrus (which intersected Mowlavi Street). The ruffians had three target areas to occupy: Sepah and Arg Squares, or the administrative and security heart of the capital housing the ministries, police headquarters, Radio Office and the Officers' Club; Baharestan Square, housing the parliament or the legislative heart of the capital; and finally Kakh Street, Mosaddeq's house or the headquarters of the executive, the Prime Minister's office. Moving north along the four streets of Pahlavi, Shahpour, Khayyam and Syrus led directly to the designated targets, or very close to them. Once they had arrived at their targets, the ruffians were to impose fear and awe with their physical presence on the ground, fill and control the streets, intimidate passers-by and bystanders, occupy key buildings and suppress any challenge to their authority.

The plan and itinerary of the roughnecks was well conceived. As they encircled the city centre by moving up the two south–north streets of Pahlavi and Syrus early in the morning, and then zeroed in on their targets in the middle that were to be attacked and destroyed, they refrained from showing themselves in areas where the ministries, sensitive offices and government strongholds were located. It is not surprising that when on 28 Mordad Gholam-Reza Sadiqi, the Minister of Interior, drove from Mosaddeq's house at around eight in the morning to the Ministry of Interior, through Sepah Street and then south on Khayyam Street, he did not notice anything unusual. At this time, the whole area around Arg Square, Bouzarjomehri and Naserkhosrow, just north of the bazaar, was quiet as the roughnecks were gradually moving up Syrus, Khayyam, Shahpour and Pahlavi Streets. Small packs travelled north along Shahpour, Khayyam and Syrus Streets, then moved along the east–west Bouzarjomehri Street, to arrive at Arg and Sepah Squares. It was not until around ten in the morning that the mob, supported by certain police units, reached the government offices around Arg Square and Babehomayoun Street.

While the common folk in Tehran did not know what awaited them on that day, a very small elite involved with one or another aspect of the coup were well informed and were already on the move. Ardeshir Zahedi reported that as of 6:00 a.m. on 28 Mordad, Parviz Yarafshar, a confidant of his father, "brought news of events that may occur on that day".[6] Zahedi's

---

[6] Zahedi, vol. 1, pp. 149–150.

reference to the fact that his father and certain anti-Mosaddeq elements knew in advance (6:00 a.m. of 28 Mordad) of the "events that may occur" on that day stand in contrast to Ardeshir Zahedi's position that 28 Mordad was an unexpected eruption or a spontaneous mass uprising of the toilers.[7] Zahedi's insistence that 28 Mordad was a purely spontaneous, endogenously initiated, religious and monarchist movement of the underclasses is the other side of the same coin, which categorically denies any participation of the CIA and the SIS in planning the events of that day at the "council of war".[8]

A general description of the ruffians' movement is well documented by Baniahmad in the semi-official account of 28 Mordad.[9] According to this Shah-approved account of the events of 28 Mordad, from the early hours of the day groups of people from south of Tehran were on the move to the north. Whereas in the past crowds were formed, demonstrations were organized and groups moved in the streets of Tehran in response to some sort of official or semi-official political invitation or initiative of a party, association or group, there had been no such previous official convocations, directives or summons for 28 Mordad. Baniahmad observes that, on that day, those who "were out of the circle of the informed" – namely ordinary Tehrani citizens – were caught by surprise. They were astounded by the number of demonstrators, by the speed at which they moved, and, most importantly, puzzled by the motive for their presence.[10]

Describing the movement of the demonstrators, Baniahmad observes that at some point, a club-wielding group ran ahead of the crowd and the taxis, which escorted them all the way from the south of Tehran. The taxis displayed photographs of the Shah behind their windshields. Both the walking demonstrators and those in the taxis, some equipped with loudspeakers, chanted pro-Shah slogans, cheered for the Shah's health, and repeated "death to Mosaddeq".[11] In the initial phase of their march to the north, the crowd were at times impeded by policemen and martial law soldiers. Baniahmad maintains that as soon as the military personnel heard the crowds cheering for the Shah, they would join them with their weapons.[12] According to Baniahmad, the bystanders were surprised at the fact that the underclass and the most disadvantaged social classes (*tabaqat-e sevvom va chaharom*) were demonstrating in favour of the monarchy; the bystanders expected this group to demonstrate against the Court and the Shah "as they usually did".[13]

---

[7] Zahedi, vol. 1, pp. 149, 158, 159, 186.   [8] Zahedi, vol. 1, p. 179, 186, 187.
[9] On the first page of this book, an official letter from the Shah's Special Office (*Daftar-e Makhsous Shahanshahi*) dated 16 April 1963 to Baniahmad states that the Shah is very pleased with the efforts of the author and conveys his Majesty's praise and appreciation of his work.
[10] Baniahmad, p. 190.   [11] Baniahmad, p. 190.   [12] Baniahmad, p. 191.
[13] Baniahmad, p. 191.

MORPHOLOGY OF THE DEMONSTRATORS

A British account of the "great demonstration" entitled "the political review of the recent events" and written less than a fortnight after 28 Mordad, states that at about 8:00 a.m. "a crowd of about 3,000 men armed with clubs and sticks started an anti-Musaddiq and pro-Shah demonstration in the southern part of the town".[14] The crowd roamed the city chanting "long live the Shah" and "death to Musaddiq the traitor". It was composed of "a large number" of the unemployed and "many well-known hooligans". According to this document, even though the demonstrators may have been inspired by royalist sentiments, they "had obviously been hired for the purpose".[15] As the crowd grew, the account noted that "a large number of well-to-do people" joined the demonstrations.

American accounts of the demonstrators are rather conflicting. Wilber acknowledges the fact that by 9:30 a.m. "really large groups, armed with sticks and stones, came from South Tehran and merged as they reached Sepah Square".[16] Yet he claims that the crowds were not composed only of hoodlums, "but included people of all classes – many well-dressed". In his confidential report to the State Department on 20 August (29 Mordad), Henderson provides a description of the demonstrating crowd. He claims that the participants "were not of [the] hoodlum type", but were "from all classes of people including workers, clerks, shopkeepers, students, et cetera".[17] According to the ambassador, "crowds seemed to be imbued with a strange mixture of resolution and gaiety". He concludes that the "speedy and easy victory" of the anti-Mosaddeq great demonstration "was achieved with a high degree of spontaneity".[18]

Henderson bases his report on the composition of the crowd on the observations of the members of the US Embassy and maintains that they had the opportunity to scrutinize the characters in the crowd.[19] The American Embassy was located on the junction of Takht-e Jamshid and Roosevelt Streets – a long way from the major hub of activities on 28 Mordad. It was three kilometres to the north of Sepah Square and also three kilometres to the north-west of Baharestan. It was also a good seven kilometres from Mowlavi Street, where the ruffians started their march. Such distances make it implausible for members of the US Embassy to have seen the demonstrators from their place of work or to have identified their social origin or profession from their apparel. It is possible that certain members of the US Embassy were present at the hot spots of 28 Mordad. However, Henderson's conclusion that the demonstration "was achieved with a high degree of spontaneity", which becomes the official position of those who present the coup as "a spontaneous national uprising", could not be in any way ascertained unless it is assumed

---

[14] FRUS, vol. x, p. 784. [15] FRUS, vol. x, p. 784. [16] Wilber, pp. 67, 68.
[17] FRUS, vol. x, p. 753. [18] FRUS, vol. x, p. 754. [19] FRUS, vol. x, p. 753.

that Henderson knew about the demonstration beforehand and could judge the degree of spontaneity of the demonstration.

Woodhouse, the head of the British MI6 in Tehran until the end of October 1952, confirms that Kim Roosevelt and the British used their respective "pairs of brothers" to muster support for the Shah, relying on "the armed forces and the ever-ready street mobs".[20] He chooses to describe the demonstrators through the eyes of two American journalists, Richard and Gladys Harkness. It is said that the information used in their article "The mysterious doings of the CIA", published in the *Saturday Evening Post*, was leaked to them by the CIA in 1954. Woodhouse claims, however, that his description of the demonstrators was made by an eye-witness, a claim that the authors of the article do not make. Woodhouse writes:

With the army standing closeguard around the uneasy capital, a grotesque procession made its way along the street leading to the heart of Tehran. There were tumblers turning handsprings, weight-lifters twirling iron bars and wrestlers, flexing their biceps. As spectators grew in number, the bizarre assortment of performers began shouting pro-Shah slogans in unison. The crowd took up the chant and there, after one precarious moment, the balance of public psychology swung against Musaddiq.[21]

Rebutting the US State Department-initiated theory of the "spontaneous" events of 28 Mordad, Woodhouse remarks ironically that "in fact probably for the first time, the Communists' technique of spontaneous demonstrations was successfully turned against them".[22] Perfectly satisfied with the outcome of the great demonstration, Woodhouse concludes that "the result showed that our organizations had done their work well".[23]

While the second-hand descriptions of the crowd given by Henderson, Wilber and Woodhouse seem rather exaggerated in different ways, more poignant and calibrated descriptions of the demonstrators are reported by Iranian eye-witnesses. In line with all Iranian accounts, one eye-witness observer wrote that:

Those riding in the trucks had an unfamiliar look. Some wore the military garb of sergeants, others wearing civilian clothes resembled roughnecks (*gardankoloftha*) and wrestlers. They carried the Iranian flag, clubs and pictures of the Shah, waving them threateningly in the air and chanting, long live the Shah, death to the sell-out (*vatanforoush*) Tudeh and death to traitorous Mosaddeq. The people passing by them would stop and watch them perplexed and consternated, without the slightest reaction.[24]

By a little after 10:00 a.m. on 28 Mordad the Iranian detectives of the Bureau of Investigation (*Edareh Karagahi*) who were dispatched to various corners of the city at around 9:00 a.m. on that day provided different

---

[20] Woodhouse, p. 128.
[21] *Saturday Evening Post*, 6 November 1954; Woodhouse, pp. 128–129.
[22] Woodhouse, p. 129.   [23] Woodhouse, p. 129.   [24] Keymaram, p. 280.

assessments of the initial crowds gathering at Sepah Square.[25] Most of the detectives described the demonstrators as "unskilled day labourers (*fa'leh*) and suspicious elements". One detective assessed them as "the unemployed who had either received a payment or were there for the fun of being involved in something". Another one who arrived a little after the others reported that "the thugs and ruffians are directing their followers to the city centre in support of the Shah".[26] After a while more news trickled in, confirming that "the ruffians of the fruit and vegetable market had brought in their men to the city centre".[27] As the detectives returned to their headquarters to brief their superiors, the news was that the unemployed and the day labourers were being paid 10 Tomans each and provided with a portrait of the Shah before being directed to Sepah Square.[28] A detective returning from Shahr-e No, Tehran's red-light district, reported that prostitutes holding pictures of the Shah and accompanied by men wielding clubs and sticks were joining the crowd, chanting "Long live the Shah".[29]

THE FOUR-PHASE PLAN OF THE DAY

Phase one of the loose plan for 28 Mordad involved the difficult task of mobilizing and organizing the unruly ruffians, having them move and occupy Tehran's key streets and squares, and finally surprising and intimidating Mosaddeq's government and his supporters by their numbers, speed of movement, sticks, clubs and slogans. This key phase involved the deployment of some 1,000 to 2,000 individuals to the central streets of Sepah, Shahabad and Shah and lasted from about 6:00 a.m. to 9:30 a.m. With the completion of phase one, the muscles, armed with clubs and sticks, having occupied the strategically significant streets of Tehran, were ready to move on. Yet this intimidating mob lacked two key resources to proceed successfully to the next phase of the plan. First, they were not armed with the guns necessary to attack government buildings and heavily guarded strategic targets, such as Tehran Radio's Broadcasting Station, the police headquarters, or the main detention centres. Second, and more importantly, the large mob needed to be guided to attain the specific objectives necessary for the success of the coup. The ruffians were mandated to occupy the key arteries of Tehran and to enforce their authority by beating back pro-Mosaddeq partisans who may have wished to re-occupy the streets, but this would not have been sufficient for overthrowing Mosaddeq. The momentum gained could only yield results if guns were employed to support the crowd and brains were employed to direct them.

The second phase of the coup plan started with the gradual injection of the two missing components into the amorphous crowd of ruffians in Sepah and

[25] Varqa, p. 16. [26] Varqa, p. 16. [27] Varqa, p. 17. [28] Varqa, pp. 16–17.
[29] Varqa, p. 17.

Baharestan Squares: armed protection, and a leadership team informed of the objectives of the loose plan for 28 Mordad. The injection of the armed personnel provided the semblance of a fraternization process and sent the important signal that the ruffians had triggered off a national insurrection. Police and military personnel gradually joined and reinforced the crowd, especially in Sepah Square, as the occupation of lightly guarded ministries required limited fire power. The leadership of the thugs, by both the infiltrated military and trained spooks injected into the crowd in phase two, was a crucial requirement for zeroing in on the planned sensitive targets. This second phase began at around 9:30 a.m., and by 10:00 a.m. the ruffians went into action at Baharestan Square where their targets were not defended by policemen or armed units. In Sepah Square, the mob entered into action later, at around 11:30 a.m., as they needed more substantial armed protection to attack the ministries.

Phase three of the coup plan, which started around noon, involved the successful occupation of the ministries and certain vital strategic buildings. As the ministries were attacked and the third phase was coming to a close, the determining factor – the big guns determined to seal the success of the operation – rolled on to the scene. Whereas during the third phase light arms were sufficient to overcome the ministries and other targets such as the Telegraph Office, and even the central police station or the headquarters of the Chief of Staff, the fourth and last phase of the operations required tanks accompanying the ruffians, and required the collaborating police and military personnel to overcome the defences around Mosaddeq's house as well as Tehran Radio's Broadcasting Station. These well-protected and heavily guarded targets could not be taken by clubs, sticks, handguns, rifles or even machine guns. During the fourth and final phase, the collaborationist military commanders and their loyal personnel needed to direct tanks amidst the ruffians who occupied the main streets and squares, have them "take over the tanks", and then have them move *en masse* to occupy Mosaddeq's house.

THE ROUGHNECKS AND THEIR COTERIE ON THE MOVE

At around 7:00 a.m. Shah and Naderi Streets were peaceful – perhaps even too calm and quiet. According to a Tudeh Party member who had set out very early in the morning to check out the city and receive his action plans for the day, when contrasted with the previous days the city was "dead, motionless and serene" around Naderi Street until ten in the morning.[30] Gholam-Hoseyn Sadiqi, Mosaddeq's Minister of Interior, who left his home on Takht-e Jamshid Street (facing the American Embassy) at 6:50 a.m. and arrived at Mosaddeq's house at 109 Kakh Street at around 7:00 a.m., found everything

---

[30] Keymaram, p. 280.

MAP 1. Phase I: The Great Demonstration. 6:00 a.m.–10:30 a.m.

calm and normal on his way. Even when Sadiqi left Mosaddeq's house and drove to the Ministry of Interior close to Arg Square at 8:00 a.m., he did not witness anything unusual.[31]

According to most accounts it was between 8:30 a.m. and 10:00 a.m. that the people living in central Tehran first encountered bands or packs of demonstrators marching north. The daily *Keyhan*'s journalist reported that crowds from Southern Tehran started converging on Sepah Square at around 9:00 a.m. chanting "long live the Shah" and "death to the Tudeh".[32] According to this reporter, another group of demonstrators, well equipped with long sticks, arrived later and joined the crowd at Sepah Square. The semi-official account of 28 Mordad maintains that at around 9:00 a.m. a couple of thousand (*chand hezar*) demonstrators congregated at Sepah Square.[33] The geographical position, centrality and accessibility of Sepah Square made it a highly strategic position. Sepah Square and its immediate surroundings, including Arg Square, some 600 metres to the south, constituted the nerve system of the Iranian government as it housed almost all of the ministries as well as important governmental offices and headquarters. These included the City Council (*shahrdari*), the police headquarters (*shahrebani*), the headquarters of the Chief of Staff, the Telegraph Office, the Radio Office, the Officers' Club, the Military Police headquarters (*dejban*), and its important detention centre. Sepah Square was naturally one of the ruffians' prime targets.

The foot soldiers of the coup needed to rapidly and forcefully impose the authority and control exercised by the anti-Mosaddeq forces over the symbols of Mosaddeq's government. This had to be done in the most blatant manner possible, sending signals to pro-Mosaddeq forces and possible bystanders that the tables had been turned. Furthermore, to lay the groundwork for attacking Mosaddeq's house, control of Sepah Square and its vicinity provided a secure and highly accessible rear base. The distance between Sepah Square and Mosaddeq's house on Kakh Street was around 2.5 kilometres, which could be travelled in about 30 minutes if walking, 20 minutes if jogging, or about five minutes if driving.

As early as around 9:00 a.m., small groups of ill-clad, club-wielding men were observed in the small streets off Hafez Street. As they washed away the anti-Shah slogans written on the walls of the narrow alleys by Tudeh Party sympathizers on the previous days, they chanted "death to Mosaddeq" and "long live the Shah".[34] However, according to most sources the chant of "death to Mosaddeq" was not heard until later. At around 10:00 a.m. trucks carrying ten to 12 ruffians each chanting "long live the Shah" also started to appear on Hafez Street.[35] At around the same time, one eye-witness standing near Serah-e Shah (the junction of Shah and Pahlavi Streets and some

---

[31] Nejati (Goftogo ba Ostad Doctor Gholamhoseyn Sadiqi), p. 540.
[32] *Keyhan*, 29 Mordad 1332.   [33] Baniahmad, p. 196.   [34] Khameh'i, 1363, p. 437.
[35] Khameh'i, 1363, p. 437.

2.5 kilometres to the north-west of Sepah Square) recalled hearing indistinct rumbles, murmurs and cries coming from Sepah and Pahlavi Streets and saw a number of trucks full of demonstrators coming up Pahlavi Street.[36] Tayyeb recalled that he and some members of his group moved to designated targets in the city on trucks and jeeps.[37] The detectives from the Bureau of Investigation also reported that at around 9:30 a.m. two trucks full of what seemed to be day labourers unloaded their human cargo at the entrance of Sepah Square and that the demonstrators were instructed by the "organizers" to chant "long live the Shah".[38] From 8:30 a.m. a group of bus and truck owners had placed their vehicles at the service of the demonstrators.[39] This perfect coordination of efforts between some of Tehran's transportation magnates and ruffian chiefs of Southern Tehran could not have been incidental.

At around the same time, a curious Tehrani, who was hanging around Naser Khosrow (south-east of Serah-e Shah and much closer to Sepah Square) noticed the distant yet ever-swelling sound of a big crowd of demonstrators chanting inaudible slogans. When he walked south on Naser Khosrow towards Bouzarjomehri, at around Arg Square, he suddenly witnessed 500 or so people with ragged clothes and bayonets in hand marching up Naser Khosrow Street, pushing towards Sepah Square.[40] In his assessment, the crowd seemed to have come from the southern part of the city, the shanty towns. Only a few in the crowd who carried pictures of the Shah were armed with clubs. They all chanted "Death to Mosaddeq, death to the Tudeh" while the police and security forces, mounted on jeeps and trucks, joined the crowd.[41]

A lawyer on his way to a court hearing at the Ministry of Justice recalled that as his taxi entered Toupkhaneh (Sepah) Square he heard chants of "Death to Mosaddeq".[42] He then saw a group armed with sticks and clubs running up Naser Khosrow Street, entering Sepah Square, before splitting into two groups: one group headed north towards Ferdowsi Street and the other turned west on Sepah Street. The chanting demonstrators commanded the passengers of a bus and a lawyer to get out of their vehicles and ordered the drivers to turn on their lights and honk their horns. The reporter of the daily *Daad* reported that at around 10:20 a.m. a group of approximately 7,000 people armed with sticks and clubs and well prepared for possible clashes moved from Eslambol Street towards Baharestan.[43] The soldiers and policemen present on their way did not move to disperse, disarm or dissuade the armed protesters; on the contrary, they all joined the crowd chanting "We want the Shah, death to Mosaddeqolsaltaneh, death to the dictator, long live Iran, the army for ever". In view of the fact that Amidi-ye Nouri, the editor of *Daad*, was a close

---

[36] Keymaram, p. 280.   [37] *Ashofteh*, 11 Azar 1333.   [38] Varqa, p. 16.
[39] *Ettela'at*, 31 Mordad 1332.   [40] *Negaheno*, Mordad 1387.
[41] *Negaheno*, Mordad 1387.
[42] A. Tafazzoli, *Sargozashti Pishnevesteh* (Tehran: Entesharat-e Atta'i, 1381), p. 271.
[43] *Daad*, 29 Mordad, 1332.

collaborator of Zahedi and became his post-coup deputy (*mo'aven-e nakhost-vazir*) in charge of the Office of Propaganda (*edareh tabliqat*), the seemingly exaggerated figure of 7,000 people should be accepted with great caution. By around 11:30 a.m. buses arriving at Sepah Square were seized by the demonstrators, who boarded them and drove towards Ferdowsi Street.[44]

ARMING AND GUIDING THE DEMONSTRATORS

Lieutenant General Hoseyn Siyasi, the head of *rokn dovom*, the army's Counter Intelligence Office, recalled that he was in contact with some of the officers involved in the "28 Mordad resurgence" and "expected certain events" on that day.[45] On the morning of 28 Mordad, Riyahi summoned Siyasi sometime after 8:30 a.m. and ordered him to conduct a fact-finding tour of the city and report back to him as there had been reports of demonstrations. Siyasi, who, due to his sensitive security position should have been the person to warn Riyahi and Mosaddeq of any irregular activities against the government, rode in a jeep to the city centre with Mohsen Mobasser, head of the inspectorate office of the army's Counter Intelligence Office. At Sepah Square and at Lalehzar and Shahreza Streets, they came across two groups of demonstrators chanting "Long live the Shah" and "Long live the army". On his return Siyasi reported that there were demonstrations but deceived Riyahi by purposefully reporting that they were numerically insignificant.[46] Siyasi, the head of the army's Counter Intelligence Office, recalled that, having given his first false report, he returned to the areas where the demonstrations were in full swing, "participated in the demonstrations", and was successful in concealing the real magnitude of the demonstrations from the Chief of Staff's office until 12:30 p.m.[47]

It was probably after Siyasi's report on the demonstrations that Riyahi called upon another "reliable" military personality to deal with the situation. Colonel Daftari recalled that Riyahi called him at around 9:00 a.m., informed him that conditions in the city were rather unusual, and asked him to use the Armed Custom Guards under his command to deal with the situation. Daftari went to his garrison at Bagheshah, mobilized some 100 soldiers, mounted them on to between ten and 15 trucks and headed out into the city.[48] The initially half-hearted and irresolute crowd, brought to the streets from Southern Tehran, took flight and dispersed whenever the military and police forces loyal to Mosaddeq fired in the air.[49] Faced with such a crowd, during the early hours of 28 Mordad Daftari could have turned the situation around in favour of Mosaddeq. Instead, he did not instruct his troops to disperse,

---

[44] Baniahmad, pp. 202, 204.   [45] Bozorgmehr, p. 427.   [46] Bozorgmehr, p. 427.
[47] Bozorgmehr, p. 427.
[48] Mohammad Daftari, Iranian Oral History Collection, Harvard University, Transcript 2, p. 13.
[49] Baniahmad, pp. 201–202, 204, 206.

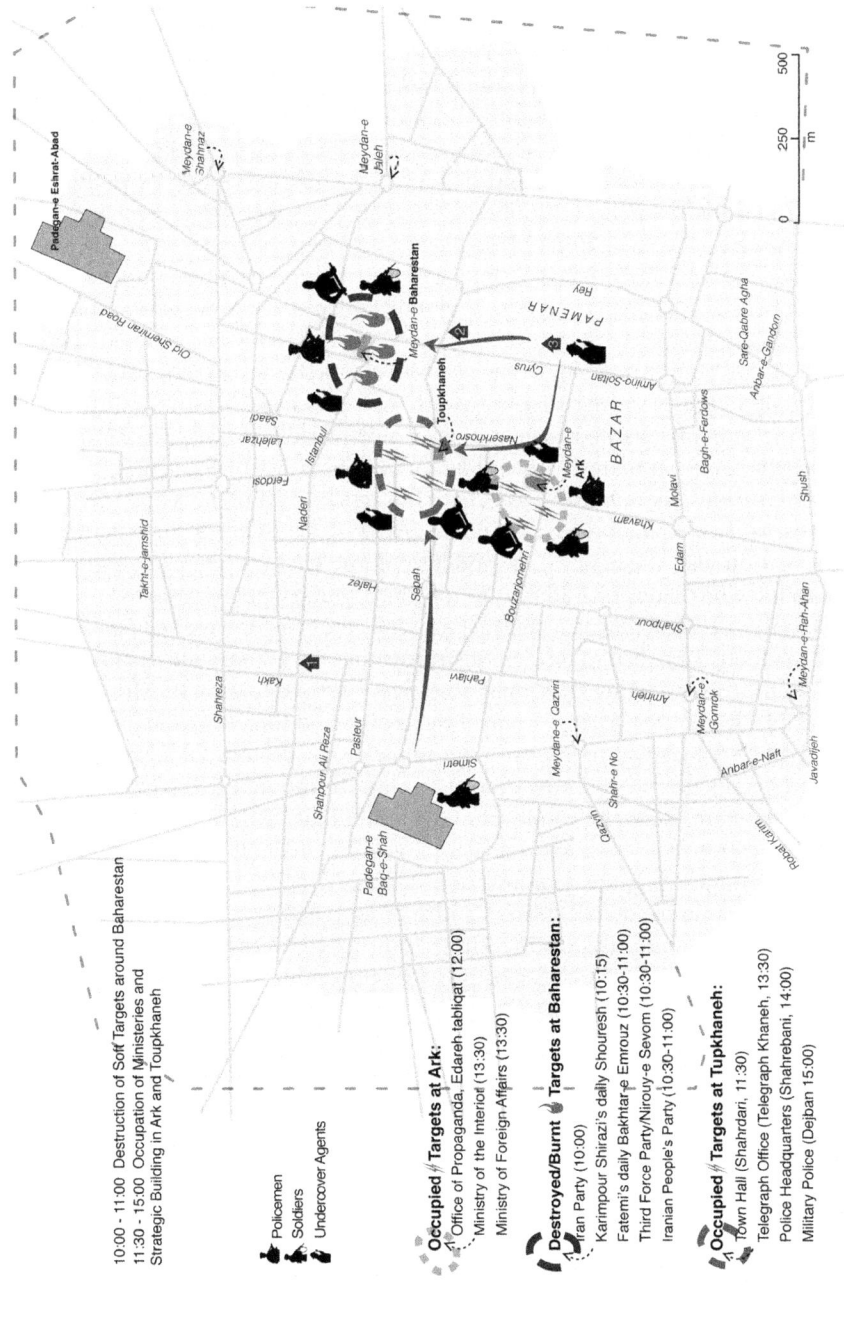

MAP 2. Phase II: The injection of the armed forces and under cover agents. 10:00 a.m.–15:00 p.m.

let alone repress the anti-Mosaddeq demonstrators. While on the previous night Major Akbar Zand had given a good beating to the Tudeh demonstrators and boosted the morale of his pro-Shah troops, displaying the effectiveness of tough repression, Daftari's inaction must have boosted the morale of the ruffians, sending the crucial signal that officers and soldiers would stand by and tolerate pro-Shah and anti-Mosaddeq demonstrators.

It must have been around 9:30 a.m. when Daftari drove from Bagheshah to Sepah Square, a distance of approximately 2.5 kilometres (or a five-minute ride). After the coup he remembered that on his route along Sepah Street he heard chants of "Death to Mosaddeq" and "Long live the Shah". Daftari described the demonstrators as a "bunch of bearded riffraff, ruffians (*yek mosht az in rishouha va az in lat o pareh pourehha*)" and added that there "was no one respectable among them that I would know".[50] When the crowd chanted "Long live the Shah" and cheered his troops, Daftari claimed that his troops kept silent. According to the eye-witness report of an employee of the Ministry of Interior, while the ruffians chanted their anti-government slogans, two trucks full of policemen waved at them.[51] According to Baniahmad's government-approved account, Daftari, mounted on a jeep, led a few truck-loads of the Armed Custom Guards to Toupkhaneh (Sepah) Square. After having circled the square "in coordination with the people", he and his column left Sepah Square. Daftari is said to have neither approved nor disapproved of the demonstrators.[52]

Daftari's decision to play a neutral part while the crowds were yelling "Death to Mosaddeq" signalled to the demonstrators that the military did not intend to stop them from attaining their final objective – the occupation of Mosaddeq's house. Neglecting his order to control the crowd and forgetting the purpose of his mission – which was to maintain the public peace, protect public and private property, and defend the government – Daftari adopted a bystander, non-military posture. Later, he would candidly admit that "we had no quarrel with the demonstrators".[53] Riyahi, the Chief of Staff, maintained that under the pretext of suppressing the demonstrators Daftari ordered the troops under his command to join the demonstrators and enter into action against Mosaddeq.[54]

Somewhere around 10:00 a.m. Daftari returned to his garrison, dismissed his troops and went to Mosaddeq's house to report on his military mission in the city.[55] Earlier in the morning Daftari had been informed by Riyahi of the unusual conditions in the city and he had actually witnessed them personally. There remains no justification for why he dismissed his troops instead of keeping them in the garrison, to be dispatched or to defend the garrison if it were to come

---

[50] Mohammad Daftari, Iranian Oral History Collection, Harvard University, Transcript 2, p. 13.
[51] Nejati (Goftogo ba Ostad Doctor Gholamhoseyn Sadiqi), p. 540.
[52] Baniahmad, p. 232.
[53] Mohammad Daftari, Iranian Oral History Collection, Harvard University, Transcript 2, p. 13.
[54] Nejati, p. 441.
[55] Mohammad Daftari, Iranian Oral History Collection, Harvard University, Transcript 2, p. 13.

under attack. It is most likely that at the behest of their commander, Daftari's dismissed troops of about one hundred joined the demonstrators.

According to the British Memorandum on the events of 28 Mordad, Tehran's Chief of Police, Modabber, had also instructed his troops not to intervene in the demonstrations, which explains why the crowds moved unhampered and unchallenged when destroying their designated targets.[56] Based on the accounts of one reporter, the police were the first of the armed forces to join the ruffians, with their pistols in their pockets and chanting "Long live the Shah".[57] From approximately 9:30 a.m., as the number of demonstrators on foot, in open trucks and buses swelled, their slogans became more consistently anti-Mosaddeq and pro-Shah.[58] It was also around this time that an increasing number of police and soldiers joined the crowds.[59]

An eye-witness observer who was around Toupkhaneh (Sepah Square) recalled that after 10:00 a.m. a few soldiers (numbering less than ten) were indiscriminately beating up passers-by with the butts of their rifles.[60] Nobody seemed to know why the soldiers were on a beating spree. When the observer took shelter in the Telegraph Office adjacent to Sepah Square, a truck-load of ruffians (*latha*) armed with sticks and yelling "Long live the Shah" arrived and took over the task of beating up the passers-by from the soldiers, who then left the scene. According to this observer, after about an hour the number of club-wielding thugs swelled, with no one to oppose them.

By around 11:00 a.m., when Daftari was reporting to Mosaddeq, the situation at both Sepah and Baharestan Squares had evolved dramatically. The operation had entered its second phase. Two key developments demonstrated the scope of the operation and the real objectives of the coup planners – developments which were not clear to the bystanders at around 9:00 a.m. First, from around 9:30 a.m. it had become clear that elements in the police force were actively cooperating with the demonstrators. At this stage, however, the full extent of their collaboration was not manifest. As of around 9:30 a.m. one of Tehran's police station commanders rushed into Mosaddeq's house and informed him that police trucks were collecting and transporting demonstrators from Southern Tehran to the heart of the city.[61] This indiscreet level of open assistance to the coup effort by the police force must have been the result of Modabber's open alignment with the coup forces. It is highly possible that the direct and indirect logistical support provided to the ruffians by the police was with the prior knowledge and consent of Modabber, if not under his direct orders. Second, by this time there were reports of a few army trucks filled with soldiers who had joined the demonstrators.[62] The detectives of the Bureau of Investigation also confirmed

---

[56] FRUS, vol. x, p. 784.   [57] *Khandaniha*, 31 Mordad, 1332.
[58] *Ettela'at*, 31 Mordad 1332.   [59] *Ettela'at*, 31 Mordad 1332.
[60] *Kelk*, No. 41, Mordad 1372 (Ebrahim Golestan, Bisto Hasht-e, panj-e, Siy o do).
[61] Baniahmad, p. 188.   [62] *Ferdowsi*, 3 Shahrivar 1332.

reports that, later in the day, army sergeants in civilian clothes and corporals in uniforms were among the crowd, actively participating in the "great demonstration".[63]

Once Sadiqi, the Minister of Interior, was informed of the police force's collaboration with the demonstrators; he called Modabber (the Chief of Police) and enquired about the facts. From Modabber's reaction, Sadiqi concluded that he was fully aware of what was going on and was dissimulating his betrayal. Sadiqi became even more suspicious of Modabber's collusion with the plotters when the Chief of Police promised to immediately enquire about such episodes and report back to him – something he never did.[64]

Convinced of Modabber's betrayal, on the morning of 28 Mordad Mosaddeq appointed Daftari (his grandnephew and the brother of his son-in-law) to this position, believing that he was conferring the highly sensitive position of the Chief of Police to a loyal and trustworthy relative. At 11:00 a.m. Mosaddeq also appointed Daftari to the most sensitive position of the Military Governor of Tehran.[65] The nomination of Daftari as Chief of Police went against Riyahi's counsel.[66] Daftari was in the unique position of having a decree as Iran's Chief of Police both from Mosaddeq and from his conspiring enemies.[67] The events of 28 Mordad proved that Mosaddeq's close relative was worthy of Zahedi's trust, but not of his own. When the Shah returned to Tehran after the coup, at the airport Daftari threw himself at his feet.[68]

From around 10:00 a.m. designated agents clearly distinct from the Southern Tehran crowd and their ruffian chiefs, who had been injected into the crowd, began taking charge of demonstrators by directing them to lay siege to key buildings.[69] Also by about 10:30 a.m., elements of the police and the military were openly "joining" the demonstrators and supporting them in their attacks against government and pro-Mosaddeq offices. At this time, a noticeable shift occurred in the conduct and comportment of the demonstrators. The ruffians, who had reached their primary targets and were aimlessly loitering and shouting in the squares and streets they had occupied, were suddenly guided to more specific and strategic targets by civilian employees of the CIA station in Tehran (Jalali and Keyvani's lads) and by elements within the police and military establishment, all of whom were well informed of the chronology of the main plan for the day. These developments signalled the start of phases two and three.

The fact that at around 9:00 a.m. groups of police and army personnel were intentionally let loose in areas occupied by the ruffians was an important step towards phase two. Daftari had dismissed around 100 soldiers of the

---

[63] Varqa, p. 17.   [64] Nejati (Goftogo ba Ostad Doctor Gholamhoseyn Sadiqi), p. 540.
[65] Nejati (Goftogo ba Ostad Doctor Gholamhoseyn Sadiqi), p. 541.
[66] Nejati, pp. 441, 604.
[67] For Daftari's account of the events of 28 Mordad see: Mohammad Daftari, Iranian Oral History Collection, Harvard University, Transcript 2, pp. 12–17.
[68] *Ettela'at Haftegi*, 6 Shahrivar 1332.   [69] Baniahmad, p. 206; *Taraqi*, 2 Shahrivar 1332.

Armed Custom Guards at a close distance from Sepah Square. The account of Major Akbar Zand's soldiers on the morning of 28 Mordad demonstrates how other soldiers were let loose on strategic streets. On Ashrafi's orders, Major Zand was arrested at 8:00 a.m. on 28 Mordad and brought to the police headquarters a few hundred metres from Sepah Square.[70] Major Zand's elite soldiers, who had ruthlessly repressed the demonstrations of the previous night, had also been arrested late at night on Tuesday 18 August (27 Mordad) and detained at the Military Governor's headquarters.[71] The detained soldiers were not fed until the next morning and were further told by their corporals that they would all be facing the firing squad for their excessive zeal on the previous night.[72] When Major Zand was brought into the headquarters of the Military Governor, his loyal forces were delighted to see him and began demonstrating in his favour, chanting slogans in favour of the Shah as they had done on the Tuesday night. Faced with the unrest, Ashrafi ordered the arrested Major Zand to take his detained platoons out of the building.[73] Ashrafi may have panicked, but in view of what was to happen later, it seems as if he had shrewdly planned "accidentally" to re-unite Major Zand with his troops and set them free right in the middle of Sepah Square. Major Zand, who found himself at the helm of his handpicked troops and free to move around the city, ordered his troops to join and support the demonstrators.[74] Thus, an experienced and zealous pro-Shah military unit was injected into the midst of the ruffians. Major Zand and his troops played a key role in the occupation of Tehran Radio's Broadcasting Station (*bisime Pahlavi*) later on that day.[75]

Major Zand had been in contact with and taken an oath of allegiance to the plotting officers: Colonel Rowhani, Major Moradiyan and another captain.[76] Even though Major Moradiyan was arrested on the Tuesday night, he was set free that same night. Once freed, Moradiyan, a member of the "Devotees of the Shah", met his fellow officers and obtained their pledge of cooperation for the activities on Wednesday (28 Mordad).[77] The officers had sworn to move ahead with their plans, coordinating their activities with the demonstration that was to occur in favour of the Shah.[78] Zand and Moradiyan's activities on 28 Mordad clearly demonstrated that the arrest of certain key liaison coup officers after the first coup did not in any way disrupt or break the coup network's chain of command as established for the first coup. Zand, a Major in the Naderi Battalion, was under the command of Rowhani, who was in turn directly connected with Colonel Nasiri and Colonel Zand Karimi. Zand Karimi was a member of the Military

---

[70] *Tehran Mosavvar*, 6 Shahrivar 1332.
[71] Baniahmad, p. 195; *Tehran Mosavvar*, 6 Shahrivar 1332.
[72] *Tehran Mosavvar*, 6 Shahrivar 1332.   [73] *Tehran Mosavvar*, 6 Shahrivar 1332.
[74] *Tehran Mosavvar*, 6 Shahrivar 1332; Baniahmad, p. 195.
[75] *Tehran Mosavvar*, 6 Shahrivar 1332; Baniahmad, p. 195.
[76] *Tehran Mosavvar*, 6 Shahrivar 1332.   [77] *Tehran Mosavvar*, 6 Shahrivar 1332.
[78] *Tehran Mosavvar*, 6 Shahrivar 1332.

Secretariat which was also attended by Carroll, Farzanegan, Akhavi and sometimes Batmanqelich. Akbar Zand was one of those young officers on whom Zand Karimi and Carroll depended for the success of TPAJAX. In the absence of Nasiri, Zand Karimi and Rowhani, through the good offices of Farzanegan and his collaborators within Mosaddeq's military apparatus, conditions were provided for Zand to carry out his responsibilities on 28 Mordad. The manner in which Akbar Zand and his troops blended with the ruffians to move the coup to its final phase provides one example of how segments of the police and the armed forces joined the demonstrators, guarded them and participated in the attacks, ransacking, looting and incineration of government offices and headquarters of pro-Mosaddeq organizations in and around the strategic centres of Tehran on 28 Mordad.[79]

Around Sepah Square, confusion reigned during the second phase of the operation, as the ruffians and segments of the police and military personnel were seeking to identify and connect with one another, consolidate forces, figure out the designated targets and move towards them. One episode best exemplifies the situation. The soldiers guarding the City Council (*shahrdari*) adjacent to Sepah Square first fired into the air to disperse the crowds that had gathered around the pillar upon which had once stood a statue of Reza Shah, which had been dismantled on 26 Mordad. Terrified by the gunshots, the crowd fled to the north and took refuge in Lalehzar Street. Suddenly, an armed soldier ran towards the retreating crowd and conveyed to them the excuses of his captain.[80] The soldier explained that they had thought the demonstrators were members and sympathizers of the Tudeh Party. "Now that we know otherwise", he said, "you gentlemen are free to do as you please".[81] Reassured by the message of the soldier, the "gentleman" ruffians returned to Sepah Square, climbed the pillar, and placed a picture of the Shah and the tri-colour flag of Iran on it.[82]

It was between 10:00 a.m. and 12:30 p.m. that civilian and military operatives with a clear agenda gradually joined the ruffians and began taking control of the demonstrators around Sepah Square, directing them to their main targets. Baniahmad's semi-official account of events on 28 Mordad is most helpful in confirming, corroborating and adding greater detail to Wilber's accounts of how the necessary civilian and military leadership was injected into the crowd. According to Baniahmad, by around noon the crowd at Sepah Square and Ferdowsi Street was gradually losing heart as it was aimlessly moving from one government office to another. The ruffians were too diffuse and unruly, and moreover did not know exactly what to do once they had gathered in the centre of the city, other than to chant slogans against Mosaddeq and in favour of the Shah and to intimidate the bystanders. The absence of clear directives was sapping their energy, until suddenly outsiders appeared and took control.

---

[79] Baniahmad, pp. 196, 201.   [80] Baniahmad, p. 201.   [81] Baniahmad, pp. 201–202.
[82] Baniahmad, p. 202.

While the crowd was becoming frustrated at its inability to take over the police headquarters or the Officers' Club, or even move towards Mosaddeq's house, "two men who had joined those present *from the outside* climbed on a stool and encouraged the people to attack Mosaddeq's house and Tehran's Radio Station".[83] "Suddenly someone walked in front of the crowd and said, oh people, I am a devotee of the Shah all those who are worshippers of the king and country should follow me".[84] At that point the final targets were clearly mapped out for the ruffians; the person addressing them led them to the north. Wilber too confirms that at about noon the crowds started "to receive direct leadership from the military and police. Those army officers previously alerted to take part in the military operations provided by TPAJAX were now taking separate but proper individual action".[85]

Who were these civilian operatives who appeared among the crowd and led the mob to the designated targets? They could have been members of SUMKA, under the TPBEDAMN umbrella. Daryoush Homayoun, an active member of SUMKA, maintained that he had no prior information about the events of 28 Mordad. Yet he recalled that Monshizadeh was in contact with associates of the Zahedis before 28 Mordad.[86] On 28 Mordad, Homayoun and Monshizadeh, who had been released from prison just the day before, arrived at SUMKA headquarters, got into a jeep and drove through the city.[87] On that day Monshizadeh spoke to the crowds on several occasions. Homayoun recalled that on 28 Mordad "we [SUMKA] were very active during the demonstrations".[88] The civilians could have also been employees of TPBEDAMN and TPAJAX. Jalali, Keyvani, Majidi, Afshar and Reza-Ali were criss-crossing the hubs of mob activity on 28 Mordad, providing "needed leadership".[89] Wilber was proud of the accomplishments and exploits of the local CIA station agents as guides and leaders of the mob: they ended up destroying and setting fire to pro-Mosaddeq and pro-Tudeh newspapers, and attacking the radio station and Military Police headquarters (*dejban*), where the military prisoners of the 25 Mordad (16 August) coup were being held.[90]

And who were the military officers previously alerted by the TPAJAX operation plan, to whom Wilber referred? Colonel Damavand[i], was involved in the early staff planning of the coup with Carroll and appeared at Baharestan early in the morning of 28 Mordad with a tank belonging to the Second Battalion of Colonel Shahrokh's Second Armoured Brigade, a battalion which Wilber points out was originally committed to the operation. Wilber also mentions Colonel Khosrowpanah, commanding officer of the Second Mountain Brigade's Infantry Regiment (*Bahador*), and Captain Ali Zand, who were joined by two trucks of the same battalion.[91] There is a very high chance that Wilber got Zand's first name wrong and that he was in fact referring to Akbar Zand.

---

[83] Baniahmad, p. 206. [84] Baniahmad, p. 206. [85] Wilber, p. 69.
[86] Homayoun, p. 57. [87] *Ettela'at*, 27 Mordad 1332; Homayoun, p. 51.
[88] Homayoun, p. 51. [89] Wilber, p. 66. [90] Wilber, pp. 66–70. [91] Wilber, p. 67.

Aside from the selected officers cited by Wilber, scores of other Iranian officers, alerted to the new plans by Farzanegan and Gilanshah, participated in the anti-Mosaddeq activities of 28 Mordad in a coordinated and systematic manner. Yet the main nucleus of those officers with prior knowledge of the plans was logically the approximately 30 collaborationist "line commanders", most of whom were also the "Devotees of the Shah" and their associates. These officers were informed, to various degrees, of a second plan to overthrow Mosaddeq. Baniahmad provides a detailed account of the activities of "a team" of such pro-Zahedi officers on 28 Mordad.[92] Baniahmad implies that this four-man team was part of the "Devotees of the Shah" network.

On the morning of 28 Mordad four officers – Lieutenants Shoja'i, Manouchehr Khosrowdad, Mazaheri and Amir Khosrowdad, all members of a "team" – gathered in front of the Officers' Academy (*daneshkadeh afsari*) on Sepah Street (between Pahlavi and Simetri Streets). Even though according to their previous plans they were to start the pro-Shah demonstrations on Thursday 29 Mordad (20 August), once they "assessed the conditions as conducive" and witnessed the demonstrating "people" they immediately entered into action on Wednesday 28 Mordad. Mazaheri taught at the Officer's Academy. Colonel Zangeneh, the President of the Officer's Academy, was a close friend of Zahedi. Right before the first coup, Zangeneh had been contacted and informed of the anti-Mosaddeq activities of the collaborationist officers by Ardeshir Zahedi. Zangeneh, who occupied a key post in terms of the influence and authority that he could bring to bear upon the young officers at the Academy, had promised Zahedi that he would collaborate with the anti-Mosaddeq officers.[93] The fact that this team of officers chose to meet in front of the Officers' Academy on 19 August could hardly have been coincidental.

Having discussed strategies, the team members divided up, each following a particular objective. Mazaher went towards Mosaddeq's house. The Khosrowdad brothers headed to the army staff headquarters and the police headquarters and later on ended up going to Mosaddeq's house. And Shoja'i walked to Sepah Square, to incite the "people" in favour of the Shah.[94] However, Shoja'i first returned to his house and changed into civilian clothes. Then, on his way to Sepah Square he met a few other officers, also wearing plain clothes, and together they decided to gather the "people" in one spot and set out to place a picture of the Shah on the pillar where once had stood a statue of Reza Shah. It was again this group of officers who decided to stop all the vehicles entering Sepah Square, seizing them, packing them with demonstrators, and dispatching them to distant strategic targets, most importantly Tehran Radio's Broadcasting Station (*bisime Pahlavi*), seven kilometres to the north.[95]

---

[92] Baniahmad, p. 231.   [93] Baniahmad, p. 172; Zahedi, p. 113.
[94] Baniahmad, pp. 231–232; Javanshir, p. 309.   [95] Baniahmad, p. 232.

12

Attacking ministries and pro-Mosaddeq buildings

At around 11:00 a.m. the third phase of the plan was initiated as a crowd of approximately 300 people marched down Babehomayoun Street and passed in front of the Ministry of the Interior.[1] According to Sadiqi, Mosaddeq's Minister of the Interior, who at the time was watching out of the window of his office, some of the demonstrators who were chanting slogans were seated in three or four trucks that drove slowly by; "a group of barefooted and bareheaded" people running around the trucks chanted pro-Shah slogans, while a truck full of policemen accompanied them.[2] At around 11:30 a.m. the mayor of Tehran, Mohsen Nasr, called Sadiqi to inform him that the city council had fallen to the demonstrators.[3] Soon after, a picture of the Shah was placed on the City Council building by a policeman and a soldier.[4] On three occasions, between 11:30 a.m. and 1:00 p.m., the demonstrators tried to occupy the Ministry of the Interior, but they were repulsed by six defenders of the building.[5]

From around 12:30 p.m. the demonstrators started attacking the Officers' Club, the police headquarters and the Ministry of Foreign Affairs, which were adjacent to one another, but they were repelled by shots fired by the military forces defending the buildings. Leaving behind three injured, the demonstrators moved on to Ferdowsi Street.[6] According to Varqa, head of the Surveillance Office (*sho'beh moraqebat*) of the Bureau of Investigation, the fact that shots fired in the air by the military defenders of the Ministry of Foreign Affairs led to the flight of a few hundred assailants proved that if commanders of military units had remained loyal to Mosaddeq, the soldiers under their command would

---

[1] Nejati (Goftogo ba Ostad Doctor Gholamhoseyn Sadiqi), p. 541.
[2] Nejati (Goftogo ba Ostad Doctor Gholamhoseyn Sadiqi), p. 541.
[3] Nejati (Goftogo ba Ostad Doctor Gholamhoseyn Sadiqi), p. 542.   [4] Baniahmad, p. 202.
[5] Nejati (Goftogo ba Ostad Doctor Gholamhoseyn Sadiqi), p. 542.   [6] Baniahmad, p. 204.

have followed suit and repelled the belligerent forces.[7] After their failure to take over these key buildings, the demonstrators tried to make headway towards Mosaddeq's house but were pushed back by the soldiers, who blocked their way up Ferdowsi Street.

Later, regrouping at Ferdowsi Street and Sepah Square, the demonstrators "were directed by a few individuals" to attack the unguarded offices of *Shahbaz* newspaper, the organ of the Anti-Colonialism Society (*jam'iyat-e mobarezeh ba este'mar*) affiliated with the Tudeh Party, and the daily *Besouy-e Ayandeh*, the Tudeh Party's newspaper.[8] Having looted and destroyed equipment and furniture, the offices were set on fire and workers were chased out and beaten.[9] According to Wilber, an Iranian CIA operative called Afshar was the person leading the attack on the offices of the Tudeh papers including *Shahbaz*, *Besouy-e Ayandeh* and *Javanan-e Demokrat*.[10] Even the news-stands selling Tudeh Party newspapers around Ferdowsi Street, such as Rahimi's kiosk, were set on fire by the ruffians and the policemen – who had by this time united. So too was the Donya news-stand on Shahabad Street, which also sold Tudeh Party newspapers and publications.[11] In their anti-Communist rampage, the Sa'di theatre, located on Shahabad Street and associated with the Tudeh Party, was attacked; the metal door of the theatre was broken down with bars and hammers. In the dark, as the electricity in the theatre had been cut off, the mob started by smashing and tearing apart the chairs and the curtains and then finally set fire to the building.[12] Soon flames and smoke engulfed the theatre.

ASSAULTING GOVERNMENT OFFICES AROUND SEPAH SQUARE

Around noon a crowd of around 500 entered the Office of Propaganda (*edareh tabliqat*), ransacked the rooms, and threw out all of the documents and files.[13] The Office of Propaganda (which later, during the Shah's rule, became the Ministry of Information) housed the Pars News Agency and the Radio Office (*edareh radio*) where radio programs were recorded for broadcasting. Convinced that they could now broadcast to the whole of Iran, the crowd that occupied the building started making speeches in front of the microphones. To their chagrin they discovered that the connection between the Radio Office and Tehran Radio's Broadcasting Station, the transmission post which effectively broadcasted the programs, had been severed.[14] Upset by the setback, the ruffians destroyed furniture and equipment and then

---

[7] Varqa, pp. 17–19.   [8] *Taraqi*, 2 Shahrivar 1332; Baniahmad, p. 204.
[9] *Taraqi*, 2 Shahrivar 1332; Baniahmad, p. 204.   [10] Wilber p. 66.
[11] Baniahmad, p. 205.   [12] *Taraqi*, 2 Shahrivar 1332; Wilber, p. 68.
[13] Nejati (Goftogo ba Ostad Doctor Gholamhoseyn Sadiqi), p. 542.   [14] Baniahmad, p. 208.

decided to set fire to the building. It was only after an employee interceded and pleaded with them not to destroy public property that they contented themselves with tearing up all the files and papers which they found in the office and placing the Shah's picture at the entrance of the building.[15] The disappointed crowd then set out towards Tehran Radio's Broadcasting Station or the Pahlavi Wireless Station (*bisim-e Pahlavi*) on the Old Shemiran Street.[16]

It was not until 1:00 p.m. that the Telegraph Office fell to the royalist crowd.[17] In their usual manner of marking their victory over a governmental office, they attached a picture of the Shah on the façade.[18] With the Telegraph Office in the hands of anti-Mosaddeq forces, the coup forces could dispatch whatever news they wished to the provinces. From somewhere between 1:30 p.m. and 2:00 p.m. the police and military forces loyal to Mosaddeq could no longer control the multi-dimensional crowd of thugs, political agents and military personnel which had been brought together and had morphed into one powerful coup force controlling the city centre. It was at this time that groups of demonstrators returned to Toupkhaneh, Baharestan, Rah-Ahan and Bistochahar-e Esfand Squares, where the royal statues had been brought down on the previous days, and replaced the empty spaces with pictures of the Shah and wreaths of flowers.[19] These symbolic acts, marking the return of the Shah, indicated that phase three of the coup plan was successfully unfolding.

At approximately 2:00 p.m. Daftari, who by this time had been officially appointed as Chief of Police and Military Governor by Mosaddeq, entered the police headquarters near Sepah Square, which was also the headquarters of the Military Governor. He recalled that the place was chaotic and that all of the personnel were chanting "Long live the Shah".[20] Daftari went among the policemen gathered in the open space behind the police headquarters building, mounted a truck, brought out his handkerchief and started crying while the policemen cheered him.[21] When a few policemen in the crowd asked him the embarrassing question of whether he was Mosaddeq's Chief of Police or Zahedi's, Daftari remained silent. Daftari claims that at this time, the police headquarters were effectively in the hands of anti-Mosaddeq forces, that the policemen chanted slogans against Mosaddeq, and that they prompted one another to attack Mosaddeq's house.[22]

Varqa, who claims to have been present at the police headquarters, presents a report which is similar to Daftari's in its broad contours, but which differs in its details. Varqa does not report pro-Shah chants as Daftari entered the police

---

[15] Baniahmad, p. 208. [16] Baniahmad, p. 208. [17] Wilber, p. 69.
[18] *Ettela'at*, 31 Mordad 1332. [19] *Taraqi*, 2 Shahrivar 1332.
[20] Mohammad Daftari, Iranian Oral History Collection, Harvard University, Transcript 2, p. 15.
[21] Baniahmad, p. 215. [22] Baniahmad, p. 216.

headquarters. According to Varqa, 50–60 junior and senior police officers and policemen had gathered in the large open space inside the police headquarters, discussing issues among themselves, when Daftari arrived and presented himself to the personnel.[23] Varqa attributes the question of whether Daftari was Mosaddeq's Chief of Police or Zahedi's to one of the arrested officers, a Lieutenant Moqadam, who was incarcerated at the headquarters of the Military Governor overlooking the space where the police personnel had gathered.[24] Moqadam, who acted as an *agent provocateur* with the objective of whipping up support for Zahedi and against Mosaddeq, was one of those officers who openly claimed his allegiance to the retired Anglophile General Arfa and was among the 32 officers promoted in rank after the success of the second coup.[25] According to Varqa, Daftari did not respond to Moqadam's provocative question. In a most ambiguous manner, Daftari had assured the police personnel present that things would soon become clear and problems would be resolved.[26] Varqa concurs with Daftari and maintains that the police headquarters had effectively sided with Zahedi before the arrival of Daftari, even though the latter seemed to be playing both sides.[27]

With the fall of the police headquarters, the only other sensitive targets left in the Sepah neighbourhood were the Military Police headquarters (*dejban*) and its prison. At around 2:00 p.m. the demonstrators, who by this time enjoyed the support of armed military personnel and were led by Major Zamanian, began their attack on the Military Police headquarters.[28] According to Wilber, it was the CIA station agent, Jalali, who had mobilized the crowd on Ferdowsi Street to attack the Military Police headquarters.[29] The first round of attack was repulsed by Colonel Sarreshteh's forces.[30] The corporals inside the Military Police prison had been incited by Colonel Azizollah Rahimi, who had on the previous day made a moving speech in support of the Shah before the soldiers and corporals gathered at the mess hall.[31] It was these same corporals who came to the assistance of the belligerents, with one of them attacking Sarreshteh with a knife.[32] It was not until 3:00 p.m. that the doors of the Military Police's prison were opened by Colonel Majid Naqdi and Fatollah Amir Ala'i with their gang of pro-Shah zealots.[33] Fatollah Amir Ala'i was a teacher at the Officers Academy and an employee of Colonel Ahmad Zangeneh, the President of the Officers Academy and Zahedi's friend, who had joined forces with the collaborationist officers.

After the successful assault on the Military Police prison, Nasiri, Batmanqelich, Rowhani and other high-ranking officers who had been

---

[23] Varqa, p. 27.   [24] Varqa, p. 27.   [25] Varqa, p. 27, *Shahed* 9 Shahrivar 1332.
[26] Varqa, pp. 27–28.   [27] Varqa, p. 33.   [28] *Tehran Mosavvar*, 6 Shahrivar 1332.
[29] Wilber, p. 70.   [30] Nejati, p. 451.   [31] Baniahmad, p. 217.
[32] Nejati, p. 451; Javanshir, p. 309.
[33] Nejati, pp. 451–452; Javanshir, p. 309; Baniahmad, p. 218.

arrested after the first coup were released. Batmanqelich, who is said to have been shaken up by the events and was not quite willing to come out of his cell, had to be nudged to put on his military attire and occupy his designated post of the Chief of Staff.[34] Batmanqelich was finally conducted to his nearby headquarters by his supporters and was installed in Riyahi's place.[35] He was now giving the military orders. He sent Nasiri along with Naqdi to arrange for the deployment of loyal forces at Sa'dabad palace.[36] Preparing for the last phase of the operation, Batmanqelich then commissioned Colonel Nasrollah Hakimi, who had been active on 9 Esfand and had been arrested for his activities to relieve Colonel Shahrokh at Jay garrison, to take command of his military unit and dispatch the tanks stationed there to attack Mosaddeq's house.[37] At around 4:00 p.m., accompanied by Colonel Behafarid and Major Movasaqi, Colonel Hakimi drove to Jay garrison, presented his credentials as the new commander of the garrison to Shahrokh, and took command of it without any resistance from Shahrokh or the soldiers stationed there.[38] Without a shot being fired, Hakimi drove away from Jay garrison and headed towards Mosaddeq's house, accompanied by 12 tanks.[39]

SMASHING PRO-MOSADDEQ PARTY HEADQUARTERS AND NEWSPAPER OFFICES IN BAHARESTAN

While one group of ruffians converged on Sepah Square between 9:00 a.m. and 10:00 a.m., those led by Tayyeb and Ramezoun Yakhi arrived at Baharestan Square at around 10:00 a.m.[40] This group was armed with sticks and clubs; its members brandished pictures of the Shah attached to their sticks and yelled "Shahanshah (the king of kings) is victorious".[41] The two main targets of the ruffians in the heart of Tehran, Sepah and Baharestan Squares were only 1.5 kilometres apart.

The demonstrators who had moved north from Mowlavi first occupied Baharestan Square and, having secured their base, fanned out into the small streets connected to Baharestan Square, which housed almost all the pro-Mosaddeq parties and organizations. Even the headquarters of Baqa'i's Iranian People's Toilers Party, which was once a pro-Mosaddeq party and had subsequently turned against Mosaddeq, had its headquarters right next to that of the Iran Party and the dailies *Bakhtar Emrouz* and *Shouresh*. On 28 Mordad, while all pro-Mosaddeq party headquarters and newspapers in the neighbourhood were ransacked and destroyed, Baqa'i's headquarters remained unscathed. The specific and precise selection of the targets to be

---

[34] Nejati, p. 452.   [35] Nejati, p. 452, Javanshir, p. 309.   [36] Baniahmad, p. 218.
[37] *Ettela'at Haftegi*, 6 Shahrivar 1332.   [38] *Ettela'at Haftegi*, 6 Shahrivar 1332.
[39] *Ettela'at Haftegi*, 6 Shahrivar 1332.   [40] *Taraqi*, 2 Shahrivar 1332.
[41] *Taraqi*, 2 Shahrivar 1332.

attacked by the ruffians demonstrated that once they were in Baharestan Square they were provided with the necessary leadership, just as they were in Sepah.

The attacks on the pro-Mosaddeq organizations, clubs and newspaper offices in the Baharestan area started at around 10:00 a.m. The fact that the occupation of Sepah and Baharestan Squares by the ruffians was taking place almost simultaneously in two different yet highly strategic locations of central Tehran took Mosaddeq's government and his non-collaborationist military personnel by surprise. In the meantime, Tehranis – the majority of whom remained loyal to Mosaddeq and were unable to see the whole scale and scope of the ruffians' north-bound thrust, but only the movement of packs of 50–100 thugs through the streets which they crossed – thought that this was another isolated demonstration typical of what had happened in the aftermath of the first coup. The fact that the main actors of the "great demonstration", namely the approximately 1,000 to 2,000 ruffians, were almost permanently on the move in small groups of 50–100, and then divided up into smaller packs of 25–50 depending on their operation, before converging on their strategic locations, provided them with great mobility, flexibility and limited visibility.[42] By breaking up, attacking and then re-uniting they succeeded in controlling a perimeter which effectively contained the military, political and administrative centres of the Mosaddeq government, before attacking the two jugulars, namely Mosaddeq's house and Tehran Radio's Broadcasting Station.

As contrasted with the ministries and key government and military installations around Sepah Square, the symbolically and politically important offices and buildings around Baharestan Square were guarded neither by police nor military personnel. As such they were easier prey for the ruffians, who were armed only with sticks and clubs. The ruffians coming from the south were joined by CIA station operatives – Jalali, Keyvani, Majidi and Reza-Ali – who had been waiting in vain around the bazaar area for Borujerdi's *fatwa* against Mosaddeq. Disappointed by the non-arrival of the *fatwa*, the native CIA operatives made themselves useful and joined the pro-Shah crowd that was heading towards the Majles in Baharestan.[43] What happened at Sepah Square was replicated at Baharestan. The ruffians, under "proper" leadership, attacked the buildings, ransacked and laid waste to them, beat up and chased out those in the buildings and finally set fire to them.

The headquarters of the influential Iran Party, Hezb-e Iran, on Shahabad Street was the first building to be attacked and set alight.[44] At around 10:00 a.m. demonstrators armed with sticks and chanting "Long live the Shah and death to the Tudeh" attacked, climbing over the walls and breaking

---

[42] Bozorgmehr, p. 310.   [43] Wilber, p. 66.
[44] *Ettela'at*, 31 Mordad 1332; Amir-Khosravi, p. 646.

down the doors and windows of the pro-Mosaddeq Iran Party headquarters, injuring those inside.[45] The crowd was incited to attack the Iran Party by Corporal Reza Hasanzad, who was in his fifties, and a boy of around ten or 12 years old.[46] The duo called on the crowd to capture the "centre of opposition to the Shah"; the ruffians, carrying "long clubs", entered Shahabad Street, right off Baharestan, and swiftly took over the Iran Party's headquarters.[47] One of the assailants used his machete to cut up a picture of Mosaddeq and the rest ripped up pictures of Allahyar Saleh, Hasibi and Zirakzadeh.[48] Pictures of Mosaddeq, the furniture, paintings on the wall and the equipment in the building were promptly destroyed; four party members inside the building who tried to put up some resistance were thrown off the balcony on to the ground.[49] The attack on the Iran Party was politically significant as the party was a major player in Mosaddeq's government. Even Riyahi, Mosaddeq's Chief of Staff, was said to be a secret member of the Iran Party.[50] While the attack took place, the police and soldiers either stood by and watched or joined the mob.[51]

Almost around the same time, two separate groups of ruffians – one from Baharestan and the other from Ekbatan Street and Sepah Square – converged on the controversial daily *Shouresh* ("Insurgence").[52] Karimpour Shirazi, the editor and director of *Shouresh*, was a staunch Mosaddeq supporter and an acerbic critic of the Court and Ayatollah Kashani. The headline in his newspaper, "Ayatollah Kashani is a British Spy", had made a lot of waves back in March 1953. At 10:15 a.m. Karimpour Shirazi called Mosaddeq to inform him that his newspaper had been plundered and then set on fire and the ruffians, armed with sticks and clubs, were on their way to the office of the daily *Bakhtar Emrouz* and the headquarters of Foruhar's Iranian People's Party.[53]

The attack on Fatemi's well-known daily, *Bakhtar Emrouz*, was psychologically and symbolically important. Fatemi was not only Mosaddeq's Foreign Minister but, most importantly, after the Shah's departure he and his paper had become outspoken critics of the Shah, his Court and his family. After the first coup *Bakhtar Emrouz* had become a virulent anti-Shah paper, calling for the dismantling of the monarchy. It is even believed that Fatemi's anti-Court speech and his editorial in *Bakhtar Emrouz* after the Shah's departure played a key role in polarizing the people, who subsequently felt as though supporting Mosaddeq and his government meant opposing the Shah and the monarchy. The anger of the military on the evening of 27 Mordad and

---

[45] *Keyhan*, 29 Mordad 1332; *Ettela'at*, 31 Mordad 1332; Javanshir, p. 304.
[46] Baniahmad, p. 196.   [47] Baniahmad, p. 196.   [48] Baniahmad, p. 198.
[49] *Khandaniha*, 31 Mordad, 1332; Baniahmad, p. 198.   [50] Mossavar Rahmani, p. 229.
[51] *Ettela'at*, 31 Mordad 1332; *Khandaniha*, 31 Mordad 1332.
[52] *Taraqi*, 2 Shahrivar 1332.   [53] *Taraqi*, 2 Shahrivar 1332; Baniahmad, p. 188.

their strong pro-Shah sentiments on 28 Mordad is said to have been rooted in their reaction to Fatemi's verbal assault on the Shah, his father and the Court.[54]

Wilber again credits Jalali for having led the mob that set fire to Fatemi's *Bakhtar Emrouz*.[55] The mob leaders made believe that Fatemi was in the building and that the ruffians could arrest him.[56] The offices of *Bakhtar Emrouz* received the same treatment as the headquarters of the Iran Party and the offices of *Shouresh*: it was gutted, its windows were smashed, and then it was set on fire.[57] Flames and smoke filled the Nezamiyeh Alley which housed the daily.[58] Safari, a well-known journalist at *Bakhtar Emrouz*, was at his office at the time of the attack. After the building was set on fire, Safari and his colleagues fled for their lives. Safari made his way towards Sepah Square as Baharestan Square was still occupied by the mob and the military.[59]

After gutting *Bakhtar Emrouz*, the ruffians headed back to Baharestan Square, their secure base of operations that now served as their meeting place after every mission. It was at Baharestan that once again "someone from crowd" incited the crowd to attack the daily *Keshvar*.[60] The self-proclaimed leader of the crowd – probably someone from the group of Jalali and Keyvani – argued that whenever the supporters of Mosaddeq's National Front (*Jebhey-e Melli*) held a rally at Baharestan, they would use the offices of *Keshvar*, and that therefore it had to be destroyed. The thugs subsequently proceeded to smash the furniture and the building, but did not set fire to it.[61]

The next target of the ruffians who had regrouped at Mokhberodowleh junction was the headquarters of Khalil Maleki's Third Force Party (*Hezb-e Nirouy-e Sevvom*). Khalil Maleki had first splintered from the Tudeh Party and, having formed the Iranian People's Toiler Party with Baqa'i, had subsequently left Baqa'i to form the Third Force Party. Maleki's decision to splinter from Baqa'i's Toilers Party has been attributed to different causes. First, it was strongly rumoured that Baqa'i's party was founded at the behest of the British.[62] Second, it was revealed that while backing Mosaddeq during the 30 Tir events Baqa'i was secretly negotiating with Qavam through his close associate Isa Sepahbodi.[63] Finally, when Baqa'i turned against Mosaddeq's camp, Maleki, a socialist and an avid opponent of the Tudeh Party's blind obedience to Soviet geo-political interests, remained a staunch supporter of Mosaddeq. The young intellectual supporters of Khalil Maleki constituted a viable left-leaning, pro-Mosaddeq and anti-Tudeh political

---

[54] *Ferdowsi*, 3 Shahrivar 1332.   [55] Wilber, p. 66.   [56] Baniahmad, p. 198.
[57] *Ettela'at*, 31 Mordad 1332; *Keyhan*, 29 Mordad 1332.   [58] *Taraqi*, 2 Shahrivar 1332.
[59] Safari, p. 868.   [60] *Taraqi*, 2 Shahrivar 1332.   [61] *Taraqi*, 2 Shahrivar 1332.
[62] *Ashofteh*, 12 Bahman 1334.
[63] Abadiyan, pp. 145–146; J. Al-e Ahmad, *Dar Khedmat va Khiyanat-e Rowshanfekran* (Tehran: Ravaq, n.d), p. 365.

force. The ruffians, who were directed by the loose coup plan of 28 Mordad to demolish all pro-Mosaddeq political organizations in their preventive attack, proceeded to neutralize the headquarters of Maleki's Third Force Party. They initially ripped up all the posters, flags and pictures in the building; then they piled up all of the party newspapers, publications and books in the courtyard and set fire to them. Soon there was nothing left of the furniture or of the building itself, which had also been set on fire.[64]

Daryoush Foruhar's Iranian People's Party (*Hezb Mellat Iran bar Mabnay-e Pan Iranism*) was also located on Safialishah Street. Foruhar's party was staunchly pro-Mosaddeq and equally anti-Tudeh. The uniformed members of the Iranian People's Party's defence squads regularly clashed with Tudeh sympathizers and after the first coup, sensing the greater threat of the Tudeh Party, their anti-Tudeh posture hardened. On 28 Mordad Foruhar met Mosaddeq, at the latter's request, at around 8:00 a.m. and was told by the Prime Minister to restrain his supporters from engaging Tudeh Party partisans in street fights.[65] At this same meeting, Foruhar raised an idea common among Mosaddeq's supporters after the failure of the first coup: he requested that Mosaddeq arm the people. The Prime Minister refused on the grounds that such an act would imply that he did not trust the army.

On his way out of Mosaddeq's house, Foruhar encountered Colonels Modabber and Ashrafi in the Prime Minister's courtyard and pleaded with them to free his supporters, who had been arrested along with Tudeh partisans a few days previously for having clashed on the streets. Having obtained the verbal assurance of the colonels, Foruhar returned to his party's headquarters at around 9:00 a.m. There, he ordered his supporters to disperse and reminded them to avoid all confrontation. He subsequently returned to the police headquarters to secure the release of his arrested partisans. Foruhar was at Modabber's office when the latter informed him about disturbances at Baharestan and the fact that his party headquarters had been attacked.[66] By the time Foruhar took a taxi and arrived at his party headquarters, the place was in flames. The task of the ruffians, however, had not been as easy as before.

The members of the Iranian People's Party had defended their headquarters with stones and bricks, until the demonstrators were able to occupy it and forced them to escape across the rooftops. The battle for Foruhar's headquarters left casualties.[67] Foruhar recalled that after the destruction of his

---

[64] *Tehran Mosavvar*, 6 Shahrivar 1332; Khandaniha, 31 Mordad 1332.
[65] Amir-Khosravi, p. 646, Baniahmad, p. 187; Foruhar's interview with Mehran Adib: http://enghe labe-eslami.com/%D8%B5%D9%81%D8%AD%D9%87%D8%A7%DB%8C-%D8% A7%D8%B2%D8%AA%D8%A7%D8%B1%DB%8C%D8%AE/16180————28- 32—————html.
[66] Amir-Khosravi, p. 646; Foruhar's interview with Mehran Adib.
[67] Amir-Khosravi, p. 646; Baniahmad, p. 198.

party's headquarters, he could not imagine that a second coup was unfolding, and so thinking that it had been the work of random ruffian groups who had been active the night before, he went to Baharestan Square in the hope of mobilizing the people in favour of Mosaddeq. Foruhar recalled that he and a few of his supporters were beaten up by a crowd of around 100, at least 80 of whom were policemen.[68] During this frenzy of violence aimed at intimidating and silencing pro-Mosaddeq supporters, the mob looted and destroyed the offices of publications suspected of pro-Mosaddeq tendencies. *Haji Baba*, *Towfiq* and the daily *Ettela'at* were also gutted.[69]

By around noon, the city centre was under the full control of the coup forces. The symbolically significant government offices were occupied, the pro-Mosaddeq and pro-Tudeh political headquarters were burnt down, and their newspaper offices were vandalized or destroyed. Most importantly, the supporters of both Mosaddeq and the Tudeh Party who were capable of putting up resistance were muzzled and stunned. They were either intimidated by the previous night's events, reluctant to engage in any altercations because of Mosaddeq's directive that his partisans should keep off the streets, or surprised and shocked by the unexpected unfolding of events. Whatever the reasons, Mosaddeq's supporters were disoriented, paralysed and almost shell-shocked. Their subdued state clearly played into the hands of the coup planners.

On Saturday 31 Mordad – or three days after the coup d'état – Baqa'i's *Shahed* placed an interesting spin on the thugs, ruffians and lumpen-proletariat who spearheaded the coup. *Shahed* attributed the uprising to the hungry, the barefooted and the ragged who had revolted against the bullying government of Mosaddeq, and affirmed that on 28 Mordad, "the Iranian people, the people of Tehran, the barefooted people of South of Tehran, the toilers, those who do not have houses, cars, property and titles revolted".[70] By presenting the hired thugs as the impoverished working class and toilers of Southern Tehran, Baqa'i's paper propagated a key notion that lingered for many decades after the coup, especially among the coup collaborators: 28 Mordad was a spontaneous popular uprising of the underclasses, supported by the army.

This official version of an "uprising" rather than a "coup" was conceptualized only five days after the events, but was repeated many decades later by Ardeshir Zahedi, who would maintain that "the main players of 28 Mordad were the toiling masses" who "started their anti-Mosaddeq and pro-Shah demonstrations from the South of Tehran and moved to the North".[71] Baqa'i's very close friend and comrade in arms, Ali Zohari, schematized the events of 28 Mordad in *Shahed*'s editorial, dispelling any doubts about a

---

[68] Foruhar's interview with Mehran Adib; Amir-Khosravi, p. 646.
[69] Baniahmad, pp. 198, 201; *Taraqi*, 2 Shahrivar 1332; *Shahed*, 29 Mordad.
[70] *Shahed*, 31 Mordad 1332.   [71] Zahedi, vol. 1, pp. 186–187.

premeditated plan by Iranian and foreign forces interested in overthrowing Mosaddeq.[72] According to Zohari, groups of people from Southern Tehran first demonstrated against the Communists and Mosaddeq's government. As time went by the crowd became swollen. The Military Governance (*farmandariy-e nezami*) sent in troops and tanks to confront the people. After the first shots were fired in the air, the police, the military and the tanks joined the people. There was no plan; there was no central command. The only thing that united these people was their resolve to rid the country of anarchy, the threat of Communism and opposition to Mosaddeq. The popular uprising was not the work of any particular party or group; the army, with the cooperation of the people, overthrew the government of the allies of the Communists.[73] This version of the coup was what Baqa'i's paper called the "truth about the 28 Mordad uprising".

---

[72] *Shahed*, 2 Shahrivar 1332.   [73] *Shahed*, 2 Shahrivar 1332.

13

The enigma of the tanks: betrayal or incompetence?

The successful conclusion of the fourth phase of the coup, or the final assault on Mosaddeq's house and Tehran Radio's Broadcasting Station, required tanks as these two buildings were heavily protected. The manner in which the tanks were to be put at the disposal of the demonstrators or dispatched to the designated areas was not planned down to the finer details. The police, the Armed Custom Guards and the army personnel instructed to support the great demonstration joined the ruffians in an irregular manner whenever they found a window of opportunity. The tank units involved in the "great demonstration" operated in almost the same way. Those tank personnel who had previously been instructed on collaborating with the activities of 28 Mordad were given a final objective and were left free almost to improvise according to their intuition, and assessment of the prevailing conditions and the evolving circumstances once they were in the city centre. No precision in targeted operations, specific deadlines or timely connections was expected of the collaborating tank personnel. They were instructed only to combine forces with the other agents of the "great demonstration" by the end of the day and seize Mosaddeq's house as well as Tehran Radio's Broadcasting Station. The absence of any specific and rigid centralized task assignments for the collaborating tank personnel gave the tank units considerable latitude to fulfil their final mission.

Various reports of tank movements and deployments abound, along with different accounts of the manner and process by which tank units fraternized with the crowds or were shrewdly won over by collaborationist tank and non-tank officers. From early in the morning there were reports of tanks appearing in front of the Majles in Baharestan.[1] By noon, "truckloads of soldiers, armoured cars and tanks were dispersed throughout the city".[2] Wilber's account is sketchy on the deployment and operation of the tank units which came to the help of the ruffians and the soldiers that had fraternized with them

---

[1] Wilber, p. 67.   [2] FRUS, vol. x, p. 785.

The enigma of the tanks: betrayal or incompetence?

on 28 Mordad. Reading Iranian sources, it seems most likely that the tanks which did play a definitive role in the fourth phase of the operations came from units primarily at Saltanatabad and subsequently at Qasr garrisons, both under the command of Colonel Nowzari. Reports after the fall of Mosaddeq's government revealed that Colonel Nowzari and the tanks under his command were also intended to play a key role in the first coup.[3] Preparations had been under way from 11:00 p.m. on 24 Mordad (15 August) to deploy some 45 tanks from Saltanatabad under the command of Batmanqelich in order to occupy the army and police headquarters as well as the Officers' Club.[4] This did not happen on 24 Mordad as the first coup did not unfold as planned. On 28 Mordad, however, these tanks entered the scene and were injected into the great demonstration at different intervals. The fact that the tanks used in the 28 Mordad coup d'état came from the Saltanatabad garrison indicated that the collaborating network operating in that garrison since the first coup continued to operate undetected and unmolested until it finally succeeded in overthrowing Mosaddeq. Ironically, however, while during the 28 Mordad operation most of the tank squadron commanders involved had a reputation for being Mosaddeq loyalists, all "lost" their tanks to the demonstrators without any recorded resistance. Their tanks were overrun and taken control of by the military, police personnel, and the ruffians. These same tanks, which were in every case bloodlessly and almost consensually hijacked, were eventually used to occupy Tehran Radio's Broadcasting Station, transport Zahedi to the Radio Station where he delivered his victory speech and finally to attack Mosaddeq's house.

SQUADRON A MANNED BY MOSADDEQ LOYALISTS AND ANTI-MOSADDEQ INFILTRATORS

Chronologically, the first tank Squadron – A – which set off for central Tehran was composed of four M-4 Sherman tanks. The M-4 Shermans have a crew capacity of five (commander, gunner, loader, driver and co-driver), weigh 30 tons, and travel at a speed of 40–48 kilometres per hour. They are armed with a 76 millimetre gun, a .50 calibre Browning machine gun, and two .30 calibre Browning machine guns. Squadron A is said to have left Saltanatabad garrison any time between midnight and 5:00 a.m. on 28 Mordad.[5] In those early hours of the morning the Mosaddeq government and its loyal military brass had no clue about what was planned for the day. There is no evidence that Riyahi had given orders that tank units be deployed. It can only be surmised that the orders to bring tanks into the city at that time of the night

---

[3] *Tehran Mosavvar*, 6 Shahrivar 1332; *Salnameh Donya*, Dahomin Salnameh, 1333. The *Donya* article is a replica of a part of the *Tehran Mosavvar* article.
[4] *Tehran Mosavvar*, 6 Shahrivar 1332; *Salnameh Donya*, Dahomin Salnameh, 1333.
[5] Mohammadi, p. 63.

came from collaborating officers who knew of the coup plan for that day. According to the existing military hierarchy and line of command, only Riyahi or Nowzari could have given permission for the tanks to leave their base. It is believed that it was Nowzari, who, in collusion with the conspirators, gave the order for the tanks to leave Saltanatabad.[6] Given that the distance between Saltanatabad and Shahreza Street was about 12 kilometres, and from Shahreza to Mosaddeq's house was another five kilometres, even if it is assumed that Squadron A left Saltanatabad at 5:00 a.m. and travelled at 40 kilometres per hour, it would have reached Shahreza in about 25 minutes. Squadron A left Saltanatabad under the command of Lieutenant Iravani, Captain Hojjat and a few other officers.[7] It is not clear whether Captain Jahanbani left Saltanatabad with Iravani and Hojjat or with another squadron of tanks, but we do know that later in the day they all regrouped at Sa'di Street.

As their supposed mission was to protect Mosaddeq's house, the tanks descended Saltanatabad Street and then took the Old Shemiran Street southbound. When they arrived at Shahreza Street, instead of turning west towards Pahlavi and then Kakh Street, they turned east and descended Abualisina Street towards Baharestan, one of the strategic points on which the pro-Shah roughnecks were converging from the southern neighbourhoods. The tanks proceeded to Jaleh Street, just north of Baharestan, to refuel, and radioed their location to headquarters.[8] At this key location the tanks were surrounded by the mob coming from the south. At around 11:00 a.m. the demonstrators boarded the tanks and took control of them without any reported resistance.[9] Subsequently, all contact between this squadron of tanks and their headquarters was lost and the tanks could effectively be manoeuvred and used as their new commanders pleased.

At this moment the thugs, supported by powerful Sherman tanks, could proceed to the other key militarily points in town. The dispatching of four tanks right in the midst of ruffians was an excellent entrapment plan. Captain Mohammadi is convinced that Colonel Nowzari (commander of the First Armoured Brigade) was in collusion with the coup planners and had set the execution of this operation in motion from the previous night.[10] However, Captain Arbabi believes that Nowzari was a good officer and loyal to Mosaddeq.[11] Based on the events of 28 Mordad and Nowzari's career advancement after the coup, it would be safe to assume that Colonel Nowzari was indeed in collusion with the collaborationist officers.[12] Colonel Nowzari controlled both the Saltanatabad garrison, where Iran's

---

[6] Mohammadi, pp. 44, 63, 73.   [7] Mohammadi, p. 34, 62.   [8] Mohammadi, p. 34.
[9] Mohammadi, p. 34.   [10] Mohammadi, pp. 55–61   [11] Mohammadi, p. 33.
[12] Nowzari became a general and the commander of the 5th Corps (*farmandeh sepah 5*) and was decorated on 26 November 1961, the occasion of the Shah's birthday with the 3rd class Taj Medal. See: http://www.22bahman.ir/ContentDetails/pageid/153/ctl/view/mid/364/Id/N-72388/language/fa-IR/Default.asp.

The enigma of the tanks: betrayal or incompetence?

most advanced tanks were stationed, and the Qasr garrison, which also housed tanks and was located very close to Tehran Radio's Broadcasting Station. Nowzari's military command position enabled him to dispatch tank units to any point in the city. He could also assign collaborationist officers to any tank units he wished. Therefore, tanks could be sent to any strategic streets or squares that the demonstrators had already occupied. Once the dispatched tank units arrived at the designated mob-controlled areas, the collaborationist officers inside each tank could begin fraternizing with the demonstrators and the police and military personnel that now accompanied them.

In view of Lieutenant Iraj Iravani's ideological tendencies (the Tudeh Party's Military Organization) it would be reasonable to assume that as the commander of Squadron A he believed that he was leading his tanks to buttress the Mosaddeq government against any threats. Iravani was an official member of the Tudeh Party and was given a life sentence with hard labour after the Military Organization of the Tudeh Party was discovered in the summer of 1954.[13] Why, then, did the tanks moving south on the Old Shemiran Street suddenly turn away from Mosaddeq's house when they reached Shahreza Street and proceed to Jaleh Street to refuel? Did Captains Jahanbani and Hojjat, the collaborationist officers, effectively take control of the tanks at an opportune moment as they both out-ranked Iravani? Or did they order Iravani to refuel at the petrol station on Jaleh Street? Is it possible that the drivers and the co-drivers of the four tanks (about whom not much is known) were collaborators or were taking their cue from the collaborationist officers? A few tanks (probably three) from Squadron A operated by Iravani and Hojjat ended up first on Sa'di Street, where they were joined by Amir Khalili, the commander of Squadron B and by Kiyani's assault force (Squadron D), which was hijacked by Khosrowdad and Shoja'i.[14] Around the gas station on Sa'di Street where some of the tanks were refuelling, Major Mihanpey, Major Amir Khaliqi (Khalili), Captain Jahanbani, Lieutenants Shoja'i, Khosrowdad, and Iravani, along with a couple of other civilians, decided to lead the tanks towards Mosaddeq's house and break down any resistance that might be put up by Mosaddeq's supporters.[15]

What is both puzzling and revelatory is that among the six officers mentioned by Baniahmad, who had gathered and who were colluding to use the tanks against Mosaddeq, there are three – Shoja'i, Khosrowdad and Jahanbani – collaborationist junior officers and two – Iravani and Amir Khalili – pro-Mosaddeq officers.[16] Were the two pro-Mosaddeq officers intimidated or forced to go along with the plans of the collaborationist

---

[13] *Ketab-e Siyah dar bareh Sazeman-e Afsaran-e Tudeh*, n.p, Esfand 1334, p. 352.
[14] Baniahmad, p. 235.   [15] Baniahmad, p. 235.
[16] Mohammadi, pp. 54, 65, 66; Davarpanah maintains that Amir Khalili may have been a collaborationist officer: see *Ettela'at*, 29 Mordad 1358).

officers? Is it possible that they were totally ignorant about what was going on? Did they hope to use their tanks in favour of Mosaddeq at the right time, when and if the circumstances were to change? Were they just overwhelmed by the crowds and swept away by the mood which prevailed at the locations occupied by the demonstrators? Were they consenting against their will and loyalties? Could they have been collaborators as well? What is known is that Hojat, Iravani and Jahanbani of Squadron A ended up at Mosaddeq's house, where their tanks were used to destroy it.[17] According to Arbabi, the officer on guard at the Saltanatabad garrison on the eve of 28 Mordad and who was subsequently replaced by Iravani, of the four tanks which left Saltanatabad very early in the morning on 28 Mordad, two eventually went to Mosaddeq's house on Kakh Street, one went to the Officer's Club on Qavamolsaltaneh and Forughi Street (close to Sepah Square), and one broke down on the way.[18]

THE STRANGE ACCOUNT OF SQUADRON B

At 9:00 a.m. a group of colonels from the Chief of Staff headquarters entered Saltanatabad garrison, from where Squadron A had left earlier on that day, and ordered Major Amir Khalili to dispatch two different tank squadrons to the city centre.[19] Amir Khalili led one squadron of eight tanks (Squadron B) to the city centre and ordered Lieutenant Houshang Qorbannejad to take another squadron of four tanks (Squadron C) to the Qasr garrison.[20] The fact that at 9:00 a.m. a group of colonels appeared at Saltanatabad garrison, 12 kilometres away from the city centre, and directly ordered the immediate deployment of tanks seems unusual. What is even more peculiar is that the orders given by the mysterious colonels were promptly carried out. The dispatch of tanks into the city, assuming normal conditions, would have required the respect of a standard chain of command. The fact that the orders of the mysterious colonels were carried out without any hesitation indicates that their instructions must have had the support of Nowzari, the commander of the garrison. If it is assumed that the colonels were members of the collaborationist network implementing the part of the coup plan that involved the participation of the tanks, then the account begins to make more sense. Anxious about the ability of loyal Mosaddeq officers or Tudeh infiltrators in the army to report on unusual military preparations and movements, the coup planners minimized the lag time between issuing their military command and its execution by going and personally overseeing the departure of the tanks. Cutting out the normal chain of command for such deployments assured the plotters that their plans would remain secret. The same method of minimizing the possibility of being uncovered had also been employed with the dispatch

---

[17] Mohammadi, p. 35. [18] Mohammadi, p. 35. [19] Javanshir, p. 308.
[20] Javanshir, p. 308; Mohammadi, pp. 73, 74.

of Squadron A. One of the reasons why the first coup failed was that planning too far ahead had alerted the pro-Mosaddeq forces. The swift and ad hoc command system employed by the collaborationist high-ranking officers on 28 Mordad assured success in putting much-needed tanks into the hands of anti-Mosaddeq forces.

Events proved that the colonels who came to Saltanatabad in effect ordered the tanks and their crews into another ingenious trap. The tanks were ordered to proceed to designated areas which had already been occupied by the ruffians, where the tanks would be encircled, boarded and hijacked. Among this group of military officers could have been those who intervened at Saltanatabad on the eve of 28 Mordad to change the officers on guard and ensure that Squadron A would be infiltrated by collaborationist officers.[21] The colonels' presence at Saltanatabad and their orders at that time could not have been at the behest of pro-Mosaddeq officers, since it was not until about 9:30 a.m. that Mosaddeq and Sadiqi started receiving news about the disturbances in the city and began making calls to Riyahi, Ashrafi and Modabber.

Major As'ad Amir Khalili's Squadron B left Saltanatabad after 9:00 a.m. He commanded eight tanks composed of M-4 Shermans and M-24s. It is not known where Amir Khalili was ordered to lead his tanks. His specific mission remains equally unknown. It can only be inferred that Amir Khalili, very much like Iravani of Squadron A and Qorbannejad of Squadron C, set out thinking that his mission was to ensure public order and peace and ended up entrapped by the ruffians. How he lost control of his eight tanks is an enigma. What is known is that Amir Khalili (he is at times referred to as Shah Khalili and sometimes as Khaliqi) was at the fuel station on Sa'di street along with commanders and hijackers of Squadrons A, C and D.

At around 4:30 p.m. Amir Khalili went to Colonel Momtaz at Mosaddeq's house and requested a meeting with Mosaddeq.[22] According to Colonel Momtaz, whose loyalty to Mosaddeq always remained irreproachable, Amir Khalili (Shah Khalili) was eager to report on the ill fate of his tank squadron, his "mismanagement", and how the tanks under his command had become dispersed.[23] By reporting to Mosaddeq, who at the time was still the Minister of War and the Prime Minister, Amir Khalili wished to get off his chest the ordeal of the loss of his tanks. Amir Khalili was not a collaborationist officer – on the contrary, he was considered to be a most loyal officer to Mosaddeq.[24] By going to Mosaddeq's house to report on his misfortunes, when Mosaddeq's house was under heavy fire by some of Amir Khalili's own tanks, Amir Khalili was proving his personal loyalty to Mosaddeq. Yet the key question remains regarding what happened to the eight tanks of Squadron B, as commanded by Amir Khalili.

[21] Mohammadi, p. 74.   [22] Nejati, p. 449.   [23] Nejati, p. 449.   [24] Mohammadi, p. 54.

Colonel Momtaz maintained that Amir Khalili's tank Squadron B was part of the "assault column" led by Lieutenant General Kiyani's Squadron D.[25] This would imply that at some point Amir Khalili handed over the command of his tanks to his superior officer, Lieutenant General Kiyani, the commander of the infantry and tank "assault column". On the basis of this report, then, the tanks of Squadron D (Kiyani's) were made up of Amir Khalili's tanks (Squadron B) and the two in effect became one and the same.

SQUADRON C DELIVERED TO THE COUP FORCES

After Amir Khalili left Saltanatabad, it was Qorbannejad who was ordered to lead Squadron C from Saltanatabad towards the Qasr garrison, the headquarters of the First Armoured Brigade commanded by Colonel Nowzari. Like Iravani, the commander of Squadron A, who was a clandestine member of the Military Organization of the Tudeh Party, Houshang Qorbannejad was a member of this same organization, and therefore it would be safe to assume that he was opposed to a Shah–Zahedi coup.[26] Qorbannejad was also given a life sentence with hard labour after the Military Organization of the Tudeh Party was discovered in 1954.[27] Qorbannejad and his four tanks had to cover six kilometres. On his way to Qasr garrison, Qorbannejad was contacted and ordered to place two of his tanks at the entrance of Tehran Radio's Broadcasting Station (*bisime Pahlavi*), only a few hundred metres away from the Qasr garrison, and to take his other two tanks to the garrison.[28] At around noon Qorbannejad witnessed the arrival of a bus filled with demonstrators chanting "Long live the Shah" in front of the garrison on the Old Shemiran Street.

At this time, an officer from the Qasr garrison approached Qorbannejad and informed him that Colonel Nowzari, commander of the First Armoured Brigade, had summoned him. In his absence, Qorbannejad appointed a corporal to take charge of his tanks and the protection of Tehran Radio's Broadcasting Station, and rushed to Nowzari. Having waited a long time in vain to meet with Nowzari, Qorbannejad was then told to go back to Tehran Radio's Broadcasting Station.[29] By the time Qorbannejad returned to the Broadcasting Station he realized that Nowzari's simple ruse had worked, as he was told by the corporal he had put in charge that in his absence Prince Gholamreza Pahlavi and Zahedi had come to the Station, seated on a tank, and had subsequently sent their messages.[30] Qorbannejad concluded that

---

[25] E. Sahabi, *Mosaddeq, Dowlat-e Melli va Kudeta* (Tehran: Tarh-e No, 1380), p. 268; Nejati, p. 449.
[26] Javanshir, p. 308.   [27] *Ketab-e Siyah dar bareh Sazeman-e Afsaran-e Tudeh*, p. 353.
[28] Javanshir, p. 308.   [29] Javanshir, p. 308.
[30] Javanshir, p. 308; It was Prince Hamidreza and not Gholamreza who spoke after Zahedi on 28 Mordad: see *Ettela'at*, 31 Mordad 1332.

The enigma of the tanks: betrayal or incompetence?

luring him away from his post was part of a plan.[31] The fact that Zahedi had already sent his message meant that, without any resistance from the two tanks supposedly defending the Broadcasting Station, the station had fallen into the hands of the insurgents.

Qorbannejad recalled that he was once again summoned to Nowzari's office. Suspicious of the motives and plans of those who were summoning him, Qorbannejad requested a formal written order, and upon its receipt he went to meet Nowzari.[32] This time Nowzari commanded him to take two of his four tanks to Riyahi at the Chief of Staff's headquarters on Sevvom-e Esfand Street, close to Sepah Square. Qorbannejad carried out his orders. On Naderi Street "a group composed of military and non-military personnel" blocked his way and his tanks came to a stop.[33] Among the demonstrators obstructing his path was Amir Khosrowdad, a member of one of the teams of the "Devotees of the Shah" actively engaged in the anti-Mosaddeq activities on that day. Khosrowdad, who was a classmate of Qorbannejad, tried to convince him to allow the ruffians to ride on his tanks to Mosaddeq's house.[34] Qorbannejad refused, but as a compromise to secure his safe passage to his destination, he promised to return after he had presented himself to Riyahi. Upon arrival, Qorbannejad was ordered by Riyahi to drive his two tanks into the Military Police (*dejban*) headquarters. The most important military prisoners from the first coup were kept at the detention centre of the Military Police. When Qorbannejad argued that if he drove the tanks into an enclosed area and then the doors were closed, his tanks would be trapped, Riyahi retorted "Do as you are told".[35] By this time Riyahi had thrown down the gauntlet and embraced the coup, believing that the Shah had the right to appoint Zahedi as Prime Minister.

By around 3:00 p.m. the Military Police (*dejban*) headquarters had been occupied by the demonstrators and the prisoners from the first coup were freed. Colonel Rasti, the commander of the Military Police, is said to have been a collaborating officer.[36] Once Qorbannejad's tanks were parked inside the Military Police headquarters, the anti-Mosaddeq military personnel boarded them and ordered him to head out. At first he refused, arguing that he had not received any such orders. However, when the first tank was boarded by Colonel Azizollah Rahimi, who had played a key role in inciting the corporals at the Military Police headquarters to rebel against their officers and who was therefore instrumental in occupying this strategic location, Qorbannejad felt compelled to comply. Qorbannejad also noticed Colonel Rowhani, who had just been freed, standing in front of the Chief of Staff headquarters and directing the tanks.[37] Arriving at Mosaddeq's house, he found that bullets were flying from all directions, and Qorbannejad

---

[31] Javanshir, p. 308.   [32] Javanshir, p. 309.   [33] Javanshir, p. 309.   [34] Javanshir, p. 309.
[35] Javanshir, p. 309.   [36] Sahabi, p. 269.   [37] Javanshir, p. 309.

observed a few M-9 armoured personnel carriers in front of Mosaddeq's house.[38]

Several points need to be highlighted in Qorbannejad's account of his adventures on 28 Mordad. First, the order to move his Squadron C of four tanks (probably composed of M-24s) came from the same colonels who personally arrived at Saltanatabad at around 9:00 a.m. M-24 tanks have a crew capacity of 5 (commander, gunner, loader, driver and co-driver), weigh about 18 tons and travel at about 40–56 kilometres per hour. Each tank is equipped with a 75 millimetre gun, a .50 calibre Browning machine gun and two .30 calibre Browning machine guns. Again, it is important to bear in mind that according to the plan for the first coup on 25 Mordad, Saltanatabad or Jamshidiyeh was supposed to provide the tanks for the operations.[39] So, it would be reasonable to assume that reliable senior and junior collaborationist officers were identified and ready to act at Saltanatabad or Qasr before the first coup; since their covers had not been blown after the first coup flopped, it was safe to draw upon them for the second coup. Second, Qorbannejad was ordered by Nowzari (commander of the First Armoured Brigade) to divide up his squadron. Third, we do not know what happened to his other two tanks, although there are reports of two stray tanks rushing down Pahlavi Street later in the afternoon, commanded by Captain Hajebi, an officer of the Imperial Guard, and Captain Monajemi.[40] Along their way these two tanks rallied the people against Mosaddeq as they chanted pro-Shah slogans. So, it is possible that Qorbannejad's two other tanks, left behind in front of Tehran Radio's Broadcasting Station, "somehow" fell into the hands of pro-Zahedi officers. Fourth, Qorbannejad, who was not a collaborationist officer, was lured away from Tehran Radio's Broadcasting Station by either Nowzari or by members of his military staff in order to prevent him from putting up any resistance to the occupation of the radio station and Zahedi's speech over it. Fifth, Qorbannejad was ordered by Nowzari to conduct his tanks straight into an area which had been occupied by the ruffians and their military and police supporters. Sixth, once Qorbannejad was able to successfully lead his tanks to the Chief of Staff's headquarters, Riyahi ordered him to drive his tanks back into the enclosed space of the Military Police headquarters, where they were eventually hijacked by the freed military prisoners of the first coup. Qorbannejad's experience fits into the general pattern of how the day unravelled for the other tank squadrons on 28 Mordad. A group of mysterious superior officers appeared at the garrison, gave specific deployment orders to the tank squadrons, which seemed to be in line with enforcing the public peace and order, and yet ultimately the tanks were led into a situation whereby they were expropriated by the anti-Mosaddeq demonstrators.

---

[38] Javanshir, p. 309.   [39] Nejati (Vasiyatnameh Sargord Doctor 'Elmiyeh), p. 526.
[40] Baniahmad, p. 236.

SQUADRON D ENTRAPPED BY THE COORDINATED ACTIVITY OF THE COLLABORATIONIST NETWORKS

The account of how the fourth tank squadron dispatched on 28 Mordad with the firm command to restore order in the city also ended up being hijacked and used against Mosaddeq's house is complex and most informative. The story of Squadron D, supposedly the main assault force commissioned to quash the insurgents, is a slightly varied repetition of the pattern of what happened to the other tank squadrons. The fate of Squadron D, from start to finish, along with the chronicle of the other tank squadrons, sheds light on how the last phase of the coup on 28 Mordad was conceived by the "council of war". The way in which tanks were drawn into the theatre of operation and then entangled in the web of the insurgents provides a clear picture of a broadly defined, well-coordinated, multiple-actor, loose plan with one specific objective. Within this plan, sloppiness and carelessness counter-balanced by blind obedience to orders coming from superior officers were factored in and even promoted as they helped camouflage the real intentions of the plotters. The mess and the confusion were important smokescreens allowing the actors to find one another and integrate and synchronize their activities, while giving the perplexed bystanders the impression that the hustle and bustle was nothing but another random demonstration typical of those days, until it was too late. As long as the three main actors – the thugs, the turncoat army and police personnel, and the hijacked tanks – coalesced into a powerful offensive force at some point in the day, and the political, governmental and military targets were randomly, yet successfully, assaulted and over-run, the end result of overthrowing Mosaddeq was only a matter of time. With the element of surprise and confusion on their side, the loosely coordinated main actors of the "great demonstration" were poised to attain their goal by early evening on 28 Mordad.

At around 11:30 a.m., upon receiving a phone call, Riyahi, the Chief of Staff, stormed into Lieutenant General Ataollah Kiyani's office and gave him important orders for the day.[41] It has been suggested that the phone call to Riyahi, which triggered the transfer of another squadron of tanks to the anti-Mosaddeq insurgents, came from Colonel Ashrafi.[42] Lieutenant General Kiyani was the deputy Chief of Staff and was arrested by Nasiri at Bagheshah during the first coup, then released after the failure of that coup. Kiyani had the reputation of being an honest and reliable pro-Mosaddeq officer, yet he was not a combat officer and was therefore not best-suited for the rather difficult job which required nerves, audacity, quick and astute reactions, initiative, and forcefulness – if not aggressiveness.[43] By the time

---

[41] Nejati (Vasiyatnameh Sargord Doctor 'Elmiyeh), p. 527.   [42] Mohammadi, p. 104.
[43] Nejati, p. 446; Sahabi, p. 268.

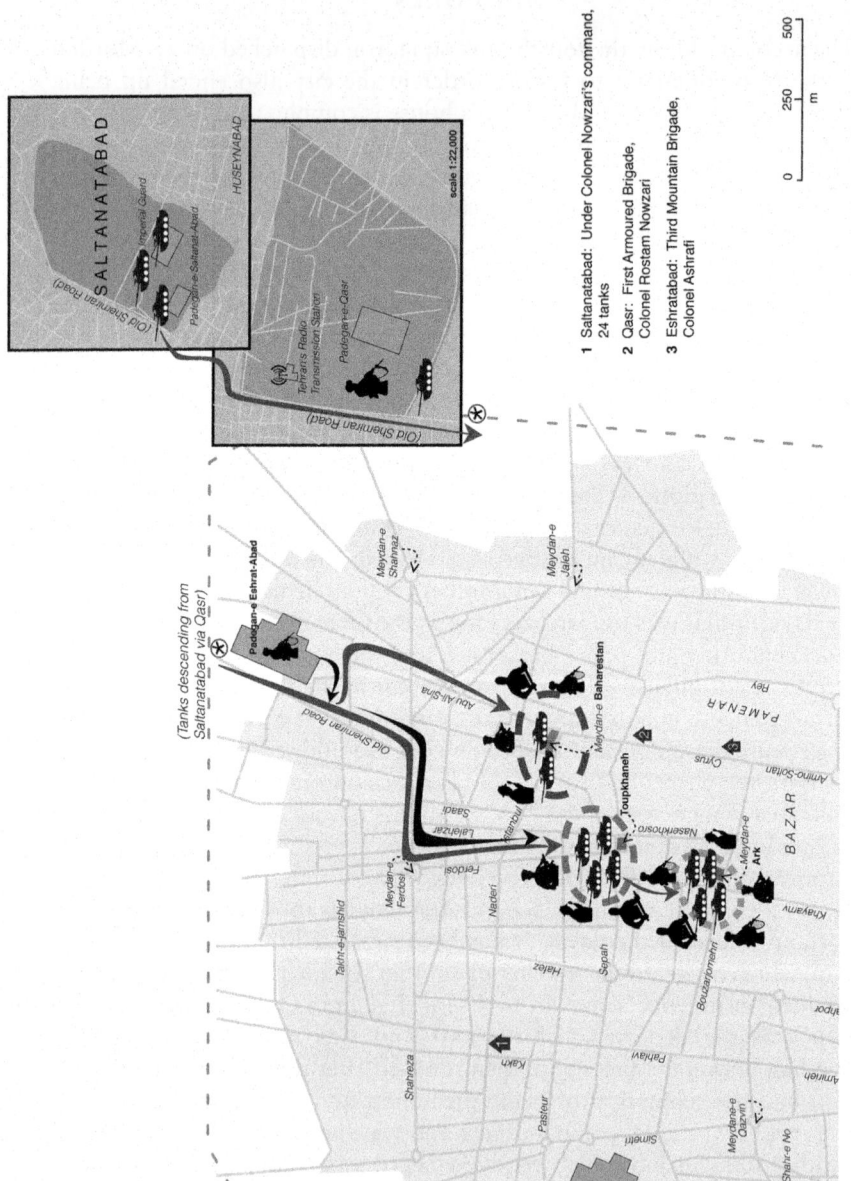

MAP 3. Phase III: Tank deployment and entrapment. 5:00 a.m.–14:30 p.m.

The enigma of the tanks: betrayal or incompetence? 215

Kiyani was called in to "deal with" the anti-Mosaddeq insurgents, the thugs occupying the key arteries of Tehran had merged with the junior collaborationist officers, policemen, army and Armed Custom Guards, rendering difficult any operation aimed at quelling them as it would require soldiers to take action against other military and police forces.

Lieutenant General Kiyani was ordered to prepare and lead the most significant assault force deployed against the demonstrators on 28 Mordad. His orders were different from those given to Squadrons A, B and C as his mission was clearly to confront and contain the insurgents, whose threat to the Mosaddeq government was by now evident. Kiyani's forces included a squadron of tanks and an infantry company of probably around 80 soldiers.[44] The infantry company which Kiyani was to lead against the insurgents was stationed at 'Eshratabad garrison and was under the command of Colonel Ashrafi, while the 12 tanks of Squadron D were coming from Saltanatabad garrison.[45] At some point Amir Khalili's tanks (Squadron B), which had left Saltanatabad at around 10:00 a.m., became integrated with or joined Squadron D under the command of Kiyani.

It must have been between 12:30 p.m. and 1:00 p.m. that Kiyani led his impressive infantry and armoured forces to Sepah Square, the main base of the ruffians. He rode in the back seat of a jeep right behind the tank leading his column. As soon as Kiyani's forces entered the Square, the demonstrators began cheering in favour of the Shah. They appealed to the soldiers in their trucks, who had orders to repress them, to join them. Subsequently, the insurgents tried to board the army trucks and vehicles.[46] Confronted with the warm reception of the pro-Shah insurgents, Kiyani's forces, who were not in a heightened offensive state of mind, were rather emotionally and psychologically destabilized. The soldiers and tanks were not ordered to take an offensive posture by dispersing the crowd, nor were they commanded to defend their arms and vehicles by all possible means. Kiyani's truck-load of soldiers and his tanks simply drove right into the midst of the welcoming insurgents, who pleaded with them to join the Shah-loving and patriotic anti-Mosaddeq forces.

Lieutenant Shoja'i, a member of the "Devotees of the Shah", along with a group of other officers wearing civilian clothes, was already among the welcoming ruffians. Earlier on that day, junior officers implicated in the coup had mingled with the ruffians converging on Sepah Square, imposing their leadership on small groups of them and leading them into small insurgency operations. As Kiyani's forces entered Sepah Square and made their way slowly through the crowd, Shoja'i mounted Kiyani's jeep and sat next to the driver.[47] Infuriated by the fact that a civilian had dared to board an army jeep, Kiyani ordered him to disembark. At this time the colonel

---

[44] Nejati, p. 446. [45] Nejati, pp. 445–446; Mohammadi, p. 114.
[46] Baniahmad, pp. 232, 233. [47] Baniahmad, p. 233.

accompanying Kiyani in the back seat recognized Shoja'i and vouched that he was indeed an officer.[48] Shoja'i then pulled out his identity card, assuring Kiyani that in plain clothes he could carry out his orders and fulfil his military objectives more effectively. Unconvinced, Kiyani reminded Shoja'i that his action of mounting an army vehicle as a civilian only encouraged the crowd to follow suit, making it impossible for the column to take any action against the demonstrators.[49]

By this time the insurgents had begun boarding the vehicles of Kiyani's military column, meeting with no resistance. Elements amongst the demonstrators – not the ruffians, but the collaborating officers who had infiltrated them – told Kiyani's soldiers that: "We are your brothers, do not fire on us. They want to overthrow your Shah. Help us prevent the Shah from becoming separated from his people".[50] In vain Kiyani ordered Shoja'i to get the demonstrators off the military vehicles. Acting as if he were complying with his superior's instructions, Shoja'i climbed off the jeep and ran to Captain Mar'ashi, himself a confederate and a "line commander". Shoja'i instructed Mar'ashi to make sure that the insurgents did not disembark from the army trucks and tanks which they had boarded, remarking that in the meantime he would keep a close eye on Kiyani.[51]

Having ensured that the insurgents would not abandon the precious booty they had won so easily, Shoja'i returned to Kiyani's jeep. Faced with the bloodless takeover of his trucks, tanks and even his own jeep by the thugs and their military supporters, Kiyani abandoned his offensive mission of confronting and containing the insurgents and decided to beat a retreat in order to save his vehicles. His plan was to conduct his column back to the army and police headquarters which he thought were "safe zones" and where he hoped to regain control of his vehicles with the help of the military and police personnel loyal to Mosaddeq. At this time Shoja'i disembarked the jeep again, ran to the tank driving in front of Kiyani's vehicle – the first tank in the column – and ordered it not to turn right (west) towards Sepah Street, which would have led to the army and police headquarters, but to go down Babehomayoun Street, away from Kiyani's intended destination.[52] To facilitate the hijacking and total control of the tanks, Mar'ashi and his team of civilian-clad junior army officers, who acted in coordination with Shoja'i, directed the demonstrators to block Sepah Street and make way for the first tank to drive away from the army and police headquarters and toward Tehran's Radio Office.[53]

Shoja'i then returned to Kiyani and informed him that the crowd would not allow the military column to move along Sepah Street, saying it was best if they went south through Khayyam Street, parallel to Babehomayoun Street,

---

[48] Baniahmad, p. 233. [49] Baniahmad, p. 233. [50] *Taraqi*, 2 Shahrivar 1332.
[51] Baniahmad, p. 233. [52] Baniahmad, p. 233. [53] Baniahmad, p. 233.

where it was less crowded.⁵⁴ Following the total paralysis and indecision of Kiyani and the smooth coordination between the collaborationist junior officers and the ruffians at this time, the tanks were split up and headed in the opposite direction to the army and police headquarters. The last step in the complete takeover of Kiyani's mighty "assault force" was to chase him from the scene, since he continued to symbolize a military and moral authority among his troops, and risked preventing the insurgents from taking full command of his column. To this end, a few among the demonstrators surrounding the tanks and the trucks, most probably the civilian-clad junior officers who knew Kiyani, began agitating the crowd against him. They shouted: "O people this is the same Kiyani, who saved Fatemi, Mosaddeq's Minister of Foreign Affairs, arrest him".⁵⁵ Fearing for his own life, Kiyani is said to have left the scene in a hurry, leaving his soldiers and his tanks behind for the insurgents. At this time Amir Khalili, who was second-in-command, took on the "leadership" of the tanks, which he no longer controlled and which were eventually directed towards Mosaddeq's house by the collaborationist officers. The only thing Amir Khalili could do was to stall by claiming that his tanks were running out of petrol and needed to be refuelled.⁵⁶ This is how Amir Khalili's tanks found themselves at the Sa'di Street petrol station accompanied by other collaborationist officers, some of whom were at this time commanding hijacked tank units.

There are three other Iranian accounts of how Squadron D lost its tanks to the insurgents. The first two are based on testimonies, while the third is based on circumstantial evidence and therefore needs to be considered with caution. According to the first account, once Colonel Mohammad Daftari, who had been nominated as the Chief of Police, received news of Kiyani's mission, he along with a number of other retired officers caught up with Kiyani's "assault column". Daftari and his collaborators followed Kiyani's "assault column", and when it entered the streets occupied by the insurgents, they were the ones who reminded Kiyani's soldiers that they were are all brothers and loyal to the Shah, the Chief of the Armed Forces. The passionate pleas of Daftari's group gradually affected Kiyani's forces and they began to fraternize with the demonstrators. It is subsequent to the fraternization of Kiyani's troops with the demonstrators that Kiyani is reported to have abandoned his troops and effectively handed them to the insurgents.⁵⁷

According to this scenario, Colonel Daftari was the main culprit in the failure of Kiyani's assault force. However, according to the second account, this one based on Colonel Momtaz's memoirs, Kiyani, who had been chosen by Riyahi, probably at the behest of Ashrafi, was not a suitable choice for this last-ditch effort against the coup forces. Momtaz believed that instead of repressing the insurgents, Kiyani lost his nerve and his authority when faced

---

⁵⁴ Baniahmad, p. 234.   ⁵⁵ Baniahmad, p. 234.   ⁵⁶ Baniahmad, p. 234.
⁵⁷ Nejati, pp. 445–446.

with the emotional slogans and speeches of the agitating officers, and ended up fraternizing with the perpetrators of the coup.[58] According to Momtaz's assessment, with the loss of Kiyani's "assault column" at around 2:30 p.m., control of Tehran slipped out of the hands of Mosaddeq's forces.[59]

The third account of what became of Kiyani's tanks is based on circumstantial evidence. In this account, the description and number of the tanks and soldiers provided resembles that of Kiyani's "assault column". The time when the tanks and soldiers entered Ferdowsi Street and Sepah Square also corresponds to the hour at which Kiyani's forces entered Sepah Square. This report, therefore, may be another account of what happened to Kiyani's forces. However, there are other factors which indicate that this account may be unrelated to Kiyani's column. The two main discrepancies between this account and the others is that in this one, first, the tanks entering the crowded areas of Ferdowsi Street and Sepah Square were already in possession of anti-Mosaddeq forces, and second, the collaborating officer responsible for bringing the soldiers and the tank crew to the anti-Mosaddeq side is not Shoja'i, Mar'ashi or Daftari.

At around 12:30 p.m. the demonstrators who had gathered at Ferdowsi Street and Sepah Square were startled – terrified, even – by the unfamiliar roar of eight tanks, followed by the noise of several truck-loads of soldiers.[60] As the demonstrators were about to disperse, fearing for their lives, soldiers appeared from inside the tanks chanting "Long live the Shah" and yelling at the crowd not to be scared of them. As soon as the demonstrators realized that the tanks had come to support them and not to quell them, they ran towards the tanks and mounted them.[61] The officer seemingly commanding the tanks at this time, Colonel Gholam-Hoseyn Afkhami, called on the demonstrators to use the tanks as shields and proceed to destroy the enemies of the Shah, wherever they might be. He pledged that they would all sacrifice their lives for the Shah and the independence of their country.[62] Supported by the tanks, the demonstrators set out to occupy Tehran's Radio Office (*edareh radio*) at the nearby Arg Square, but discovered that it was already under attack by another group.[63] Once the first group of assailants discovered that they could not broadcast from Tehran's Radio Office, both groups mounted the tanks and headed for Tehran Radio's Broadcasting Station.[64]

In relation to Afkhami's activities on 28 Mordad, *Nabard Mellat* praised him as one of those honourable Muslim soldiers who, along with Colonel Dadsetan, had played an important role in guiding the "revolutionaries".[65] In the evening of the second coup Farhad Dadsetan was appointed as Tehran's Military Governor. Amir-Abdollah Karbaschian, the editor of *Nabard Mellat*, was once very close to Navvab Safavi and his newspaper was

---

[58] Nejati, p. 448. [59] Nejati, p. 448. [60] Baniahmad, pp. 204, 206.
[61] Baniahmad, p. 206. [62] Baniahmad, p. 206. [63] Baniahmad, p. 207.
[64] Baniahmad, p. 208. [65] *Nabard-e Mellat*, 7 Shahrivar 1332.

effectively the mouthpiece of Fadaiyan Eslam or "the Devotees of Islam". But by the time this piece was published, Karbaschian had fallen out with Navvab Safavi and had become a staunch supporter of Zahedi and the Shah. Karbaschian's newspaper claimed that Colonel Afkhami, who had somehow taken command of the tanks at Shahreza Street, was responsible for commanding the tanks and troops in his possession to move towards Mosaddeq's house.[66] The fact that Afkhami did not serve in a tank unit at the time and, according to *Nabard Mellat*, was a traffic police officer (*afsar rahnema'i*) makes his feat on 28 Mordad even more impressive and more enigmatic. According to this account, Afkhami had walked to Shahreza Street, where he "had taken over the leadership of Northern Tehran's revolutionaries".[67]

According to a third account, Benjamin Nehura (known as Ben to his friends) was instrumental in placing Afkhami at the command of the tanks.[68] Ben was a rather mysterious Jewish-Iranian, who had lived with his aunt in Antwerp during the Second World War and subsequent to the invasion of Belgium had moved to Britain, returning to Iran only after the war. Ben was well connected to a variety of circles in Iran and was on friendly terms with the Shah. On 28 Mordad Ben witnessed the tanks which were stuck in the midst of the crowd with their hatches open and their crew leaning out and staring aimlessly at the demonstrators surrounding their tanks and chanting pro-Shah slogans.[69] To Ben, it looked as though the tanks were just sitting there without a commander. He therefore decided to get into his car, license plated 1001, and call on a few officers, one of whom was Afkhami. Ben drove to Afkhami's house, gave him a report of the situation, had him put on his military attire, drove him to Serah Shah, and mounted him on the tank.[70] It is quite possible that the three accounts of Afkhami's seizure of eight Sherman tanks are unrelated to the seizure of Kiyani's tanks, as in none of the accounts about Afkhami is any direct mention made of either Kiyani or the "assault column". What is of importance, however, is a pattern that could be extrapolated from such incidents on 28 Mordad.

The episodes on 28 Mordad involving police and military personnel positioned in strategic spots of the city previously occupied by the ruffians and subsequently taking leadership roles to neutralize and co-opt potentially hostile military forces are too recurrent to be assumed to be spontaneous activities or haphazard events. These episodes seem like a series of well-coordinated coincidences, and it would therefore be all too easy and fortuitous to assume that they happened by chance on Wednesday 28 Mordad. If it is assumed that the last phase of the coup, involving tanks, was "unplanned", then the behaviour of the tank squadron commanders driving their tanks into the areas already occupied by the thugs and those accommodating them, such as Mar'ashi, Shoja'i and Afkhami, would become totally inexplicable. Were

---

[66] *Nabard-e Mellat*, 7 Shahrivar 1332. [67] *Nabard-e Mellat*, 7 Shahrivar 1332.
[68] Varqa, pp. 48–49. [69] Varqa, p. 49. [70] Varqa, p. 49.

Mar'ashi and Shoja'i in the Sepah area just by chance? Was Afkhami strolling aimlessly along Shahreza Street when he suddenly took command of eight tanks passing by? Was he really resting at home and only taken to the tanks by Ben Nehura? When account is taken of the events which occurred and the individuals involved in them at a few strategic assembly points on 28 Mordad, it becomes apparent that the events and their sequence were not accidental happenings, and that the actors were not present and undertaking particular tasks by chance.

The fact that, on 28 Mordad, almost all of the tank squadrons dispatched to the city centre under rather irregular circumstances were "seized" in a similar style establishes another pattern of a pre-conceived and orchestrated plan. The tank squadrons which played a key role in the late-afternoon events of 28 Mordad were dispatched from Saltanatabad garrison, organizationally under the command of Colonel Nowzari. This was not the only garrison around the city centre with tanks, but it must have been the garrison in which the coup planners had the safest, most dependable, and most administratively well-positioned senior and junior collaborators.

Three different groups of collaborationist officers were required to guarantee the success of the last phase of the coup: first, on the dispatch side, a senior commanding officer or a small group of them giving the orders for the tanks to leave the garrison; second, a number of collaborating junior officers accompanying the dispatched units to assure the safe transfer of the tanks to the anti-Mosaddeq forces, since not all the tank crews or even commanders were collaborating officers; third, on the receiving side, a number of collaborationist officers, having taken command of the ruffians at the designated congregation zones, enveloping the tanks and taking control of them. The fact that collaborator military personnel were present among both the tank crews and the thugs guaranteed a smoother coordination for the hijacking of the tanks. Once the collaborating dispatched tank officers connected with their receiving counterparts, the thugs surrounding the strategic locations simply boarded the tanks, fraternized with the tank crews and took control of them. From early in the morning of 28 Mordad until around 2:00 p.m. the network of collaborationist officers was able to take over some 24 tanks. From around 4:00 p.m. the hijacked tanks converged on Mosaddeq's house for the final assault.[71]

---

[71] Nejati, p. 447.

14

Mosaddeq overthrown

It must have been around 1:30 p.m. when the insurgents discovered that it was impossible to broadcast from the Radio Office at Arg Square and boarded a few tanks, hijacked from Squadron D, which were heading north toward Tehran Radio's Broadcasting Station on the Old Shemiran Road. To the coup planners, "Radio Tehran was a most important target, for its capture not only sealed the success at the capital, but was effective in bringing the provincial cities quickly into line with the new government".[1] Earlier, Major Akbar Zand had set out towards Tehran Radio's Broadcasting Station, with strict orders to occupy it.[2] Zand and his zealous pro-Shah soldiers from the Naderi Battalion encircled and disarmed the soldiers protecting the Broadcasting Station. Wilber reports that early in the afternoon the crowd started moving north towards Tehran Radio's Broadcasting Station.[3] "Buses and trucks" transported "full loads of civilians, army officers and policemen" to the second most important target of the anti-Mosaddeq forces.[4]

The responsibility for guarding the Broadcasting Station fell under the jurisdiction of Ashrafi, and therefore its occupation by the insurgents must have been facilitated by him and his collaborators, assuming that Ashrafi was in league with the coup-makers. The soldiers guarding the Station did not have orders to shoot at possible assailants, be they military or civilians. It is not clear if Riyahi ever gave orders to shoot on 28 Mordad. At his trial, after the coup, Riyahi confirmed that he had given orders to shoot if necessary, but added that to his knowledge only a few shots had been fired, and those into the air.[5] Mohammad Mohanna, Mosaddeq's Undersecretary of War, recalled that on that day he distinctly remembered Riyahi refusing to give orders to shoot to an officer who had requested permission.[6] So, the insurgents, transported by trucks, buses and taxis from Sepah Square, had a relatively easy time entering

---

[1] Wilber, p. 70. [2] Baniahmad, p. 208. [3] Wilber, pp. 70–71. [4] Wilber, p. 71.
[5] Bozorgmehr, p. 549. [6] Bozorgmehr, p. 548.

Tehran Radio's Broadcasting Station.[7] There was, however, a reported attack by pro-Mosaddeq army personnel on the insurgents from the Abbasabad hills overlooking the Broadcasting Station. As a result of this mortar attack, the pro-Shah insurgents are said to have taken flight until Captain Zand and his forces counter-attacked and forced the lone fighter to retreat.[8] Aside from this seemingly insignificant event, the Broadcasting Station fell to the anti-Mosaddeq insurgents without much fighting.[9] The victory was facilitated by the fact that the two tanks under the command of Qorbannejad (Squadron C) and which were supposedly defending the Broadcasting Station were completely neutralized by Nowzari's shrewd machinations.

TEHRAN RADIO FALLS

Between 2:00 p.m. and 2:30 p.m. the music that was being broadcast over Tehran Radio came to an abrupt end.[10] The takeover of the Broadcasting Station did not imply its immediate use. The insurgents who occupied the Station were faced with a few technical complications that were believed to be last-minute acts of sabotage by pro-Mosaddeq employees of the Broadcasting Station.[11] Tehran Radio resumed broadcasting somewhere between 2:30 p.m. and 3:30 p.m.[12] It is now almost certain that the first indication of the fall of the Broadcasting Station came at around 3:30 p.m. Tehran time.[13] At this time the station began broadcasting news of the royalist victory, along with a reading of the royal edict appointing Zahedi as Prime Minister. The first speaker on the air victoriously claimed that the Mosaddeq government had been defeated; Fatemi and Sanjabi, Mosaddeq's ministers of Foreign Affairs and Education, had been arrested and killed; all government offices had been occupied; and that Mosaddeq had fled.[14]

It must have been sometime between 4:30 p.m. and 5:30 p.m. that Zahedi arrived at the Broadcasting Station and addressed the Iranian people.[15] Zahedi announced that he was the legal Prime Minister of Iran, as appointed

---

[7] Baniahmad, p. 210.   [8] Baniahmad, p. 210.   [9] *Ettela'at*, 31 Mordad 1332.
[10] *Taraqi*, 2 Shahrivar 1332; Khameh'i, 1363, p. 440; *Khandaniha*, 31 Mordad 1332.
[11] *Ettela'at*, 31 Mordad 1332; Baniahmad, p. 210.
[12] Based on three sources (*Dad*, 29 Mordad 1332; Sadiqi in Nejati, p. 544; Bozorgmehr, pp. 387, 417) the radio resumed operation around 3:30 p.m., while based on three other sources (Wilber, p. 71; *Tehran Mosavvar*, 30 Mordad 1332; Khameh'i, 1363, p. 440) Tehran radio resumed operation at 2:20 p.m.
[13] National Security Archives, S.A. Koch, Zendebad Shah, Central Intelligence Agency, 1998, p. 65: http://www2.gwu.edu/~nsarchiv/NSAEBB/NSAEBB435/docs/Doc%204%20-%20CIA%20-%20Zendebad%20Shah%20-%202000%20release.PDF.
[14] FRUS, vol. x, p. 785; Nejati (Goftogo ba Ostad Doctor Gholamhoseyn Sadiqi), p. 544.
[15] *Taraqi*, 2 Shahrivar 1332 cites 4:00 p.m.; on the basis of Sadiqi's account in Nejati (p. 544), which seems like a more accurate account, at 4:00 p.m. it was Ahmad Faramarzi who was speaking on the radio and since Zahedi spoke after Faramarzi, he must have arrived at the

by his Majesty the Shahanshah and would remain in this position until the new parliament was elected.[16] He then briefly outlined the programme of his government, which began with reinstating the rule of law. In the interval between the resumption of Tehran Radio's broadcasting and Zahedi's arrival and speech, numerous pro-Shah figures had the historic opportunity of addressing the people. Most Iranians of the time remembered the voice and speech of the first speaker, Mehdi Mirashrafi, the fiery editor of the daily *Atash* and an early advocate of a coup d'état against Mosaddeq. He said, "Hello, Hello (*Allo, Allo*) here Tehran, people, good news *besharat amiz*, in a few moments General Zahedi the Prime Minister will read the Shahanshah's message for you, people of the provinces rejoice the treacherous Mosaddeq has taken flight... today the people of Tehran revolted... *qiyam kardand*"[17]

Among the relatively long list of prominent pro-Shah militants who had made their way to the Broadcasting Station some were euphemistically referred to by Wilber as "elements upon whom reliance had been placed in the TPAJAX planning".[18] These were collaborationists with whom the CIA station agents, Iranians, and Americans and their liaisons had reached an agreement to overthrow Mosaddeq. These individuals formed the first circle of contacts around TPAJAX planners. Wilber's classification is important as it distinguishes between three types of pro-Shah activists during 28 Mordad. First, there were the local CIA station planners and masterminds such as Colonel Farzanegan, who spoke before Zahedi.[19] Second, there was a hardcore nucleus of directly or indirectly CIA-affiliated and CIA-connected individuals, whose actions were coordinated with the general plan of the day as conceived by the members of the "war council". These individuals "on whom reliance had been placed" by the TPAJAX planners and who spoke over the radio were: Mostafa Kashani, Ayatollah Kashani's son; Malekeh 'Etezadi, the leader of the Zolfaqar Party; General Arfa', the spiritual father of the Ariya Party; and Poure'tezadi, the editor of the daily *Zelzeleh*.[20] Third, there were the affiliates of the direct collaborationists, whom Wilber calls the "spontaneous" pro-Shah elements, such as Colonel Ali Pahlavan and Major Husand [Hushang] Mirzadian, of whom it is claimed that they joined the demonstration as the day evolved.[21]

Station at around 4:15–4:30 p.m.; in *Ettela'at*, 29 Mordad 1358, Iraj Davarpanah (a defendant of Mosaddeq's house) recalls that Zahedi started his speech at 5:00 p.m.; *Shahed*, 31 Mordad 1332 also refers to 5:00 p.m., and finally Wilber (p. 73) cites 5:30 p.m. as the time when Zahedi spoke on the air.

[16] *Ettela'at*, 31 Mordad 1332.
[17] Quotation taken from http://history.persianblog.ir/post/121/   [18] Wilber, p. 71.
[19] Wilber, p. 73.
[20] Wilber, pp. 70, 73; Rahnema, p. 955; *Daad*, 29 Mordad 1332; M. H. Salemi, *Tarikh Nehzat-e Melli Shodan Naft-e Iran az Negahi Digar* (Tehran: Markaz-e Asnad-e Enqelab-e Eslami, 1388), p. 497.
[21] Wilber, p. 71. For an account of Colonel Pahlavan in front of the Broadcasting Station, see Amir-Khosravi, p. 636.

The majority of those who spoke on Tehran Radio from 3:30 p.m. to about 7:00 p.m. fell in to one of these three types of coup activists. In addition to the key personalities whom Wilber knew about directly and considered worthy of mentioning in his report, there were other equally key coup actors (as well as lesser-known ones) who willingly and proudly marched up to the microphone to celebrate the anti-Mosaddeq coup. They were Mehdi Mirashrafi, Mozaffar Baqa'i, Mehdi Pirasteh, Ahmad Faramarzi, Mahmud Shervin, Prince Hamidreza Pahlavi (the Shah's half-brother), Mas'oud Pahlavan, Soltanpour, Ali Moshiri, Reza Sajadi and Major Na'ini.[22] Mehdi Mirashrafi was one of the first to approach Sam Falle of the British Embassy in July 1952 to suggest that a coup d'état was a feasible and desirable means of getting rid of Mosaddeq.

WHERE IS ZAHEDI?

The conflicting reports on how General Fazlollah Zahedi was brought to the Broadcasting Station have their roots in the controversial issue of where he was staying between 26–28 Mordad (17–19 August). According to Ardeshir Zahedi (the general's son) and those analysts basing their information on him, during this tense period General Zahedi was given refuge, shelter and protection by his Iranian friends and supporters. CIA sources say otherwise. Wherever Fazlollah was, the security apparatus of Mosaddeq could not find him, even though a memorandum was issued to arrest him on 25 Mordad and another on 26 Mordad with a large prize for information on Zahedi's whereabouts.[23] Wilber, Roosevelt and, most importantly, Hotchkiss (the CIA operative in Iran who lodged General Zahedi in the basement of his house) maintain that from Monday 26 Mordad until the afternoon of Wednesday 28 Mordad, Fazlollah Zahedi was a guest of American authorities in Tehran and was given shelter on property owned or rented by the American Embassy.[24] The issue of who was giving refuge and protection to the designated Prime Minister after Mosaddeq weighs heavily in determining whether 28 Mordad was a CIA-backed and planned coup d'état or a national uprising.

According to Ardeshir Zahedi, from the early hours of Sunday 16 August, once it became clear that Mosaddeq had "rebelled" against the Shah's royal edict, General Zahedi first went into hiding at Azizollah Farzanegan's house (Abbas Farzanegan's brother) and then moved to Mrs. Molukosadat Moshir-Fatemi's house, on the Old Shemiran Road, below Qeytariyeh.[25]

---

[22] *Ettela'at*, 31 Mordad 1332; *Daad*, 29 Mordad 1332; Baniahmad, p. 210; *Negaheno*, Mordad 1387; Javanshir, p. 308; Khameh'i, 1363, p. 440.
[23] *Ettela'at*, 26 Mordad 1332; Bozorgmehr, pp. 358, 436.
[24] Ahmad Ashraf's interview with Theodore Hotchkiss (1926–2001), the CIA Station Operative at the US Embassy in Tehran on 22–23 December 1990 in Spencer (West Virginia).
[25] Zahedi, vol. 1, pp. 119, 121, 123, 125.

In the afternoon of 16 August (25 Mordad) Ardeshir Zahedi claims that his father participated in a "historical" six-hour meeting at Seyfosaltaneh Afshar's house on Bahar Street.[26] Bahar Street runs almost parallel to Roosevelt Street and very much closer to Takht-e Jamshid Street, the location of the American Embassy compound and Hotchkiss' house. The General is said to have returned to his own estate in Hesarak to spend the night of Sunday 16 August.[27] However, Ardeshir Zahedi maintains that his father returned to Afshar's house on Bahar Street from Monday 17 August and stayed there until the afternoon of 19 August, when Ardeshir drove his father from Afshar's house to an unspecified location on the Old Shemiran Street.[28] Faced with the unanimous position of all the CIA sources that General Zahedi was in the custody of the CIA in Tehran and was brought clandestinely into the embassy compound for the important "war council" on Monday 17 August, Ardeshir Zahedi claimed that such assertions were mere "rubbish".[29]

According to Ardeshir Zahedi, around noon on 19 August (28 Mordad), he toured the city and then reported to his father on his observations. Fazlollah Zahedi then "consulted with his councillors", and decided to take control of the situation. Ardeshir Zahedi maintains that Colonel Khal'atbari, deputy of the police who had joined the insurgents, was called upon to send a tank to General Zahedi's residence.[30] Without any reference to the whereabouts of General Zahedi, Baniahmad maintains that Gilanshah and *mohandess* (Ardeshir) Zahedi, along with a tank and a number of Air Force corporals, arrived at Zahedi's residence. At that time Zahedi is said to have boarded a tank and, accompanied by Colonel Khal'atbari riding in his own car, set out towards the Broadcasting Station. Lieutenant Shoja'i, who had been active all day, led the convoy on a motorbike.[31]

According to Wilber's report, however, at about noon, "Roosevelt went to the houses where Generals Zahedi and Gilanshah were in hiding"; they were informed of the events during the day and were "*told to wait for instructions*".[32] Wilber refers to General Zahedi and Gilanshah as Roosevelt's "valuable charges". After "Carroll and the Persian-speaking Major William Keyser (Assistant US Military Attaché) reported on the military situation" in the city, and pro-Zahedi activists began broadcasting from Tehran Radio, Roosevelt went back to the hiding place of the generals and told them that "*it was time* for them to play an active role".[33] Gilanshah was driven from Zahedi's hideout in search of a tank by Major Keyser. Having found a tank, Gilanshah was to meet with Zahedi at 16:30 p.m. "on a certain street corner", from where they would proceed to Tehran Radio's Broadcasting Station on a tank.[34] On their way Gilanshah and Keyser came across two Air

---

[26] Zahedi, vol. 1, p. 128.   [27] Zahedi, vol. 1, p. 135.   [28] Zahedi, vol. 1, pp. 148, 149, 150.
[29] Zahedi, vol. 1, p. 136.   [30] Zahedi, vol. 1, p. 150.   [31] Baniahmad, p. 236.
[32] Wilber, p. 69.   [33] Wilber, pp. 69, 72.   [34] Wilber, p. 72.

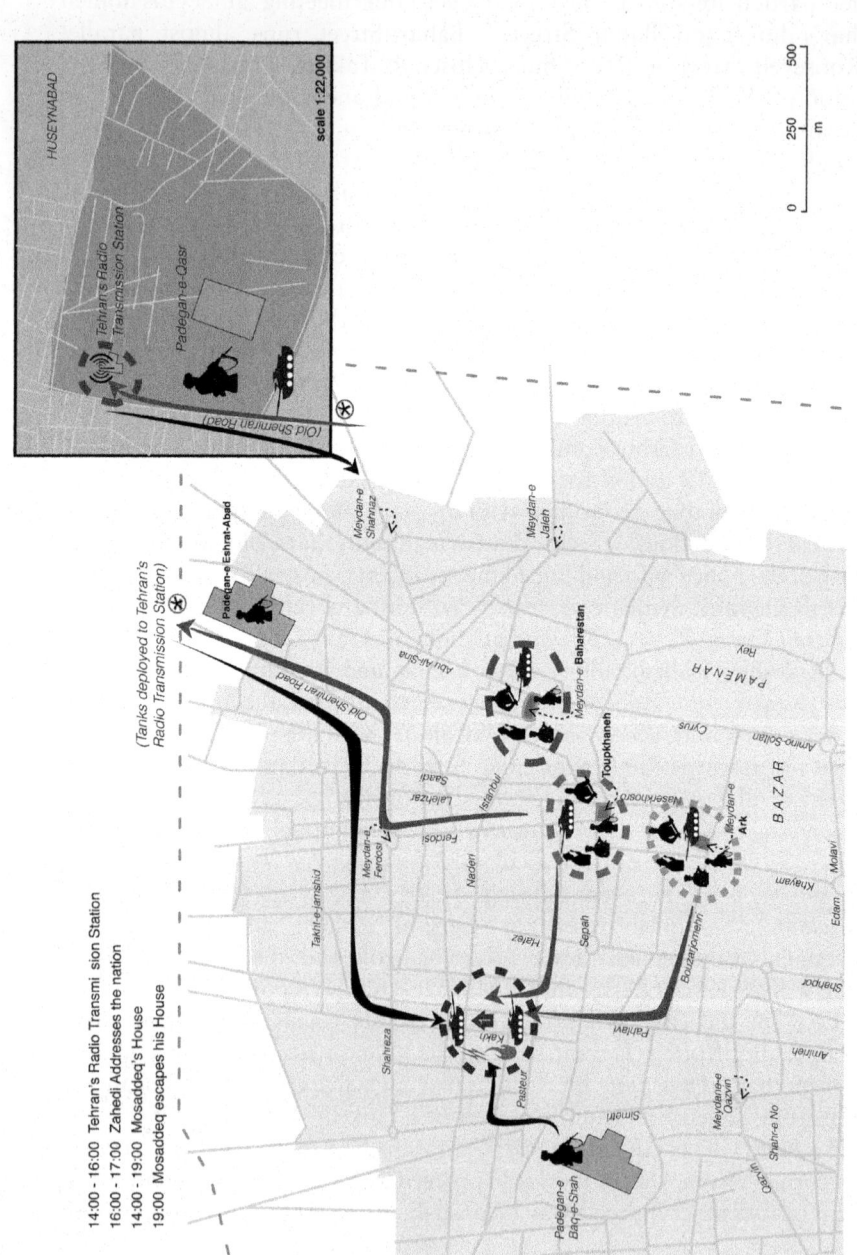

MAP 4. Phase IV: Attaining the targets. 14:00 p.m.–19:00 p.m.

Force officers, asked them for a tank, and were provided with one. Gilanshah, accompanied by the Air Force officers and a tank, met Zahedi at 16:30 p.m. At this time Zahedi boarded the tank, drove triumphantly to the Broadcasting Station and addressed the nation as the new Prime Minister.[35] Roosevelt's account of how General Zahedi emerged from his hideout to take control of the situation is similar to that of Wilber.[36] In the absence of precise information on the origin of the tank used by General Zahedi, it would be safe to assume that it originally belonged to Kiyani's Squadron D, since Lieutenant Shoja'I, who played a key role in hijacking those tanks, was also the officer who escorted the tank delivering Zahedi to the Broadcasting Station.[37]

CONVERGING ON THE ULTIMATE TARGET: MOSADDEQ'S HOUSE ATTACKED

With the fall of Tehran Radio's Broadcasting Station at around 14:20 p.m., the coup forces had one final target to converge on. The impressive army that set siege to Mosaddeq's house comprised: the ruffians; the injected military personnel of the police; soldiers of the Armed Custom Guards, the Army, the Air Force and the Imperial Guard; teams of the "Devotees of the Shah"; the tank squadrons and their personnel; the local friends of CIA operatives Jalali and Keyvani; and collaborationist organizations such as Monshizadeh's SUMKA, Malekeh E'tezadi's Zolfaqar Party, Sepehr's Ariya Party, Baqa'i's Toilers Party, Kashani's Society of Moslem Mojaheds and Parvin Ajdanqezi's gang.

By this time, Sha'ban Ja'fari and his ruffian friends who had been released from Qasr prison by the insurgents were also on the loose and desperately needed to play out their patriotic and Shah-worshipping role in the overthrow of Mosaddeq. Sha'ban Ja'fari recalled that at around 2:15 p.m. Boyouk Saber, the leader of the fourth column of ruffians, along with Colonel Khal'atbari, the Deputy Chief of police, came to Qasr prison and set him free.[38] According to eye-witness reports, as late as 2:00 p.m. cars and trucks were still transporting pro-Shah children, policemen, Armed Custom Guards, and Air Force personnel north through Shahpour Street and Amiriyeh.[39]

The destruction of Mosaddeq's house was the prime goal fixed for the various participants in the "great demonstration". All other acts of violence committed on that day by the insurgents were means to the gradual occupation and consolidation of those strategic positions which they needed to secure before embarking on their final assault. By the end of the day, the government's headquarters and Mosaddeq's house had to be demolished. The coup forces succeeded in demolishing the symbol of Iran's relentless challenge to neo-colonialism.

[35] Wilber, pp. 72–73.   [36] Roosevelt, pp. 188–192.   [37] Baniahmad, p. 236.
[38] Sarshar, pp. 160–162.   [39] Nejati (Vasiyatnameh Sargord Doctor 'Elmiyeh), p. 527.

A summary account of the fall of Mosaddeq's house and the successful completion of the last phase of the operation to overthrow Mosaddeq's government is provided by the anonymous British Memorandum to the US State Department. According to this report, at first "a large crowd" attacked Mosaddeq's residence, but was repulsed by the machine gun fire of those defending it. Then, the ruffians launched another round of attacks, but this time supported by pro-Zahedi troops. This second wave also failed, and the assailants were repulsed. It was not until the arrival of the Sherman tanks and their heavy bombing that the insurgents succeeded in overrunning Mosaddeq's house. At about 6:00 p.m. "the defense of the house was given up, and the gate was broken down".[40]

The details of the attack on Mosaddeq's house confirm the succinct account of the British Memorandum and demonstrate that as Behbudgar, one of the ruffian leaders of Southern Tehran, recalled, the mission of the hired hands on 28 Mordad was to "cause disorder in the city and loot Mosaddeq's house".[41] The assault on Mosaddeq's house occurred in three main waves: the ruffians; the ruffians and lightly armed military personnel, along with armed members of various athletic organizations; and finally the tanks. The battle for Mosaddeq's house is said to have lasted five hours and to have produced anywhere between 50 to 300 casualties.[42] While the number of dead on 19 August was initially reported at 35–42, by 25 August the head of the National Coroner's Office claimed that 41 were killed and 75 wounded.[43]

The main resisting figure was Colonel 'Ezatollah Momtaz. He was a member of the pro-Mosaddeq Organization of Nationalist Officers, commander of the Second Mountain Brigade, the officer who arrested Colonel Nasiri on 25 Mordad, and was in charge of protecting Mosaddeq's house. After Momtaz was ordered by Mosaddeq to end his military activities at around 5:30 p.m., a second circle of officers loyal to Mosaddeq continued to fight against the insurgents to the bitter end. This circle was composed of Captains Fesharaki (Mousa Mehran) and Iraj Davarpanah, both members of the Military Police (*dejban*), and their personnel as well as Lieutenant Shoja'iyan.[44]

Momtaz later recalled that he had stationed ample troops, supported by armoured vehicles, around the streets leading to 109 Kakh Street, the location of Mosaddeq's house.[45] Four tanks were positioned around Mosaddeq's house to assure the safety of the Prime Minister's office.[46] At around 10:30 a.m. sporadic shots were fired from Princess Shams Pahlavi's palace.[47] Fire was also opened from two military trucks: one parked in front of the Officer's Academy, the other parked at the junction of Kakh and Pasteur Streets.[48] The

---

[40] FRUS, vol. x, p. 785.   [41] Manzarpour, p. 196
[42] Sahabi, p. 258; *Keyhan*, 29 Mordad 1358; FRUS, vol. x, p. 786.
[43] *Keyhan*, 31 Mordad 1332, *Ettela'at*, 31 Mordad 1332.
[44] Nejati, pp. 448–449; *Keyhan*, 29 Mordad 1358.   [45] Nejati, p. 446.   [46] Sahabi, p. 268.
[47] *Keyhan*, 29 Mordad 1358; Khameh'i, 1363, p. 438.   [48] *Keyhan*, 29 Mordad 1358.

two trucks from which Mosaddeq's house came under fire in the morning were destroyed by Lieutenant Shoja'iyan's unit, after which a temporary calm returned.[49] By around 10:30 a.m. the coup planners had learnt that gunshots would not suffice to overrun Mosaddeq's house.

The first round of more organized attacks against Mosaddeq's house began at around noon.[50] The assailants, chanting "Long live the King of Kings", took flight as soon the tanks guarding Mosaddeq's house began manoeuvring and a few gun shots were fired into the air.[51] The second round of attacks started around 3:00 p.m.[52] By this time, the injected armed military personnel were well-integrated with the ruffians, providing them with leadership and light firepower support. Tehran Radio's Broadcasting Station had been seized by the insurgents, and the coup forces were in possession of tanks, even though not all of the tanks had been able to converge on Mosaddeq's house.[53] Faced with a formidable offensive force, the defendants of Mosaddeq's house started opening fire. From around 3:00 p.m. the sound of incessant bullets echoed around Mosaddeq's house.[54] Confronted with the superior fire-power of the defenders of Mosaddeq's house, the assailants retreated again.[55] From around 4:00 p.m. the streets leading to Mosaddeq's house were gradually surrounded by the ruffians and the military personnel who had successfully completed their siege and seizure of all other strategic buildings. At this time the hijacked tanks began rolling in.

A fresh group of zealous pro-Shah combatants, namely the soldiers of the Imperial Guard forces, also joined the assailants. The personnel of the Imperial Guard, under Colonel Nasiri, who had acted as the main engine of the first coup, were disarmed after it failed in the early hours of Sunday 16 August. These loyal pro-Shah soldiers were subsequently incarcerated at Bagheshah garrison, with their weapons stashed in the room adjacent to them.[56] The decision to place this most ardent pro-Shah military corps at Bagheshah garrison, and under the command of Daftari, was most curious. Bagheshah was the closest military garrison to Mosaddeq's house, being only a 15-minute walk away. Keeping this devout anti-Mosaddeq corps, which had already participated in the first coup, under very loose surveillance, with their weapons in the room adjacent to them and at a 15-minute walking distance from Mosaddeq's house, remains a riddle, unless it is assumed that the decision was intentional and a part of the plot. At 3:45 p.m., when gunshots were heard around Mosaddeq's house, the Imperial Guard soldiers moved against their gaolers, disarmed them, locked them up, emptied the armoury and, under the leadership of Lieutenant Agahian, marched north

---

[49] *Keyhan*, 29 Mordad 1358.   [50] *Taraqi*, 2 Shahrivar 1332.
[51] *Taraqi*, 2 Shahrivar 1332, *Khandaniha*, 31 Mordad 1332.   [52] *Taraqi*, 2 Shahrivar 1332.
[53] *Taraqi*, 2 Shahrivar 1332.   [54] *Tehran Mosavvar*, 6 Shahrivar 1332.
[55] *Keyhan*, 29 Mordad, 1332; Khameh'i, 1363, p. 440; Baniahmad, p. 213.   [56] Sahabi, p. 266.

towards Mosaddeq's house.⁵⁷ According to Momtaz, Mosaddeq's house subsequently came under fire from the Imperial Guard soldiers.⁵⁸

Bagheshah garrison was one of the key hubs of anti-Mosaddeq activities on 28 Mordad. Parviz Khosrovani, who had played an important role in the 9 Esfand demonstration against Mosaddeq, was freed from prison around 15 Mordad.⁵⁹ Khosrovani was informed of the events that were going to take place on 28 Mordad by the officers of the Imperial Guards at Bagheshah garrison. He was asked to join forces with the collaborationist officers of the Imperial Guard. It must have been around 4:00 p.m. when Khosrovani led the members of his athletics club to Bagheshah garrison, where they were armed by the Imperial Guard soldiers who had taken over the garrison.⁶⁰ In the company of the Imperial Guard soldiers, Khosrovani's armed "athletes" made their way to Mosaddeq's house. According to Fardust, on 28 Mordad Khosrovani was successful in mobilizing the athletes of his club, Taj, to join forces with other groups demonstrating and marching against Mosaddeq's house.⁶¹

The third – and decisive – wave of attack on Mosaddeq's house started at around 4:30 p.m., when the insurgents could bring in the full force of the tanks they had appropriated during the day. The deadlock between the numerically superior yet insufficiently armed insurgents and the small yet relatively heavily armoured defence force around Mosaddeq's house was broken with the entrance of these tanks. Five Sherman tanks first came from the direction of Eslambol and Naderi Streets.⁶² As they moved towards Serah-e Shah from Shah Street they turned south, moving down Pahlavi Street towards Pasteur and Kakh Streets.⁶³ These tanks, which were the remnants of Squadrons A, B and D and had last congregated at the petrol station on Sa'di Street to refuel, came to the scene of operations around Mosaddeq's house with ruffians sitting and standing on them. Some of the collaborating officers involved in hijacking them, such as Shoja'i and Mar'ashi, and who had been in civilian clothing, had already gone home and changed back into their military uniforms before re-joining the tank column heading towards Mosaddeq's house.⁶⁴

The first machine-gun volleys were fired at Mosaddeq's house from a tank stationed in front of the Point Four (*asl-e chahar*) building.⁶⁵ The two tanks of Squadron C, under Qorbannejad's command, also appeared in front of Mosaddeq's house. Two tanks accompanied by Lieutenants Naraqi, Kazem Khaza'i and Hamid Jahanbani of Squadron A started attacking Mosaddeq's house.⁶⁶ From 4:30 p.m. to around 6:00 p.m. the tanks

---

⁵⁷ *Tehran Mosavvar*, 6 Shahrivar 1332. ⁵⁸ Nejati, p. 447; Sahabi, p. 266.
⁵⁹ Parviz Khosrovani, Iranian Oral History Collection, Harvard University, Transcript 1, p. 11.
⁶⁰ Parviz Khosrovani, Iranian Oral History Collection, Harvard University, Transcript 1, p. 12.
⁶¹ Fardust, p. 182. ⁶² *Taraqi*, 2 Shahrivar 1332. ⁶³ *Khandaniha*, 31 Mordad 1332.
⁶⁴ Baniahmad, p. 235. ⁶⁵ Baniahmad, p. 212. ⁶⁶ *Keyhan*, 29 Mordad 1358.

attacking Mosaddeq's house were primarily relying on their .30 and .50 calibre Browning machine guns, blasting at the defendants on the rooftop of Mosaddeq's house.[67]

After the first wave of attack by the belligerent tanks, the pro-Mosaddeq tanks and troops riposted with equal vigour, destroying one of the insurgent tanks that had started attacking them from the south.[68] Momtaz recalled that while his main attention was focused on the fire coming from the south of Mosaddeq's house, his forces also came under attack from the north.[69] Fire was pouring in from all sides and Mosaddeq's house was being blown apart piece by piece. In the meantime, one of the defending tanks was silenced by the superior fire-power of the Sherman tanks.[70] The impressive resistance put up by Momtaz's forces was respectfully acknowledged in the published reports which followed the success of the second coup – and this in a press intent upon endearing itself to the new men in power.

From 6:00 p.m. the belligerent tanks surrounding Mosaddeq's house started using their heavy 75 millimetre guns. The shells pounded the roof of Mosaddeq's house, and as parts of it collapsed the dust from the debris rose to the sky.[71] By 6:30–7:00 p.m. the first Sherman tank rammed through the iron-gated entrance to the compound of Mosaddeq's house and entered it.[72] As the tanks rolled over the gates of Mosaddeq's house, the objective of the day and the operation was at hand. By this time, Mosaddeq and members of his cabinet had left the house on 109 Kakh Street.

NEGOTIATING MOSADDEQ'S SURRENDER

At around 3:00 p.m. a new and unexpected development accelerated the fall of Mosaddeq. At his trial after the coup Riyahi recalled that it was only after the Broadcasting Station fell to the demonstrators and pro-Shah speakers went on the air that he realized that the demonstrators were partisans of the Shah. It was at this moment that he immediately ordered all the troops under his command to stand down.[73] At his trial, Riyahi argued that based on the information he had received from the Second Bureau, until 3:00 p.m. on 28 Mordad he was under the impression that the demonstrators were members of the Tudeh Party "camouflaged" as pro-Shah elements.[74] While all the participants were mustering their forces and converging on Mosaddeq's house, Riyahi not only ordered the troops under his command to cease fire, but also ordered his officers to send their soldiers and tanks

---

[67] *Khandaniha*, 31 Mordad 1332.
[68] *Tehran Mosavvar*, 6 Shahrivar 1332; Baniahmad, p. 214.   [69] Sahabi, p. 267.
[70] Baniahmad, p. 243.
[71] *Khandaniha*, 31 Mordad 1332; *Taraqi*, 2 Shahrivar 1332; Baniahmad, p. 214.
[72] *Khandaniha*, 31 Mordad 1332.   [73] Bozorgmehr, pp. 417, 548.
[74] Bozorgmehr, pp. 417, 548.

back to their barracks.[75] By 4:30 p.m., when the first wave of attacks by the belligerent tanks against Mosaddeq's house began, Mosaddeq's Chief of Staff had already surrendered the forces under Mosaddeq's command to the pro-Zahedi forces.

Having disbanded the forces under his own command, Riyahi called Mosaddeq in his besieged house and asked him to issue a decree ordering the pro-Mosaddeq forces to cease resistance.[76] Mosaddeq refused to issue such a decree, upon which Riyahi informed him that Brigadier Fouladvand was on his way with sound advice.[77] At around 4:45 p.m. Fouladvand entered Mosaddeq's house, strongly recommending that Mosaddeq issue an order whereby the armed forces would cease resistance and in effect surrender. Mosaddeq refused to give such an order and insisted that he would stay at his house and accept the consequences.[78] At his trial after the coup Mosaddeq recalled that Fouladvand was sent by the pro-Shah officers to secure his resignation.[79] Was Mosaddeq insinuating something about Riyahi's loyalty?

Based on Ahmad Razavi's suggestion, Mosaddeq agreed to declare that his house would cease resistance, even though he still considered himself the legal Prime Minister of Iran. The declaration was signed by Razavi, Shayegan, Nariman and Zirakzadeh, and handed to Fouladvand. It was at 5:00 p.m. that Razavi grabbed the white bed sheet from Mosaddeq's mattress, took it out to the soldiers guarding the house, and asked them to hoist it as a sign of non-belligerence, as Mosaddeq's house had become undefendable.[80] The white bed sheet discouraged neither the assailants nor the defenders from firing upon one another. At this time it became evident to Mosaddeq and his 15 close followers, who remained in the house, that the object of the assailants was to occupy the house and do away with its occupants.[81]

While Mosaddeq's house was under attack, Zahedi's Chief of Staff, Batmanqelich, issued a communiqué ordering the commanding officers of the units defending the army, police and Military Police headquarters to lay down their guns. Momtaz, who continued to defend Mosaddeq's house, was also ordered to capitulate.[82] Surrounded from all sides, out-gunned, running out of ammunition, and with more tanks under the control of insurgents coming on the scene, Momtaz went to report on his precarious military condition to Mosaddeq.[83] Having heard Momtaz's report, Mosaddeq ordered him to carry out the orders of the new Chief of Staff and return his personnel to their garrisons.[84] Momtaz obeyed, and from that moment the

---

[75] Bozorgmehr, p. 417.
[76] Nejati (Goftogo ba Ostad Doctor Gholamhoseyn Sadiqi), pp. 544–545.
[77] Nejati (Goftogo ba Ostad Doctor Gholamhoseyn Sadiqi), p. 545.
[78] Nejati (Goftogo ba Ostad Doctor Gholamhoseyn Sadiqi), p. 545.   [79] Nejati, p. 454.
[80] Nejati, p. 456.
[81] Nejati (Goftogo ba Ostad Doctor Gholamhoseyn Sadiqi), pp. 546–547.
[82] *Keyhan*, 29 Mordad 1358.   [83] Sahabi, p. 267.   [84] *Keyhan*, 29 Mordad 1358.

bulk of the forces defending Mosaddeq's house withdrew. The departure of Momtaz's troops must have happened at around 6:00 p.m.

According to Davarpanah, one of the defendants of Mosaddeq's house after Momtaz's departure, had Momtaz refused to obey Mosaddeq's orders and continued to defend his house, the assailants would not have been able to over-run Mosaddeq's house so easily. Davarpanah argues that the majority of the collaborationist officers were from the Second Mountain Brigade, which Momtaz commanded. Had Momtaz stayed behind, collaborationist officers such as Captains Yavari, Majlesi and Sa'edi would not have been able to lead the personnel of the Second Mountain Brigade into battle against their commander.[85] Davarpanah believed that the loyalty of the rank and file of the Second Mountain Brigade to their commander would have prevented the collaborationist officers from easily manipulating the soldiers. Once Momtaz and his troops left, Davarpanah and Fesharaki continued to defend the Prime Minister's office with about 60 soldiers perched on the rooftops of Ahmad and Gholam-Hoseyn Mosaddeq's house.[86]

The defence of Mosaddeq's house continued until around 7:00 p.m. when Davarpanah went to Mosaddeq and reported that his troops were almost out of ammunition and that the military situation was untenable.[87] It was at this time that Mosaddeq and some 15 of his close associates and ministers decided to leave the house by climbing over the walls and crossing into the neighbour's house.[88] The belligerent tanks entered Mosaddeq's empty and demolished house. As the night fell and the shame of the day was veiled, the final scene of the "great demonstration" began.

FEASTING HYENAS

Ecstatic at their victory, the insurgents entered Mosaddeq's house chanting "death to Mosaddeq" and began looting. In less than an hour they gutted the house, taking with them whatever they could.[89] The thugs and the military personnel accompanying them left Mosaddeq's house carrying every conceivable object: tables, chairs, curtains, refrigerator, mattresses, wardrobes, decorative objects, jewellery, bathroom utensils, carpets, cutlery and even personal objects such as the Qur'an from the house.[90] Half an hour after Mosaddeq's house was plundered, one of his precious carpets was sold for 1,500 Tomans.[91] The sale of the valuable items looted from Mosaddeq's house by the thugs and military personnel reached such embarrassing proportions that Zahedi's head of the army's Second Bureau was forced to issue

---

[85] *Keyhan*, 29 Mordad 1358. [86] *Keyhan*, 29 Mordad 1358.
[87] *Keyhan*, 29 Mordad 1358. [88] *Keyhan*, 29 Mordad 1358.
[89] *Khandaniha*, 31 Mordad, 1332.
[90] Khameh'i, 1363, p. 441; Bozorgmehr, pp. 120, 146, 206; *Taraqi*, 2 Shahrivar 1332.
[91] *Taraqi*, 2 Shahrivar 1332.

a directive threatening those military personnel engaging in such sales with disciplinary action.[92] In the pillage of Mosaddeq house, the safe in which he kept sensitive state documents, including the original version of the royal edict which Nasiri had handed to him in the early hours of 16 August, was opened and its contents disappeared.[93] At around 7:30 p.m., when nothing was left inside Mosaddeq's house to loot, the assailants and the military personnel set fire to it.[94] The burning of Mosaddeq's house continued until 9:00 p.m.[95]

That very same night, Colonel Farzanegan, the official CIA agent actively involved throughout all stages of both coups and one of the military men in the new cabinet – Undersecretary of Post, Telegraph and Telephone – received orders from Zahedi, (the new Prime Minister) and Carroll to wrap up the operation.[96] As his final duty of the day, Farzanegan "placed known supporters of TPAJAX in command of all units of the Tehran garrison, seized key military targets and executed the arrest lists".[97] The new appointees of the coup d'état government were: Farhad Dadsetan as Military Governor; Mohammad Daftari as Chief of Police; Eskandar Azmudeh as commander of the First Mountain Brigade; Zand Karimi as commander of the Second Mountain Brigade; Ali-Mohammad Rowhani as commander of the Third Mountain Brigade; and Karimi as commander of the First Armoured Brigade. Nowzari was reinstated as commander of the Second Armoured Brigade.[98]

Two days after the fall of Mosaddeq's house, a young supporter of the nationalist movement who had been absent from Tehran during those four momentous hazy days of August 1953, went to visit 109 Kakh Street. He saw a white banner hanging from Mosaddeq's house. On it was written: "At nightfall he was thinking of pillage, by sunrise the body was headless and the head wore no crown".[99] The one-line poem accused Mosaddeq of being a plundering monarch, and rejoiced in his overthrow. The banner was signed by Baqa'i's Toilers Party, one of the main confederates of the insurgents who had attacked and looted Mosaddeq's house. This same poem appeared on the morrow of the coup on the first page of *Shahed*, below Baqa'i's picture.[100] On that same Friday (30 Mordad), when the anti-Mosaddeq allies were basking in the glory of their victory, General Zahedi went to visit Ayatollah Kashani at his Shemiran residence. At this meeting with Zahedi, Kashani's close circle of friends – Shams Qanatabadi, Baqa'i, Nadali-ye Karimi and Haerizadeh – were also present.[101]

---

[92] Bozorgmehr, p. 120.   [93] Bozorgmehr, pp. 119, 120, 187.
[94] *Taraqi*, 2 Shahrivar 1332.
[95] Nejati (Goftogo ba Ostad Doctor Gholamhoseyn Sadiqi), p. 549.   [96] Wilber, p. 75.
[97] Wilber, p. 75.   [98] *Tehran Mosavvar*, 30 Mordad 1332.
[99] N. Pakdaman *in Arash*, August–September 2003.   [100] *Shahed*, 29 Mordad 1332.
[101] *Khandaniha*, 3 Shahrivar 1332.

15

Religious representatives and the coup

Overthrowing Mosaddeq required making a case against his government, on religious grounds, that would placate his religious supporters and provide a justification for the actions of the thugs, the military and the police collaborators. The religious demonization of Mosaddeq and sanctification of the coup d'état would not have been possible without the active collaboration of certain religious leaders. By consistently portraying Mosaddeq's government as the harbinger of Communism and atheism, the coup planners believed that they were providing Iran's religious leaders with the necessary excuse to openly call for Mosaddeq's ousting. In preparation for the coup, the planners had originally placed their hopes in four key clerical figures of the period. These religious figures, however, were of very different theological statures. Their levels of respectability within the traditional Shi'i hierarchy and the numbers of their religious followers also varied significantly.

According to the "London Draft of the TPAJAX Operational Plan" (Appendix B), hammered out between 15 and 17 June 1953 at the SIS main office, the masterminds of the coup believed or were told that "nearly all important religious leaders with large followings are firmly opposed to Mossadeq"; they were also told that "the pro-Zahedi capabilities in this field are very great".[1] Even though in Wilber's report the names of the four clerical leaders are left blank, their identity is fairly easily discerned in view of the characteristics employed to introduce them. Two of them are identified as "non-political", leaving two as political clerics, where one of the two political clerics is identified as possessing a "terrorist gang". The two "non-political" key clerics referred to are probably Ayatollahs Borujerdi and Behbahani. The political clergy with a "terrorist gang" is Navvab Safavi, and the political clergy without a particular description is Ayatollah Kashani.[2] At the time Ayatollah Kashani was known as a political clergy (*akhund*

---

[1] Wilber, p. 13; Wilber, Appendix B, p. 20, 21.
[2] In his main report, Wilber refers to Behbahani, Borujerdi and Kashani by name: pp. 57, 71.

siyasi), while Behbahani, in spite of his well-known political orientations, did not have such a reputation. There is very little doubt that the assumption of the coup planners, based on their domestic and foreign informants, was that the four "influential" religious figures – Grand Ayatollah Borujerdi, Ayatollahs Behbahani and Kashani – as well as Navvab Safavi were supportive of Mosaddeq's overthrow.[3]

The planners of the first coup hoped that "during the period of intensive anti-Mossadeq publicity before the coup day the leaders and their henchmen will" collaborate with the coup by carrying out six steps.[4] They would: first, "spread word of their disapproval" of Mosaddeq; second, "give open support" to the Shah; third, "stage pro-religious anti-Mossadeq demonstrations"; fourth, "threaten pro-Mossadeq deputies and members of Mossadeq's entourage and government"; fifth, "ensure full participation of themselves and their followers" in efforts to overthrow Mosaddeq; sixth, after the change of government "give the strongest assurances over Radio Tehran and in Mosques that the new government is faithful to religious principles".[5] Even though two of the four religious figures, namely Behbahani and Kashani, did participate in the overthrow of Mosaddeq by collaborating with the coup and becoming involved in many of the anti-Mosaddeq steps outlined by the coup planners, two other figures, namely Grand Ayatollah Borujerdi and the once fiery and radical Navvab Safavi, did not behave as expected by the planners and refused to enter the game.

Being erroneously informed, the coup planners assumed that the four religious figures were homogeneous in their hostility towards Mosaddeq and love of the foreign-domestic plotters, and that they would therefore participate with equal zeal and commitment in the overthrow project. Perhaps the coup planners hoped that once their anti-Mosaddeq smear campaign was in full swing Borujerdi and Navvab Safavi, under pressure from Behbahani and Kashani or their followers, would be compelled to rally to the anti-Mosaddeq camp. The emphasis of the deceptive anti-Mosaddeq propaganda accusing him of paving the path to a Soviet annexation of Iran was chosen with the objective of intimidating the non-compliant religious dignitaries, namely Borujerdi and Navvab Safavi, and forcing their hands to join the coup project. The assumption that Borujerdi and Navvab Safavi could be bullied, against their beliefs, into a religio-political position demonstrated a lack of familiarity with their personalities.

The position of each of the four religious figures in relation to cooperation with the coup plan was coloured by their respective political backgrounds and dispositions, their position in relation to British colonialism, their personal relationships with Mosaddeq, the Shah and the British and, finally, the contraction or expansion of their respective political power and influence

---

[3] Wilber, Appendix B, p. 21.   [4] Wilber, Appendix B, p. 21.
[5] Wilber, Appendix B, pp. 21, 22.

during Mosaddeq's premiership. Openly siding with the plotters against Mosaddeq was synonymous with publicly admitting their alliance with foreign interests. The only religious figure who may have been insensitive to being identified as a British collaborator was Ayatollah Behbahani, who already had such a reputation.

AYATOLLAH BEHBAHANI

Ayatollah Behbahani was close to the young Shah and at this time supported him unreservedly. Whenever the Court felt politically anxious or threatened, word was sent out to Behbahani to rally his troops and stage a strong show of "popular" support for the Shah.[6] Behbahani was a man of many resources. He was not only influential among pro-Shah politicians and notables, but was also closely connected with leaders of the *meydan* (the South Tehran fruit and vegetable market). Even though he had some following among merchants at the bazaar, the leading figures in the bazaar were staunch followers of Mosaddeq. Overall, Behbahani was well positioned to get a considerable "mass" mobilized for or against an issue, especially when funds were made available to him. Behbahani did not believe in political Islam as such, but was convinced that the long-term political and economic interests of the clergy and the crown were intertwined and that it was incumbent upon the clergy to support the crown when the latter was threatened and demanded such help. Behbahani's political interventions in favour of the Shah at critical moments gave the public the impression that he was the foremost religio-political puppeteer of the land.[7]

Behbahani was also known for his very close ties to the British. Among both the Iranians and the British it was reputed that Behbahani listened closely to what the British said, and that a single word from their embassy was sufficient to have him change his mind.[8] Behbahani was indeed in contact with the British Embassy in Iran and candidly discussed political matters with its employees. In a meeting with Major R. Jackson, Behbahani informed him of his deep opposition to the Mosaddeq government and to Communism, and then proceeded to explain why he needed to be reappointed as the "head of the religious Bequests Department so that he could draw upon that fund for the purpose of opposing communism and incidentally Mussadeq".[9] Just as the Shah called on Behbahani for political favours, the British Embassy also contacted Behbahani with similar expectations. When in the summer of 1952 Mosaddeq demanded extraordinary legislative

---

[6] M. Tafreshi and M. Taherahmadi, *Gozareshhay-e Mahramaneh Shahrebani*, vol. 2 (Tehran: Entesharat-e Sazeman-e Asnad-e Melli, 1371), p. 154.
[7] *Farman*, 18 Aban 1330.   [8] British Petroleum Archives, File 071068, 12 December 1950.
[9] FO 248/1531, 19 May 1952.

powers from the Majles, the British sought Behbahani's assistance to bring pressure to bear upon his clerical friends, "the mullahs", to "express their opposition to Musaddiq's request".[10]

Ironically, some 18 years after Ayatollah Behbahani helped bring the Shah to power, the Shah confided in Asadollah 'Alam, his Minister of Court, that Behbahani was "an old servant of the English" (*kohneh nokar*).[11] Later still, in January 1972, he again referred to Behbahani as a special servant and the agent (*ayadi*) of the British.[12] In May 1976 the Shah characterized Behbahani as a "corrupt" man.[13] Given the role of Ayatollah Behbahani in organizing the events of 28 Mordad, the Shah seems to have been concurring with the idea that Behbahani was acting according to the wishes of the British for a reasonable financial reward, to overthrow Mosaddeq, reinstate General Zahedi and ensure the return of the Shah to power.

AYATOLLAH KASHANI

As contrasted with Behbahani, Ayatollah Kashani was a firm believer in the inseparability of religion and politics. For him, clerical leaders only concerned with spiritual Islam and aloof from socio-political issues and problems were quietists collaborating with injustice and unworthy of a religious leadership role. Kashani was a renowned anti-British cleric and had been imprisoned by the Allies for his pro-German and anti-British activities. Kashani was also a main supporting political pillar of Mosaddeq and the oil nationalization movement. During the bloody 21 July 1952 (30 Tir) showdown between Qavam and Mosaddeq, Kashani threw all of his religio-political weight and support behind Mosaddeq. Kashani's support at that crucial historical moment was instrumental in bringing Mosaddeq back to power. However, Kashani was a shrewd politician, and, since November 1951, according to Middleton's report to the Foreign Office, he had "established contact with the Court" and had "also been in touch with the American Embassy".[14] His main argument, according to Middleton, was "the danger of Communism and the need for immediate American aid".

Once the two men fell out and he began to move against Mosaddeq, Kashani had no option but to move into the pro-Shah, pro-Zahedi and pro-British camp. Kashani had witnessed the gradual erosion of his power and influence during the premiership of Mosaddeq and held Mosaddeq responsible for this. Zaehner, of the British Embassy, believed that "the detaching of Kashani and Makki from Musaddiq were 'due to the factors' created and directed by the brothers Rashidiyan".[15] Kashani hoped that by siding with

---

[10] FO 248/1531, 14 July 1952. [11] 'Alikhani, vol. 2, p. 129. [12] 'Alikhani, vol. 2, p. 387.
[13] 'Alikhani, vol. 6 (Bethesda: Ibex Publishers, 2008), p. 65.
[14] FO 248/1514, 14 November 1951. [15] FO 248/1531, 15 May 1952.

the coup planners he would regain his religio-political status in the aftermath of Mosaddeq's overthrow. This awkward political shift placed Kashani in a fragile and ambivalent position from which he never recovered. Kashani was reluctantly pushed into allying himself with the pro-British political forces, which he had previously always opposed because of their ultimate objective to undo Iran's oil nationalization. Aligning himself with the pro-Shah forces was not as bitter as joining the British camp. For a cleric who had established his public image and reputation as an anti-colonial bulwark, participating in the overthrow of Mosaddeq and becoming closely associated with British politico-economic interests in Iran was religio-political suicide. As much as he had come to dislike the Prime Minister, Kashani's cooperation with the effort to overthrow Mosaddeq turned to dust all his efforts at chasing out the political and economic dominance of the British from Iran. Most humiliating of all, however, was that Kashani came to be seen by the public as a friend of the British.

From August 1952 Kashani settled his old disagreements and quibbles with Behbahani.[16] Simultaneously, in September of 1952 – over-confident of his popularity and political clout and disappointed with Mosaddeq's attempts at curbing his arbitrary meddling in the affairs of the state – Kashani moved closer to Zahedi.[17] At this time, Middleton observed that "Kashani would like to see Musaddiq removed, if he could be quite certain that this would not damage his position".[18] Events such as 9 Esfand, the Afshartus Affair, the provision of sanctuary to Zahedi in the Majles and the unsuccessful bid to retain his presidency of the Majles hardened Kashani's anti-Mosaddeq stance. Kashani's justification for his enmity towards Mosaddeq was one that had been previously voiced by Baqa'i and was very much in line with the excuse which justified British and American intervention in Iran. Mosaddeq was presented as an apostate who had "rebelled against Islam" and was accused of "dragging Iran into the Communist trap" by ensuring the hegemony of the "Bolshevik Tudeh Party".[19] The simple formula repeated by Kashani's entourage – that Mosaddeq's rule was synonymous with Communist rule – was exactly in tune with the propaganda of the coup planners. Kashani and his newspapers did not shy away from demanding that Mosaddeq be hanged for having rebelled against the constitution.[20]

As the date of the coup approached, Kashani's tone sharpened. Kashani issued a communiqué on the occasion of Mosaddeq's proposed referendum on dissolving the Majles, labelling the referendum a "foreign plot", and reiterated that "patriotic Muslims" would not participate in it.[21] He also

---

[16] *Ettela'at*, 3 Shahrivar 1331; *Bakhtar Emrouz*, 24 Shahrivar 1331.
[17] FO 248/1531, 30 September 1952.   [18] FO 248/1531, 30 September 1952.
[19] *Mellat-e Ma*, 22 Mordad 1332.
[20] *Siyasat-e Ma*, 10 Tir 1332; *Mellat-e Ma*, 7 Tir 1332; *Atash*, 9 Tir 1332.
[21] *Ettela'at*, 10 Mordad 1332.

used his religious status and labelled it as *"haram"* (or forbidden) and "despised by the 12th Imam".[22] Whereas Behbahani's opposition to Mosaddeq was cool-headed, tempered and calculated, Kashani, who had swung from full support for Mosaddeq to contemptuous animosity towards the man, was unable to conceal his emotional antagonism. While Behbahani had his heart and mind in the overthrow project and did not question its ethical propriety, Kashani was a reluctant accomplice whose pride and temperamental disposition had pushed him into an uncomfortable alliance with partners whom he loathed on principle.

After the coup, Kashani's conscience, and probably his sense of guilt at having sided with British interests, pushed him along a collision course with Zahedi and the regime. On 19 January 1956 the 79-year-old Kashani was charged with "instigating the people to arm against the monarchy", and he was imprisoned.[23] While Ayatollah Kashani was in prison, charged also with ordering the assassination of General Razmara by the Fadiyan Eslam ("Devotees of Islam"), his son, Mohammad Kashani, wrote a revealing letter to Ardeshir Zahedi, reminding him of the Ayatollah's consistent support for and services to Fazlollah Zahedi, at a time when Kashani was at the peak of his power and Zahedi was politically isolated and under pressure. Mohammad Kashani wrote: "If you want to know the truth, it was because of your father that my father fell out with Mosaddeq". He pleaded with Ardeshir Zahedi to implore the Shah for Ayatollah Kashani's pardon.[24] At this time Behbahani was also actively petitioning the Shah for clemency towards Kashani.[25] Kashani was finally released in March 1956 after the intercession of Ayatollah Borujerdi, and died six years later in isolation.

GRAND AYATOLLAH BORUJERDI

It would be safe to suggest that both Behbahani and Kashani were implicated in the coup by their support for and aid towards it. The coup planners were therefore justified in relying on their involvement in and contribution to the overthrow operation. However, their reckoning that Ayatollah Borujerdi and Navvab Safavi would also actively cooperate with the coup effort was flawed. The Grand Ayatollah Borujerdi did not believe that his role as the highest Shi'i authority was to intervene in politics and the everyday political haggling in the country. He deliberately avoided taking sides in domestic political rivalries and clashes as he firmly believed that entangling the spiritual beliefs of the people with a particular political platform, interest or faction could lead to the demise of religious beliefs when political tides turned. Borujerdi stood above political brawls and derived his popular religious authority and respect from

---

[22] *Ettela'at*, 10 Mordad 1332.
[23] *Rowhaniy-e Mobarez Ayatollah Seyyed Abolqasem Kashani*, vol. 2, p. 744.
[24] *Ashofteh*, 26 Bahman 1334.   [25] *Ashofteh*, 26 Bahman 1334.

this position. Borujerdi's style of keeping politics out of the seminary schools and insisting on the separation of religion and politics bothered the partisans of political Islam – namely Kashani and Navvab Safavi, who accused him of being passive and a quietist. Yet when Borujerdi felt that the general welfare of the Shi'i or the national integrity of the country was threatened, he reacted firmly.

It is revealing that whereas the reports from British Embassy officials in Tehran to the Foreign Office reflected an impressive level of acquaintance with Iranian notables, politicians and politico-religious leaders such as Kashani, Behbahani and Navvab Safavi, when it came to Borujerdi the Iran experts at the embassy seemed ill-informed. Borujerdi's name very seldom came up in their reports, and when it did, it was curiously in passing. Clearly, Borujerdi had no need to establish any ties with the British Embassy officials, nor did these officials find any reason to become interested in him as he was a religious man and did not play the everyday game of politics. Pyman, the "Oriental Counsellor" at the British Embassy in Iran whose reports reflected his intimate knowledge of and acquaintance with Iranian notables, writes: "Naser Qashqa'i had suggested to Kashani that he should stick to religion and keep out of politics, and should try to establish himself as the chief Shi'ah divine. (Incidentally, the position of leader of the Shi'ah sect is already held by one Burujerdi, who lives in Qum)".[26] Unlike Behbahani, Borujerdi, had no desire to be known to or in contact with the British, and was probably perfectly happy to be referred to as "one Burujerdi".

The British took an interest in Ayatollah Borujerdi when he surprised them, the Anglophile Iranian notables and the Shah with his opposition to their anti-Iranian machinations and his open support for Mosaddeq. In the summer of 1951 the Shah and the British had come to the conclusion that Mosaddeq had to go.[27] The British Cabinet, having abandoned the idea of attacking and taking the Iranian oilfields on 12 July, began reconsidering their military options of invading and holding onto Abadan. By mid-September, "Operation Buccaneer" was closely considered by the British as a viable solution to attain this end. While on 27 September 1951, the British forces were ready to launch "Operation Buccaneer", the cabinet, faced with staunch American opposition, backed off.[28] In his report of 1 October, Zaehner of the British Embassy in Tehran informed the Foreign Office that according to Salman Assadi, a well-informed Iranian contact, "Ayatollah Burujerdi has sent a message to Dr. Houman for presentation to H.I.M [the Shah] in which Burujerdi says that the Musaddeq government has his entire support".[29]

Almost simultaneously, on 29 September 1951, Henderson, the new American Ambassador to Tehran, met with the Shah, whereupon the monarch

---

[26] FO 248/1493, 23 June 1950. [27] FO 248/1514, 28 June 1951.
[28] Louis, 1984, pp. 686–687. [29] FO 248/1514, 1 October 1951.

informed him that Ayatollah Borujerdi had sent him a message reiterating that "all Iran must stand together in face of British threats and if Britain should invade Iran the country must present a solid front".[30] According to the Shah, Borujerdi's message was a clear indication that he was "aligning" himself with Mosaddeq, at least on the oil issue. The Shah lamented to Henderson that Borujerdi's message was delivered to him in the presence of a number of other people, leading him to believe that news of Borujerdi's support for Mosaddeq's government would be widely circulating among Iranians.[31] Borujerdi's inside information about the threat of invasion by the British is interesting and impressive, as is his decisive *prise de position* and intervention in political matters at crucial and decisive moments of national crisis.

While the 28 February 1953 (9 Esfand) events over the Shah's departure from Iran consolidated the alliance between Ayatollahs Kashani and Behbahani against Mosaddeq and brought their partnership into the open, the two clerics knew full well that without the presence of Borujerdi in their camp, their anti-Mosaddeq position and propaganda would not have much religious weight. From the end of February 1953 to the coups in August of that year the Kashani–Behbahani axis sought to convey the idea that Ayatollah Borujerdi was indeed in their camp. However, Borujerdi systematically demonstrated his independence from the anti-Mosaddeq front by disclaiming their propaganda and even displaying his irritation at their insinuations and innuendos.[32]

After 9 Esfand, when the anti-Mosaddeq axis consciously drove an irreversible wedge between the Shah and Mosaddeq, Ayatollah Borujerdi chose to neutralize the efforts of this axis by building bridges between the Shah and Mosaddeq for the sake of Iran's independence. The non-political Borujerdi, who raised himself above the micro-political fray, proved to be much more politically astute when it came to Iran's long-term self-sovereignty and right of self-determination. While the Kashani–Behbahani axis was beating on the polarizing drum of the Shah against Mosaddeq, Borujerdi consulted at length with emissaries from the both Shah *and* Mosaddeq. Borujerdi then sent a public message inviting the Shah and Mosaddeq to unite and work together as they had done before for "the independence and grandeur of Iran".[33] Borujerdi chided the "deviant and rabble-rousing elements" who had "caused disruption and turmoil" on 9 Esfand.[34] In this carefully worded public announcement, typical of Ayatollah Borujerdi's style, there is no indication of his displeasure towards Mosaddeq, yet there is an undeniable reprimanding of the pro-Shah demonstrators, mobilized by Behbahani and Kashani, who had rioted against Mosaddeq and broken down the door to his house.

---

[30] FRUS, vol. x, p. 186. [31] FRUS, vol. x, p. 186. [32] Rahnema, pp. 874–876.
[33] Rahnema, p. 875. [34] Rahnema, p. 875.

In spite of Borujerdi's clear position on the events of 28 February (9 Esfand) and his lack of involvement with Behbahani and Kashani's political ploys, the Kashani–Behbahani axis conducted a wide propaganda campaign to try to convince Borujerdi's followers that he too supported the anti-Mosaddeq and pro-Shah camp. During the last five months of Mosaddeq's government, Ayatollah Kashani and Shams Qanatabadi tried very hard to convince the general public that Borujerdi was in the same anti-Mosaddeq camp as Behbahani and Kashani.[35] The Kashani–Behbahani camp knew that without Borujerdi's support, the religious aspect and appeal of their anti-Mosaddeq position would not seem convincing to the pious majority.

At the end of March 1953, when consensus was reached among the members of the anti-Mosaddeq camp on General Zahedi as the future Prime Minister, Hoseyn 'Ala, the Minister of Court, went to visit Borujerdi "in order to ascertain the latter's attitude regarding Zahedi".[36] 'Ala subsequently reported to the American Ambassador in Iran on his visit with the Grand Ayatollah. During this visit 'Ala admitted that Borujerdi had not committed himself to anything and had informed 'Ala that he would re-contact him. Ala then opined that he thought Borujerdi had "seemed sympathetic".[37] In this meeting with Henderson, 'Ala seemed to be the spokesman of the "group who [was] interested in [the] overthrow [of the] Mosaddeq government".[38] 'Ala was honest in reporting his conversation with the Ayatollah, but could not hide his wishful thinking that Borujerdi would eventually join the anti-Mosaddeq camp. By mid-April, Borujerdi sent a message to counter the rumours circulating in the anti-Mosaddeq press speculating on his discontentment with the Mosaddeq government and its so-called "appeasement policy" towards the Communists.[39] In spite of constant pressure on Borujerdi by various pro-Shah newspapers to side with Behbahani and Kashani against Mosaddeq, Borujerdi refused to comply.[40]

Mosaddeq, in turn, was cognizant of the manner in which Ayatollah Borujerdi was in fact supporting his government by refusing to join or even tacitly acknowledge the claims of the Kashani–Behbahani axis against him. As a sign of his gratitude towards Borujerdi, and seeking to neutralize future plots by the Kashani–Behbahani axis that could turn Borujerdi against him, Mosaddeq used his discretionary powers and added three items to the Press Laws already in place. The three items were intended for the protection of Ayatollah Borujerdi at a time when the press was going wild with injurious and disparaging literature against their political opponents. The new items stipulated that in the case of any disrespectful or defamatory comments or statements about "the highest religious dignitary of the land, who is the public's Source of Imitation", both the author and the newspaper publisher

---

[35] *Democrat-e Eslami*, 17 Esfand 1331.   [36] FRUS, vol. x, p. 720.
[37] FRUS, vol. x, p. 720.   [38] FRUS, vol. x, p. 720.   [39] *Ettela'at*, 27 Farvardin 1332.
[40] *Vahemeh*, 2 Ordibehesht 1332.

would be held responsible and could receive a sentence of anywhere between three months to one year of imprisonment.⁴¹ Mosaddeq protected Borujerdi from all kinds of abuse that were customary in the press at the time, but purposefully worded the law in such a way that it could protect neither Behbahani nor Kashani.

Around mid-July 1953, as the D-day against Mosaddeq approached and the necessity of a united anti-Mosaddeq religious front including Borujerdi loomed, the anti-Mosaddeq press pushed once again to pit Borujerdi against Mosaddeq.⁴² Borujerdi actively sought to neutralize the fabricated animosity which was presented to the public by the anti-Mosaddeq press. Late in June of 1953, Borujerdi, a master at avoiding undesirable visitors, met with Mosaddeq's envoys, even though he was ill, simply to display his support for the Mosaddeq government.⁴³ Relentless in their effort to draw Borujerdi into the anti-Mosaddeq camp and frustrated by their inability to do so, the anti-Mosaddeq press adopted a more aggressive posture, directly calling on Borujerdi to take a stand.⁴⁴ The real pressure on Borujerdi to join the anti-Mosaddeq religious camp came when Behbahani and Kashani categorically condemned the referendum on dissolving the parliament, and Borujerdi refused to position himself against Mosaddeq. The fact that Kashani had called the referendum an "Islamically prohibited act" (*haram*), and Behbahani had written against it, while Borujerdi had not uttered a word on its un-Islamicness, placed Kashani and Behbahani in a precarious religious position.

Seventeen days before the first coup an important petition in support of Mosaddeq was sent to the Majles. The importance of this statement of support, some two weeks before the first coup, stemmed from the fact that it was coming from the province of Lorestan, the real power-base and home of Borujerdi. Furthermore, the petition was sent by Ayatollah Ruhollah Kamalvand, Borujerdi's official representative and right-hand man in Khoramabad (capital of Lorestan).⁴⁵ This important development sent a clear signal to those who were familiar with the subtleties of Borujerdi's manoeuvrings. Kamalvand's petition demonstrated that while the machine to overthrow Mosaddeq was in high gear, Ayatollah Borujerdi was not only ignoring the calls for alliance by Behbahani and Kashani, but was also indicating his continuing support for Mosaddeq's government.

Borujerdi's consistent non-aggressive, if not favourable, disposition towards Mosaddeq and his refusal to say a word against his government was becoming increasingly bothersome and injurious to the anti-Mosaddeq religious claims of the Kashani–Behbahani axis. Four days before the first coup Shams Qanatabadi, Kashani's closest confidant and associate at the time, employed a surprisingly pushy and almost irreverent tone with regard to

---

⁴¹ *Ettela'at*, 10 Ordibehesht 1332.   ⁴² *Atash*, 11 Tir, 31 Khordad 1332.
⁴³ *Ettela'at*, 6 Tir 1332.   ⁴⁴ *Atash*, 11 Mordad 1332.   ⁴⁵ *Ettela'at*, 8 Mordad 1332.

Borujerdi. In his newspaper, Qanatabadi wrote: "Your holiness, Ayatollah Borujerdi: Are you aware of the fact that Mosaddeq has delayed the implementation of the law against the consumption of alcoholic beverages for another year?"[46] Just as Borujerdi refused to react to the stirrings, invitations and incitation of the anti-Mosaddeq camp right before the coup, so too he frustrated the coup-makers by not issuing an edict "calling for a holy war against Communism", thereby failing to legitimize the coup d'état against Mosaddeq.[47]

When Borujerdi refused to religiously sanction the coup against Mosaddeq, the Kashani–Behbahani axis reacted with anger and disapproval. The headline of the Kashani and Shams Qanatabadi daily tells the simple story of Borujerdi's refusal to ally himself with the anti-Mosaddeq camp right up until the day of the coup d'état. In big print at the bottom of the first page of *Mallat-e ma*, dated 28 Mordad 1332 (19 August 1953), it reads: "Your holiness (*hazrat-e*) Ayatollah Borujerdi! Tehran is in the hands of the Bolsheviks and Mosaddeq has tied the hands of the Muslim people behind their backs, again you continue to remain silent?"[48] Borujerdi was not to rubber stamp the coup d'état in the name of the Shi'i Islam he represented. Borujerdi was a cleric, but not of Behbahani and Kashani's ilk. The article in Qanatabadi's newspaper confirms that, right up until the coup on 28 Mordad, the Kashani–Behbahani camp were highly distraught by Borujerdi's refusal to collaborate with them in a British–American initiated and planned coup d'état. Through his acts, decisions, words and significant silences, when notable men of the cloth pressured him to utter just a single word against Mosaddeq, the Absolute Source of Imitation (*marja' taqlid motlaq*) of the Shi'i informed his followers (*moqaledin*) that he would not consent to the removal of Mosaddeq, and that his religious followers should not move against Mosaddeq as they did not have his approval for such an act.

Some time between the evening of the 28 and 29 Mordad, telegrams were exchanged between Ayatollah Behbahani and the Shah. In his telegram to Behbahani, the Shah thanked the Iranian people for their "kindness" towards him. Ayatollah Behbahani wrote back informing his Majesty that everyone was eager to see their glorious and popular king. In this telegram Behbahani petitioned God for the Shah's health and "the endurance" of his "illustrious Islamic monarchy".[49] Aside from the telegraphs between Behbahani and the Shah after 28 Mordad, Behbahani had sent the Shah a highly supportive telegram while he was in Bagdad. In this telegram Behbahani had wished that "the holy spirits of the guardians of the faith" would help the king to maintain the independence of the country and "cut off the hands of foreigners".[50]

---

[46] *Mellat-e Ma*, 21 Mordad 1332. [47] Wilber, p. 57. [48] *Mellat-e Ma*, 28 Mordad 1332.
[49] *Ettela'at*, 31 Mordad 1332. [50] *Atash*, 31 Mordad 1332.

The Shah returned to Iran on 22 August (31 Mordad). Three days after his return, Borujerdi answered the telegram that the Shah had sent him from Rome (sometime between 27 and 30 Mordad). Borujerdi's response to the Shah came with four to seven days of delay. Borujerdi answered the Shah only after the coup, and not before. The Shah must have hoped to receive a response much sooner and in a style similar to Behbahani's. In his measured and almost dry response, Borujerdi wrote that since the Shah had written to him that he would be back immediately, his response was delayed. Borujerdi wrote that he was delighted to hear that the Shah was in good health while in Rome and added that he "hoped that the Shah's auspicious (*masood*) entrance (*vorood*) to Iran would be a fruitful/joyful (*mobarak*) one, resulting in the betterment of religious objectives (*eslah-e maqased diniyeh*), the glory of Islam and the welfare of Muslims".[51] In the body of Borujerdi's message, a veiled cynicism with respect to the past conduct of the Shah may be detected: Borujerdi begins the important part of his message by saying "I hope that" (*omid ast*), implying that what he expects of the Shah's return to the country is merely a wish, with no expectation that it become a reality. In the text of Borujerdi's formal telegram there are no signs of adulation, exuberance at the return of the Shah or expression of hope that his rule and dynasty endure indefinitely.

In his telegram, Borujerdi addressed the Shah as *Ala hazrat* (his royal title) and added the clerical expression *khalad ollah taala molkaho* ("May God the Almighty protract your realm eternally"). This title is one of the many standard and generic titles used by the clergy when addressing Shahs and does not imply praise for them on any particular occasion or act. It is the body of the message which presents the substance of the correspondence, not the ceremonial title used for a particular king. Mirza Hasan Shirazi addressed Nasereddin Shah in exactly the same manner (*khalad Ollah taala molkaho*) when he was warning and chiding the Shah on the use of tobacco in his Court. Ayatollah Ha'eri, the founder of the Qom Seminary School, addressed Reza Shah in the same way (*khalad Ollah taala molka*) when he informed him that the prevailing conditions in the country were against the Shari'a.

Attempts at presenting Ayatollah Borujerdi as a proponent of the anti-Mosaddeq collaborationist axis and a supporter of or a contributor to the coup d'état is not founded on historical facts.[52] Such mis-representation seeks to provide a religious legitimization for the coups. The necessity of presenting a religious justification for the coup was highlighted in the

---

[51] *Ettela'at*, 3 Shahrivar 1332. Attempts have been made to replace Borujerdi's original telegram to the Shah, as reproduced in the daily *Ettela'at*, with fabricated versions glorifying the Shah's return. See D. Bayandor, *Iran and the CIA* (NY: Palgrave Macmillan, 2010), p. 233; Homayunfar, p. 326.

[52] See Zahedi, pp. 179, 185; Bayandor, pp. 78–81, 150–154.

Nicosia version of Operation Ajex and promoted by the domestic anti-Mosaddeq forces. Explaining the coup as the consequence of the religious sentiments of Iranians and their loyalty to Iran's main Source of Imitation (*marja' taqlid*) gives the false impression that Borujerdi finally succumbed to the barrage of foreign and domestic propaganda accusing Mosaddeq of anti-religious and Communist tendencies. As simple and as politically convenient as the homogenization of Shi'i clergy may be, it is historically and analytically erroneous. Consequently, to argue that Borujerdi finally aligned his politics in relation to Mosaddeq with Behbahani and Kashani is unfounded.

Two days after the coup, General Zahedi met Ayatollah Kashani, who had been instrumental in his victory, at his house in Shemiran.[53] Later, General Zahedi repaid his debt to Ayatollah Kashani by having Mostafa Kashani, his son, and Shams Qanatabadi, his right-hand man, "elected" to the first post-coup Majles.[54] In contrast, no such meeting between Zahedi and Borujerdi was ever reported in the Iranian press. Some two weeks after the coup, when Zahedi wrote a telegram to Borujerdi congratulating him on the occasion of the Eyd Qadir, Borujerdi once again returned a dry telegram, simply wishing that God would assist Zahedi in fulfilling his religious responsibilities at such a difficult point in time.[55]

SEYYED MOJTABA NAVVAB SAFAVI

Just as the coup planners' assessment of Ayatollah Borujerdi turned out to be incorrect, so their expectations of Navvab Safavi also proved dated. Mojtaba Mir-Lowhi, better known as Navvab Safavi, was the founder of the "Devotees of Islam" (*Fadaiyan Eslam*). The "Devotees of Islam" had become a much-feared organization after it had proudly accepted responsibility for the assassination of Abdol-Hoseyn Hajir (the powerful Minister of Court) on November 1949 and General Razmara (the Prime Minister) in March 1951. The young cleric, Navvab Safavi, and his fervent band of followers had at one point been effectively under the spiritual leadership of Ayatollah Kashani. After the assassination of Razmara, Navvab Safavi felt shunned and betrayed by both Ayatollah Kashani and Mosaddeq's National Front, with whom he believed he had an alliance. Navvab Safavi's reaction was one of threats and intimidations. He accused Mosaddeq and Kashani of collusion with the Court and threatened to assassinate them both. In June 1951, or some five weeks after Mosaddeq became Prime Minister, Navvab Safavi was arrested and remained in jail until January 1953 – or about seven months before the coup.

---

[53] *Shahed*, 1 Shahrivar 1332; Salemi, p. 499.   [54] FRUS, vol. x, p. 895.
[55] *Ettela'at*, 10 Shahrivar 1332.

While in prison, Navvab Safavi, feeling isolated and abandoned, adopted a more conciliatory posture towards Mosaddeq and Kashani. Navvab Safavi restrained his aggressive invectives and moderated his belligerent discourse, sending word to both men that if the imprisoned members of the "Devotees of Islam" were released he would promise to withdraw from the political scene.[56] While in prison, Navvab Safavi became more politically cynical and withdrawn. He gravitated towards a more spiritual Islam rather than the hard-line violent political Islam which he had previously espoused.

After his release from prison, Navvab Safavi pursued a policy of détente and peaceful coexistence with Mosaddeq's government. In his statements and declarations after his release, Navvab Safavi reiterated his political disengagement and disinterest in the political squabbles of the times. He often repeated that he did not sympathize with any of the competing political forces as he did not consider any of them interested in implementing the *Shari'a*.[57] From early May 1953, Navvab Safavi's organization was confronted with a series of factional secessions and expulsions.[58] The fissures within the "Devotees of Islam" were due to more than one reason, but a key one was the difference of opinion between engagement and non-engagement in politics. Two months before the coup against Mosaddeq, while Kashani and his followers were committed to ousting Mosaddeq from power, Navvab Safavi was not yet ready to mend fences with Kashani and join the anti-Mosaddeq religious axis.[59] Some 20 days before the first coup, the "Devotees of Islam" sent an important message to the Court, to Mosaddeq and to Kashani that they did not intend to support any of them and preferred to continue with their policy of non-interference.[60]

On 26 Mordad, one day after the first coup, when all competing political forces, supporters and opponents of Mosaddeq were taking stock of what had happened and planning their next political move, Navvab Safavi and his followers were mourning the untimely death of Navvab Safavi's young wife at the Abuzar Mosque in Tehran.[61] According to Navvab Safavi, on 28 Mordad he chose to stay put and wait. He had reached the decision not to become involved with the events of 28 Mordad by a divination through the Qur'an (*estekhareh*).[62] So, Navvab Safavi played no political role in the events that led to the coup and remained an unaligned observer. Whereas both Behbahani and Kashani did fulfil the expectations of the coup planners and did mobilize their followers to overthrow Mosaddeq, Navvab Safavi desisted from joining forces with the anti-Mosaddeq religious collaborationists.

---

[56] *Tolu'*, 1 Mehr 1330; M. Hoseyni, *Khaterat-e Mohammadmehdi 'Abdkhoda'i* (Tehran: Markaz-e Asnad-e Enqelab-e Eslami, 1379), pp. 91–92.
[57] *Ettela'at*, 15, 25 Farvardin, 5 Ordibehesht 1332.   [58] *Ettela'at*, 6, 7, 9, Khordad 1332.
[59] Golmohammadi, pp. 510, 614.   [60] *Khandaniha*, 3 Mordad 1332.
[61] *Ettela'at*, 26 Mordad 1332.
[62] *Goftogo*, Seyyed Mohammad Hoseyn Manzourolajdad, Pa'iz 1379, no. 29.

16

Why did the second coup succeed?

The looming question of why, if Mosaddeq was so popular, the people did not take to the streets and undo the coup, as they had done on 30 Tir and 9 Esfand, may never obtain a comprehensive and satisfactory response. The mere fact that the coup d'état did succeed does not prove that the people had lost faith in the leadership and policies of Mosaddeq and no longer supported him. The ousting of Mosaddeq on 28 Mordad was not the result of a peaceful referendum but of a coup d'état launched because all other political and parliamentary means of replacing him had failed. The success of the second coup may be analysed and explained from five different angles: first, the efficiency and innovativeness of the multi-actor, multi-force coup d'état plan; second, the socio-political and psychological environment and condition which followed the first coup; third, alienation and desertion in Mosaddeq's camp; fourth, the political flaws in the anti-coup forces and in Mosaddeq in particular; and fifth, money matters.

FIRST EXPLANATORY FACTOR: THE EFFICIENCY OF THE MULTI-ACTOR COUP

The first explanatory factor for the success of the primarily home-spun second coup was that it was imaginative, resourceful and original in many aspects. However, it continued to employ the tools and agents that had been clearly articulated and identified in the CIA/SIS-drawn TPAJAX plans. In its initial phase, the coup plan relied on the mobilization of the ruffians and their cortège, giving it the impression of a "popular" uprising of the disinherited. This skilful tactic sowed confusion among the supporters of Mosaddeq. The movement of pro-Shah packs of demonstrators yelling "Long live the Shah" did not give the impression that a military coup was underway. The ruffians' early morning slogans and chants, before they arrived at their designated targets in the heart of the city, were wisely confined to "Long live the Shah" and "Death to Tudeh sympathizers", which did not necessarily reveal their anti-Mosaddeq intentions. To the Tehranis of that day, accustomed as they were to a variety of such demonstrations with chants of "Death to" and "Long live", the walking, running or truck-driving demonstrators were not unusual, causing immediate suspicion and reaction. The thugs demonstrating on 28 Mordad could initially pass for any other group of civilian demonstrators. This created the ideal camouflage for them to attain their targets and once they started attacking their objectives, they intended to be noticed and feared.

Mosaddeq's supporters interpreted the early morning demonstrations as yet another muscle-flexing exercise on the part of pro-Shah and anti-Communist forces and failed to realize that the agitations were a prelude to the overthrow of Mosaddeq. Camouflaging the afternoon military coup in the guise of "another" innocuous street demonstration rendered the second coup difficult to detect and prevent. The innovative plan relied heavily on the element of surprise after the second phase of the coup unfolded and slogans were directed at Mosaddeq. Had the coup forces occupied the sensitive spots of the city in full force or had the tanks suddenly rolled out onto the empty streets and squares of Tehran on the morning of 28 Mordad, the intention and objective of the coup planners would immediately have become manifest. The early appearance of the troops or tanks would have alerted the pro-Mosaddeq forces to the threat of an impending military coup, resulting in their mobilization in defence of Mosaddeq's government.

The gradual injection of the military personnel and the tanks into the "great demonstration" enabled the coup forces to attain their military objectives and impose their hegemony before the Tehranis could fully realize that a military coup d'état was underway. While the "great demonstration" veiled the military coup, a seemingly spontaneous popular movement camouflaged the hired thugs and their retinue who had planned trajectories and assigned targets of attack, destruction and occupation. The resourceful coup, wrapped in layers of subterfuge, befogged the minds of pro-Mosaddeq forces, confusing and finally paralysing them. The Rashidiyan brothers should be credited for correctly identifying the thugs, their retinues and the lumpen-proletariat as the necessary ingredients which would produce a successful regime-change recipe, which the first coup clearly ignored.

The unorganized and decentralized nature of the common people, Mosaddeq's socio-political base, placed them at a major disadvantage when it came to deciphering the events and preparing a timely riposte. The pro-Mosaddeq political organizations also suffered from an inability to understand the 28 Mordad events as they too were taken by surprise. On 9 Esfand the pro-Shah forces did not yet possess a camouflaged military plan following the initially successful demonstration of the thugs. The 28 Mordad plan corrected the error that a demonstration without immediate military support was incapable of overthrowing Mosaddeq. The domestic and foreign coup planners had learnt from their experiences at destabilizing Mosaddeq, while

Why did the second coup succeed?

the same could not be said about the popular pro-Mosaddeq forces, which were devoid of a coordinated and centralized network or command headquarters. The amorphous pro-Mosaddeq forces, coming from different walks of life, were dispersed, disjointed and disconnected. If the eye-witness information and observation of Tehranis scattered throughout the city on the numbers and the deployment of the various packs and columns of thugs coming from South of Tehran had been reported to a centralized headquarters and analysed, a clearer picture of what was in stock for the day might have emerged and perhaps have been responded to in the early hours of the morning.

The second coup plan benefitted from another clever feature, for which the members of the "council of war" are to be credited. This was an integrated operation, relying heavily on the military network and plans that remained intact after the first coup. The uncompromised collaborationist "line commanders" of Operation TPAJAX were also included, contacted and reactivated for the second coup. While the military loyal to Mosaddeq may have believed that the key coup agents had been arrested and therefore that their network had been dismantled or neutralized after 25 Mordad, the facts demonstrated that the military network involved in the 25 Mordad coup was still well connected, potent and operational. The approximately 30 surviving "line commanders" were well positioned within their respective garrisons and properly briefed on what was expected of them. The 28 Mordad coup plan simply grafted the second phase of the original military plan, already built into Operation TPAJAX, on to a demonstration by the thugs and their followers. In retrospect, it can be said that the coup planners relied on the fact that clear alarm signals had been put in place and explained to the team leaders in case the original plan failed – which it did. According to Wilber, this signalling mechanism, which "automatically" called "for movement from one phase to the other", was a major factor in the success of the second coup.[1]

The second military phase of the coup, in case of the failure of the first coup, was known to the "team heads" and the "line commanders". Only the new action date and approximated time of engagement, along with the necessary fine-tunings and calibrations, had to be re-set and coordinated with the planned activity of the ruffians. On the evening of 17 August, the general plan for the "great demonstration" was cobbled together and the date was set by the "council of war" for 19 August. The military "team heads" had to convey the date and any last-minute revisions to the uncompromised "line commanders". Without the active participation and contribution of the military identified and recruited within Operation TPAJAX, the key military objectives necessary for the overthrow of Mosaddeq on 19 August would not have been secured.

---

[1] Wilber, Appendix E, p. 20.

The second coup on 28 Mordad would have remained inconclusive had the ruffians acted alone. Without the CIA's native employees (TPBEDAMN), the collaborationist political groups (SUMKA, Ariya, Zolfaqar, Toilers Party, Society of Moslem Mojaheds) and the secret military organization of the "Devotees of the Shah", the smooth coordination and integration of the parts played by the thugs, the military personnel and the tank units would not have been possible. The crucial role played by this triad – CIA's native lads, collaborationist political groups and "Devotees of the Shah" – on 28 Mordad orchestrated, manipulated and directed the unruly ruffians, who were incapable of self-management, to attain their strategic objectives and, most importantly, to coalesce with the military personnel and tank units. While the civilians of TPBEDAMN provided the necessary leaderships and footwork, the military personnel of Operation TPAJAX provided the much-needed fire-power, without which Mosaddeq's partisans would have been back on the offensive on 29 Mordad just as they had been on 10 Esfand.

Apart from the inventiveness of the second coup in drawing upon different reliable key actors and packing different objectives and targets into one coup plan, the strategy was also original in its flexibility and expectations from its participating agents. Having learnt from the mistakes of the first coup, the foreign and domestic masterminds drafted a loose but well-adapted plan which best employed the skills and capabilities of the different coup agents available and involved. The plan was also perfectly tailored to the behavioural pattern, mood, temperament and character (*kholqiyat*) of each group of participants. The participants were not expected to carry out precise, tightly coordinated or detailed tasks that they were inept at. The ruffians and their entourage were expected only to intimidate and scare Tehranis with their numerical strength and rough demeanour. They were then required to use their muscles and clubs when attacking opponents, their headquarters or government buildings. In the meantime they were supposed to shield and protect the military personnel joining them and the tanks they were to hijack. Finally, they were expected to participate in setting siege to Tehran Radio's Broadcasting Station and Mosaddeq's house.

Whereas the tank units involved in the military aspect of the coup plan had to keep to a loose and approximate timetable, the thugs and the infantry units were free of any such obligations. They were expected neither to be punctual nor to act in a disciplined or coordinated manner. The coup was planned to last the whole day. The elastic, malleable and ad hoc character of the premeditated operation minimized high-risk bungling and botch-ups which could have jeopardized it. Yet the time gap between the decision to execute and the operation date was very tight. The "line commanders" in charge of tanks and military personnel involved in the second coup were only informed on 17, 18 or even early 19 August, and were expected to commence operations at some point on 19 August. The very short preparation lag precipitated a large degree of creative improvisation on the part of the "line commanders" and their subordinate officers, as well as keeping the coup plot a very well-guarded secret.

The seemingly mysterious appearance of a group of officers at the Saltanatabad garrison early on the morning of 19 August (28 Mordad) and the equally enigmatic orders changing the officers on guard during the evening of 18 August (again at Saltanatabad) could be explained as the creative initiative of the collaborationist military officers working under the stress of a very tight schedule. Reflecting on the lessons learnt from the coup d'état in Iran, Wilber wrote: "In some cases it is possible to arrange for the replacement and reassignment of officers who are in the wrong position from our point of view. The placing of the right man in the right spot at the right time is of course the most important factor in all military operations".[2] The military network established by the coup planners seemed successful at placing anti-Mosaddeq and pro-Shah officers at sensitive theatres of operations on 28 Mordad. It seemed equally successful at distancing pro-Mosaddeq officers from those same theatres of operation at decisive moments. The experiences of Major Akbar Zand and Lieutenant Houshang Qorbannejad (commander of tank Squadron C) provide examples of how effectively the coup planners were able to move officers around through assignments and re-assignments, pulling them out of and pushing them into the theatre of operations so as to assure success. Having the right pro-Shah and anti-Mosaddeq officers in the right place at the right time played a key role in the success of the morning operations.

SECOND EXPLANATORY FACTOR: THE REIGN OF CONFUSION

The second factor explaining the success of the 19 August coup can be sought in the socio-political and psychological environment which followed the first coup. The political atmosphere of limbo and uncertainty between Sunday 16 August and Wednesday 19 August worked to the advantage of the coup forces and the disadvantage of the pro-Mosaddeq forces. During those three interim days, the Iranian state came under a volley of unprecedented shocks, rendering it almost dysfunctional. A coup d'état was foiled, the Shah fled the country and the parliament was dissolved. Mosaddeq's government, recovering from a coup, was divided on the highly sensitive issue of how to proceed politically in the absence of the Shah. Competing political forces within Mosaddeq's government and in society spoke and acted irresponsibly and recklessly, while the news circulated that the Shah had appointed Zahedi as Prime Minister and that Mosaddeq's rule was illegal.

The rapid pace of unusual political events disoriented the ordinary people, who witnessed a gradual social slippage towards increasing disorder,

[2] Wilber, Appendix E, p. 13.

unpredictability and even chaos. To the common people, the string of events in Tehran demonstrated that the state was out of control. While the opponents of the Shah, of all shades and colours, celebrated his departure in demonstrations, poured invectives on him and his Court in their fiery speeches, called him a traitor and a house-servant of the British, chanted "Death to the treacherous Shah" in their marches, demanded that he be deposed, called for republics of all sorts, tore down the statutes of him and his father and clashed violently among themselves, insecurity and anxiety rose among ordinary Tehranis, irrespective of their political tendencies.

During these messy days "members" of a bogus Tudeh Party were also at work in Tehran, intentionally provoking a state of social hysteria and frenzy. These fake Tudeh Party members were CIA *agents provocateurs* who were psychologically preparing the people not to react against the overthrow of Mosaddeq on the forthcoming Wednesday. The CIA operatives Keyvani and Jalali, along with their band of hired hands, were following instructions from Roosevelt and Carroll.[3] Under the guise of Tudeh Party members, the gang of Keyvani and Jalali implanted the "red scare" in the hearts of Tehranis by looting and smashing shops in the city centre.[4] The simple message of the CIA's *agents provocateurs* to the Tehranis was that should the Communists – the real enemies of the Shah – come to power, such gruesome acts of vandalism would become everyday occurrences. Keyvani and Jalali also sought to convey the old message that Mosaddeq's government did not wish to control the Tudeh Party as it was in league with it. The theme of Mosaddeq as the Trojan Horse of the Communists was the leitmotif of the coup planners and was strongly conveyed to the ordinary people in order to lure them away from defending Mosaddeq on Wednesday.

Between Sunday and Wednesday the non-militant partisans of Mosaddeq – the real backbone of his authority – came under great psychological pressure. Those who admired their Prime Minister for his efforts on oil nationalization, the sense of national pride he had generated, his unauthoritarian and democratic politics and his personal honesty and uprightness, and yet who were *not* strongly opposed to the young Shah – who himself was very different from what he became after the coup – or *did not* oppose a constitutional monarchy, were torn apart, neutralized and pushed to the side-lines. The uncontrolled excitement and excesses of militant opponents of the Shah worried the common people. The successful operation of the CIA's *agents provocateurs* added to the misgivings of the common people about an unpredictable future without a visible central authority enforcing law and order. In view of the magnitude, weight and speed of the events between Sunday and Wednesday, the common people who traditionally supported Mosaddeq by taking to the streets and spontaneously demonstrating in his support became more and more estranged from what was going on in the streets. During these days, the

---

[3] Wilber, p. 59.   [4] Wilber, p. 63.

common supporters of Mosaddeq were becoming alienated from the street politics of anti-Shah militants and not necessarily from Mosaddeq. The sense of security and solidarity felt by Mosaddeq's supporters suddenly gave way to a debilitating state of insecurity, undermining their resistance and resolve. The political dichotomy and contradiction between the Shah and Mosaddeq, as highlighted between Sunday and Wednesday by the opponents and supporters of the Shah, unsettled and confused a good number who, in the past, had not seen their support for Mosaddeq as opposition to the Shah.

The indecision, uncertainty and inertia of Mosaddeq's popular support base were exacerbated by the Prime Minister's silence after the first coup attempt. Neither a public statement explaining his thoughts or position on the current political crisis nor a public communique on what he thought should be done came from 109 Kakh Street, the Prime Minister's office. Mosaddeq fell silent when he should have spoken. The *pishva* (or leader), as Mosaddeq was called, either felt no pressing need for a public address or was no longer in the mood to provide leadership for his followers. At his trial, Mosaddeq recalled that those days were extremely busy with just managing the country. It seems as though Mosaddeq feared that a directive inviting the people to take to the streets would have caused a bloodbath.

Mosaddeq was not oblivious to the impact of political chaos and its negative consequences on ordinary Tehranis. From Tuesday afternoon (18 August) Mosaddeq's government abruptly took a tough stand against lawlessness in Tehran. Following two days of lawlessness the government decided to impose public peace with all its might. As positive as this firm position was in assuaging the fears and insecurities of the common people, Mosaddeq's popular base, it had an adverse effect on the hardcore pro-Mosaddeq and anti-Shah militants. The government's decision on Tuesday played right into the hands of the coup planners as its effect was not enough to sway the common people to react immediately to the coup d'état on Wednesday; yet it certainly discouraged the hardcore militants from coming out in force against the anti-Mosaddeq insurgents. The police communiqué which appeared in the newspapers of Tuesday 18 August warned that any activity that disturbed the public peace would be severely dealt with by the forces of law and order.

Mosaddeq's government forbade demonstrations in the hope of keeping Tudeh Party sympathizers off the streets. When on Tuesday evening the Tudeh Party sympathizers came out demonstrating on Eslambol and Naderi Streets as well as on Sepah Square, military units led by collaborationist pro-Shah officers clashed with them forcefully, giving them a beating and dispersing them. The violent clashes boosted the morale of the pro-Shah military personnel, who were said to be angry at the anti-Shah provocations of the Tudeh sympathizers. The harsh repression sent a clear signal that street clashes were no longer tolerated by the government. But the clampdown was also interpreted by Tudeh sympathizers as Mosaddeq's new policy of containing and crushing the Tudeh Party.

The violent confrontations of the Tuesday evening, which lasted until midnight, impacted upon the state of mind of the Tudeh rank and file on the following day. The Tudeh sympathizers who may have come on to the streets against the thugs, even without a directive from their superiors, were intimidated and scared. They were reluctant to be beaten up ruthlessly again by what they believed was Mosaddeq's army. The argument has been made that the first stage of Mosaddeq's overthrow actually started with the assault of the army on the Tudeh demonstrators.[5]

Mosaddeq's instruction to both Kalil Maleki and Daryoush Foruhar to keep their members off the streets helped empty the streets of Tehran of Mosaddeq's important fighting forces. The militant partisans of Maleki's Third Force Party and Foruhar's Iranian People's Party constituted an important organized assault team engaged in street clashes whenever there was a need to come out in support of Mosaddeq. Mosaddeq's instructions to Maleki and Foruhar, which were intended to reduce political tensions on the streets of Tehran, in effect prevented the pro-Mosaddeq partisans of these two parties from actively opposing the ruffians on Wednesday and perhaps foiling the second coup. The events of Tuesday evening ensured the absence of organized and militant pro-Mosaddeq or anti-Shah forces on the streets of Tehran and effectively emptied the streets for the thugs to take over on the Wednesday.

On Wednesday a good number of Mosaddeq's supporters chose the sidewalks. The growing public weariness caused by social unrest and uncertainty between the two coups, along with a growing sense of suspicion about the long-term objectives of the Tudeh Party, gnawed at the resolve of Mosaddeq's popular base. The neutralization and inactivity of Mosaddeq's mass supporters throughout 28 Mordad was the best-case scenario the coup planners could hope for. While Mosaddeq's combative supporters were muzzled on Wednesday, the zealous pro-Shah soldiers, policemen and officers were excited and on the offensive to expel Mosaddeq and bring back the Shah.

THIRD EXPLANATORY FACTOR: DESERTION IN MOSADDEQ'S CAMP AND THE PRIME MINISTER'S STUBBORNNESS

Whereas on 30 Tir (21 July 1952), after Mosaddeq's resignations and Qavam's appointment as Prime Minister, a broad wave of instinctive popular support returned the absent Mosaddeq to power, a year later some of those key national figures who were instrumental in supporting Mosaddeq were keenly lending a hand to his opponents. The fact that Mosaddeq's old allies had gradually turned into his bitter enemies had emboldened those who were never fond of him but had been too intimidated by his popular support to

---

[5] *Ferdowsi*, 3 Shahrivar 1332.

oppose him. By the summer of 1953, some of the major political and religious forces which had systematically supported Mosaddeq in the parliament and on the streets and had fended off threats to his government from the day he became Prime Minister, had not only withdrawn their support but also openly opposed his government.

Since October 1949, when he was in exile, Ayatollah Kashani had thrown in his full political and religious weight behind the candidacy of Mosaddeq's National Front members to the 16th parliament. When Kashani triumphantly returned to Tehran in June 1950, he was already a member of parliament. Mosaddeq, the deputy from Tehran with the highest vote, and members of the National Front were all at the airport to greet him. Kashani was a public figure with an impressively wide social, political and religious network. His influence was not limited to Qanatabadi, Navvab Safavi or Baqa'i's political organizations – he had connections with politicians from a wide spectrum of tendencies and allegiances, from royalists and anti-Communist Anglophiles, to sympathizers and members of the Communist Tudeh Party. Apart from Ayatollah Borujerdi, he had close ties with all other prominent religious figures, including Ayatollah Behbahani in Tehran and Ayatollah Khonsari in Qom. The assassination of Prime Minister Razmara on 7 March 1951 by Khalil Tahmasebi (a member of Navvab Safavi's "Devotees of Islam") was at the behest of Kashani.[6] One week later, the Iranian Parliament ratified the nationalization of the oil industry. When on 27 April 1951 Mosaddeq became Prime Minister, he hurried to Kashani's house to consult the Ayatollah and subsequently carried Kashani with him to the pinnacle of power.

The exact date and reason for the rift, estrangement and eventual enmity between Mosaddeq's old allies and the Prime Minister are hard to pinpoint. Except for Mozaffar Baqa'i, whose intentions for joining Mosaddeq were rather dubious from the beginning, Mosaddeq's other allies seem to have joined forces with him to ensure free elections to the parliament and, most importantly, to nationalize the oil and chase away British colonialism. Baqa'i seems to have been primarily concerned with his own power and position and is said to have been intent on setting Kashani against Mosaddeq so as to pave the road for his own political ascendency.[7] After he became Prime Minister, Mosaddeq refused to base his government on the coalition of forces in the National Front. Abdol-Qadir Azad, a vocal member of the 15th Majles and an influential member of the National Front, was the first politician to object to Mosaddeq's obstinacy in acting independently of his old allies. When Mosaddeq refused to give two portfolios in his government to members

---

[6] M. Hoseyni, *Khaterat Mohammad Mehdi Abdekhoda'i* (Tehran-e Markaza-e Asnad-e Enqelab-e Eslami, 1379), p. 88; Be Ravayat Asnad, *Rowhaniy-e Mobarez Ayatollah Seyyed Abolqasem Kashani*, vol. 1, p. 401.

[7] Be Ravayat-e Asnad, *Rowhaniy-e Mobarez Ayatollah Seyyed Abolqasem Kashani*, vol. 1, p. 230.

of Azad's Independence Party, Azad became the first of the apostles to turn his back on Mosaddeq and join the opposition camp.

While Mosaddeq rejected the demands of his old political allies for a share or a say in his government, he was much more lenient towards Kashani's claims. The sensitive position of the head of the Religious Endowments (*owqaf*), which had a religious significance, went to Mahmud Shervin, a very close associate of Kashani. It would be safe to assume that when Mosaddeq began his government, he gave Kashani the impression that he was more equal than others. As long as the Ayatollah benefitted from a privileged position, he remained a very close ally of Mosaddeq, without whom Mosaddeq might have either voluntarily resigned or been removed from power well before 19 August 1953. It would be fair to say that Mosaddeq almost relegated the internal affairs of the country to Kashani while he focused his attention on the oil issue and the protracted negotiations, correspondences and meetings with various British and American delegations that it entailed. In Mosaddeq's absence on the national scene, the political and organizational backbone of his movement, namely the National Front, became crippled by internal rivalries and jealousies. The domestic political vacuum which Mosaddeq's focus on the oil nationalization issue and his subsequent international official trips created was filled by Kashani, whose affable character made him the arbiter and decision-maker on key domestic policies.

On 6 October 1951, accompanied by some key politicians and members of both the Senate (upper house) and Majles (the lower house), Mosaddeq flew to New York to address the Security Council of the United Nations. He left behind hard feelings, distrust and rumours among his old allies and members of the National Front. The fact that Ahmad Matin-Daftari and Saham-Soltan Bayat, Mosaddeq's close relatives, were accompanying him on this trip as representatives of the Senate (upper house), while Hoseyn Makki was not in attendance, created long-lasting resentment and bitterness. Some National Front figures (such as Ha'erizadeh) were opposed to Matin-Daftari accompanying the Iranian delegation and criticized the "exclusion" of Makki.[8] This occasion provided grounds for Makki, a figure highly popular among the people, and a loyal and old supporter of Mosaddeq and the Secretary (*dabir*) of the National Front, to feel estranged from Mosaddeq. Makki was known as the selfless soldier of the oil nationalization movement: he needed a pat on the back. Mosaddeq seemed too preoccupied with oil matters or too insensitive to such seemingly insignificant issues. While he energetically pursued the oil negotiations, for one reason or another his formerly staunch political followers became distanced from, if not hurt by, him. As a result of what Makki perceived to be his exclusion, he moved one step away from Mosaddeq and two steps closer to Kashani. Possessing excellent human relations and grasping Makki's discontent, Kashani moved to appease him

---

[8] Safari, p. 534.

and save face for him by publishing a letter in the newspapers. In his letter Kashani praised Makki for his contribution to the oil nationalization movement and claimed that Makki's presence was much more important in Tehran, stating that it was the Ayatollah who had wished him to stay behind.[9]

The elections to the 17th Parliament strengthened the political position of Kashani within the National Front, further fuelled the rivalries and jealousies within the organization and brought about the main cause of the rift between Mosaddeq and Kashani. The election campaign and the jockeying for power among the candidates began in December 1951. According to certain accounts, in order to prevent infighting and individual jockeying for power within the National Front during the elections, the members of the National Front accepted Kashani's leadership and agreed to comply with his directives on the fielding of candidates.[10] In view of the vast political prerogatives extended to Kashani, it was not surprising that at the end of the election there was a general perception that Kashani had sought to guarantee the election of his very close associates, frustrating other National Front members who were also seeking election. Kashani was still Mosaddeq's staunch ally, and his patronizing interventions in favour of some and against others gave the impression that Mosaddeq tolerated and supported cronyism in elections. Accounts proliferated of Kashani's meddling in the elections and the increasing roles of his sons, Abolma'ali, Mohammad and Mostafa, designating themselves as candidates for election, while benefitting from their father's patronage system. During this period the peddling of influence by Kashani and his close associates became so rife that Amir-Teymur Kalali, Mosaddeq's Minister of Interior, resigned. According to Amir-Teymur, his resignation was due to the fact that not only had he been under pressure from Kashani to facilitate the election of Shams Qanatabadi (the Ayatollah's right-hand man), but that even Mosaddeq seemed to be nudging him to reach a compromise with Kashani.[11] Reports of Kashani's meddling in the election was so rife that Makki, a close friend of the Ayatollah, began criticizing the extent of Kashani's patronage system during the elections to the 17th Majles. What had been promised to be a free election was turning out to be not so free and the press were holding Mosaddeq responsible. Mosaddeq seemed to be paying a heavy price for keeping the friendship and support of Kashani. Mosaddeq's misgivings about the consequences of Kashani's excesses during the elections should be considered the beginning of the rift between the two men.

The departure of Qavam and the return of Mosaddeq after 21 July 1952 (30 Tir) could be considered a threshold in the political balance of power

---

[9] Ettela'at, 17 Mehr 1331.
[10] A. Maleki, *Tarikhcheh Jebhey-e Melli* (Tehran: Taban, n.d), p. 34.
[11] H. Lajevardi, *Khaterat Amir Teymur Kalali* (Bethesda, Markaz Motale'at Khavarmiyaneh Daneshgah Harvard, 1977), pp. 76–77.

between Kashani and Mosaddeq. Kashani justifiably believed that he had played a crucial role in returning Mosaddeq to power, and therefore felt that he should be consulted more directly in running state affairs. At this point Kashani must have thought that he was almost the senior partner, and he certainly began acting that way. However, Mosaddeq felt that if he consulted with Kashani and other key political allies, it was out of common courtesy and not because he was obliged to. Mosaddeq was neither an organizational person nor was he inclined to traditional patron–client relations. Open intervention, intercession and meddling in the affairs of the state by "irresponsible" personalities irritated him. The first signs of open disagreement began when Mosaddeq introduced his new government to the parliament on 27 July 1952. Kashani was opposed to the appointment of Hoseyn Navvab as Minister of Foreign Affairs and to Ali-Akbar Akhavi as Minister of the Economy. Kashani, Baqa'i and Makki were also opposed to the appointment of General Ahmad Vosouq as the Undersecretary of the Ministry of War.[12] Even though, in a letter, Mosaddeq brushed off Kashani's objections to his appointees, both Akhavi and Navvab were forced to resign under pressure from Kashani.

Mosaddeq's request for extraordinary legislative powers (*ekhtiyarat*) from the Majles to expedite the plans and policies of his governments for the duration of six months, and its subsequent ratification by the Majles on 3 August 1952, strengthened his hand at the cost of the parliament. However, once Kashani was elected to the position of Speaker of the Majles on 8 August, he found an important platform from which he could challenge Mosaddeq's power. On 8 January 1953, when Mosaddeq renewed his demand for the extension of the extraordinary legislative powers by another year, Kashani's opposition became open. Kashani and his allies – including Baqa'i, Makki and Ha'erizadeh – now opposed Mosaddeq on the grounds that as true defenders of Iran's constitution they were rallying against what amounted to a *dictatorship*. The ratification of the extension of the extraordinary legislative powers on 19 January 1953 by the Iranian Parliament further empowered Mosaddeq while infuriating Kashani and his allies. The fact that the Iranian Parliament sided with Mosaddeq over the enabling act deeply disturbed Kashani and his allies, who thought they controlled the Majles.

From 19 January, Mosaddeq's old and influential allies were on a collision course with the Prime Minister. As the opposition to Mosaddeq spread from the traditional Anglophiles, conservatives and royalists to his old friends who possessed some popular support, instead of realizing the gravity of the situation Mosaddeq dug in his heels and insisted on his old ways. In one of their last official meetings, on 28 January 1953, when attempts were made to mediate between the two estranged leaders, Mosaddeq informed Kashani:

---

[12] M. A. Movahhed, *Khabe Ashofteh Naft* (Tehran: Karnameh, 1378), vol. 2, p. 558.

"This is my mode of operation. I will continue to work if you wish, but if you do not wish me to continue, I will go and I will bow to the wish of the parliament. But we have to be careful and avoid chaos in the country".[13]

Just as Mosaddeq seemed insensitive to the pragmatic political consequences of his old friends turning into his bitter enemies, he seemed equally oblivious to the importance of keeping the young Shah on his side. Immediately after the events of 9 Esfand (28 February 1953) Mosaddeq lost all trust in the Shah, becoming convinced that the Shah not only opposed him but also that he wanted him dead. Mosaddeq incorrectly believed that the Shah was responsible for the events of that day and that he had plotted it in advance.[14] The old politician took the events so personally that from that moment on he refused to meet with the Shah. As much as the young Shah, who until the last days before the coup was not at ease with antagonising Mosaddeq, tried to meet with the Prime Minister, Mosaddeq adamantly refused. Sulking and hurt though he was, his refusal to meet the Shah was a political mistake of dire national consequences. Gholam-Hoseyn Mosaddeq, his son, recounted how the Shah desperately sought to see Mosaddeq and even offered to come to his house. Mosaddeq's curt response to the Shah, through his own son, was that "it would be below the dignity of his Majesty to come to our house".[15] Mosaddeq's stubbornness reflected his lack of political pragmatism. Refusing to see the Shah while his new enemies were presenting themselves as the defenders of the Shah's rights against his autocratic Prime Minister pushed the Shah into the arms of his enemies. The new opposition to Mosaddeq, led by Kashani and Baqa'i, was astutely trying to present Mosaddeq's relation towards the Shah as an antagonistic one, claiming that he wanted to overthrow the monarchy. Mosaddeq could have talked to the Shah, exposing their lies. Had Mosaddeq been sensitive to the clear signals of support and solidarity that the Shah was sending him in May 1953 through his close emissaries such as Qa'em-Maqam Rafi', and had he been less stubborn (or even paranoid) towards the Shah, he might have been able to prevent the hesitant Shah from entering into the covenant that brought about the coup against him.[16]

FOURTH EXPLANATORY FACTOR: MOSADDEQ'S IDIOSYNCRASIES

The success of the coup was partially attributable to the political and military shortcomings of those forces that could have prevented the coup, including Mosaddeq and the Tudeh Party. Yet Mosaddeq's burden of responsibility is more significant as he was in power and therefore legally responsible. The assumption that Mosaddeq, the legalist and non-revolutionary, would not

---

[13] *Ettela'at*, 12 Esfand 1331.
[14] G. Mosaddeq, *Dar Kenar Pedaram* (Tehran: Rasa, 1369), p. 65.
[15] G. Mosaddeq, p. 66.   [16] Rahnema, p. 941; *Ettela'at*, 7 and 10 Ordibehest 1332.

call on the people to take to the streets and resist the coup must have given the coup planners some degree of assurance that if they could put on a quick and strong show of force, occupying the city centre and key strategic targets, they would attain their objective before the people could spontaneously organize and re-take the city. Mosaddeq could have sent a radio message inviting the people to come on to the streets. He did not, and he was often reproached for this by his young and zealous supporters at the time. Those of his supporters who expected him to confront the coup with equal force expected something of him that was not in his nature.

For Mosaddeq, political differences – and even conflicts – had to be settled through disputation and negotiation, not through physical violence. Mosaddeq firmly believed that calling on the people to resist the coup d'état would have caused a civil war and a bloodbath. He and his close political advisors did not wish to have blood on their hands.[17] At his trial, Mosaddeq said, "the country develops in the shadow of freedom, not of the club".[18] The coup planners, by contrast, had accepted the possibility of civil war and were prepared to shed blood in order to oust Mosaddeq.[19] The diametrically opposed ethical position of Mosaddeq and his antagonists in relation to the price of political power placed the coup forces in a clearly superior military position. Mosaddeq believed that the responsibility for enforcing law and order in the city was the job of the police and, in the last recourse, the military, but not of the people. Mosaddeq's silence between the confusing days of the first and second coups undoubtedly disoriented his partisans. The country seemed to have no one at the helm: his calm demeanour gave the impression of a hesitant or even a reluctant Prime Minister incapable of making important decisions. For Mosaddeq, the days after the first coup may have been business as usual; the Tehranis did not feel the same way.

In retrospect, Mosaddeq's military appointees can be seen not to have been the most suitable officers for a time of acute political crisis. Some of them were honest and well-educated men, but they did not possess the firmness, resolve or courage required to make difficult decisions at critical times. According to the coup planners, Riyahi (the Chief of Staff) was weak "from a military point of view" as he lacked "command and combat experience".[20] In their assessment of the military capacities of the "hostile government" which they wished to overthrow, the coup planners concluded that Riyahi "and most of his staff had been French-trained and were very thorough in staff work and very green in the field".[21] Even though the pro-Mosaddeq "Nationalist Officers Organization" had suggested Lieutenant General Mahmud Amini, a seasoned military officer, for the post of Chief of Staff, Mosaddeq had decided

---

[17] Nejati (Goftogo ba Ostad Doctor Gholamhoseyn Sadiqi), p. 537.
[18] Bozorgmehr, p. 205. [19] Wilber, Appendix E, p. 20. [20] Wilber, Appendix E, p. 9.
[21] Wilber, Appendix E, p. 9.

to appoint Riyahi.[22] At the time of the two coups, there were only a few military commanders appointed by Mosaddeq who had the nerve, boldness and conviction to rise to difficult military situations requiring judicious and audacious combat decisions. The murder of Lieutenant General Mahmud Afshartus by a group of collaborationist officers and civilians in late April 1953 clearly indicated that the appointment of a forceful, energetic and patriotic military officer to the important position of Chief of Police could not be tolerated by the pro-coup forces as it seriously jeopardized their future plans.

One day before he went missing, Afshartus had informed the heads of police that he possessed a complete list of those officers who were spying for the Americans. He threatened that before the week was over the traitors would be imprisoned or executed.[23] While military appointments that were inappropriate from a professional and technical point of view by Mosaddeq could be one factor explaining the success of the coup d'état, the other – and probably more important one – relates to Mosaddeq's poor judgement of character. Mosaddeq refused to take sound advice about the unreliability of certain key military personnel and continued to follow his misplaced conviction in the trustworthiness of those who ultimately betrayed him. At the end of 28 Mordad, Mosaddeq's unwillingness to call on the people, the inaptitude and incompetence of some of his military personnel, along with the treachery of others, sealed the success of the second coup.

The first failed coup d'état sent the clear signal that a hard nucleus of military opposition to Mosaddeq had been formed within the army and police. Furthermore, it demonstrated that this insurgent nucleus had not only plotted but had also attempted the coup; this should have shed light on its organizational capabilities, and, most importantly, on the possibility of foreign support for the coup. The lenient and almost lethargic reaction of Mosaddeq, the judiciary system and his military appointees to the perpetrators of the first coup clearly manifested the fault-lines of Mosaddeq's liberalism when faced with an aggressive and determined foe. Mosaddeq's legalism rendered his enemies ever more bold and aggressive. The laxity with which the perpetrators of Afshartus' murder were treated repeated itself after the first coup. In the absence of a serious crack-down on the obvious culprits, not only did the coup network remain almost intact, but the perpetrators were given a second chance – an opportunity usually denied in coups d'état.

Mosaddeq was not an expert on coups d'état, but his military and state security appointees should have taken all possible precautions by taking the initiative, rather than passing every decision by Mosaddeq for his approval. Mosaddeq, his military staff, his administration and his followers were completely taken off guard as they did not expect a second coup in such a

[22] Mossavar Rahmani, p. 216. [23] Mossavar Rahmani, p. 387.

short time, nor one so well-organized and so well camouflaged. Mosaddeq and his military and security apparatus did not take into serious account the information that was being provided by the arrested officers involved in the first coup. The fact that the military's legal officers were put in charge of the interrogations demonstrates Mosaddeq's legalistic approach to the first coup. Furthermore, Mosaddeq's police and security apparatuses were so well infiltrated at the most vital positions that the flow of information leading to firm action became impossible.

On the evening of August 17, while the legal office in Mosaddeq's military and security establishment moved at a snail's pace to clumsily interrogate the captured officers, process the information gleaned and make further arrests, the plotters were planning their second modified plan. Faced with the perpetrators of the failed coup, Mosaddeq's government acted cautiously and according to the fine letter of the law. The coup-makers, however, rapidly prepared for a second lightening assault. The time lag between the evening of 17 August when the date for the second coup was decided and the execution date (early morning of 19 August) was less than 36 hours, minimizing the risk of any breach in confidentiality and secretiveness on the part of the plotters.

Mosaddeq's indecision, wavering and procrastination between the first and the second coups had their roots in his state of perplexity over the departure of the Shah and were aggravated by his own political ethics, his legalism, his pacifism and his pre-modern gentlemanly code of conduct. Politically, Mosaddeq held dear certain fixed principles, which were compatible so long as he could serve as the Prime Minister of a constitutional monarch, but which became difficult to reconcile as soon as he found himself confronted with an absent monarch whom he wished to protect, yet who himself had dismissed him and fled. Mosaddeq was committed to Iran's constitutional monarchy and loyal to the young Shah, who was supposed to reign and not to rule. During these four crucial days, Mosaddeq was juggling hard to protect the crown of the absentee man who had unsuccessfully tried to fire him through a coup. What made Mosaddeq special as a politician was a stubbornness rooted in his sense of self-righteousness. In the political realm this quality was both a virtue and a vice. His inflexibility did alienate many of his friends, but it also gave him the aura of a resolute quixotic national hero in search of Iran's independence.

On the morning of 16 August, members of Mosaddeq's cabinet and inner circle were requested to gather at the Prime Minister's home/office to assess the previous night's coup. Among those who arrived were Fatemi and Haqshenas, who had been arrested and mistreated that night and who were only released after the coup flopped. According to Mehdi Azar, Mosaddeq's Minister of Education, most of those present were extremely upset about the coup and demanded rapid and harsh reprisals. Seyfollah Mo'azzami argued that those directly involved in the coup, such as Nasiri, should be executed lest the threat that the Shah would try to oust the government again in the future should linger.[24] As the idea of executing those who had been involved in the coup was floated, Mosaddeq, wearing his traditional cloak (*aba*) and standing in the doorway, asked, "Gentlemen, according to which legal article can we execute these people? Yes they intended to commit a crime, but the crime has not occurred. Where in the world does the intention to commit a crime count as a crime? And therefore how can we execute these people for the crime that did not materialize?"[25] When those present insisted on their position, Mosaddeq turned to his Ministers of Justice and Interior and said: "Please find one article in our laws which enables me to arrest these individuals let alone execute them and I will comply with your wishes". That was the end of the meeting. Later that day, the two ministers reported that Mosaddeq was right and that there was no law that permitted the execution of those who had attempted the coup.[26] Mosaddeq's ethical legalism after the first coup was what distinguished him from other politicians, but it was also what precipitated his downfall.

Mosaddeq's democratic inclinations were primarily a product of his premodern ethical politics. These same ethical politics, without which he could not function in the long run, deprived him of the ability to exercise any long-term pragmatism, a necessity for modern-day political survival. Mosaddeq's in-built ethical compass in politics almost automatically "corrected" or "neutralized" his forays into political expediency. No sooner would he demonstrate political pragmatism, as in his early alliance with Ayatollah Kashani and the peripheral political organizations around Kashani such as the "Devotees of Islam", than he would pull the plug on his opporune political move, alienating the "real politicians" such as Kashani and Baqa'i. In times of tense political disorder and strife such as 30 Tir, Mosaddeq's ethical politics could paralyse him. When a decision needed to be made which could involve the possibility of violence and death, Mosaddeq's humane calculus could not compute how the sacrifice of a few could be worth the saving of the many. Callous feasibility analysis had no place in his ethical politics.

At decisive and critical historical moments, leaders may have a difficult time properly gauging the voice of the people. Another kind of a politician, different from Mosaddeq, might have heard the people's message after 16 August as one demanding the execution of those involved in the coup, the deposing of the Shah, the arming of the people, the proclamation of a republic and assuring the security of the young republic through a secret alliance with the Tudeh Party. Even though the coup planners had succeeded in intimidating the sympathizers of the Tudeh Party on the evening of 27 Mordad, had the party leadership called upon its members and sympathizers – which it did not – their intervention might have changed the course of events. But, once

---

[24] Mehdi Azar, Iranian Oral History Collection, Harvard University, Transcript 2, pp. 14–15.
[25] Mehdi Azar, Iranian Oral History Collection, Harvard University, Transcript 2, p. 15.
[26] Mehdi Azar, Iranian Oral History Collection, Harvard University, Transcript 2, pp. 15–16.

again, Mosaddeq was not the man to break his oath to the Shah, renege on his firm belief in a constitutional monarchy, or seek a behind-the-scenes deal with the Tudeh Party and jeopardize the national sovereignty of his country in the name of "hearing the message of the people". It is highly possible that even though Mosaddeq's opponents kept hammering at the fact that he was paving the path for a Communist takeover, they knew full well that Mosaddeq's ethical politics would prevent him from any collusion with the Tudeh Party, reassuring them of their success on 28 Mordad.

When the stakes were so high, as they were in oil-rich and geo-strategically important Iran, Mosaddeq's political propriety in the midst of a serious confrontation was construed as wide-eyed naivety, weakness and indecisiveness, thus rendering his enemies more audacious and bold. The tedious legalism which Mosaddeq demonstrated after 30 Tir, 9 Esfand, and the murder of Afshartus and the first coup sent a simple message to his enemies: anyone challenging him, shooting innocent people in the process, besieging the Prime Minister's house and breaking down his door, murdering his Chief of Police, and seeking to arrest him and members of his government, could count on effectively going unpunished or spending at most a few months in prison before being released. Mosaddeq's ethical politics minimized the risk of rebellion against him. Yet Mosaddeq's principles of selflessness, honesty and patriotism enhanced his popularity and became the best guarantee against a real popular and spontaneous movement against him. It was Mosaddeq's unwavering domestic popularity that forced the conspirators to rely on generous financial incentives and promises of political power and career advancement to certain segments of those who needed to be persuaded to rebel against him. The coup d'état of 28 Mordad against Mosaddeq, plotted, supported, perpetrated and partially executed by the US and British governments, was the best testimony to the hard fact that in the absence of forceful extra-legal means, as Seyyed Zia had astutely observed, there was no immediate alternative to removing the Prime Minister from power.

FIFTH EXPLANATORY FACTOR: MONEY MATTERS

Inciting segments of the population against Mosaddeq and securing their participation in the premeditated plan of the "council of war" for 28 Mordad required financial, ideological and religious incentives. As Western officials were forced to report on the political realities in Iran after 28 Mordad, Mosaddeq was a highly popular leader at the time and after the coup. He had become the symbol of the oil nationalization movement, resisted the bullying British and was viewed by Iranians as a true patriot and anti-colonialist. His showdown with the British and his exercise of national self-determination through internationally recognized institutions had returned to Iranians a deep sense of pride, self-respect and dignity. Mosaddeq and his administration were known for their incorruptibility and honesty in a country where notables seldom differentiated between state coffers and their own pockets, and when the occasion rose did not necessarily turn down sweet offers from foreign powers.

The British Memorandum, written on 2 September 1953 (exactly two weeks after the coup) clearly stated that "the success of the coup" was due to three factors, one of which was that "plenty of money was made available to carry it out".[27] As would be expected in a highly secretive affair such as a coup d'état promoted and orchestrated by a foreign country against another sovereign state, no one asked for receipts and no one provided them. There are no accounts or debit and credit columns indicating who exactly spent what and who received what. The British Memorandum indicates two points. First, money was used in staging the "great demonstration"; and second, the sums were high according to the standard of covert operations at the time. These high sums could have been used for bribes, hiring hands and services, and purchasing necessary material, hardware and equipment to assure the smooth flow of the operation. The exact sum spent by the foreign masterminds directly involved in the coup d'état of 19 August 1953 is therefore subject to much speculation.

According to one account, "one hundred thousand dollars was put at the disposal of four plotters: the two Rashidiyan brothers, Malekeh E'tezadi, who supervised some of the Southern Tehran houses of ill repute, and Ayatollah Qanatabadi".[28] Ayatollah Qanatabadi is none other than Shams Qanatabadi, a low-ranking cleric and Ayatollah Kashani's right-hand man at the time. It is reported that "around $100,000" was "paid for the mob in the final days".[29] Some "$900,000" is said to have "remained unspent from the originally appointed funds" and these "were handed over to the Zahedi regime".[30] These figures do add up to the $1,000,000 budget approved by the Director of the CIA on 4 April 1953 "to be used by the Tehran Station in any way that would bring about the fall of Mossadeq".[31] There is no indication of how much was expended from the sum of $150,000 budgeted "to create, extend, and enhance public hostility and distrust and fear of Mossadeq and his government".[32]

According to Felix Aqayan, a member of the Shah's close entourage and privy to the murmurs, facts and gossip of the Court, on 24 Mordad 1953 four suitcases full of Dollars were handed over by CIA operatives in Tehran to four individuals: Zahedi, Gilanshah, Fardust and Nasiri.[33] Aqayan maintained that these suitcases loaded with Dollars were for the expenses of the coup d'état. Even though between 24 and 27 Mordad, Zahedi, Nasiri, Gilanshah and their associates had plenty of time to convert their Dollars into the national currency, it has been widely rumoured that on 28 Mordad Dollar notes were being extensively passed around in Tehran. The common phrase

---

[27] FRUS, vol. x, p. 786.   [28] Dorril, p. 592.   [29] Dorril, p. 594.   [30] Dorril, p. 594.
[31] Wilber, pp. 3, 18, 19.   [32] Wilber, Appendix B, p. 15.
[33] Felix Aghayan, Iranian Oral History Collection, Harvard University, Transcript 1, pp. 4–5.

"Behbahani's dollars", heard during the days before and after 28 Mordad, referred to Ayatollah Behbahani's Dollar-denominated hand-outs to the roughneck leaders who participated in the "great demonstration" of 28 Mordad.[34] Even Mohammad Daftari admits that the throngs that poured out from Southern Tehran were induced by the money spent by the Americans, though he believes that the sums were not very significant.[35]

Kennett Love, who was in Tehran until 25 August, recalled that immediately after the second coup "large amounts of American currency began to flow into the foreign exchange market". He maintains that these sums were reportedly coming from sources in Southern Tehran.[36] Love reports that after the second coup the US currency entered the market in such quantities that it depreciated the Dollar from its pre-coup parity of about $1=128 rials to about $1=50 rials.[37] According to Love, "it can be reasonably inferred that the glut of Dollars was coming from the '*chaqu keshan*' (knife-wielders) and that it represented their wages for the work on 19 August".[38]

Wilber emphasizes the point that not a single cent was spent on "the purchase of officers".[39] This corroborates Dorril's general statement that the main sums expended from the budget were paid out to the mob. Even though Wilber asserts that officers were not bribed during 28 Mordad, it would be prudent to distinguish between some of the top brass involved in the coup d'état, the 40 line commanders, those officers who were members of the "Devotees of the Shah", and other associated officers. One would assume that Colonel Farzanegan, who was an official CIA station agent, would have had some sort of a "contract" with a clearly stipulated salary or financial stipend.[40] As a "contractual employee" of the CIA he would not therefore be considered as an officer who was bribed or purchased for the particular project of overthrowing Mosaddeq. It is probable that the 40 line commanders, the members of "Devotees of the Shah" and other associated officers did not directly receive a penny from the CIA budget. In view of the CIA-orchestrated propaganda campaign focused on Mosaddeq's intention to hand over the country to the Communists, chase out the Shah and declare a republic, the reason for the military and police officers to side with Zahedi and against Mosaddeq may have been ideological, patriotic or have derived from authentic loyalty to the Shah and the country. The events between 25 and 28 Mordad could have added some credibility to the existing phobia of Communists among the military. A good number of the collaborating officers may have

---

[34] R.W. Cottam, Nationalism in Iran (PA: University of Pittsburgh Press, 1979), p. 226.
[35] Mohammad Daftari, Iranian Oral History Collection, Harvard University, Transcript 2, p. 14.
[36] Love, *The American Role in the Pahlavi restoration on 19 August 1953*, p. 40.
[37] Safari, p. 792. Ayatollah Kashani claimed that on 22 June 1953, the Dollar was worth 110 rials.
[38] Love, p. 41.   [39] Wilber, Appendix E, p. 22.   [40] Wilber, Appendix D, pp. 4, 5.

expected promotions and even appointments to key positions in the Iranian military establishment. Finally, "according to a British account, the coup d'état cost £700,000, though a most recent estimate with access to the participants and CIA accounts has put it as much as 10 to 20 million dollars".[41]

In April 1955, after 19 months in office, General Zahedi was forced to resign as Prime Minister. One of the issues that clouded his departure was rumoured to have been certain financial improprieties on the part of himself and Farzanegan. These charges of wrong-doing seemed to be intertwined with the coup d'état and its immediate aftermath. As mentioned before, Ayatollah Behbahani is said to have complained to the Shah that "since Zahedi's tenure as Prime Minister whatever [money] was in the country and came into the country found its way into the accounts of some, frustrating the people with the scale of bribes and inflation".[42] It was even rumoured that at a state dinner in Washington, President Eisenhower had warned the Shah about the financial misconducts of General Zahedi and Farzanegan.[43]

One of Zahedi's friends, Reza Keynejad, believed that the Shah was the source of the rumours of financial impropriety against the General. Keynejad remembered that even though the Shah knew that "the five million dollar check in Zahedi's personal name was immediately handed over to Amini, to be credited to the national accounts", the Shah told everyone that "Zahedi received money".[44] Keynejad does not explain the reason why Zahedi received such a sum after the coup or when this was given to him. Depending on when the money was given to Zahedi, it could be hypothesized that it may have been in recognition for the services he rendered during 28 Mordad, and that a part of it was intended for redistribution by him among other key contributors to the coup effort. The fact that presumably the Americans gave $5,000,000 to the person of Fazlollah Zahedi must clearly have disturbed the Shah. He may have become wary of Zahedi's importance in the eyes of the Americans, given the handsome sum, or jealous of the substantial gift to the general. The news of monetary payment to Zahedi may have also revived the Shah's well-placed suspicions that perhaps the Americans were once again greasing palms in preparation for another regime change.

---

[41] Dorril, p. 594.   [42] *Ashofteh*, 24 Farvardin 1334.   [43] *Ashofteh*, 21 Day 1334.
[44] Askari, p. 311.

17

Mosaddeq's exit: legal transfer of power or coup d'état?

On 22 August (31 Mordad) the Shah's plane, escorted by three Iranian Air Force planes, appeared on Tehran's skyline. It landed at 11:00 a.m. at Mehrabad Airport where the Shah, wearing his blue air-force uniform, descended the steps.[1] He returned triumphantly from Rome via Baghdad, claiming that his departure from Iran had been a calculated tactical move. He publicly labelled the events a "miracle", a "national uprising" and a "liberating insurrection". Privately, however, to US Ambassador Henderson, the Shah "expressed [his] deep appreciation of [the] friendship which [the] US had shown him and Iran during [this] period".[2] General Zahedi became Prime Minister, Ali Amini became his Minister of Finance and the mysterious Abdol-Hoseyn Meftah, who had been Mosaddeq's Undersecretary of Foreign Affairs, was reinstated in his post. A document entitled "Summary of events in Persia", written by the Eastern Department of the British Foreign Office, candidly enumerated the benefits of Mosaddeq's overthrow. It observed that

> General Zahedi formed a government. Supported by an immediate grant of United States aid, he was able at least to check the deterioration of Persia's economy ... by the end of the year he had put the extreme nationalists more or less in their place, had resumed diplomatic relations with the United Kingdom, and was approaching the oil problem in a manner which at least offered far better hopes of a settlement than had existed at any time since 1951.[3]

This document clearly indicated that from the Eastern Department of the British Foreign Office's point of view the coup had successfully attained Britain's economic objectives.

As has already been mentioned, some four months after the coup Dennis Wright, who had been in Tehran for less than a month, reported to Anthony Eden that "There is a considerable body of opinion here which holds that Dr. Musaddiq and other extreme nationalists still enjoy a greater measure of

---

[1] *Ettela'at*, 31 Mordad 1332.   [2] FRUS, vol. x, p. 762.   [3] FO 416/107.

popular support than the present regime".[4] A month and a half later, the more informed Wright wrote that "There seems little doubt that there is still much latent support for Musaddiq throughout the country ... the present Government appears to be well in control, but they lack popular support".[5] The theme of Mosaddeq's broad popularity among Iranians after the coup, in contrast to the unpopularity of the coup d'état government which had been put into place by a US–British plan, was embarrassing to the British diplomats in Tehran and was often repeated in their dispatches to London.[6] Nearly six months after the coup, British officials in Tehran were at pains to admit that "leaving aside the Tudeh, the majority of the people probably still favour Dr. Mussadiq in spite of his policies or lack of them".[7] Wright warned that "The nationalist hysteria of the last two years will not easily be forgotten, nor will its pre-dominantly anti-British focus. Outward appearances are misleading ... Amongst the masses of the people ... Dr. Mosaddeq's action against the AIOC and the embassy was regarded as a national victory". "This", he wrote, "is a fact that we should not forget".[8]

The spectre of Mosaddeq was haunting the coup-makers. The old man's persistent popularity after the coup could not have been a secret to the Shah. In spite of his haughty declarations about a national and liberating insurrection, the Shah felt politically fragile and indebted to an array of political and military fixers, peddlers and turncoats, whom he one by one eliminated in time, until he felt comfortable at home. In relation to his foreign friends who had brought him home triumphantly, he had a more difficult time shaking off his indebtedness and dependence.

If Mosaddeq remained popular among "the majority of the people" months after the coup, and if his popularity as compared with Zahedi's unpopularity was so stark that British officials in Iran had to begrudgingly admit it, then how could he have been overthrown by a "spontaneous" and "popular uprising" on 28 Mordad? One of the requirements of an autonomous grassroots mass movement leading to a spontaneous national uprising in the tradition of Rosa Luxemborg is the persistence and accumulation of unresolved economic, social and political problems and grievances. Pent-up antagonism towards and exasperation with unpopular policies of a government are usually expressed through protests, marches, demonstrations, strikes and finally street clashes of the disgruntled with government forces. Socio-political opposition to an unwanted government is vented in a variety of forms with some regularity before it reaches its threshold and becomes a spontaneous national uprising. In the absence of peaceful political solutions, the big explosion in the form of a national uprising is usually preceded by smaller scale grassroots socio-political signals.

---

[4] FO 416/106, 31 December, 1953.   [5] FO 416/107, 7 January, 1954.
[6] FO 416/107, 8 January, 1954; FO 416/107 13 March, 1954.
[7] FO 416/107, 12 February, 1954.   [8] FO 416/107, 13 February, 1954.

During Mosaddeq's 28 months of government protests, strikes, demonstrations and marches in Tehran were by no means directed primarily against his government. These strong expressions of public emotion were predominantly of two kinds. Either they were in support of Mosaddeq's domestic and foreign policy positions, or they were ideological and political muscle-flexing and sabre-rattling by one party or political organization, essentially against its political and ideological opponents – and not necessarily directed against Mosaddeq. The Tudeh Party sympathizers, irrespective of their changing position in relation to the Mosaddeq government, systematically clashed with a variety of anti-Tudeh organizations, including pro and anti-Mosaddeq forces. During his tenure, there were, however, anti-Mosaddeq public expressions from particular quarters. The demonstrations by the Tudeh Party in July and December 1951 and the small and random anti-Mosaddeq demonstrations of the Fadaiyan Eslam ("the Devotees of Islam") between June 1951 and 1952 could be considered anti-Mosaddeq public expressions. But, in retrospect, they can be seen as politically minor events as the demonstrators did not voice any significant levels of public discontent with Mosaddeq's government, or call for the resignation or ousting of the Prime Minister.

On 28 Mordad, the Tudeh Party and the "Devotees of Islam" did not officially or unofficially call on their members or sympathizers to demonstrate against Mosaddeq. Therefore, even if previously they may have had differences with Mosaddeq, by the time of the so-called "spontaneous national uprising", these had been resolved – or, given the alternatives, the Tudeh and the Devotees were content with not throwing in their lot with the anti-Mosaddeq forces. The singular and most important anti-Mosaddeq demonstration during his premiership – calling for his death, seeking to assault him and his house and aiming to destabilize his government – was that of 28 February 1953. This was a very particular demonstration and far from a plural or broad-based one. The details of the 28 February (9 Esfand) demonstration indicate that the participants were recruited, guided and managed by key clerical, military and political figures who wished to see Mosaddeq removed from power. All of the key players in the 9 Esfand demonstration were also involved in the August coups almost six months later. The participants in the 28 February demonstration did not constitute a socially all-inclusive body reacting to some unpopular policy of the Mosaddeq government. Their chant of "Death to Mosaddeq" was a novelty and expressed the single-mindedness of the demonstration. The same chant was to be heard on 19 August (28 Mordad). The process of how events began and unravelled, the manner of recruitment, mobilization and organization, and finally the mode of demonstration and dispersal of the participants during 28 February (9 Esfand) indicate that it was neither a spontaneous nor a national uprising, but rather a directed and engineered dress-rehearsal for 28 Mordad.

One could argue that while direct and indirect opposition to Mosaddeq and his government was consistently vented in the anti-Mosaddeq press and the Iranian parliament, such opposition was surprisingly absent on the streets (except on the special occasions of 9 Esfand and eventually 28 Mordad). When people of different social classes and walks of life do not take to the streets, where the culture of street demonstration exists and such demonstrations are not systematically repressed, then one may conclude that there is no major or evident opposition to the government. In the absence of any widescale and recurrent public expression of opposition to Mosaddeq's policies, it would be difficult to explain why the common people, assuming they were the actors of the so-called "spontaneous national uprising" of 28 Mordad, intuitively came to the conclusion that suddenly they were fed up with Mosaddeq and that Wednesday 19 August would be the right day for them all to take to the streets, not only to display their discontent and anger towards the Mosaddeq government, but also to topple it. A detailed study of the events leading up to and including 28 Mordad demonstrates that Mosaddeq's government was not overthrown by a spontaneous and popular burst of anti-Mosaddeq sentiments but by a cool-headed, coordinated, premeditated coup d'état plan. Both the 15 and 19 August coups were plotted.

A COUP D'ÉTAT

In his classic study, *Coup d'état*, Edward Luttwak refers to six established procedures for achieving a change of leadership: revolution, civil war, pronunciamiento, putsch, liberation and war of national liberation.[9] He concludes that "a *coup d'état* involves some elements of all these different methods by which power can be seized but, unlike most of them, the *coup* is not necessarily assisted by either the intervention of the masses, or, to any significant degree, by military-type force".[10] Luttwak argues that even though the assistance of the masses and military forces would make the seizure of power much easier, it would be "unrealistic" to assume that "they would be available to the organizers of a *coup*".[11] Some military forces would, however, need to be available to the coup organizers to mount a successful operation. Luttwak mentions that a coup "can be carried out by civilians *using* some army units" and concludes that "a *coup* consists of the infiltration of a small but critical segment of the state apparatus, which is then used to displace the government from its control of the remainder".[12] Rather than distinguishing a coup from other means of changing a leadership on the basis of its participants or the "who", Luttwak places the emphasis on the mechanics and the "how".

---

[9] E. Luttwak, *Coup d'état* (Cambridge : Harvard University Press, 1979), pp. 24–26.
[10] Luttwak, p. 26.   [11] Luttwak, p. 26.   [12] Luttwak, pp. 25, 27.

A coup d'état needs to be identified through its principal causes and context (the "why" question); through its main participants (the "who" question); and through its method and mechanics of execution (the "how" question). Irrespective of the important "why" and "how" questions, a coup d'état needs to be distinguished from other forms of change in leadership, first through its actors. The "why" and "who" questions are usually related. In the case of Iran, the vital economic and financial interests of a foreign country – the UK – were severed by an Iranian act of nationalization. This exercise of national self-sovereignty by the government in place – Mosaddeq's – was intended to prevent any back-peddling to the pre-nationalization period. To safeguard their financial interests, first the UK and then the US reviewed options to regain their foregone interests. Once the option of direct foreign military intervention by the British – Operation Buccaneer – was shelved in June 1951 and the domestic anti-Mosaddeq forces proved incapable of removing Mosaddeq, the option of a coup d'état remained the only possible alternative. A foreign intended and premeditated intervention without the use of foreign troops necessitated heavy reliance on the collaboration of domestic civilian and military anti-Mosaddeq forces.

The reason for the coup d'état in Iran was primarily an exogenous one, rooted in the immediate oil interests of the UK and the potential oil interests of the US. To veil the crassness of the simple financial reason, an ideological justification, popular at the time with average UK and US citizens, namely the imminent threat of Communism, was evoked to make an act of imperialism seem like a humanitarian intervention with the aim of safeguarding freedom and the free world. If the reason for the coup d'état was primarily domestic, one would have to look for domestic popular expressions of dissatisfaction towards Mosaddeq's government. The activities of the TPBEDAMN organization were aimed precisely at giving the impression of such discontent and generating some genuine discontent. Had there been sufficient domestic grievances against Mosaddeq, the opposition would not have needed to employ such tactics. Faced with the dominant perception that the people supported Mosaddeq's "bothersome" insistence on his terms of negotiation with the British over oil matters, the foreign plotters and their collaborators had no option other than staging a coup d'état against a government representing the popular will.

Revolutions or wars of liberation are different from coups in that the role of the popular masses is determinant in the first two, while it is almost negligible in the last. Planning a coup implies that those aiming to change the leadership do not believe they have the support of the broad masses, otherwise they would rationally privilege a low-risk political and parliamentary road over a high-risk extra-legal, forceful and violent means of obtaining political power. By definition a coup d'état requires the participation of some military units to overwhelm by force or the threat of force the target government and the people supporting it. To arrive at the solution of a coup d'état also implies that the masterminds do not believe that existing socio-political conditions could generate the necessary level of domestic grievance which would in turn remove the target. They would therefore need to impact, change and re-constitute the existing conditions as much as possible through "grey propaganda" – deceptive political and religious rumours and character assassinations – in addition to bogus demonstrations coordinated by their own *agents provocateurs*.

The events on 19 August 1953 in Iran do qualify as a coup d'état based on Luttwak's general theory. The curious fact that Luttwak does not mention the coup in Iran in his important study may be because certain crucial aspects of the coup in Iran undermine at least one of Luttwak's most important criteria for judging a coup d'état. Luttwak considers a coup feasible only when "the permanent machinery of the state", as distinct from political leadership, could be infiltrated and controlled to change the political leadership. The coup, he suggests, "operates in that area outside the government but within the state which is formed by the permanent and professional civil service, the armed forces and police".[13] According to Luttwak, the aim of the coup is "to detach the permanent employees of the state from the political leadership".[14] Explaining the coup in Iran within Luttwak's neat separation between "the political leadership" (as the target of change) and the "permanent state machinery" (as the body which needs to be infiltrated to mobilize the perpetrators of the coup) presents a formidable problem. In the Iranian case, "the political leadership" was both the perpetrator *and* the target of the coup.

The domestic coup forces hiding behind the Shah – the traditional symbol of power, authority and national cohesion as well as an intricate part of "the political leadership" – sought to wrench away power from the Shah's Prime Minister, customarily and constitutionally nominated by the parliament and endorsed by the Shah. The coups d'état (25 and 28 Mordad) were constructed to pit one wing of the political leadership against the other, with each possessing its own followers and "permanent employees" within the state. This particularity of the coup in Iran is not accounted for by Luttwak's theoretical framework. Furthermore, Luttwak's theory is focused on the actors of the formal modern state apparatus composed of "the permanent and professional civil service, the armed forces and the police" as the potential agents of the coup d'état. The second coup d'état in Iran demonstrated the political power of the informal actors of the modern state apparatus, namely the thugs and the ruffians, the motor of the second coup, gainfully employed by "the council of war".

At his trial Mosaddeq maintained that "any military operation conducted by military personnel with the objective of a regime change or the overthrow

---

[13] Luttwak, p. 20.   [14] Luttwak, p. 20.

of a government is defined as a coup d'état".[15] As proof of his claim that on both 25 and 28 Mordad a coup d'état was carried out against his government and that the events of 28 Mordad were the consequence of 25 Mordad, he presented the Court prosecuting him with a memorandum by Lieutenant General Dadsetan, Zahedi's Military Governor. This official memorandum requested that retired Colonel Fatollah Litkouhi be promoted in rank and indemnified for his active role in "the *coup d'état* of 25 to 28 Mordad" and for his "important role in toppling the government of Doctor Mosaddeq both in Qom and Tehran".[16] To Mosaddeq, this was irrefutable evidence that even the perpetrators of his overthrow believed that they had toppled his government through a coup d'état.

JUSTIFYING THE COUP

The coup d'état in Iran needed a domestically justifiable rationale. Claiming that the Mosaddeq government needed to be overthrown simply because it did not comply with the economic wishes and interests of Western powers would have stripped the domestic perpetrators of all legitimacy and presented them as they were in truth. Therefore an auxiliary rationale had to be conjured so as to camouflage the primary motive. The difference in interpretation of the Iranian Constitution on the powers and responsibilities as well as on the rights of the Shah in relation to his Prime Minister provided the best domestic pretext for the coup. Almost six months before 28 Mordad the domestic opposition to Mosaddeq had begun working on and propagating the idea that Mosaddeq was arrogating all executive powers to himself, while the lion's share of it belonged to the Shah, and that he sought to expel the Shah from the country in order to finalize his absolutist powers. This was the pretext for the demonstrations against Mosaddeq on 28 February (9 Esfand).

Mosaddeq believed that under the constitution the Shah was a symbolic sovereign with no executive rights and powers. He was therefore exempt from political accountability and authorized to reign indefinitely as political disasters and successes were not of his doing. The executive responsibility of running the state, according to Mosaddeq's interpretation of the constitution, rested with the government. The debate over the constitutional role of the Shah and the Prime Minister was conducted and settled in favour of Mosaddeq's interpretation in mid-March 1953, or five months before the coup d'état, by an eight-man parliamentary committee including two of Mosaddeq's staunchest enemies, Baqa'i and Ha'erizadeh.[17] After having consulted with the Shah and Mosaddeq, the parliamentary committee based its ruling on articles 35, 44 and 45 of the Iranian Constitution, concluding that it was obvious that the administration and responsibility of state affairs

---

[15] Bozorgmehr, p. 116.   [16] Bozorgmehr, p. 117.   [17] Rahnema, pp. 859–861.

in political and military domains was not within the brief of the sovereign. The committee report reiterated that the person of the Shah was free of all responsibilities, while the ministers and the government were responsible for running affairs of state.[18] Ministers and government were charged with administering the law and exercising their functions in the name of the Shah and were accountable to parliament.

This ruling on the interpretation of the constitution by a bi-partisan parliamentary committee acceptable to both parties did resolve the problem between the Shah and the Prime Minister. At the time, both the Shah and Mosaddeq agreed to respect the findings of the eight-man committee. Yet the anti-Mosaddeq partisans of the Shah who were actively plotting to overthrow him and who wanted to see the Shah take a firm and hostile position against Mosaddeq, found themselves in an uncomfortable position. Hoping to sway the Shah against the findings of the eight-man committee, 'Ala (the Minister of Court) reminded the Shah that the ratification of the ruling of the committee in parliament would enhance Mosaddeq's power and undermine his own. To 'Ala's dismay, the Shah responded that he thought the report "was in accordance with the spirit of the Constitution".[19] The Shah's upholding of the decision of the eight-man committee deprived the domestic and foreign plotters against Mosaddeq of a domestic quasi-legal case for their plans: the Shah accepted that his job was to reign and not to rule, and he was therefore not in the position to oust Mosaddeq by a royal edict.

It took the domestic and foreign coup planners five months to change the Shah's mind and obtain a quasi-legal excuse: the royal edicts. The Shah had to be convinced that it was his constitutional right and prerogative to exercise executive powers such as appointing or dismissing a Prime Minister. It was not until late July 1953 – or less than a month before the coup – that the Shah became convinced that constitutionally he could be a ruling monarch.[20] Once the Shah was almost forced to act as an autocratic sovereign, a domestic rationale for removing Mosaddeq was available for the coup planners, enabling them to pretend that the coup attempt against Mosaddeq was due to the Prime Minister's political and constitutional insubordination and not because of his intransigence on the oil issue.

OPTIONS FOR OVERTHROWING MOSADDEQ: QUASI-LEGAL AND/OR MILITARY COUP

The idea that the Shah should dismiss Mosaddeq through a royal edict (*farman*) and appoint Zahedi as his replacement was put forward and relentlessly pursued by the foreign coup planners as early as mid-May 1953.[21] This was the "quasi-legal" option to overthrow Mosaddeq, foreseen in the

---

[18] *Ettela'at*, 21 Esfand 1331. [19] Rahnema, p. 865. [20] Rahnema, pp. 894–896.
[21] Wilber, pp. 25–26; Wilber, Appendix A, p. 3.

TPAJAX plan, which was attempted on 16 August and failed. Yet the royal edicts played a key role in the success of the second coup. After the failure of the first coup, the royal edict appointing Zahedi and the wide publicity it received in the press provided the coup masterminds with the justification to argue that Mosaddeq's government was illegal and that the Prime Minister was a rebellious outlaw as he had not complied with the Shah's "legal" use of his political prerogatives. The smokescreen of a domestic political crisis rooted in a constitutional crisis was effectively used to camouflage the foreign-perpetrated coups d'état. This excuse could make believe that the events on 19 August simply resulted from the refusal of Mosaddeq's government to comply with the Shah's royal edict. This was presented as the last straw to be added to the general dissatisfaction of the popular masses with the performance of Mosaddeq.

The modality of mounting the coup against Mosaddeq was openly addressed in the "Initial Operational Plan for TPAJAX" drafted in Nicosia between 13 and 30 May, and subsequently in the "London draft of the TPAJAX Operational Plan" drawn up by the CIA–SIS team between 15 and 17 June 1953. In the first document (the Nicosia plan) it was clearly stipulated that there were two ways to put Zahedi in office: first, "quasi-legally, whereby the Shah names Zahedi Prime Minister by [a] royal firman" [edict]; second, "military coup".[22] This document suggested that the "quasi-legal method" (using the royal edict) be tried first and "if it fails, [a] military coup will follow in matter of hours".[23] In both the Nicosia and London documents, the "quasi-legal" and then "military coup" sequence was confirmed and the important role that the royal edicts would play, as instruments of the "quasi-legal" form of removing Mosaddeq, was highlighted.[24]

Having assessed the possible conditions which could create a coup situation, the London draft dropped the necessity of the quasi-legal step as a prerequisite to a military coup. It clearly stipulated that "However, with or without the possession of a royal edict naming him as Prime Minister, Zahedi will take over the government and will execute the various requirements of coup day".[25] Worried that the Shah might not sign the royal edicts, the coup planners wished to persevere with the military option, irrespective of the quasi-legal step. It would be safe to suggest that as of 25 June 1953, the coup clock was ticking against Mosaddeq's government after the 11 top-ranking American conspirators, including Allen Dulles (director of the CIA), agreed to give Operation TPAJAX the thumbs-up and the Secretary of State, John Foster Dulles, adjourned the meeting by exclaiming: "that's that, then let's get going".

At his trial Mosaddeq presented an elaborate case, arguing that his dismissal by the Shah was contrary to the constitutional customs and traditions

---

[22] Wilber, Appendix A, p. 3. Underline in the original.   [23] Wilber, Appendix A, p. 3.
[24] Wilber, Appendix B, p. 7.   [25] Wilber, Appendix B, p. 14.

of the state and therefore illegal. Mosaddeq evoked the notion of *maslahat* (expediency or public interest) and argued that "even if we assume that the royal edict was legal it was against the public interest (*maslahat*) of the country and that which is to the benefit of the country takes precedence over all other considerations".[26] Mosaddeq's explanation of why he did not comply with the royal edict dismissing him, delivered to him in the early hours of 16 August (25 Mordad), is important as it sheds light on the charge of rebellion and insubordination brought against him after the coup. After 19 August (28 Mordad), the regime argued that Mosaddeq's insubordination towards his dismissal by the Shah brought about and justified the second coup. The fact that Mosaddeq did not divulge his dismissal by the Shah to Henderson and flatly denied it when Henderson directly questioned him about it on 27 Mordad reveals that Mosaddeq was ill at ease with the public's interpretation of his reaction to the content of the *farman*.[27] During his meeting with Henderson, Mosaddeq reiterated that even if there had been a dismissal edict he would have considered it null and void.

Mosaddeq's dilemma, based on his record of dealings with the Shah, was that he did not want to foreclose the possibility of bringing the Shah back to Iran as a constitutional monarch. There is hardly any doubt that Mosaddeq was a firm believer in Iran's constitutional monarchy. Acknowledging his own dismissal by the Shah would have shed doubt upon the legitimacy of the office that he claimed to hold, if he believed that the Shah had the right to dismiss him (which he did not). Mosaddeq believed that his legitimacy came from the people, and in his eyes the results of the referendum on the dissolution of the parliament proved this. Furthermore, the first coup, camouflaged in its quasi-legal wrapping, had failed and Mosaddeq was still in power. Disclosing the content of the edict and refusing to carry out its content, with the backdrop of the failed coup, could have been interpreted as Mosaddeq's rejection of the Shah's authority as the monarch, and could thereby have played into the hands of those in his own camp who wished to see a republic and of those in the opposition who had consistently argued that Mosaddeq sought to overthrow the monarch. Denying the content of the edict, once the first coup had failed, saved face for the Shah, while it gave him the time and opportunity to return to his country and regain the throne as a constitutional monarch.

Acknowledging his dismissal by the Shah after the failure of the first coup would have placed Mosaddeq in a precarious political position. Since he was not prepared to hand power over to Zahedi, he would have been forced to openly challenge the Shah's edict on legal or pragmatic grounds. To have done so would have meant that he considered the Shah to have acted illegally. Back on 6 March 1953, Henderson had reported that the Shah was frightened at the thought of a military coup in his name and believed that the

[26] Bozorgmehr, p. 310.   [27] Bozorgmehr, p. 402.

"miscarriage of an attempted coup would be likely to complete the ruin of Shah and his dynasty".[28] This had now happened, though Mosaddeq sought to prevent the complete ruin of the Shah and his dynasty. If Mosaddeq wished to dethrone the Shah and vilify him as a traitor, the military activities of the anti-Mosaddeq plotters, along with the Shah's edict, provided him with a golden opportunity on the morning of 16 August. But Mosaddeq was not after the Shah's throne or a regime change. He remained loyal to the concept of a constitutional monarchy wherein the Shah remained a symbolic figure. He had sworn allegiance to the constitution according to which Mohammad Reza was the monarch, and he had also made a personal promise to the young Shah to this effect.[29] The fact that he separated the Shah as the constitutional monarch from the first coup – whereas almost everyone around him directly associated the Shah with the coup and demanded his removal – made Mosaddeq's task even more delicate and difficult. Mosaddeq knew that the coup plotters were hiding behind the Shah's legitimacy and that the Shah had unenthusiastically thrown his support behind them. It is not surprising that after the first coup Mosaddeq kept asking "what am I to do?"

MOSADDEQ'S ETHICAL, LEGAL AND POLITICAL DILEMMA

In the early hours of 16 August, given the exceptional circumstances under which he received the royal edict, Mosaddeq must have reflected on the legality of rejecting the Shah's edict, dismissing him and appointing Zahedi. The ethical legalist in Mosaddeq would have prompted him to accept the royal edict and hand over power to Zahedi if he had not thought that the edict and the coup were part of a foreign plot to undo his efforts at implementing the nationalization of Iranian oil. Accepting the Shah's edict and stepping down from power after the first coup was foiled would have meant abandoning the popular will after having defeated the aggressor. In Mosaddeq's mind, after the first coup, Iran's opponents had two distinct heads: the Shah, and the foreign and domestic plotters. As late as it may have been, Mosaddeq was trying to salvage the Shah and the monarchy, while severing the other head – a task which proved impossible.

Mosaddeq's reaction to the royal edict hinged on his assessment of five key issues. Through numerous previous political crises Mosaddeq had demonstrated that he was not really attached to maintaining power at all costs and had wilfully offered his resignation. Mosaddeq had to assess: a) whether the edict was authentic and represented the Shah's un-coerced will; b) whether the Shah had the legal right to dismiss him; c) why the edict was accompanied by an attempted military coup; d) if he were to accept the edict, what would

---

[28] FRUS, vol. x, p. 701.   [29] Bozorgmehr, p. 308.

become of the oil nationalization issue, the successful resolution of which, in the interest of Iranians, had become Mosaddeq's covenant with the Iranian people; and finally e) how he could acquit the Shah of the coup attempt against his government and convince him to return to the country?

The circumstances surrounding the delivery of the royal edict played a key role in Mosaddeq's reaction to its content. Making a quick, lucid and well thought-out decision, with clear reports of a coup being under way, irregular tank movements and armed military men acting as mailmen and possible future gaolers knocking on his door at very late hours of the night must not have been easy. Mosaddeq's reaction may have been very different had he been handed the royal edict by the Shah's Minister of Court during regular working hours over a cup of tea, had there been no coup attempt, and had the Shah remained in Iran so that he could be contacted and consulted.

In order to find out if the edict was authentic and un-coerced, Mosaddeq needed to meet with the Shah, but he was not to be found. Mosaddeq sought to contact the Shah for clarification on his *farman* on 16 August but he was informed that the Shah had left the country.[30] According to Gholam-Hoseyn Mosaddeq, his father sought in vain to locate the Shah, while he grappled with numerous unsettling questions which seemed to have paralysed him. Mosaddeq wondered why the Shah had sent him such an edict, as he had agreed to the ruling of the eight-man committee that he did not have the legal right to do so; now that he had done so, to whom was Mosaddeq supposed to hand the country?[31] In view of Zahedi's associations with foreign interests, Mosaddeq did not see him as fit to take over as Prime Minister. The Shah's departure seems to have thrown Mosaddeq completely off balance, perhaps explaining his silence between the two coups. According to his son, Mosaddeq kept asking, "what am I to do now?"[32] Unable to contact the Shah, Mosaddeq decided that a text (the royal edict) had been signed by the Shah, but that its content was not known to him or fully in accord with his will. Mosaddeq knew the irresolute young king and was aware of how he could be convinced to do something against his will.

In relation to the legality of whether the Shah could dismiss the Prime Minister, as he had done in his royal edict, some five months previously the eight-man Committee of the Majles looking into the dispute between Mosaddeq and the Shah had ruled that the Shah was a symbolic monarch void of any executive powers. Mosaddeq firmly believed that the Shah was not entitled to directly dismiss or appoint ministers, let alone the Prime Minister, within a constitutional monarchy. At his trial Mosaddeq evoked articles 35, 44,

---

[30] Bozorgmehr, p. 266.
[31] Gholam-Hossein Mosaddeq, Iranian Oral History Collection, Harvard University, Transcript 2, p. 12.
[32] Gholam-Hossein Mosaddeq, Iranian Oral History Collection, Harvard University, Transcript 2, p. 12.

45, 46, 60, 61 and 67 of the Iranian Constitution, just as the eight-man Committee had done, to prove that the Shah was not empowered to dismiss him or appoint a replacement.[33] According to Mosaddeq the power of appointment and dismissal of the Prime Minister lay only with parliament.

But, by 16 August, circumstances were different from five months earlier. Mosaddeq's referendum of 3 August 1953 (in Tehran) and 10 August (in the provinces) had put an end to the parliament, the highest body in the land according to the constitution. In the absence of a parliament, did the Shah have the right to appoint a new Prime Minister? Or was it the responsibility of the Prime Minister to conduct elections for a new parliament and then have the new parliament vote on a new Prime Minister? The absence of the Majles allowed for different interpretations. Moreover, the Shah's sudden departure after the failure of the first coup confronted Mosaddeq with a state of confusion and paralysis only because he wished to maintain the constitutional monarchy; otherwise the situation was ideal for ending the Pahlavi dynasty.

Aside from the issue of whether the Shah had the legal right to dismiss his Prime Minister, the manner in which the royal edict was written generated serious doubts about its authenticity, which in turn strengthened Mosaddeq's suspicions that the content of the edict did not represent the Shah's will. The handwriting, style, spaces between the words on certain lines, the distance between certain lines, and finally the date of the royal edict presented serious problems and irregularities for him. At his trial Mosaddeq argued that he was suspicious of the authenticity of the royal edict and had concluded that the Shah had not signed its contents willingly.[34] To Mosaddeq the royal edict, which was dated 22 Mordad (13 August) and delivered to him in the early hours of 25 Mordad (16 August), was not written by the Shah, but was a text that had been inserted into a blank letter signed by him.[35] The issue of why the *farman* (royal edict) dismissing him was delivered at 1:00 a.m. by armed officers and soldiers three days after it was signed, and of why the last lines were written with unusually wide spaces between the words to fill out the page, made the text and its controversial content highly suspect. Mosaddeq was convinced that the Shah had signed a blank official letterhead for the plotters to fill in.[36]

As Abbas Towfiq has appropriately pointed out, it is rather bizarre that there exists no trace of the royal edict dismissing Mosaddeq. In a smiling photograph of him taken immediately after the second coup, Nasiri holds an illegible document, which is said to be the royal edict addressed to Mosaddeq.

---

[33] Bozorgmehr, pp. 210–214. For an excellent account of the legality or illegality of the *farman*, see Abbas Towfiq, *Qanouni boodan ya nabodan-e farman-e azl Mosaddeq* (Paris: Entesharat Sahand, 2008).

[34] Bozorgmehr, p. 204.   [35] Bozorgmehr, p. 266.

[36] There are two different accounts by Mosaddeq on why the text was added to the already signed royal letterhead: see Towfiq, p. 22. and Bozorgmehr, p. 266.

In this document, the words in each line are widely spaced, as are the lines. Nasiri is reported to have referred to the document in his hands as the *farman* which dismissed the old Prime Minister.[37] Copies of the text appointing Zahedi do exist: it is equally irregular in its writing. Whereas in the first two lines of the four-line text the words in each line are almost equidistant, the words in the last two line are gradually squeezed in to finish the text just before the royal signature. The irregular spacing between the words is clearly visible in the document. Furthermore, the date on the *farman* – 23 Mordad (14 August) – seems to have been tampered with. The suspicious circumstances surrounding the penmanship of the royal edict and its integrity are accentuated by the fact that the Iranian press reported that the document was dated "22 Mordad".[38]

In response to those who argued that the dissolution of parliament by Mosaddeq created a constitutional crisis and legally entitled the Shah to dismiss his Prime Minister, Mosaddeq made the argument that the edict dismissing him was dated 22 Mordad (13 August) while the Iranian Parliament was still technically in session. On 13 August the Shah was still legally obliged to seek the voice of the parliament, which was officially dissolved three days later. Mosaddeq based his argument on the fact that it was only in the early afternoon of 16 August (25 Mordad), after the edict had been written and delivered to Mosaddeq, that the parliament was officially dissolved through an announcement to that effect publicized in the Iranian press.[39] During his trial Mosaddeq maintained that the royal edict was not in the handwriting of the Shah and was furthermore dated three days before its delivery date, when the parliament had not yet been officially dissolved.[40]

The fact that, concurrent with the delivery of the edict to his house, a series of military operations aimed at overthrowing his government was launched convinced Mosaddeq that the attempt against his government was a violent coup d'état orchestrated by foreigners under the guise of a "legal" royal edict.[41] The circumstances clearly reflected a coup and not a constitutional transition of power. In defence of his decision to ignore the royal edict, Mosaddeq argued that he believed that he could manage the country without the assistance of foreigners and that he needed to stay in power to bring the people's movement to a successful conclusion. This, he believed, was to the greatest benefit of Iran. At his trial, however, Mosaddeq said that had it not been for safeguarding the oil nationalization movement he would have "kissed the royal edict and resigned".[42] Was Mosaddeq insinuating that

---

[37] Bozorgmehr, p. 159; Towfiq, pp. 21–24.
[38] *Ettela'at*, 25 Mordad 1332; Towfiq, pp. 17–20 provides a detailed and original account of why the *farmans* had been tampered with.
[39] Bozorgmehr, p. 296. [40] Bozorgmehr, pp. 160, 204, 266.
[41] Bozorgmehr, pp. 116–17. [42] Bozorgmehr, p. 205.

irrespective of the authenticity of the edict he was so fed up with the situation that he would have welcomed the excuse of the edict and resigned, had it not been for his commitment to safeguard Iran's nationalized oil industry?

DID DISSOLVING THE 17TH PARLIAMENT LEGITIMIZE THE COUP?

On more than one occasion Mosaddeq must have thought that the 17th Majles was becoming ever more hostile toward him and his government: it was manipulated by foreign interests, dysfunctional in carrying out its responsibilities, a source of dissonance, and was weakening his position in his negotiations over the oil issue. He was convinced that whenever there was a crisis in parliament, its negative impact was immediately manifested in the hardening tone, comportment and stance of Iran's counterparts in the oil negotiations.

From the end of March 1953, 'Ala, the Minister of Court, was trying hard to replace Mosaddeq with Zahedi. In his meeting with Henderson, 'Ala, who must have been worried about the ratification of the ruling of the eight-man committee in parliament, reiterated that "unless energetic steps [were] taken to overthrow Mosadeq in the immediate future, such influence as the Shah still had would disappear".[43] 'Ala conveyed a sense of urgency to the US Ambassador that unless the Shah was convinced to take action, "it might be too late to save Iran". In this same meeting of 30 March 1953, on behalf of "the group who was interested in overthrowing Mosadeq", 'Ala asked Henderson whether "the US government was still supporting Mosadeq", and if in the ambassador's opinion "Mosadeq would be able to effect [the] settlement [of] the oil problem, they might decide [to] postpone taking action".[44] The balance of power between the foreign and domestic perpetrators of the coup, and the reasons for ousting Mosaddeq, are manifest in the conversations between 'Ala and Henderson.

By 15 April 1953, Ala reported to Henderson that the Shah believed that there were only two ways to remove Mosaddeq: 1) a vote of no confidence by the Majles; or 2) a vote of inclination for a successor to him.[45] The fact that the Shah was not comfortable with a forceful ousting of Mosaddeq posed a problem for the opposition, which needed the Shah's blessing to remove Mosaddeq rapidly, irrespective of the means. In 'Ala's conversations with Zahedi, who had declared himself ready to remove Mosaddeq, the latter had also spoken about "peaceful means" of overthrowing Mosaddeq.[46] At this time 'Ala seemed obliged to pursue a parallel objective: to force Mosaddeq out of office legally, which was more to the liking of the Shah, and to continue to explore the possibilities of pushing him out by force.

---

[43] FRUS, vol. x, p. 719. [44] FRUS, vol. x, p. 720. [45] FRUS, vol. x, p. 723.
[46] FRUS, vol. x, pp. 719–720.

Mosaddeq's exit: legal transfer of power or coup d'état? 285

On the same day that 'Ala informed Henderson that if Mosaddeq was to be removed then the Shah wanted him out through the soft, parliamentary way, 'Ala also informed the US Ambassador that he would try to influence certain members of the parliament to cripple the Majles by preventing it from attaining a quorum.[47] If 'Ala really wished to remove Mosaddeq through a vote of no confidence in the Majles, then crippling the parliament could not further his cause. Unless he sought to undermine the Shah's wish of peacefully removing Mosaddeq, it must be assumed that 'Ala was trying to cripple the parliament in the hope of preventing the ratification of the ruling of the eight-man committee on the constitutional status of the Shah; he sought to buy time until his friends could muster forces in parliament sufficient to oust Mosaddeq.

The day after 'Ala met Henderson and spoke about his plans to halt the official activities of the Majles, the Majles failed to obtain a quorum.[48] Ha'erizadeh, the leader of the "Freedom" faction in parliament, openly echoed 'Ala's policy of crippling the Majles and promised that members of his faction would continue their policy of preventing the formation of a quorum until such time as the "fate of the government was determined".[49] Once the Majles resumed its activities on 10 May 1953, its sessions were constantly agitated by deputies opposed to Mosaddeq insulting, abusing and even physically assaulting the pro-Mosaddeq deputies. It was very clear that opposition deputies were intent upon preventing the normal functioning of parliament, and Iranian newspapers reported regularly on the brawls, fist-fights and insults in the Majles.[50]

At this time Mosaddeq was faced with a parliament manipulated by the Court, but probably not by the Shah. Every day the deputies opposed to Mosaddeq put on an impressive show, publicizing the legislative dysfunctionality of the country and the un-governability of Iran so long as Mosaddeq was in power. Furthermore, Mosaddeq had come to know that 30 opposition deputies of the 17th Majles were bought by the British, and that negotiations were underway to pay off another ten deputies; this would have then formed a solid block which could have censured, given a vote of no-confidence and ultimately brought down his government.[51] Mosaddeq had told Henderson that the reason he decided to dissolve the Majles was that "the British-purchased Majles was unworthy of [the] Iranian people and should be eliminated".[52]

Even though Mosaddeq's pre-occupation with 40 deputies being bought out by the British to censure and then vote out his government may seem rather farfetched, both the Nicosia and London drafts of the TPAJAX Operational Plans confirm his suspicions. Both documents discuss the exact

---

[47] FRUS, vol. x, p. 725.   [48] *Ettela'at*, 27 Farvardin 1332.
[49] *Ettela'at*, 3 Ordibehesht 1332
[50] *Ettela'at*, 20, 22 Ordibehesht; 5, 7, 17 Khordad; 2, 4, 15, Tir; 1332.
[51] FRUS, vol. x, p. 750.   [52] FRUS, vol. x, p. 750.

modality of how deputies in the Majles should be bought in order to prepare for the change in government. The Nicosia document mentions that for the "quasi-legal effort" deputies had to be purchased, and adds that the "SIS considers 20 deputies now not controlled must be purchased".[53] The London plan mentions that "it is yet to be decided whether the purchases are to be made by the British group or directly by Zahedi."[54]

The CIA–SIS plan was to secure a majority plus one vote against Mosaddeq, and it estimated that "at least 30 deputies are prepared to vote against Mosaddeq if they think there is a good chance that they will be in a majority".[55] The London draft on how to overthrow Mosaddeq referred to "a list of deputies with the amounts required for the purchase of each" and "a special funding operation". There is also mention of the necessity to "purchase additional deputies solely to have them remain in the Chamber to ensure the quorum".[56] Once the necessary deputies were purchased and other pre-conditions were fulfilled, the coup planners hoped that the Majles would "pass a motion to censure the government ... followed by the dismissal of Mosaddeq and the appointment of Zahedi as successor". They predicted that "if successful the coup would be completed by early afternoon". The CIA–SIS planners had also thought of a backup plan: "failing success, the coup would be mounted later that evening".[57] It may be assumed that the evening plan included a military operation. The authors of the Initial Operational Plan (TPAJAX), drafted in Nicosia, referred to their quasi-legal method of overthrowing Mosaddeq as a coup.

On 6 July 1953, Mosaddeq saw signs of how his government could be toppled by the Majles. His anxiety about purchased deputies ousting his government seems justified now that the facts about the operational plans of his overthrow have been made public. The events on this day strengthened the idea that the foreign-purchased Majles needed to be dissolved. On this day Ali Zohari, an anti-Mosaddeq deputy and the right-hand man of Baqa'i, moved that the Prime Minister should be censured. To Mosaddeq it was clear that the opposition deputies were initiating the processes of bringing down his government at the behest of the British. The second important issue which troubled Mosaddeq was that Makki, another staunch anti-Mosaddeq deputy, was elected as one of the two members of parliament sitting on the committee overseeing the National Bank's printing of money (*heyat nezarat andoukhteh eskenas*). Makki's new position as a controller of the National Bank (*bank melli*) would have enabled him to discover that the government had been printing money and running a budget deficit. To deal with the country's financial difficulties and obligations resulting from the embargo on the sale of nationalized Iranian oil, Mosaddeq had been printing money,

---

[53] Wilber, Appendix A, p. 4.   [54] Wilber, Appendix B, p. 19.
[55] Wilber, Appendix B, p. 19.   [56] Wilber, Appendix B, p. 20.   [57] Wilber, Appendix A, p. 8.

but without publicizing it. Makki's publicizing of this fact would have placed greater economic and political pressure on Mosaddeq's government.

These two developments, added to all of the previous problems he had encountered with the Majles, convinced Mosaddeq that he could no longer work with the parliament and needed to dissolve it through a referendum before the foreign-controlled Majles ousted him. It was not until 12 July that Mosaddeq publicly expressed this idea. On 14 July his cabinet agreed on putting the question of continuation or dissolution of the 17th Majles to a national referendum. Ten days later Mosaddeq announced the decision of his government to proceed with a referendum, and on Thursday 13 August the Ministry of Interior announced the final results of the referendum: 2,043,389 votes in favour of dissolving the Majles and 1,207 votes against it.[58] Mosaddeq's official announcement that the 17th parliament had been dissolved and that the election date for the 18th parliament would be announced later appeared simultaneously with the news of the first coup in Iranian newspapers.[59]

The ethical legalist in Mosaddeq may have clashed with the politician in him over the dissolution of the Majles. In view of Mosaddeq's long-held belief in the primacy of parliamentary democracy, the thought of dissolving the parliament could not have been an easy one. Was it not Mosaddeq who in December 1951 had hammered home that "without a parliament, representative of the will and tendencies of the majority of the people nothing can be attained and without such a parliament, the existence (*mojoudiyat*) and independence of our country will be confronted with a great danger"?[60] How could Mosaddeq explain his swing from parliamentary democracy to direct democracy – the national referendum – only once the parliament began to undermine the attainment of his political objectives? The Mosaddeq who decided to dissolve the Majles did so not only for political expediency and pragmatism, but also because he was convinced that a significant number of deputies had been purchased by foreign interests. His decision to dissolve the Majles through a national referendum may have betrayed the aspirations of the parliamentarian Mosaddeq, who had made free elections in a parliamentary democracy and the unfettered activity of the parliament the raison d'être of his political career, especially in the 1950s. Yet he remained loyal to the oil nationalization movement, to neutralizing foreign political pressures and plots, and to seeking the direct vote of the people. As an ethical legalist Mosaddeq made a difficult choice: yet he was convinced that his decision was for the good of the people, on whose support he could count.

Dissolving the Majles through a referendum was highly fortuitous for the coup planners as it created a political vacuum which could justify the legality of the Shah's edict dismissing Mosaddeq. In the absence of the Majles, the

---

[58] *Ettela'at*, 24 Mordad 1332.   [59] *Ettela'at*, 25 Mordad 1332.   [60] *Ettela'at*, 26 Azar 1330.

Iranian Constitution did not foresee whether the Prime Minister could be dismissed, who had the legal power to do so, and on what grounds. Mosaddeq argued that only parliament could dismiss him and his government, but in the absence of the parliament the coup planners could argue that the right to dismiss the Prime Pinister returned to the Shah. The dissolution of the Majles created a legal deadlock. To the coup planners this was an unexpected gift which strengthened the quasi-legal semblance of the Shah's right to dismiss Mosaddeq through his royal edict. The CIA–SIS team pointed to the dissolution of the parliament and argued that it "clearly revealed [the] abuse of the constitution" by Mosaddeq. This convenient event provided a golden opportunity "on which Mossadeq could be relentlessly attacked by the CIA–SIS subsidized press".[61]

Those members of Mosaddeq's government, such as Hasibi, Parsa, Mo'azzami, Razavi and Sanjabi, who are said to have disagreed with the idea of dissolving the Majles at the time may have been correct in their opposition: little did they know that the coup was being mounted irrespective of whether the Majles was in session or not. The facts remain that as much as the supporters of the coup wished to make a legal case for it, the coup plan was conceived, authorized and set into motion by the foreign conspirators well in advance of Mosaddeq's decision to dissolve the parliament. According to the London draft of the TPAJAX Operational Plan (15 June), it was highly preferable if the Shah would issue his royal edicts, but, in the case that he refused to do so, the coup was to go ahead anyway.[62] Whereas Mosaddeq's cabinet decided on the referendum on 14 July, the CIA Director approved the $1,000,000 budget for Tehran's CIA station to bring about the fall of Mosaddeq on 4 April 1953 – or more than three months previously.[63] However, the fact that the results of the referendum, heavily favouring the dissolution of the Majles, were announced before Nasiri presented Mosaddeq with the text signed by the Shah certainly helped the cause of the coup planners by giving a semblance of legitimacy to their coup attempt.

---

[61] Wilber, p. 32. [62] Wilber, Appendix A, p. 8. [63] Wilber, p. 3.

Conclusion

The "Iranian Englishmen", the majority of the British Embassy staff in Tehran as well as Miss Lambton were correct in their assessment that, in view of British interests in Iran, Mosaddeq had to be removed instead of negotiated with. The longer Mosaddeq remained in power the more he laid bare the simple fact that the manner in which the British were pursuing their economic and political interests in Iran rendered their interests fundamentally incompatible with Iran's national interests. Mosaddeq's tenure also demonstrated to Iranians as well as the colonized and semi-colonized countries of the world that pursuing Iran's benefit at the cost of Britain or any other foreign power was the right and responsibility of a nationalist government putting the welfare of its people first. The anti-Mosaddeq foreign and domestic coalition understood that, given the tenuous historical relationship between Iran's rulers and the ruled, it was neither easy nor common for Iranians to trust a political leader, let alone come to believe in his honesty, uprightness, patriotism and justice. Even if such qualities were to be combined in a politician, it was difficult for Iranians to reach any sort of an agreement on that one person during his lifetime.

Mosaddeq had many defects, but during his tenure he had become that unique politician with whom more Iranians than usual had entered into a part affective and part rational relationship based on love and respect. This almost unprecedented political and emotional bond between the majority of Iranians and Mosaddeq provided him with spectacular popularity, which continued even after his overthrow. Yet a good part of Mosaddeq's appeal was based on his untiring, perhaps quixotic quest, to return to Iranians what he believed was their expropriated rights, dignity and wealth. The history of the AIOC's financial dealings with Iran, combined with the record of British foreign policy towards Iran, imposed an imperative clash between a Britain which did not wish to change its bullying ways and a stubborn and incorruptible politician bent on reclaiming the pride and the rights of Iranians. If Britain were to regain its past interests in Iran it needed to expedite the overthrow of

Mosaddeq, as time would show that "the old man", despite his errors, did indeed embody those features that Iranians respected in their leaders.

The British drive to demonize Mosaddeq on the international scene, thereby putting more pressure on the US to approve of and assist in his removal, was a hazardous move if the process were to drag on for long. Mosaddeq's interaction with the international community left a very different common impression than that longed for by the British. In the prevailing political atmosphere of decolonization, Mosaddeq's style of battling against neo-colonialism was rather different from other anti-colonial leaders. He was neither a soldier nor a revolutionary. In his language and mannerisms one could detect neither xenophobia nor cultural nativism. On the contrary, he was a non-provincial Westernized man fully at ease with a Western public. He believed in social justice and equity, but was far from being a Marxist or a Communist. He came very close to being a social democratic liberal, believing in the democratic electoral rules and processes and the peaceful circulation of power based on the people's voice. The West at the time was more interested in strong "freedom-loving" leaders – a euphemism for strictly "anti-Communist" leaders who ruled in an authoritarian way – rather than "wishy-washy" liberal democrats guided by the unpredictable moods of their people. Iron-fisted anti-Communists, keeping a tight reign over their people and indulgent with Western economic interests in their own countries, were preferred profiles. There was something of the tradition of the *javanmardan* (the chivalrous) in Mosaddeq's politicking that made him so attractive to his people and so disliked by those who favoured Iran only for what they could exploit and gain from it.

President Truman, who did not believe in overthrowing governments, even when it was highly recommended by his British allies, saw Mosaddeq for what he was, and valued him. The Eisenhower administration, guided by a different worldview, did not see much merit in a non-authoritarian social democratic leader who, irrespective of his popularity, was not committed to uprooting the Communists. Mosaddeq's most important vice from the point of view of his Western antagonists was that internationally he remained an inflexible and dogmatic leader on the issue of Iran's oil. As such, he was setting a bad international example. Mosaddeq was neither against Iran's integration within the world economy, nor was he an economic protectionist. He was a believer in the ideal free market system, demanding fair play through the application of perfect competition. The real danger he posed was that he sought to use Iran's oil on the international markets to put an end to the extra-market and political rents and benefits accrued to the super-powers through their political and military dominance and muscle. The inability of Britain in June 1951 to impose economic terms through gun-boat diplomacy erroneously convinced Mosaddeq that Britain had abandoned military solutions and replaced these with diplomatic reasoning. Little did he know that a change in US administration would allow for a new convergence of interests in favour of overthrowing governments – especially if these were believed to be turning red.

The chronology of events does not indicate that Eisenhower was hostile to the Mosaddeq administration from the moment he assumed power. On the contrary – initially Eisenhower shared with his predecessor the same feeling towards the British. Both the Democrats and Republicans found the British to be the main hurdle to the solution of the oil problem and what they believed to be the deteriorating situation in Iran. Like the Truman administration, Eisenhower initially believed that the US should provide economic assistance to Iran to prevent the country from falling to Communists, irrespective of the British–Iranian dispute and the intransigent position of the British. On 4 March 1953, during the 135th meeting of the National Security Council in Washington, Eisenhower pressed for supporting Mosaddeq's government against the possibility of a Communist takeover by trying to persuade the British to leave the Americans to deal with the Iranians and permit the US to put the Iranian oil industry back in operation. At this meeting Eisenhower made the interesting comment that "if I had $500,000,000 of money to spend in secret, I would get $100,000,000 of it to Iran right now".[1] Eisenhower's position, seemingly eager to help Mosaddeq financially and thereby support his government, suddenly changed.

This abrupt change occurred within a week. On 11 March 1953, during the 136th meeting of the National Security Council, Eisenhower said that "he had very real doubts whether, even if we tried unilaterally, we could make a successful deal with Mosaddeq". The President "felt that it may not be worth the paper it was written on, and the example might have grave effects on US oil concessions in other parts of the world".[2] Somewhere between mid- and late March, General Walter Bedell Smith, Undersecretary of State, determined that the US government could no longer approve of the Mosaddeq government and would prefer a successor. This "change in policy was communicated to the CIA, and the NEA Division was informed that it was authorized to consider operations which would contribute to the fall of the Mosaddeq government".[3]

From late March the coup machine was put into operation. The American administration seemed to cede reluctantly to the British lobby and became the driving force behind planning and executing the overthrow of Mosaddeq. The US change of heart and direct involvement in the planning and execution of the coup d'état caused a radical shift in the Iranian public's attitude towards the US. One can speculate that with the exception of Tudeh Party members, who were always dubious of US imperialism, and sympathizers with the coup, who consistently remained loyal to the West, after 28 Mordad a relation of love and hope between Iranians and the US government was overshadowed with distrust, suspicion and a sense of betrayal. Whereas the

---

[1] FRUS, vol. x, p. 698. [2] FRUS, vol. x, p. 713. [3] Wilber, p. 2.

Attlee government was unable to manipulate the Truman administration to approve of "Operation Buccaneer" in the summer of 1951, the Churchill government succeeded in convincing the Eisenhower administration to become their coup partners. The British government succeeded in turning the US administration from a possible ally and saviour into a new predator state in the eyes of many Iranians.

The 1953 coup in Iran was the first of a series of clandestine US operations across the world. Defending the free world against Communism in the midst of the Cold War provided the ideal pretext for US administrations to intervene in the domestic affairs of different countries with impunity and overthrow governments of different types. After Iran, the US is alleged to have been involved in, engineered or orchestrated coups in Guatemala (1954), Indonesia (1965), South Vietnam (1963), Brazil (1964), Ghana (1966) and Chile (1973). The ultimate cause of these interventions was usually strongly intertwined with some sort of economic interest, justifying the accusation of neo-colonialism and imperialism.

In comparison to the colourful revolutionary politicians and leaders of the 1950s and 1960s, Mosaddeq was an elderly, fragile-looking and less flamboyant personality. He was a legalist and a believer in political righteousness, who at times frustrated his goal-oriented and more radical companions and followers. He was usually more intent on following the legal process and the ethical path than obtaining the desired end result. There were occasions during his tenure when he slipped, but he usually ended up correcting his excesses. At times, the end justified some – but not all – of the means. Mosaddeq's active political life, which ended on 28 Mordad, demonstrated that in the final analysis, if his objective of safeguarding the nationalized oil and reviving the Iranian economy by breaking the blockade against the sale of her oil, shared by the majority of his compatriots, was attained as a result of his efforts, so much the better; if not, lessons were to be learnt from this socio-political exercise, and when the next opportunity presented itself, the people would be much wiser because of this experience. This was politics as a pedagogical exercise and not necessarily for maximizing power, control and tenure. However, Mosaddeq was not willing to protect the nationalization of oil by unleashing a civil war and witnessing the spilling of Iranian blood by Iranians. The ultimate end did not justify any and all means.

A close reading of the history of the coup d'état, from the day Mosaddeq came to power through to his overthrow, leads to three broad observations on the psychological disposition and behavioural pattern of the key players. First, only six days after the Majles ratified the Oil Nationalization Law, the British threatened Iran with military retaliation. The notion that as long as Mosaddeq was in power, a return to the pre-oil nationalization conditions was impossible seems to have been ingrained in the minds of various British administrations, leading them to the inevitable conclusion that Mosaddeq needed to be got rid of before the oil nationalization law could be reversed.

In this period, British administrations were still under the impression that they could pursue their economic interests through brute force. The method for removing Mosaddeq underwent mutations, but the British determination to remove him did not waiver.

Second, the Shah and Seyyed Zia began talking about a coup d'état to British and American diplomats almost at the same time (late December of 1951 and early January of 1952). This was some six months after the discussions on replacing Mosaddeq were launched by the British. The fact that the British wished to see Mosaddeq removed, and then acted on it, emboldened and encouraged the "Iranian Englishmen" and the Monarch. Convinced as they were of the mythical power of the British to successfully attain their ends, the "Iranian Englishmen" eagerly entertained the idea of a coup d'état as an option. Ironically, even though the Shah talked to Henderson about a coup d'état as the only possible solution to remove Mosaddeq, he was psychologically incapable of following through on the idea. This was a reality that his close foreign co-conspirators consistently remarked upon and factored into their calculations when they decided to launch the coup d'état – with or without his direct involvement. The act of the coup d'état petrified him, and even after the British and American administrations launched the coup operation in April 1953 the Shah refused to become directly involved in it. Even as a reluctant coup partner, the Shah seems to have involuntary sabotaged the CIA–SIS plan by delaying meetings and, most importantly, postponing until the last minute the signing of the white sheets of paper that later become royal edicts. Had the British and American administrations, backed by the "Iranian Englishmen", not forced the Operation TPAJAX upon him, the young Shah does not seem to have been inclined to concede to a coup (with the risks that it involved). From as early as 26 December 1951, when the Shah talked to Henderson about a coup, to 19 August 1953, when the coup overthrew Mosaddeq, the Shah was a conflicted soul whose indecision and fear paralysed him, convincing the British and American administrations and their secret services that they needed to think and act for him.

Third, throughout Mosaddeq's 28-month term, the American administrations were caught in a tug of war with various British governments over how to proceed with Iran and the oil issue. Initially the Truman administration blocked any attempt by the British to intervene militarily in Iran. Subsequently, it sought to resolve the oil dispute by playing the role of an objective and trustworthy intermediary. From November 1951, having failed to convince the American administration to back their invasion initiative, the British administration retaliated by obstructing the US proposals on the oil issue, voicing their disapproval and reiterating that Mosaddeq's fall would result in "a more amenable government".[4] The British government's open obstruction of

---

[4] FRUS, vol. x, p. 257.

American initiatives to resolve the oil issue in Iran created tension between the US and Britain. By August 1952, when the American government proposed to provide Iran with a grant to partially resolve its financial problems, the British government once again opposed such a move; in turn, it informed the American Secretary of State that the Iranian army might have to intervene in the internal affairs of the country, and that the US and Britain "should not be hasty in coming to Mosaddeq's aid because we think we shall never have a better government to deal with".[5] Even the Eisenhower government initially pursued a conciliatory policy towards Mosaddeq. It mulled over the possibility of purchasing oil from Iran and providing financial aid to it while convincing the British not to oppose such initiatives. However, by the beginning of March 1953 Mosaddeq's rejection of the British proposal of 20 February 1953 on the issue of indemnities for the oil nationalization, which was also supported by the American administration, tipped the situation in favour of the British solution of intervention. At the same time, the US administration interpreted the events after 9 Esfand as ones which would probably lead to "a dictatorship in Iran under Mosaddeq". It also began to worry about the political vacuum that, in the absence of a strong replacement, "Mosaddeq's sudden absence" would provide for the Communists to take over.[6] The US shift to the British position of seeking to overthrow Mosaddeq happened in the second half of March. Once the US administration became convinced that a coup d'état was the only political and economic solution to the Iranian deadlock, it took the initiative and pursued the course to its end.

In the final analysis, the coup d'état created a long-lasting social, political and psychological malaise which was passed on from generation to generation and was not attended to, still less healed, after the 1979 revolution in Iran. The post-coup Iranian society has yet to come to grips with 28 Mordad – both the event and its consequences. The 28 Mordad coup d'état derailed the course of Iran's political and economic development, while traumatising Iranians. An equally important social and psychological consequence of the coup was that it turned certain values upside-down. From the point of view of all those who favoured and supported the oil nationalization movement, those Iranians who collaborated with the foreigners against their own national interests were being rewarded economically and politically by the post-coup regime. Iranians who continued to believe in the proud nationalist dream which Mosaddeq had helped set into motion and followed through with tenacity had to come to grips with the notion that what to them seemed treason to Iran's national interests would not only go unpunished, but would be handsomely rewarded. The post-coup regime and the governments which followed placed a tight lid on discussion of the whys, hows and whos of the coup, forcing such reflections and debates underground. Reactions to the coup were formed, but would largely remain latent, surfacing only sporadically

---

[5] FRUS, vol. x, p. 435.   [6] FRUS, vol. x, p. 693.

and in a radical form. Iranian anti-British sentiments were transformed into anti-Americanism and anti-Imperialism. Some of the pro-Mosaddeq adolescents during the coup later became the founders and active members of armed guerrilla organizations, both Marxist and Islamic. The more moderate and tempered actors in the nationalization movement introverted but did not forget the role of foreign intervention or its consequences. Some of those key collaborators in the 28 Mordad coup among the military brass, politicians, clergy and the thugs were one by one marginalized, dishonoured and even executed as the Shah regained his confidence and authority at home and sought to rid himself of the awkward feeling of being king by their grace alone.

The historical evidence that has accumulated over the years, and that has been used in the present work, points to the fact that the 1953 overthrow of Mosaddeq was effected through a foreign-hatched coup. The facts indicate that both the failed coup of 25 Mordad and the successful coup of 28 Mordad were the outcome of premeditated and intentional foreign involvement in the internal affairs of Iran. The successful 28 Mordad coup d'état, which came hot on the heels of the first unsuccessful coup attempt, was part and parcel of the British-proposed and American-directed (and supported) operation to overthrow Mosaddeq. The events of 28 Mordad were not impromptu or unprepared, but carefully and intelligently thought out, revised and planned by the key foreign and domestic masterminds who gathered at the American Embassy after the failure of the first coup. The events were steered, executed and operationalized by Iranians who were directly and indirectly carrying out modified British–US plans drawn up in Nicosia and London by British and American intelligence officers and spooks. There must have been Iranians who independently joined the activities against Mosaddeq on 28 Mordad: the point, however, is that had these Iranians constituted a significant force, it would not have been necessary for the CIA and SIS operatives and their highest echelon political representatives to opt for a messy coup.

In 1978, Henry Precht, the Country Director for Iran, informed Crowe (his British interlocutor) that due to the Freedom of Information Act he was considering the release of certain documents pertaining to the 1952–1953 period; if they were released, "there would be some very embarrassing things about the British in them".[7] Subsequently, the British attempted to persuade the State Department to withhold not only British documents, but the American ones too.[8] The British and the Americans had every reason to be embarrassed by the release of sensitive information about the coup in Iran. Direct and premeditated British–US intervention in the form of a planned

---

[7] National Security Archives, TNA:PRO FCO 8/3216. From B.L. Crowe to R.S. Gorham, 12 October 1978: http://www2.gwu.edu/~nsarchiv/NSAEBB/NSAEBB435/
[8] National Security Archives, TNA:PRO FCO 8/3216. From R.J.S. Muir to R.S. Gorham, 14 December 1978: http://www2.gwu.edu/~nsarchiv/NSAEBB/NSAEBB435/

covert coup operation aimed at removing Mosaddeq from power was a clear violation of Iran's sovereignty, an assault on its territorial integrity and a travesty of international law.

The predicament of the architects and subsequent supporters of the opinion that, on 28 Mordad, the Iranian people rose up and swept away Mosaddeq, is that – unlike people such as Seyyed Zia, Asadollah Rashidiyan or Kim Roosevelt – they find it rather embarrassing and politically incorrect to openly come out in favour of coup d'états as an acceptable way of changing governments. What makes a transparent pro-coup position in relation to the 28 Mordad coup more delicate is that espousing it implies that foreign intervention in the affairs of another country is permitted and collaboration with foreigners to attain their ends is an acceptable practice. Seyyed Zia, Rashidiyan and Roosevelt did not seem to have a fixation or a complex with regards to a coup d'état. Since they seemed neither bothered by being involved in a coup nor had many misgivings about foreign intervention and collaboration with foreigners, it would be safe to say that they saw no reason to dispute the reality of the 1953 coup.

Henderson and the Shah, as well as those who followed their complicated logic on what happened on 28 Mordad and what it should be called, were different from the unabashed proponents of the coup and rather ill at ease in their own post-coup skins. Henderson was present at the 25 June 1953 meeting when the coup was approved in Washington. He had come to be a supporter of a coup since the end of March. Henderson was also present in the grounds of the American Embassy in Tehran on 17 August 1953, when Kim Roosevelt and his fellow Iranian-American conspirators earmarked Wednesday 19 August for the "great demonstration". Even though Henderson is said to have been conferring with General McClure "a few hundred yards away" from where the conspirators were finalizing their plans, he must have immediately been briefed on the activities planned for Wednesday 19 August (28 Mordad) by Roosevelt and Carroll. So, Henderson had full knowledge of the fact that the first and second coups were planned by the CIA and the SIS. He was also informed about how the second coup was then fine-tuned, calibrated and executed with the help of Roosevelt, Carroll and their Iranian networks of collaborators.

Two days after the coup, Henderson consciously misled the public, both Iranian and American. He advised the State Department to launch a campaign stressing the "spontaneity" of the anti-Mosaddeq and pro-Zahedi movement. This misrepresented version of history turned the foreign-engineered coup into a spontaneous mass movement of the Iranians. Henderson was covering up, forgetting or denying his own direct experiences in the planning of the coups on 25 June and 17 August 1953. Henderson needed to misinform the people for "reason[s] of state". Loyal to his country, he was dissimulating what he thought the world community would consider as wrong and immoral. He was in no position to explain why the coup was essential for the immediate interests of Britain and the long-term US interests in Iran and the region. His career and loyalty condemned him to distort history. The Shah of Iran was also involved in the coup plans and was informed of the coup and the role of foreigners in it. For a long time he had resisted becoming actively and personally engaged in such a conspiracy because he was scared of the consequences of an unsuccessful foreign coup, and perhaps ashamed of his involvement in it. The Shah was therefore in a situation somewhat similar to that of Henderson. He too needed to misrepresent history publicly. This, he needed to do for a different kind of "reason of state".

Relics of nationalism, respect for the right of self-determination, shame at intervention in the affairs of other sovereign countries, the stigma attached to coups and coup-makers, and the guilt of helping foreigners against one's own national interests – these all compel the present-day advocates of Mosaddeq's overthrow to follow the lead of Henderson and the Shah and prove against historical realities that 28 Mordad was the result of the independent thought, will and action of the Iranian people. Making 28 Mordad a legal and Iranian event sanitizes the immoral foreign-planned coup, completes the dissimulation process set into motion by Henderson and the Shah, demonizes the target of the coup and sanctifies the Iranian coup-makers. It ultimately erases the traces of those who intervened and those who collaborated. It sweeps the historical reality and impact of the act under the carpet, postponing the process of coming to terms with uncomfortable realities.

That the events of 28 Mordad were a spontaneous mass movement, a national resurgence, a popular uprising, a legal counter-coup, a backlash of the people's discontent, even a jihad against atheism and Communism orchestrated by religious leaders, cannot be demonstrated or supported by historical facts. It is perhaps time for a new generation of *decomplexé* (unabashed) defenders of the overthrow of Mosaddeq to take to the stage. Their task will be most difficult, but will at least be consistent with historical facts and therefore academically defendable. They would need to accept that, irrespective of the vices and virtues of Mosaddeq and the legacy of his government, 28 Mordad was a planned coup and that it was parented by foreigners, even if its midwives were Iranians. They would subsequently have to demonstrate the comparative benefit of foreign intervention over domestic reconciliation of differences, as well as the comparative benefit of violent political change over peaceful transition. Finally, they would need to assess the long-term benefits of the foreign-perpetrated coup for both Iran and the international community. This would be the challenge of the present-day supporters of Mosaddeq's overthrow in Iran.

Biographical notes of key figures

Afshartus, Mahmud (1907–1953) Born in Tehran, he attended the Officers' Academy. In 1952 Mosaddeq appointed him as Tehran's Military Governor and subsequently as Chief of Police. He was one of the four founders of the "Nationalist Army officers", a pro-Mosaddeq organization within the army. To precipitate the downfall of Mosaddeq's government, Afshartus was abducted and later murdered by members of the pro-Zahedi "Retired Officers' Association". The masterminds behind his assassination were the enigmatic pair of Mozaffar Baqa'i and Hoseyn Khatibi. On 28 Mordad, the absence of a strong, daring and aggressive pro-Mosaddeq officer such as Afshartus occupying a sensitive military position was deeply felt.

Akhavi, Hasan (1908–?) Born in Tehran, he attended the Officers' Academy and served in numerous military posts, such as the head of the army's counter-intelligence office. By the time of the 1953 coup, he had a wide base of associates and contacts in the army. Akhavi was a protégé of General Arfa and friends with Farzanegan and Batmanqelich. He was an active member of the Military Secretariat in charge of planning the coup against Mosaddeq. After the coup, he was promoted in rank and became the vice-Chief of Staff. In 1957 he entered the Eqbal cabinet as Minister of Agriculture. He left the government in October 1960, and also retired from the army.

'Ala, Hoseyn (1882–1964) Born in Tehran to a diplomatic family, he went to London at an early age and studied law at the University of London. 'Ala spoke perfect English and good French. He began his career at the ministry of foreign affairs as "chef de cabinet" in 1906, was appointed Minister of Public Works in 1918, and was sent to London in 1934 and then to Washington in 1945 as an Ambassador. He was appointed Prime Minister for the first time in March 1951. After Mosaddeq's premiership, 'Ala became Minister of Court for the third time. He played an important role in coordinating the anti-Mosaddeq forces. After the removal of Fazlollah Zahedi in April 1955, 'Ala was again appointed as Prime Minister and escaped an assassination plot by the "Devotees of Islam". In 1957, he resigned his position of Prime Minister to Manouchehr Eqbal and became Minister of Court for a fourth time, serving in this position for the rest of his life.

Amidi-ye Nouri, Abolhasan (1903–1980) Educated in Iran, he became a lawyer. After the departure of Reza Shah, he published the daily *Daad*, which became popular because of his special articles entitled "Behind and Under the Political Curtain". He was initially a member of the National Front, but soon after Mosaddeq's premiership he joined the anti-Mosaddeq camp and his newspaper became one of the most vociferous critics of Mosaddeq. During the trial of the members of the "Devotees of Islam" in 1952, he acted as one of their lawyers. Between the first and the second coups, Amidiy-e Nouri and his newspaper played a key role in mobilizing the anti-Mosaddeq camp. After the coup, he became Zahedi's Undersecretary in charge of the Office of Propaganda as well as the spokesperson of the government. He subsequently became a member of parliament for two terms. After the 1979 revolution, Amidiy-e Nouri was arrested, condemned to death and executed.

Arfa, Hasan (1894–1985) Educated in Istanbul and Paris, Arfa graduated from the Military Academy at St. Cyr, the foremost French military academy, and subsequently entered the Iranian army. He was fluent in French, English and Turkish, but was said to be less at ease with Persian. In 1923 he met Hilda, his lifetime British wife, a leading ballerina and a highly cultured multi-lingual woman. They married in Berne. In 1925 he served as Iran's first military attaché in England. In 1944 he was appointed Chief of Staff and founded the right-wing "National Movement Party". He was known for his anti-Communist tendencies and waged a campaign against the Tudeh Party in Iran. Arfa was arrested by Ahmad Qavam in 1945 and in 1946 by his arch rival, Razmara. In Hoseyn Ala's first cabinet in 1951 he became Minister of Roads. Arfa was known for his pro-British tendencies and was said to be the mastermind behind the anti-Mosaddeq Ariya Party. Arfa had close relations with Mozaffar Baqa'i and Ayatollah Kashani. After the coup, having jockeyed to become Prime Minister, Arfa was appointed Ambassador to Pakistan and subsequently Turkey. Arfa left Iran before the 1979 revolution and spent his last days in Monte Carlo.

Ashrafi, Hoseynqoli (1908–?) He graduated from Tehran's Officers' Academy and then completed his military training at Tehran's University of War. In March 1953, he replaced Teymour Bakhtiyar as commander of the Third Mountain Brigade. Shortly afterwards Mosaddeq appointed him as Tehran's Military Governor while he continued to retain his command position of the Third Mountain Brigade. On 19 August, the day of the second coup, Mosaddeq suspected Ashrafi of being in collusion with pro-Zahedi officers. At noon, Mosaddeq deposed Ashrafi from all positions of command and arrested him. After the coup, Ashrafi was arrested again and imprisoned for his collaboration with Mosaddeq, but was released before he was put on trial. He subsequently entered private business.

Azmudeh, Eskandar (1913–?) He graduated from Tehran's Officers' Academy and completed his military training at Tehran's University of War. In 1953 he was commander of the Pahlavi Regiment, served at the Military Governor's headquarters and was a member of the "Devotees of the Shah", a secret anti-Mosaddeq organization. During the first coup he was in charge of neutralizing the telephone centre at the bazaar and then proceeding to Mosaddeq's house. After the success of the second coup, Azmudeh was promoted in rank and was given command positions in the provinces before becoming Undersecretary of the Ministry of Finance and the Head of Customs Services. In 1974 he became the Governor of Eastern Azarbayejan. He left the country before the 1979 revolution and resided in London.

Bakhtiyar, Teymur (1904–1970) Born in Shahr-e Kord, he obtained his high school diploma in Beirut and in 1923 entered the French Cavalry School at Saumur. He graduated from Tehran's University of War in 1949, at the top of his class. In 1953 he was put in command of the Third Mountain Brigade and subsequently commissioned to put down Abolqassem Khan Bakhtiyar's revolt in Isfahan, which he successfully executed. In April 1953 he became the commander of Kermanshah's Armoured Brigade. When approached by Farzanegan and Towne, a CIA station agent supporting the coup against Mosaddeq, he pledged his support. After the second coup he was promoted in rank and became Tehran's Military Governor. In 1954, he was instrumental in discovering and destroying the military wing of the Tudeh Party. Three years later he became the first head of SAVAK. In 1961, after plotting to replace the Shah, he was removed from office and forced to leave Iran. He was assassinated in Iraq in the summer of 1970.

Baqa'i, Mozaffar (1912–1987) Born in Kerman, he finished his high school education in Iran and went to Paris to study philosophy. He returned to Iran and began his career at the University of Tehran. In 1946 he joined Ahmad Qavam's Democratic Party, and became an MP in 1947. In 1949 he published the influential daily *Shahed*. When the 16th Majles was convened in 1950, Baqa'i was among the list of pro-Mosaddeq MPs elected. Baqa'i was initially one of the key members of the pro-Mosaddeq National Front. In 1951 he founded the Iranian People's Toilers Party, and from the inception of Mosaddeq's government he gradually distanced himself from Mosaddeq, befriending Ayatollah Kashani and eventually openly opposing Mosaddeq. From 28 February 1953, Baqa'i propagated the idea that Mosaddeq was paving the way for the Communists and intended to remove the Shah and overthrow the monarchy. His paper, *Shahed*, played an important role in swaying public opinion against Mosaddeq and in favour of Zahedi. After the coup, Baqa'i, who was instrumental in the downfall of Mosaddeq, was marginalized. After the 1979 revolution he tried his hand at politics again and through Hasan Ayat, an old follower of his, made some inroads. Yet he was later arrested and imprisoned, and he passed away in prison under very suspicious circumstances.

Batmanqelich, Nader (1903–1991) He attended Tehran's Officers' Academy, pursued his military studies in Germany and graduated from Tehran's University of War. In 1952 he headed the Shah's Military Office. Before the coup, Zahedi appointed him as Chief of Staff. During the first coup he and the forces under his command were to occupy the headquarters of Mosaddeq's Chief of Staff, but he is said to have lost heart and aborted his mission. He was arrested after the first coup, freed after the success of the second coup, and became the Chief of Staff. In 1954 he first became Iran's Ambassador to Pakistan and then to Iraq. In 1958 he entered Eqbal's cabinet as Minister of Interior. He passed away in the US.

Behbahani, Ja'far (1916–1987) Born in Tehran, he received his BA in law from the University of Tehran. He pursued his studies in France. He headed a public notary office and opened an office in Tehran's bazaar district. After the coup, because of Ayatollah Seyyed Mohammad Behbahani, his father and his own role in the success of the second coup, he entered the Iranian parliament on three consecutive occasions. Ja'far Behbahani was very close to the Rashidiyan brothers. In 1960, in association with Asadollah Rashidiyan, he founded the League of Defenders of the Constitution.

From January 1962, Asadollah Rashidiyan and Ja'far Behbahani, who had first supported Ali Amini, began campaigning and agitating against his government, resulting in their arrest. After their release, the two men attempted to launch a party called "The People's Party". From the mid-1960s Behbahani gradually moved out of the political limelight.

Behbahani, Ayatollah Seyyed Mohammad (1871–1963) Born in Tehran, he was the son of Ayatollah Abdollah Behbahani, one of the two prominent leaders of Iran's constitutional movement. In addition to having been a *mojtahed*, he studied philosophy for six years. After the assassination of Abdollah Behbahani in 1910, Mohammad became the influential head of Tehran's Seminary School. With the ascent of Reza Shah to power, Mohammad Behbahani became very close to the monarch. Behbahani maintained his close relationship with Mohammad Reza Shah and emerged as the religious guardian of the young king. From January 1953, when relations between Mosaddeq and the Shah began to worsen, Behbahani played an active role in supporting the Shah. He played a vital role in rallying Southern Tehran ruffians against Mosaddeq and in favour of the Shah during the second coup. After the coup, Behbahani became even more influential than before, until he fell out with the Shah over the latter's White Revolution.

Borujerdi, Grand Ayatollah Seyyed Hoseyn (1875–1961) Born in Borujerd (Lorestan), he began his preliminary seminary school studies in Borujerd and was sent to the Isfahan Seminary School at the age of 18, where he studied for nine years. In 1902 he went to Najaf, the hub of Shi'i education, studied with Shi'i luminaries such as Akhund Molla Kazem-e Khorasani and became a *mojtahed*. Hoseyn returned to Borujerd in 1911 and stayed there for 33 years, during which he revived the Borujerd Seminary School. In 1944, subsequent to the invitation of the highest ranking clergy of Qom, Borujerdi entered this city, and after the death of Ayatollah Seyyed Abolhasan Esfahani in 1947 he became the uncontested single source of emulation of the Shi'i. Borujerdi not only returned Shi'i religious leadership and authority back to Iran, but also actively engaged in the reform and development of the Qom Seminary School. Borujerdi refrained from constant interference in political matters. During the oil nationalization movement, whenever he felt a foreign threat against the national sovereignty of the country he threw his full support behind Mosaddeq. His relationship with Mosaddeq was cordial. He refrained from undermining Mosaddeq's authority and at no time sided with or aided the coup forces. Borujerdi did not appreciate the radicalism of the "Devotees of Islam" and Ayatollah Kashani. As long as Borujerdi was alive the Shah did not dare launch his land reform and the White Revolution.

Dadsetan, Farhad (1906–1977) Born in Tehran, he studied at Tehran's Officers Academy. He married the niece of Reza Shah's wife, which is said to have paved the way for his successful military career. In 1949 he became the commander of the Gendarmerie. He was subsequently appointed as the commander of the Gorgan Corps. Before the first coup, Dadsetan was among the circle of officers close to Zahedi plotting to overthrow the Mosaddeq government. Dadsetan played an important role in the second coup and was appointed as Tehran's Military Governor by Zahedi on the evening of 28 Mordad. He was subsequently promoted in rank. Within a few months he was replaced by Teymur Bakhtiyar. In his last military post he commanded the Kerman Corps.

Biographical notes of key figures

Daftari, Mohammad (1906–1987) He attended Tehran's Officers' Academy before going to France and attending the Military Academy at St. Cyr. On his return to Iran he joined Razmara's circle of friends. In 1947 he became the commander of Tehran's Military Police. During the assassination attempt on the life of the Shah at Tehran University in February 1949 Daftari helped the Shah into the car which took him to the hospital. When Razmara became Prime Minister in 1950, he promoted Daftari to Chief of Police. Daftari was subsequently placed in command of a newly created force called the Custom Guards. Even before the first coup, Daftari (who was a relative of Mosaddeq) was in close contact with Zahedi and the plotting officers and was designated as Zahedi's Chief of Police. On the day of 28 Mordad, he played an important role in publicly demonstrating the tacit compliance of his forces with the anti-Mosaddeq demonstrators. Against the advice of his Chief of Staff, Mosaddeq appointed Daftari as Chief of Police on the day of the second coup. After the coup Daftari remained as Chief of Police for a short period and was subsequently sent to Rome as a military attaché. In 1955 he was appointed to the sensitive position of the head of the army's Procurement Office. He was arrested in 1961, put on trial, and imprisoned for three years for alleged financial misconduct. He left Iran before the revolution and resided in Paris.

Esma'ilpour alias **Ramezoun Yakhi, Hoseyn** (1914–?) He was first imprisoned at the age of 20 and by 1953 (when he was 39) had spent some ten years of his life in jail and three years in banishment. In 1949 he became a partner in a bakery and also worked as a mason. He later owned a real estate agency in Bagh Ferdows. Ramezoun Yakhi was one of Southern Tehran's key knife-wielders and ruffian leaders. He was known for his physical strength and piety. Ramezoun Yakhi was very close to Asadollah Rashidiyan. On 28 Mordad, his followers constituted one of the four main columns which occupied the centre of Tehran and played a determining role in turning the events against Mosaddeq and paving the way for the success of the second coup. After the coup, he maintained his close ties with Asadollah Rashidiyan.

Fardust, Hoseyn (1917–1987) A childhood friend and close companion of Mohammad Reza Pahlavi, Fardust followed the crown prince to the Swiss boarding school La Rosey, where they stayed for five years. Fardust completed his studies at the Officers' Academy then went to Paris to study law during Mosaddeq's government and subsequently attended the University of War after his return to Tehran. After the coup, Fardust returned to Iran, and in 1959 founded and headed the very powerful "Imperial Inspectorate Organization" which reported directly and only to the Shah. Fardust was among a very select few whom the Shah trusted during his reign. After the revolution he stayed in Iran. In 1987 he appeared on a television show, and a few weeks later he was declared dead by the authorities.

Farzanegan, Abbas (1910–2004) He attended and graduated from Tehran's Officers' Academy. He spent a few years in the US as Iran's military attaché. According to Wilber, Farzanegan, a CIA station agent was trained at Fort Leavenworth. Farzanegan returned to Tehran from Washington in early July 1953 with the mission to "renew all of his old contacts within the Iranian army". Farzanegan was a member of the Military Secretariat in charge of planning the first coup. He was not arrested after the first coup and was instrumental in planning and executing the second coup. In the post-coup Zahedi government, Farzanegan became Undersecretary of Post, Telegraph and

Telephone. In 1955, with the departure of Zahedi, Farzanegan lost his post in the cabinet and left the country. He was later appointed as Ambassador to Kuwait, Saudi Arabia, Holland and Norway. He spent the last years of his life in the US.

Fatemi, Hoseyn (1917–1954) Born in Na'in, he collaborated with his brother in the publication of a daily in Isfahan. He went to Tehran in 1937 and worked with the daily *Setareh*. In 1940 he published his brother's daily *Bakhtar* in Tehran. By this time Fatemi had become well known in political and journalistic circles. In 1945 he went to Paris to pursue his studies, while he continued to contribute articles to Iranian dailies. He returned to Iran in 1948 and started publishing his own newspaper, *Bakhtar Emrouz*, in 1949. In the same year he joined Mosaddeq in the National Front, became a close adviser to him, placed his newspaper at the service of the National Front and remained loyal to Mosaddeq until the end. Fatemi became Mosaddeq's Deputy Prime Minister and escaped an assassination attempt by the "Devotees of Islam" in February 1952. In September 1952 he became Minister of Foreign Affairs. He was arrested by pro-Zahedi troops during the first coup. After his release he wrote scathing articles against the Shah and the Court. After the second coup he went into hiding and was captured in February 1954. He was subsequently put on trial and executed.

Garzan, Abbas (1897–?) He attended and graduated from the Cossack Officers School. He also attended European military schools and started his military career during the reign of Reza Shah. In 1943 he became the commander of Isfahan Army, and two years later he was appointed as deputy Chief of Staff. In 1950 he was appointed Chief of Staff by Razmara. He occupied this sensitive position until the events of 30 Tir (21 July 1952), subsequent to which he was removed by Mosaddeq and forced to retire. At this time he joined the anti-Mosaddeq officers. After the coup, Garzan became the Governor of Fars, and when Zahedi reshuffled his cabinet in 1954 he was given the portfolio of the Minister of Roads.

Gilanshah, Hedayatollah (1907–1986) He was born in Tehran and attended Tehran's Officers' Academy before being dispatched to train as a pilot in England and France. He later attended training programmes in England and the US and is considered one of the founders of Iran's Air Force. In 1949 he was appointed as the Chief of Staff of the Iranian Air Force and became close to the Shah and the Court. He was forced into retirement by Mosaddeq and became a key player among the anti-Mosaddeq officers. He accompanied Zahedi during the four crucial days between the two coups and was promoted in rank after the coup, while he was appointed to the chief of the Shah's military office. From 1954 to 1959 he was the Chief of Staff of the Iranian Air Force. He was subsequently forced into retirement.

Ha'erizadeh, Abolhasan (1888–1972) He went to seminary school in Yazd and Isfahan. He entered the 4th parliament at a young age and was closely associated with Seyyed Hasan Modarres. In 1946, along with Qavamolsaltaneh, he was one of the founders of "The Democrat Party of Iran". Once Ahmad Qavam's cabinet gave way to other Prime Ministers, Ha'erizadeh became a virulent opponent of these governments in parliament. During the elections for the 16th parliament, Ha'erizadeh was elected to the Majles from Tehran, along with a number of other National Front members. The pro-Mosaddeq Ha'erizadeh soon turned against his National Front friends and joined the opposition to Mosaddeq. Ha'erizadeh was involved with the planning of the first coup. After the coup Zahedi appointed him to the position of roving ambassador, which he had much coveted. He entered the 18th Majles, but fell out with Zahedi over the oil issue and was subsequently marginalized.

Haj Reza'i, Tayyeb (1913–1963) He was a traditional athlete, a wrestler, a street fighter and a renowned ruffian leader. He was thrown into jail on numerous occasions and banished to Bandar Abbas for disturbing the peace, street brawls, and assault and battery. In 1947, he opened a fruit store in the main fruit and vegetable market of Southern Tehran. From 1948, he organized religious mourning processions and ran a mourning centre (*takiyyeh*) next to Tehran's main granary. Tayeb and Ramezoun Yakhi were instrumental in mobilizing their followers against Mosaddeq on 9 Esfand (28 February 1953) and 28 Mordad. Tayeb, who was close to Ayatollah Behbahani, seems to have been prompted by him on both occasions. Tayeb was also close to Asadollah Rashidiyan. After the coup, Tayeb and 19 of his collaborators were decorated with the Second Class Medal of Rastakhiz (or resurgence) for their contributions to ousting Mosaddeq. Subsequently, Tayeb became a successful banana merchant, walking around with a pistol which was said to be a special gift to him by the Shah. Ten years after the coup, Tayeb was arrested, condemned to death and executed for his involvement in the 5 June 1963 pro-Khomeyni uprising against the Shah.

Haqshenas, Jahangir (1910–2000) Born in Tehran, he studied at the industrial school in Tehran and was then sent on a scholarship to the School of Polytechnic in Berlin. Upon his return to Iran he was employed at the Plan and Budget Organization and then at the Iranian Insurance Company, where he became the managing director. Along with Zirakzadeh, he was one of the founders of the politicized Engineers Association in 1944 and the Iran Party in 1945. In 1952, he became Minister of Roads in Mosaddeq's government and was arrested during the first coup. He was arrested and imprisoned for a couple of months after the second coup. Afterwards he went into private business and left Iran to live in the UK.

Hejazi, Abdolhoseyn (1904–?) He was a member of the second graduating class of Tehran's Officers' Academy in 1924. He continued his military studies at the Military Academy of St. Cyr in France. Hejazi occupied key military positions in the army. In 1951 he was appointed as the Military Commander of Tehran as well as the Chief of Police. He was removed from office by Mosaddeq and was arrested in October 1952 for plotting with Zahedi and the Rashidiyan brothers against the government. After the coup, he was appointed to the posts of Commander of the Fars Army, Commander of the University of War, Ambassador to Pakistan, deputy Chief of Staff, Commander of the Ground Forces and, finally, the Chief of Staff. After being removed from office, he committed suicide.

Ja'fari, Sha'ban (1921–2006) He was born in Tehran and dropped out of school after the fourth grade. He was around 14 when he began frequenting the traditional athletics clubs of Tehran. At the age of 15 he was arrested and imprisoned for his role in a street brawl. Ja'fari was an important figurehead of the South Tehran ruffians, a follower of Ayatollah Kashani and a close acquaintance of Navab Safavi and Hoseyn Makki. Ja'fari played an important role in mobilizing the Tehran ruffians against Mosaddeq on 9 Esfand and during the second coup. He was in prison during the morning events of the second coup and was released in the afternoon. After the coup he was decorated and generously supported to build his own traditional athletics club called the "Ja'fari Club". During the revolution, he left the country a few days before the Shah and settled in the US.

Kashani, Abolqasem (1877–1962) Born in Tehran, he travelled to Najaf and became a *mojtahed* at the age of 25. He returned to Tehran in 1921 and became the leading political cleric during 1941 and 1953. In 1925 Kashani was elected to the Iranian Constituent Assembly and voted in favour of ending the Qajar dynasty and installing Reza Shah's monarchy. In 1944 he was arrested by British forces for his alleged collaboration with the Germans, and was released in 1945. From 1945 to 1951 he formed an alliance with Navab Safavi (Mojtaba Mir Lowhi) and became the source of emulation of Navab Safavi's organization of Fadaiyan Eslam (the "Devotees of Islam"). In 1948, Kashani's close collaborator Shams-e Qanatabadi founded the "Society of Muslim Mojaheds", which became Kashani's political organization. Kashani was exiled after the assassination attempt against the Shah in 1949. From exile in Beirut he ordered his followers to campaign for the election of National Front members to the 16th parliament. In June 1950 Kashani returned to Iran and formed a strong alliance with Mosaddeq. Kashani's support for Mosaddeq during the events of 30 Tir (20 July 1952) was instrumental in the downfall of Ahmad Qavam's government and Mosaddeq's return to power. Kashani became the President of the 17th Majles after the departure of Seyyed Hasan Emami. From November 1952, Kashani fell out with Mosaddeq and gradually became his chief political opponent. Kashani was instrumental in mobilizing the anti-Mosaddeq demonstrations of 9 Esfand (27 February 1953): he vehemently opposed Mosaddeq's referendum on dissolving the 17th Majles and came to view Mosaddeq as a puppet of the Communists bent on abolishing the monarchy. By the time of the coup, Kashani had established strong ties with Zahedi and was one of the key anti-Mosaddeq clerics, along with Behbahani. He met with Zahedi two days after the coup, but fell out with him and was arrested in 1956 for two months.

Khajehnouri, Ebrahim (1896–1991) Born in Tehran he attended the French St. Louis School in Tehran. He obtained his degree in law and sociology from the University of Brussels. In 1942, he co-founded the Edalat (justice) Party along with his friends, Ali Dashti and Jamal-e Emami. He became the Director-General of the Publications and Propaganda Department and held the office of Deputy Prime Minister in 1944 and again in 1946 and 1948. In 1949 he was elected as a senator from Tehran. During Mosaddeq's premiership he was a member of the opposition and collaborated with Zahedi. After the coup he became a senator once again and strongly opposed the bill on the creation of the SAVAK. Khajehnouri was an eloquent and gripping writer and his monographs of key Iranian politicians under the title of "Bazigaran-e Asr-e Tala'i" (Players of the Golden Age) remains a classic.

Khosrovani, Parviz (1920–?) He graduated from Tehran's Officers Academy in 1942. He was the founder of the Taj (Crown) Athletics Club which had the full support of Mohammad Reza Shah. In 1953 he became actively involved in anti-Mosaddeq activities and was arrested along with Sha'ban Ja'fari after the 28 February (9 Esfand) events in front of Mosaddeq's house. Khosrovani was released about two weeks before the first coup. After the second coup, in which he and his athletes personally participated, he was promoted in rank and became a Special Adjutant to the Shah. In 1966 he became the Director of the Physical Education Organization and Assistant to the Prime

Minister. In 1971 he became deputy commander of the Gendarmerie. He went to London before the revolution.

Makki, Hoseyn (1911–1999) He was born in Meybod near Yazd and moved to Tehran to continue his education. He was an employee of the National Iranian Railroad Company while he researched and wrote on the history of Iran. He began his career as a journalist after 1941. In 1943 he founded the Iran Party and in 1946 he became one of the founding members of Ahmad Qavam's "Democrat Party of Iran". He entered the 15th Majles and joined forces with Baqa'i and Ha'erizadeh in opposing the rapidly changing governments and militating against the Supplementary Oil Agreement. He became famous for his filibuster which prevented the Agreement from being ratified during the 15th Majles. Makki was one of the key founders of the pro-Mosaddeq National Front. He entered the 16th Majles and formed a minority pro-Mosaddeq faction. After Mosaddeq's premiership, Makki remained an untiring supporter of his policies. Makki began opposing Mosaddeq in December 1952. After the coup and the assassination attempt on 'Ala's life in 1955, Makki was arrested and imprisoned for about a month. Makki spent his life after the coup on his research and publications on various aspects of Iranian history.

Mirashrafi, Mehdi (1910–1979) He was born in Tafresh and graduated from Tehran's Officers Academy. He pursued a military career in the army until his resignation in 1942. After publishing his highly controversial and polemical paper, *Atash*, Mirashrafi became well known in oppositional political circles. Mirashrafi opposed Mosaddeq after he became Prime Minister and succeeded in entering the 17th Majles. Mirashrafi was in contact with members of the British Embassy and advised them to remove Mosaddeq through a coup. Mirashrafi was close to both Seyyed Zia Tabataba'i and Ayatollah Kashani and consistently militated against Mosaddeq both in the parliament and through his newspaper. Immediately after the fall of Tehran Radio's Transmission Station, he was the first person to speak and give news of Mosaddeq's overthrow. After the coup he was elected to the 18th and 20th Majles and subsequently went into business. He became a very successful industrialist and landowner. After the revolution he was arrested, condemned to death and executed.

Monshizadeh, Davud (1915–1989) Born in Tehran, he was sent to the University of Dijon on a government scholarship in 1932. He went to Germany in 1937 and obtained his doctorate from Berlin University in 1943. Monshizadeh returned to Iran in 1950 and founded the Iranian Nationalist Socialist (Fascist) Party called SUMKA in 1951. From 1952, Monshizadeh's Brown Shirts started clashing with Tudeh (Communist) Party sympathizers and members on the streets. Monshizadeh gradually gravitated towards Zahedi. His partisans were involved in the anti-Mosaddeq demonstrations of 9 Esfand, were accused of involvement in the abduction of Afshartus, and played an active role in support of the anti-Mosaddeq forces during the second coup. After the coup, he and his party were financially aided by the police and the Court. Monshizadeh left Iran in 1963 and spent the rest of his life in Sweden and the US.

Nasiri, Ne'matollah (1910–1979) Born in Semnan, he attended military schools and graduated from Tehran's Officers' Academy. In 1949 he became the commander of the Pahlavi Regiment and was then promoted to the highly sensitive post of commander of the Imperial Guards. In preparation for the first coup, Nasiri (a key player in the plot) was dispatched to Ramsar to obtain the Shah's disputed Royal edicts dismissing

Mosaddeq and appointing Zahedi, deliver them first to Zahedi, and, having communicated it to Mosaddeq, arrest the Prime Minister. In the early morning hours of 16 August, Nasiri was arrested at Mosaddeq's house, only to be released in the afternoon of 19 August after the success of the second coup. Nasiri was promoted in rank after the coup. In 1960 he became the Chief of Police and subsequently the Military Governor of Tehran. In 1965 he became Deputy Prime Minister and the head of SAVAK, where he served for some 13 years. In 1978 he became Ambassador to Pakistan, but was recalled after three months and subsequently arrested three months before the February 1979 revolution. After the revolution Nasiri was condemned to death and executed.

Navab Safavi (Mir Lowhi), Mojtaba (1924–1956) Born in Tehran, he attended the German technical high school in Tehran and briefly worked at the British-managed Iranian Oil Company in Abadan before going to Najaf in 1943 to pursue his religious studies at the seminary school. On his return to Tehran around 1946, he founded an organization called the Fadaiyan Eslam, or the "Devotees of Islam". His organization was committed to the application of the Shari'a, the restoration of an Islamic Government and the cleansing of evil-doers and enemies of Islam. From 1945 to 1951, Navab Safavi and Ayatollah Kashani formed an alliance, and Navab Safavi threw the full weight of his organization behind Kashani's political objectives. In March 1946 his zealous followers assassinated Ahmad Kasravi. Navab Safavi's organization accepted responsibility for the assassination of Hajir, the Minister of Court (January 1950), Prime Minister Razmara (March 1951), and Fatemi, Mosaddeq's Minister of Foreign Affairs (February 1952). Navab Safavi was arrested five weeks after Mosaddeq's premiership. He remained in prison from June 1951 to January 1953. He refused to enter into any political alignments after his release and did not play a role in the two coups. In November 1956, a member of his organization fired on Prime Minister 'Ala from close range. In less than a week, Navab Safavi and some thirty members of the Fadaiyan Eslam were arrested. Navab Safavi and seven of his collaborators were put on trial, and Navab Safavi was sentenced to death and executed.

Qanatabadi, Shams (1914–1988) Born in Tehran, he pursued his high school studies in Tehran and then attended the Qom seminary school before going to Najaf. He returned to Tehran in 1946 and became a close follower and collaborator of Ayatollah Kashani. In 1949 he founded the "Society of Moslem Mojaheds" with the assistance of Mahmud Shervin. With Kashani's support, he entered the 17th Majles as a representative of Shahroud. Qanatabadi stood loyally by his mentor Kashani during the latter's conflict with Mosaddeq and alliance with Zahedi. He published the weekly *Demokrat Eslami*, in which from March to the end of August 1953 he assailed Mosaddeq's government as anti-religious, anti-monarchic and a stooge of the Communists. Qanatabadi also published the daily *Mellat Ma*. Three days after the coup, Zahedi met with Qanatabadi, Baqa'i and Ha'erizadeh at Kashani's house. After the coup, Qanatabadi took off his religious garb and continued to be a member of the 18th and 19th parliaments.

Qavam, Ahmad (1873–1956). Born in Tehran to a family of notables, he was homeschooled and well educated. Qavam spent three years studying in Europe. He started his career at the Qajar court and soon climbed the ranks. He entered the cabinet as

Minister of War in 1910 and continued to occupy various ministerial positions in subsequent governments. After Seyyed Zia's 1920 coup, Qavam, who at the time was the Governor of Khorasan, was arrested and sent to jail in Tehran. Some three months later, when Seyyed Zia was deposed, Qavam became Prime Minister. In 1923 he was exiled to Europe. After the departure of Reza Shah, Qavam returned to politics in 1941. In 1942 he became Prime Minister under the rule of Mohammad Reza Shah. He was intermittently in power as Prime Minister or out of favour and in exile. After almost three years of absence, Qavam returned to Iran in 1950. In July 1951, when Mosaddeq resigned as Prime Minister, the Shah called on the 81-year-old Qavam, who had the support of the American and the British, to become Prime Minister. Qavam's government was very short-lived and Mosaddeq returned to power on a wave of popular support. Qavam went into hiding and lived in Tehran until his death.

Rashidiyan, Asadollah (1922 – 1980?) Born in Tehran, he was the son of Habibollah Rashidiyan and the brother of Seyfollah and Qodratollah. Not much is known about his educational background. Asadollah is said to have engaged in commerce from an early age. He became politically involved with Seyyed Zia, who was a friend of his father, and remained very loyal to Seyyed Zia. Asadollah, who had close connections with the British Embassy, became actively involved in opposing Mosaddeq. After the departure of the British from Iran, Rashidiyan collaborated with the American Embassy and was one of the key figures and masterminds of the coup on 28 Mordad. Rashidiyan was close to both the Shah and Princess Ashraf, and was trusted by both. After Mosaddeq's overthrow Rashidiyan was handsomely rewarded for his activities and was allowed to establish the Bank of Cooperatives and Distribution. He is said to have also owned an insurance company. He left the country and lived in London until the end of his life.

Riyahi, Mohammad-Taqi (1910–1988) Born in Esfahan, he graduated from Tehran's Officers Academy and was sent to France on a government scholarship. He attended the prestigious School of Polytechnic (Ecole Polytechnique) in Paris in parallel with his military studies and obtained a degree in hydraulic engineering. After the nationalization of the oil industry he was appointed as the managing director of the Abadan oil refinery. Riyahi was a member of the pro-Mosaddeq Iran Party. In 1952, Mosaddeq appointed him as the deputy Minister of War, and after the events of 28 February 1953 Riyahi became the Chief of Staff. He was arrested after the coup and was condemned to three years in prison. After his release from prison he joined the private sector. In March 1979 Riyahi was appointed Minister of National Defence in Mehdi Bazargan's post-revolution Provisional Government. Riyahi resigned from his position after three months and left Iran. He spent the rest of his life in Nice, France.

Rowhani, Ali-Mohammad (1912–1983). Born in Tehran, he graduated with highest honours from Tehran's Officers Academy. He served in various military posts outside of Tehran for ten years. In 1949 he was appointed to the post of the commander of the Naderi Regiment at the Third Mountain Brigade. He was also promoted to the position of the deputy commander of the Third Mountain Brigade at 'Eshratabad. Rowhani was a member of the secret military organization of the "Devotees of the Shah" and was in close contact with Zahedi before the first coup. He was arrested on 17 August on charges of planning and participating in the first coup. He was freed during the afternoon of 19 August and played an important role in the attack on

Mosaddeq's house. After the coup he was promoted in rank and appointed as the commander of the Third Mountain Brigade. In 1956 he became the commander of the Khouzestan Corps and retired in 1966. He passed away overseas.

Sadiqi, Gholamhoseyn (1905–1991) Born in Tehran, he was sent to Paris on a government scholarship in 1929. After having obtained his doctorate in philosophy from the University of Paris in 1937, he returned to Iran and pursued an academic career at the University of Tehran. In 1948 he founded the Institute for Social Studies and Research. In 1951, he was appointed as Minister of Post and Telegraph and subsequently as Minister of Interior by Mosaddeq. During the first and second coup he was Mosaddeq's Minister of Interior and remained loyal to him. After the second coup he was arrested and imprisoned, but was eventually allowed to resume teaching at the University of Tehran. He is known as the father of the study of sociology in Iran. During the end of the Shah's reign and after the failure of Azhari's military government, the monarch invited Sadiqi to become Prime Minister, but their discussions failed to secure Sadiqi's acceptance.

Tabataba'i, Ziaeddin-Seyyed Zia (1888–1969) He is popularly known as Seyyed Zia. Born in Shiraz, he moved to Tabriz where he concluded his studies and learnt English, French and Russian. Tabataba'i moved back to Shiraz, where he published the daily *Eslam*. After Mohammad-Ali Shah Qajar closed the parliament and suspended the constitution, Tabataba'i moved to Tehran to join the Constitutionalist. He participated actively in the takeover of Tehran by the Constitutionalist and published his radical dailies, *Sharq*, *Barq* and *Ra'd*. Tabataba'i was subsequently sent to Europe to pursue his education. In 1917 he travelled to Russia, met with Lenin and then returned to Iran. From 1920 he actively entered into politics, joined forces with Reza Khan (later Reza Shah) and entered Tehran triumphantly with 1,400 soldiers as the new Prime Minister. Some three months after the 1921 coup, Tabataba'i was pushed out of office by Reza Khan and went to Switzerland and finally settled in Palestine. He returned to Iran in 1944 after 22 years of exile and began jockeying for power. He entered the 14th Majles as the representative of Yazd. Tabataba'i remained the real power behind the governments that speedily succeeded one another. In 1951, Tabataba'i was groomed to become Prime Minister after 'Ala, but this did not happen. He was known as an ardent Anglophile and was open about having received money from the British to stage the 1921 coup. Less than nine months after Mosaddeq became Prime Minister Tabataba'i counselled the British Embassy to remove him by force.

Zahedi, Ardeshir (1928) Born in Tehran, Fazlollah Zahedi's son obtained his Bachelor of Science in agriculture from the State University of Utah in 1950 after having completed his high school education in Tehran. Upon his return to Iran he worked at the United States Point Four Program in Tehran, which was administered by a special agency of the Department of State. Ardeshir Zahedi was a close aide of his father during the latter's activities against Mosaddeq. He played a key role in the second coup. After the coup and during his father's premiership he became highly influential in Iranian politics as Fazlollah Zahedi's personal assistant. In 1957 he married the Shah's daughter, Princess Shahnaz Pahlavi, and in 1959 he served as Iran's Ambassador, first in Washington and subsequently in London. In 1966 he became the Minister of Foreign Affairs in Amir Abbas Hoveyda's government and held this position until 1971. He was again appointed as Ambassador to Washington in 1973. Zahedi was retained as Ambassador until the revolution in 1979.

Zahedi, Fazlollah (1892–1963) Born in Hamedan, he entered the Cossack's Officers Academy and is said to have served under Colonel Reza Khan. Zahedi participated in numerous internal campaigns, demonstrated bravery and was quickly promoted in rank. Having participated in the defeat of Esmail Agha Simitqu in 1922, he received the prestigious Zolfaqar medal and became Reza Khan-e Sardar Sepah's adjutant. From this date Zahedi was appointed to numerous commanding posts throughout Iran. In 1940 he became the commander of Iran's Gendarmerie. In 1943 he was arrested by the British for pro-German activities and was released in 1945. In 1949 he was appointed as the Chief of Police, and during the elections to the 16th Majles he played an important role in safeguarding the integrity of the elections, resulting in pro-Mosaddeq National Front members entering the parliament. Zahedi was appointed as Minister of Interior in Mosaddeq's government but resigned after a few months. From 1951, Zahedi presented himself as a viable replacement for Mosaddeq and began opposing him. Zahedi played an important role in mobilizing the military against Mosaddeq and systematically challenging his government. He is said to have been implicated in the abduction and murder of Afshartus. Zahedi, who was instrumental in the first and second coups, became Prime Minister on the evening of 19 August. He remained Prime Minister until 1955, at which time the Shah asked for his resignation and sent him off to Switzerland, where he lived for the rest of his life.

Zirakzadeh, Ahmad (1907–1993) Born in Tehran, Zirakzadeh graduated from high school in Tehran and was sent to France in 1926 by the army to pursue his studies. He studied mathematics at the School of Polytechnic (Ecole Polytechnique) in Paris. In 1934 he entered the Iranian Navy, but was subsequently transferred to the Ministry of Roads in 1940. One year later he started teaching at the University of Tehran and became the editor of a left-leaning newspaper, *Mardan-e Kar*, which was banned in 1944. Zirakzadeh was one of the founders of the politicized Engineers Association in 1944 and the Iran Party in 1945. The Iran Party was a social democratic party with socialist and nationalist tendencies. Zirakzadeh was the first Secretary General of the Iran Party. Zirakzadeh was one of the 20 founding members of the pro-Mosaddeq National Front. In Mosaddeq's government Zirakzadeh became Undersecretary of the Ministry of Economy and entered the 17th Majles as a National Front candidate from Tehran. Zirakzadeh was arrested during the early hours of the first coup, along with Jahangir Haqshenas, Mosaddeq's Minister of Roads, and Hoseyn Fatemi by members of the Imperial Guard. After the failure of the first coup, they were all released. He remained loyal to Mosaddeq. After the success of the second coup Zirakzadeh went into hiding and was arrested afterwards. Zirakzadeh gradually distanced himself from politics. He left for the US after the revolution, but later returned to Iran and lived there for the rest of his life.

Bibliography

Archival documents

British Foreign Office: FO.
British Petroleum Archives, University of Warwick: BP.
Foreign Relations of the United States (FRUS), *Iran*, 1952–54: FRUS.
Iranian Oral History Collection, Harvard University.
National Security Archives, The George Washington University, Washington.
RAIOH (Research Association of Iranian Oral History), Berlin.

Works in Persian

Abadiyan, H., *Doctor Mozaffar Baqa'i* (Tehran: Moaseseh Motale'at va Pajoheshhaye Siyasi, 1377).
Afrasiyabi, B. and Dehqan, S., *Taleqani dar Tarikh* (Tehran: Niloufar, 1360).
Afrasiyabi, B., *Khaterat va Mobarezat-e Doctor Hoseyn Fatemi* (Tehran: Sokhan, 1366).
Aqeli, B., *Sharh-e Hal-e Rejal Siyasi va Nezamiy-e Moaser Iran* (Tehran: Goftar, 1380).
Ahmadi, M. R., *Khaterat-e Ayatollah Gerami* (Tehran: Markaz-e Asnad-e Enqelab-e Eslami, 1381).
Al-e Ahmad, J., *Dar Khedmat va Khiyanat-e Rowshanfekran* (Tehran: Ravaq, n.d).
'Alikhani, A. N., *Yaddashthay-e 'Alam*, vol. 1 (Bethesda: Iranbooks, 1992).
'Alikhani, A. N., *Yaddashthay-e 'Alam*, vol. 2 (Bethesda: Iranbooks, 1993).
'Alikhani, A. N., *Yaddashthay-e 'Alam*, vol. 3 (Bethesda: Iranbooks, 1995).
'Alikhani, A. N., *Yaddashthay-e 'Alam*, vol. 6 (Bethesda: Ibex Publishers, 2008).
Amir-Khosravi, B., *Nazar az Darun be Naqshe Hezb Tudeh Iran* (Tehran: Ettela'at, 1375).
Aqeli, B., *Roozshomar-e Tarikh-e Iran*, vol.1 (Tehran: Nashr-e Goftar, 1369).
Aramesh, A., *Haft sal dar zendan-e Ariyamehr* (Tehran: Bongah-e Tarjomeh va nashr-e Ketab, 1358).
Araqi, M., *Nagoftehha* (Tehran: Rasa, 1370).
Askari, H., *Shah, Mosaddeq, Sepahbod Zahedi* (Sweden: Arash, 2000).
Azizi, G., *Hezb-e Sosialist-e Melli-e Kargaran-e Iran* (Tehran: Markaz-e Asnad-e Enqelab-e Eslami, 1383).
Baniahmad, A., *Panj Rooz Rastakhiz-e Mellat-e Iran* (Tehran: Chapkhaneh Artesh, n.d).

Be Ravayat-e Asnad-e SAVAK, *Rowhaniy-e Mobarez Ayatollah Seyyed Abolqasem Kashani*, vols.1 and 2 (Tehran: Markaz-e Barrasiy-e Asnad-e Tarikhiy-e Vezarat-e Ettela'at, 1379).

Be Ravayat-e Asnad-e SAVAK, *Seyyed Ziaeddin Tabatabai'e* (Tehran: Markaz-e Barrasiy-e Asnad-e Tarikhiy-e Vezarat-e Ettela'at, 1381).

Be Ravayat-e Asnad-e SAVAK, *Mozaffar Baqa'i* (Tehran: Markaz-e Barrasiy-e Asnad-e Tarikhiy-e Vezarat Ettela'at, 1382).

Be Ravayat-e Asnad-e SAVAK, *Rashidiyanha*, vols 1, 2 & 3 (Tehran: Markaz-e Barrasiy-e Asnad-e Tarikhiy-e Vezarat Ettela'at, 1389).

Be Ravayat-e Asnad-e SAVAK, *Azad Mard: Shahid Tayeb Haj-Reza'i* (Tehran: Markaz-e Barrasiy-e Asnad-e Tarikhiy-e Vezarat Ettela'at, 1378),

Be Ravayat-e Asnad-e SAVAK, *Jebhey-e Melli* (Tehran: Markaz-e Barrasiy-e Asnad-e Tarikhiy-e, 1379)

Behzadi, A., *Shebh-e Khaterat*, vol. 2 (Tehran: Ata'i, 1388).

Bozorgmehr, J., *Doctor Mohammad Mosaddeq dar Dadgah-e Tajdid Nazar* (Tehran: Enteshar, 1365).

Elahi, S., *Seyyed Zia, Mard Aval ya Mard-e Dovom-e Coup d'état* (LA: Ketab Corp, 2011).

Fardust, H., *Zohur va Soqute Saltanat-e Pahlavi*, vol. 1 (Tehran: Entesharat-e Ettela'at, 1390).

Golmohammadi, A., *Jam'iyate Fadaiyan Eslam be Ravayat-e Asnad*, vol. 2 (Tehran: Markaz-e Asnad-e Enqelab-e Eslami, 1382).

Homayoun, D., *Man va Rouzegaram* (Hamburg: Nashre Talash, 1387).

Hoseyni, M., *Khaterat-e Mohammadmehdi 'Abdkhoda'i* (Tehran: Markaz-e Asnad-e Enqelab-e Eslami, 1379).

Jami, *Gozashteh Cheraq Rahe Ayandeh* (Tehran: Entesharat Niloufar, 1362).

Javanshir, F. M., *Tajrobeh 28 Mordad* (Tehran: Entesharat Hezb Toudeh Iran, 1359).

Karamipour, H., *Khaterat-e Doctor Shervin* (Tehran: Markaz-e Asnad-e Enqelab-e Eslami, 1384).

Ketab-e Siyah dar bareh Sazeman Afsaran Tudeh, n.a, (n.p, n.p, Esfand 1334).

Keymaram, M., *Rofaqaye Bala* (Tehran: Shabaviz, 1374).

Khameh'i, A., *Az Ensha'ab ta Kudeta* (Tehran: Hafteh, 1363).

Khameh'i, A., *Panjaho Seh Nafar* (Entesharat Hafteh: Tehran n.d).

Lajevardi, H., *Khaterat Amir Teymur Kalali* (Bethesda, Markaz Motale 'at Khavarmiyaneh Daneshgah Harvard, 1977).

Makki, H., *Vaqaye' Siyom-e Tir* (Tehran: Entesharat-e 'Elmi, 1378).

Maleki, A., *Tarikhcheh Jebhey-e Melli* (Tehran: Taban, n.d).

Manzarpour, A., *Dar Koucheh va Khiyaban* (Tehran: Vezarate Farhang o Ershad-e Eslami, 1386).

Mirza'i, S., *Tayeb dar Gozar-e Lutiha* (Tehran: Madiya, 1381).

Mohammadi, M. J., *Raze Piruziye Kudetaye 28 Mordad* (Koln: Forough, n.d).

Mosaddeq, G., *Dar Kenar Pedaram* (Tehran, Rasa, 1369).

Mosaddeq, M., *Khaterat va Ta'alomat* (Tehran: 'Elmi, 1365).

Mossavar Rahmani, G., *Kohneh Sarbaz* (Tehran: Rasa, 1366).

Movahhed, M. A., *Khabe Ashofteh Naft* (Tehran: Karnameh, 1378).

Nejati, G.R, *Jonbesh Melli Shodan-e Naft-e Iran* (Tehran: Enteshar, 1366).

Pahlavi, M. R., *Ma'muriyat Baray-e Vatanam*, (Paris: Parang, 1366).

Rahnema, A., *Niruhaye Mazhabi bar bastar Nehzat-e Melli* (Tehran: Gam-e No, 1384).
Safari, M. A., *Qalam va Siyasat* (Tehran: Namak, 1371).
Sahabi, E., *Mosaddeq, Dowlat-e Melli va Koudeta* (Tehran: Tarh-e No, 1380).
Salemi, M. H., *Tarikh Nehzat-e Melli Shodan Naft-e Iran az Negahi Digar* (Tehran: Markaz-e Asnad-e Enqelab-e Eslami, 1388).
Sanjabi, K., *Omidha va Naomidiha* (London : Nashre Ketab, 1368).
Sarshar, H., *Sha'ban Ja'fari* (Los Angeles: Nashr-e Nab, 1381).
Shahhoseyni, H., *An Suye Khaterehha* (Tehran: Samadiyeh, 1388),
Shifteh, N., *Zendeginameh va Mobarezat Siyasiye doctor Mosaddeq* (Tehran: Koomesh, 1370).
Tafazoli, A., *Sargozashti Pishneveshteh* (Tehran: Entesharat-e Atta'i, 1381).
Tafreshi, M. and Taherahmadi, M., *Gozareshhay-e Mahramaneh Shahrebani*, vol. 2 (Tehran: Entesharat-e Sazeman Asnad-e Melli, 1371).
Torbatiy-e Sanjabi, M., *Koudetasazan* (Tehran: Kavosh, 1376).
Torkaman, M., *Tote'eh Robodan va Qatl-e Sarlashgar Afshartus* (Tehran : Rasa, 1363).
Towfiq, A., *Qanouni boodan ya nabodan-e farman-e azl Mosaddeq* (Paris: Entesharat Sahand, 2008).
Varqa, M., *Nagoftehha'i Piramoun-e Fororiziye Hokumat Mosaddeq va naqsh Hezbe Tudeh-e Iran* (Tehran: Baztabnegar, 1384).
Zahedi, A., *Khaterat-e Ardeshir Zahedi*, vol. 1 (Tehran: Ketab Sara, 1385).
Zohtabfard, R., *Ghoghaye Naft* (Tehran: Chap Akhtar Shomal, n.d).

Works in English

Bayandor, D., *Iran and the CIA* (NY: Palgrave Macmillan, 2010).
Cottam, R. W., *Iran and the United States* (PA: University of Pittsburgh Press, 1988).
Cottam, R. W., *Nationalism in Iran* (PA: University of Pittsburgh Press, 1979).
Dorman, W. and Farhang, M., *The U.S. Press and Iran* (Berkeley: University of California Press, 1987).
Dorril, S., *MI6: Fifty Years of Special Operations* (London: Fourth Estate, 2001).
Falle, S., *My Lucky Life* (Sussex: The Book Guild, 1996).
Gasiorowski, M. J. and Byrne, M., (eds.) *Mohammad Mosaddeq and the 1953 Coup in Iran* (Syracuse: Syracuse University Press, 2004).
Louis, W. R., *The British Empire in the Middle East 1945–1951* (Oxford: Clarendon Press, 1984).
Love, K., *The American Role in the Pahlavi Restoration on August 1953* (Unpublished manuscript, Allen Dulles Papers, Princeton University Library, 1960).
Luttwak, E., *Coup d'état* (Cambridge: Harvard University Press, 1979).
Pahlavi, A., *Faces in a Mirror* (NJ: Prentice–Hall, 1980).
Roosevelt, K., *Countercoup* (New York: McGraw-Hill, 1979).
Wilber, D., *Clandestine Service History. Overthrow of Premier Mossadeq of Iran*, http://cryptome.org/cia-iran.htm.
Woodhouse, C. M., *Something Ventured* (London: Granada, 1982).

Further reading

Abrahamian, E., *The Coup: 1953, The CIA and the Roots of modern U.S.-Iranian Relations* (New York: New Press, 2013).
Azimi, F., *Iran: The Crisis of Democracy* (London: I.B.Tauris, 2009).
Bill, J. and Louis, Wm. R., *Mussadiq, Iranian Nationalism, and Oil* (London: I.B. Tauris 1988)
De Bellaigue, C., *Patriot of Persia* (New York: Harper, 2012).
Katouzian, H., *Musaddiq and the Struggle for Power in Iran* (London: I.B. Tauris, 1999).
Kinzer, S., *All the Shah's Men: An American Coup and the Roots of Middle East Terror* (New Jersey: Wiley, 2008).

Index

Abadan oil refinery, 12
Abbasi brothers, 72, 165, 168
Acheson, Dean, 14, 16
Afkhami, Gholam-Hoseyn, 161, 218–219
Afshartus, Mahmud, 28, 31, 34, 40–44, 46, 47, 48, 50, 63, 239, 263, 266
Ajdanqezi, Parvin (Roqiyeh Azadpour), 163, 164, 227
Akhavi, Hasan, 42, 54, 77, 87, 88–92, 105, 110, 121, 131, 132, 190
'Ala, Hoseyn, 18, 22, 35, 37, 243, 277, 284–285
Alam, Asadollah
  coup d'état, 9
'Alam, Asadollah, 8–9, 24, 67, 238
American Embassy, 7, 29, 32, 35, 64, 90, 98, 105, 111, 134, 170, 177, 224, 225, 238, 295, 296
Amidi-ye Nouri, Abolhasan, 36, 135, 136, 183
Amini, Mahmud, 262
Amir Khalili, As'ad, 207–208, 209–210, 215, 217
Aqayan, Felix, 267
'Arab, Hasan, 58, 168, 170–171
Arbab Zeinolabeddin, 71
Arbabi, Ali-Mohammad, 141–142, 206, 208
Arfa', Hasan, 42, 53, 54, 55, 56, 57, 86, 87, 89, 121, 223
Ariya Party, 42–43, 45, 47, 52, 53–54, 55, 56, 57, 58, 85, 86, 121, 223, 227, 252
Armed Custom Guards, 88, 91, 113, 153, 186, 189, 226, 227
Ashrafi, Hoseynqoli, 12, 88, 90, 105–106, 114–116, 121, 144–145, 151, 189, 201, 209, 213, 217, 221

Ashtiyani, Hoseyn, 32
Attlee, Clement, 13, 291
Azar, Mehdi, 264
Azmudeh, Eskandar, 46, 93, 94, 96, 97–98, 102, 110, 114, 115, 119–121, 122, 124, 234
Azmudeh, Hoseyn, ix

Bagheshah Garrison, 96–97, 103, 109, 153, 229
Baharestan Square, 18, 31, 54, 147, 156, 167, 170, 174, 175, 179, 180, 187, 197–198, 200, 202
Bakhtiyar, Abolqasem, 34–35, 36
Bakhtiyar, Teymur, 56, 71, 108, 118, 119, 121, 130
Bana'i, Asghar, 156, 160
Baniahmad, Ahmad, 119, 120–121, 176, 186, 190, 192, 207, 225
Baqa'i, Mozaffar, 24, 25–26, 30, 32–33, 41–44, 46–47, 49, 52, 53, 57–59, 62, 86, 121, 135, 170, 171, 197, 200, 202–203, 224, 227, 234, 239, 257, 260–261, 265, 276, 286
Batmanqelich, Nader, 52, 88, 89, 90, 92–93, 95, 97, 98, 108, 118–120, 121–122, 124, 125, 135, 143, 190, 196–197, 205, 232
Bayandor, Nasrollah, 41, 43, 50, 118
bazaar, 31, 37, 38, 39, 44, 49, 50, 72, 79–81, 97, 120, 124, 126, 133, 137, 167, 175, 237
Behbahani, Ja'far, 53, 140
Behbahani, Seyyed Mohammad, 37–40, 44, 45, 49, 50, 69, 70, 108, 127–128, 131, 132–133, 136–137, 139, 140–141, 158, 164, 167, 169, 170, 235–238, 239–246, 248, 257, 268, 269

315

Index

Behboudi, Soleyman, 67–68, 78
Behbudgar (Sa'lehi), Hasan, 72, 138–140, 160, 161, 171–172, 227
Behzadi, Siyavosh, 105
Borujerdi, Ayatollah Seyyed Hoseyn, 39, 40, 128, 132, 136–137, 175, 198, 235–236, 240–247, 257
Boscoe Brothers, 56, 79–81, 83, 87, 134
British Memorandum, 130, 187, 227, 267
Byrne, Malcolm, 81

Carroll, George, 63, 75, 87–93, 104, 110, 125, 130, 145, 190, 191, 225, 233, 254, 296
Central Intelligence Agency (CIA), 3, 5, 9–10, 22, 27, 29, 33, 40, 49, 53, 56, 60, 61–64, 72, 74–77, 79, 80–81, 84–88, 89, 90, 93, 100, 101, 102, 103, 106, 107, 110, 111, 112, 114, 117, 120, 123, 125, 128, 130, 134, 145, 147, 148, 154, 176, 178, 188, 191, 194, 196, 198, 223, 224, 225, 233, 249, 252, 254, 267, 268, 269, 278, 286, 288, 291, 293, 295, 296
Chaqu Keshan (knife wielders), 139, 156, 268
Churchill, Winston, 26, 27, 60, 61, 292
Constitutional crisis, 278, 283
Cottam, Richard, 141, 170
council of war, 125–126, 127–129, 130–131, 137, 141, 156, 176, 213, 251, 266, 275

Daad, 135–136, 148, 183
Dabirsiyaqi, Qodrat, 141, 142
Dadsetan, Farhad, 93, 108, 218, 234, 276
Daftari, Mohammad, 41, 48, 71, 88, 93, 94, 97, 113, 121, 153, 184–189, 195–196, 217–218, 229, 234, 268
Darbyshire, Norman, 60, 74, 76
Davarpanah, Iraj, 228, 232, 233
Dayhimi, Habibollah, 53, 54, 121
Dehqan, Ahmad, 82–83
Devotees of Islam (Fadaiyan-e Eslam), 17, 57, 219, 240, 247, 248, 272
Devotees of the Shah (Fadaiyan Shah), 23–24, 25, 40, 51, 52, 97, 102, 111, 115, 118–121, 138, 145, 189, 192, 211, 215, 227, 252
Dowlatshahi, Hoseyn-Ali, 52, 53
Dulles, Allen, 27, 60, 278
Dulles, John Foster, 60, 61, 111, 278

Eden, Anthony, 1–2, 3, 21, 29, 32, 60, 270
Eisenhower, Dwight, 5, 27, 28, 60, 61, 269, 290–291, 292, 294

Esfand 9 (February 28 1953) plot, 28, 34, 37, 39–42, 43, 44–45, 46–47, 49–55, 57, 62, 86, 106, 116, 128, 158, 161, 163, 197, 229, 239, 242–243, 249, 250, 261, 266, 272, 276, 294
Eshqi, Ahmad, 49
'Eshqi, Ahmad, 58, 72, 158, 162
E'tezadi, Malekeh, 52–53, 140, 227, 267
Extraordinary Legislative Powers (ekhtiyarat), 30–31, 59, 237, 260

failure of the first coup, 101, 102, 103, 111, 124, 125, 126, 135, 146, 201, 251, 278, 279, 282, 295
Falle, Sam, 19–20, 25–26, 28–29, 32, 118, 224
Fardust, Hoseyn, 89, 92, 131–132, 140, 229, 267
Farzanegan, Abbas, 62, 87–94, 95, 98, 99, 110–111, 112, 121, 122, 123, 125–126, 128, 129, 130, 134, 145, 190, 192, 223, 233, 268, 269
Farzanegan, Azizollah, 224
Fatemi, Hoseyn, 24, 97, 109, 199, 200, 222, 264
Fesharaki, Mousa, 228, 232
Firouzabadi, Seyyed Jalaleddin, 38
First Armoured Brigade, 88, 141, 206, 210, 212, 234
Foruhar, Daryoush, 147, 199, 201–202, 256
Fouladvand, Ali-Asghar, 102, 231–232

Garzan, Abbas, 108, 158
Gasiorowski, Mark, 81–82, 86
Gilanshah, Hadayatollah, 23, 52, 93, 96, 111, 112, 118, 122–123, 125, 128–129, 192, 225–226, 267
Gilgili, Haj Akbar, 172
Goiran, Roger, 63, 79, 81, 85
Goodwin, Joseph, 63, 87, 91, 134

Ha'eri Yazdi, Mehdi, 136–137
Ha'erizadeh, Abolhasan, 25, 93, 258, 260, 276, 285
Haj Reza'i, Taher, 138, 156, 157, 160
Haj Reza'i, Tayyeb, 50, 53, 72, 138, 156, 157–161, 162, 164–168, 169, 171, 172, 183, 197
Haji Khodadad (Khodadad Khan), 71, 72, 165–166
Hamidi, Esma'il, 90, 113, 117
Haqshenas, Jahangir, 97, 264
Hasan Khani, Naser, 72, 156, 160

Hasibi, Kazem, 161, 199, 288
Hejazi, Abdol-Hoseyn, 21, 24, 118
Henderson, Loy, 3–4, 5, 7–8, 9, 13, 14, 15, 25, 35, 36, 39, 40, 55, 118, 125, 131, 177–178, 241, 242, 243, 270, 279, 284–285, 293, 296–297
Hojjat, Esma'il, 206, 207
Homayoun, Daryoush, 55, 56–57, 83–84, 191
Homayouni, 119–121
Homayouni, Mehdi, 102, 119, 122
Hotchkiss, Theodore, 111, 112, 224, 225

Imperial Guards, 78, 88, 89, 96–97, 102, 103, 153, 229
Iran Party, 197, 198–199, 200
Iranian Constitution, xii, 276–277, 282, 288
Iranian People's Toilers Party, 32, 41, 42–43, 45, 52, 54, 58, 86, 197, 200, 227, 234, 252
Iranian People's Party, 147–148, 199, 201, 256
Iravani, Iraj, 142, 206, 207–208, 209, 210

Ja'fari, Sha'ban, 38, 49–50, 53, 72, 140, 158, 160, 162–165, 166, 168, 169, 170–171, 227
Jahanbani, Hamid, 142, 143, 206, 207–208, 230
Jalili (Djalili), Ali, 80–82, 148, 200
Jandaqi (Shahriyari), Abdollah, 156, 160, 161, 162, 164, 165, 166, 168, 169, 171

Kalali, Amir-Teymour, 259
Kamalvand, Ruhollah, 244
Karimpour Shirazi, Amir-Mokhtar, 199
Kashani, Abolqasem, 18, 25, 30–33, 35, 37–40, 41–42, 44, 45–47, 49, 52, 57–59, 63, 66, 69, 108, 128, 141, 158, 159, 162, 169, 170, 174, 234, 235–236, 238–240, 241, 242–245, 257–261, 267
Kashani, Mohammad, 240
Kashani, Mostafa, 93, 169, 223
Keyser, William, 225
Keyvani, Farrokh, 56, 62–63, 81–85, 107, 126, 127, 129–130, 137, 148–149, 174, 188, 191, 198, 200, 227, 254
Khajehnouri, Ebrahim, 24, 26
Khal'atbari, Ziaeddin, 71, 225, 227
Khameh'i, Anvar, 150, 151
Khatibi, Hoseyn, 41–44, 47
Khodayeki, Asadollah, 138

Khosrovani, Parviz, 50–51, 71, 153, 229–230
Khosrowdad, Amir, 192, 192, 211
Khosrowpanah, Ali-Farhang, 90, 91, 93–94, 95, 96, 98, 116–117, 119, 120, 125, 191
Kiyani, Ataollah, 96–97, 142, 207, 210, 213–218, 219, 226

Lambton, A.K.S, 10, 12, 14–15, 17, 73, 74, 170, 171, 289
line commanders, 91, 93, 117, 120, 145, 154, 192, 251, 252, 268
Litkouhi, Fatollah, 276
London draft of operation TPAJAX, 29, 61, 98, 235, 278, 286, 288
Louis, Roger, 15, 26, 75
Love, Kennett, 134, 146–147, 268
Luttwak, Edward, 273, 275

Makki, Hoseyn, 25, 30, 238, 258–260, 286–287
Maleki, Khalil, 147, 149, 200–201, 256
Mansurpour, 90, 95, 113–114, 119, 121
Mar'ashi, 119, 120, 216, 218, 219, 230
Marzban, Reza, 83
Matin-Daftari, Ahmad, 258
McClure, Robert, 125, 296
McGhee, George, 13
Mesgar, Mahmud, 72, 168–169, 171, 172
Meydan (fruit and vegtable market), 106, 155, 157, 167, 237
Middleton, George, 15, 18, 20–22, 24–25, 26, 27, 29, 32, 58, 238, 239
Military Secretariat, 62, 77, 89, 91, 93, 101, 103, 105, 110, 112, 122, 131, 190
Mirashrafi, Mehdi, 19–20, 29, 223, 224
Mo'azzami, Seyfollah, 264, 288
Mobasheri, Mohammad-Ali, 102
Mobasser, Mohsen, 88, 95, 121–122, 184
Modabber, Nasrollah, 48, 88, 113, 121, 131, 151, 152–153, 187–188, 201, 209
Mohanna, Mohammad, 221
Momtaz, Ezatollah, 88, 95–96, 98, 103, 153, 154, 209, 210, 217, 228, 229, 230, 232
Monazzah, Ali-Akbar, 41, 44, 50
Monshizadeh, Davud, 42, 54–57, 84, 86, 191, 227
Moradiyan, Ali, 119, 189
Morrison, Herbert, 12
Mosaddeq, Gholam-Hoseyn, 159, 233, 261, 281
Mozayyani, Ali-Asghar, 41, 50, 118

Naqdi, Majid, 196, 197
Nasiri, Ne'matollah, 71, 78, 88, 89, 93–94, 96–98, 100, 102, 118–120, 122, 124–125, 135, 189, 196, 197, 213, 228, 229, 234, 264, 267, 282, 288
National Front (Jebhey-e Melli), 10, 55, 161, 200, 247, 257–259
national resurgence, 9, 297
National Will Party, 13, 62, 65
Navvab Safavi (Mirlowhi), Mojtaba, 47, 56, 57, 218, 235, 236, 240–241, 247–248, 257
Navvab, Hoseyn, 260
Neguib, Mohammad, 21
Nehura, Benjamin, 219, 220
Nejati, Gholam-Reza, 87
Nicosia Draft of Operation TPAJAX, 61, 62
Nouri, Bahaeddin, 38
Nowzari, Rostam, 88, 141–143, 205, 206–207, 208, 210–211, 212, 220, 222, 234

Operation Boot, 27, 99
Operation Buccaneer, 12, 13, 29, 74, 241, 274
Ordubadi, Mansur, 90, 113, 119, 120
Organization of Nationalist Officers, 115, 228
Owliya'i, Karim, 169, 170

Pahlavi, Ali-Reza, 51
Pahlavi, Ashraf, 32, 67, 69, 74, 75–77, 82, 83, 159
Pahlavi, Gholamreza, 210
Pahlavi, Hamid-Reza, 224
Pahlavi, Mohammad Reza, 49, 97, 99, 109, 120, 130, 143, 144, 145, 163, 164, 188, 219, 246, 254, 270, 271
    Behbahani, Mohammad, 237, 238, 245
    coup d'état, 2–6, 8–9, 76–78, 91, 102, 126, 127, 172, 253, 284–285, 293, 297
    Kashani, Abolqasem, 37–39
    Khatibi, Hoseyn, 41
    Mosaddeq, Mohammad, 13–14, 16, 17, 18–19, 35–36, 40, 52, 109, 135, 147, 150, 183, 255, 261, 276, 277, 278, 279, 281–284
    Qavam, Ahmad, 18
    Roosevelt, Kermi, 75
    The British, 22, 27, 60
Pahlavi, Reza Shah, 174, 190, 192, 246
Pan-Iranist Party, 56
Parsa, Ali, 88
Popular uprising, 7, 9, 202, 203, 271, 297

Qanatabadi, Shams, 41, 47, 49, 57–58, 108, 158, 159, 174, 234, 243, 244–245, 247, 257, 259, 267
Qarani, Vali, 52
Qorbannejad, Houshang, 208, 209, 210–212, 222, 230, 253

Rahimi, Azizollah, 50, 196, 211
Ramezoun Yakhi (Esma'ilpour), Hoseyn, 72, 161–165, 167, 168, 169, 171–172
Rashidiyan, Asadollah, 64, 65, 66–67, 68–71, 296
    Baqa'i, Mozaffar, 32
    Behbahani, Mohammad, 127, 140
    coup d'état, 19, 29–30, 64, 107, 122, 123, 125, 126, 140, 267
    Fazlollah Zahedi, 68
    Kashani, Abolqasem, 238
    Mohammad Reza Shah, 66–67, 69, 73, 74, 75–78, 80, 91, 102, 139, 164
    Southern Tehran ruffians, 62, 71–72, 126, 139, 140, 159, 160, 163, 164, 165, 166, 168, 250
    The British, 73–75, 99
    Zahedi, Ardeshir, 112
Rashidiyan, Habibollah, 64–66
Rashidiyan, Qodratollah, 24, 65
Rashidiyan, Seyfollah, 65, 73, 140
Razavi, Ahmad, 232, 288
Razmara, Haj Ali, 58, 89, 240, 247, 257
Retired Officers' Association, 23, 24, 25, 34, 40, 41, 42, 43, 45, 47, 50
Reza'i, Ali, 156, 157, 160
Riyahi, Mohammad-Taqi, 96, 97, 98, 105, 110, 115, 121, 124, 131, 143, 144, 150, 152, 153, 184–186, 188, 197, 199, 205, 209, 211, 212, 213, 217, 221, 231–232, 262–263
Roosevelt, Kermit, 3–7, 26, 28, 60–61, 63, 73, 74–75, 77–78, 79–82, 83, 84, 87, 88, 98, 100, 104, 111, 122, 125–126, 134, 178, 224, 225–227, 254, 296
Rostami, Amir, 42, 43
Rostami, Ja'far, 43
Rowhani, Ali-Mohammad, 90, 91, 93, 98, 116–119, 121, 145, 189–190, 196, 211, 234
Royal Edict (farman), 77, 78, 84, 88, 91, 92, 93–94, 277–279, 280–283, 288, 293

Saber, Boyouk, 72, 138, 168–169, 227
Sadiqi, Gholam-Hoseyn, 115, 175, 180, 188, 193, 209
Saleh, Allahyar, 35, 199
Saltanatabad garrison, 141, 142, 143, 144, 205, 206, 208, 215, 220, 253
Schwarzkopf, Norman, 76–77
Schwind, Don, 134
Second Armoured Brigade, 88, 143, 153, 191, 234
Second Mountain Brigade, 88, 90, 95, 98, 116, 117, 191, 228, 233, 234
Sepah Square (Toupkhaneh), 148, 166, 168, 174, 177, 179, 180, 182, 183, 184, 186, 187, 189, 190, 192, 194, 195, 197, 198, 199, 200, 208, 211, 215, 218, 221, 255
Sepahbodi, Isa, 200
Sepahpur, Mehdi, 99
Shahed, 41, 58, 135, 202, 234
Shahrokh, Naser, 88, 153, 154, 191, 197
Shayanfar, Ali-Naqi, 106, 114, 119
Shepherd, Francis, 11, 12, 13, 62
Shervin, Mahmud, 42, 57, 58, 224, 258
Shoja'i, 71, 192, 192, 207, 215, 216, 218, 220, 225
SIS (Secret Intelligence Service), 5, 9, 10, 22, 27, 40, 53, 60, 61, 63–64, 67, 72–76, 80–81, 84, 88, 100, 101, 106, 107, 114, 126, 154, 176, 235, 286, 288, 293, 295
Siyasi, Hoseyn, 121, 184
Society of Moslem Mojaheds (Majma' Mosalmanan-e Mojahed), 42, 43, 45, 52, 57, 58, 227, 252
success of the second coup, 107, 114, 130, 196, 231, 249, 251, 263, 278
SUMKA, 42, 47, 52, 54–57, 58, 84, 86, 191
Supplemental oil agreement, 11, 66

Tabataba'i, Seyyed Ziaeddin, 13, 15–20, 21, 22, 24, 29, 53, 56, 57, 58, 62, 65–67, 68–69, 73, 82, 86, 171, 266, 293, 296
Taheri brothers, 164–165
Taj Athletics Club, 51, 153
Taleqani, Seyyed Mahmud, 132, 133
Tehran Radio's Broadcasting Station (bisime Pahlavi), xxi, 114, 179, 180, 189, 192, 194, 195, 198, 204, 205, 207, 210, 212, 218, 221, 222, 225, 227, 229, 252

Third Force Party, 147, 149, 200, 256
Third Mountain Brigade, 88, 90, 95, 98, 105, 113, 116, 144, 145, 152, 234
Tir 30 (21 July 1952) uprising, 18, 19, 200, 238, 249, 256, 259, 265, 266
TPAJAX, 4, 53, 60–63, 73, 75, 77, 79, 84, 87, 88, 91, 93, 99, 100, 104, 106, 117, 120, 190, 191, 223, 234, 249, 251–252, 277–278, 285–286, 293
TPBEDAMN, 56, 62, 85, 86, 107, 129, 133, 191, 252, 274
Tudeh Party, 18, 41, 43, 46, 54–55, 62, 79, 80, 84, 86, 96, 100, 102–103, 108, 109, 118, 119, 127, 129, 132, 144–146, 147–151, 152, 157, 159–160, 161, 171, 180, 182, 190, 194, 200–202, 207, 231, 239, 254, 255, 256, 257, 261, 265–266, 272, 291
  Military Organization, 142, 207, 210

Vahedi, Abdol-Hoseyn, 47, 56
Varqa, Mashallah, 151, 193, 195–196
Vosouq, Ahmad, 260

Wilber, Donald, 60, 63, 64, 73, 74, 80–82, 83–84, 87, 91–92, 101, 108, 112, 117, 125, 126, 130–131, 134, 136, 148, 153, 177, 178, 190–192, 194, 196, 200, 204, 221, 223–224, 225–227, 235, 251, 253, 268
Woodhouse, Christopher Montague, 4, 6, 27, 28, 29–30, 60, 63–64, 72–74, 80, 81, 83, 84, 87, 100, 134, 178
Wright, Dennis, x, 3, 10, 270, 271

Yarafshar, Parviz, 175

Zaehner, Robert Charles (Robin), 66, 73–74, 75, 238, 241
Zahedi, Ardeshir, 92, 93, 99, 112, 134, 175, 224–225
  Afshartus, Mahmud, 42
  American Embassy, 35, 98
  Carroll, George, 130
  coup d'état, 63, 112, 125, 192
  Esfahan, 130
  Goodwin, Joseph, 134
  Kashani, Mohammad, 240
  popular uprising, 202
  Southern Tehran ruffians, 138–139

Zahedi, Fazlollah, 8, 9, 24, 26, 35, 44, 48, 88, 92, 93, 100, 111–112, 122, 125, 133–134, 143, 148, 205, 222–223, 224–227, 269
Afshartus, Mahmud, 42
Ala, Hoseyn, 284
American Embassy, 7
Ashrafi, Hoseynqoli, 114
Behbahani, Mohammad, 128, 132, 269
British Embassy, 21, 24–26
Carroll, George, 234
CIA, 63, 267
coup d'état, 29, 61–62, 278
Daftari, Mohammad, 113, 121, 195
Devotees of the Shah, 118–119
Falle, Sam, 20
Farzanegan, Abbas, 92
Kashani, Abolqasem, 32, 63, 234
Middleton, George, 20, 239
Mosaddeq, Mohammad, 23, 118, 284
Nasiri, Ne'matollah, 97
open letter, 136
Pahlavi, Mohammad Reza, 78, 269
Rashidiyan, Asadollah, 19, 32
Retired Officers' Association, 23
Roosevelt, Kermit, 5
Royal Edict, 84, 135–136
Southern Tehran ruffians, 172
The British, 286
Zangeneh, Ahmad, 192, 196
Zand Karimi, 90–94, 95, 98, 105, 110–111, 113, 115–117, 119, 120–121, 124–125, 145, 189, 234
Zand, Akbar, 119, 120, 145–146, 152, 186, 189–190, 191, 221, 222, 253
Zargham, Amirqoli, 108, 119, 121, 130
Zarrinkia, Amir, 49, 58
Zirakzadeh, Ahmad, 97, 161, 199, 232
Zohari, Ali, 202, 203, 286
Zolfaqar Party, 52–53, 55, 57, 85, 159, 223, 227

Lightning Source UK Ltd.
Milton Keynes UK
UKOW04n1625291217
314985UK00001B/2/P